No. 380
$18.90

Make Your Own Camping Equipment

By Robert Sumner

How to Survive in the Wilderness

MAKE YOUR OWN CAMPING EQUIPMENT

By
Robert Sumner

DRAKE PUBLISHERS INC.
NEW YORK • LONDON

Published in 1976 by
DRAKE PUBLISHERS INC.
801 Second Avenue
New York, N.Y. 10017

Library of Congress Cataloging in Publication Data

Sumner, Robert.
    Make your own camping equipment.

    1. Camping--Outfits, supplies, etc. I. Title.
GV191.76.S85   646   76-4523
ISBN 0-8473-1152-X

ISBN: 0-8473-1152-X
LC : 76-1205

Printed in The United States of America

CONTENTS

Introduction

This book is for anyone who ever wanted to make their own down parka, tent, sleeping bag, or backpack—either for reasons of economy or enjoyment—but didn't for lack of knowledge of materials and sources, techniques, or patterns. All the information needed to make your own lightweight camping equipment is here. Section One covers materials, with information such as the best fabrics for a certain job, how to gauge down quality, choosing good hardware, and where to get your hands on it all. Section Two goes into design and sewing techniques, with enough information and basic instruction for the non-sewer to do the job right, and without getting bogged down in all the byplay of a sewing manual. In the third and main section of this book are the equipment patterns.

All of the patterns in this book have been designed for easy home construction without sacrificing the features and engineering that set off the sophisticated and functional equipments from the run-of-the-mill products. Prototypes were constructed for all of the patterns, both to insure the functional merits of the designs and to facilitate the writing and illustrating of clear and concise assembly instructions. Everything is spelled out to make the fabrication of the equipment as simple and fail-safe as possible.

Making your own gear is a lot more fun than work. And a good measure of satisfaction comes from the self-sufficiency of tending your own needs. Add to this the fact that your new down parka which costs $75 in the store will cost you only about $15 to make, and the matter is surely sweetened.

SECTION ONE

MATERIALS

Chapter 1

Fabrics

Probably the least understood part of elemental equipment is the fabrics from which it is made. Equipment function and strength are just as dependent on materials as design. Since synthetic fabrics have been around for less than forty years, it is understandable that most of us know little about them and how they work.

The key to the development of fully synthetic fibers is a chemical process called polymerization. Various ingredients are mixed, causing a molecular reaction forming larger, long and stable chain molecules or *polymers*. This is the substance from which the fibers are formed and its basic ingredients determine the generic fiber type. This substance is melted and forced through a device resembling a shower head, called a *spinneret*. This device is a man made approximation of the organ used by silk worms and spiders to spin their secretions.

During or after extrusion through the spinneret and cooling, the resultant monofilament fibers are stretched. Stretching serves the dual purpose of shrinking the fibers to a more workable diameter for a particular fabric application, and of orientating the polymer chain molecules to achieve a desired strength to stretch trade off. This orientation process is used to make fibers for climbing ropes, which must have an accurate and ample amount of stretch or elongation potential to prevent injurys from rapid deceleration in falls. The more a fiber is stretched, the stronger it becomes. However, its ability to stretch without breaking decreases. Hence, climbing ropes which have sustained a bad fall should be discarded.

Next the processed monofilament strands are prepared for weaving as filament yarn, tow, staple, staple yarn, or, as existing continuous monofilament. Most light-weight nylon fabrics used for elemental equipment are woven from untwisted filament yarns.

The different types of yarn, or the monofilament alone, are measured by what is called the *denier*. This is the weight in grams of nine thousand meters of the yarn. The larger the denier, the larger the diameter of the yarn. The denier is used to compare the relative sizes of yarns of the same generic type. However, because the measurement is based on weight, it should only be used for comparing different generic types of fibers of a comparative specific gravity.

Generic names refer to the chemical compositions of the fibers, such as nylon, polyester, rayon and olefin. Whereas manufacturers trade names refer to their own specialized renditions. For example, "Dacron" is the registered trademark of Du Pont for their polyester fiber, commonly known for its use as a sailcloth.

Different generic fibers may be *blended* in staple or filament yarns, or *combined* in the weaving of the fabric to attain performance characteristics not common to a single fiber. A popular mix for parka applications is what is commonly called 60/40 cloth, a combination of cotton and nylon. The nylon contributes strength, while the cotton serves to allow breathing for ventilation. When the cotton becomes wet is swells to tighten the weave and impart some water repellency. A similar material 50/50 fabric may be made by mixing the fibers before they are spun into yarns.

How a particular fiber yarn is woven also determines the performance characteristics of the finished fabric. Variations on a plain weave are used for most elemental equipments made of synthetic fibers. A plain weave packs the filament yarns very closely together, a necessity with nylon because, unlike natural fibers, it is very smooth and slippery. A tight weave is desirable for our purposes to control porosity, downproofness and wind resistance. However, while a tighter weave increases these properties of the fabric, it lessens the tear strength. This is a result of the fibers being bent in a greater angle around one another. The tearing forces are concentrated on individual threads which are immobilized and unable to stretch. This problem is overcome in the lighter weight nylon fabrics through the use of stop threads; two threads woven as one, every ¼" or so, in the warp and the fill. Such is ripstop nylon. Another way to increase tear strength is to weave the fabric with double yarns, as in duck and oxford weaves. These are sometimes referred to as two-ply fabrics.

The tightness of the weave is measured by the thread count. This indicates the number of threads in the warp and fill in one square inch of fabric. The thread count may be used to compare fabrics of identical denier yarns as to porosity or downproofness. Lower thread counts indicate a greater porosity, desirable for a tent wall, while the higher thread counts indicate a tighter weave and a lower porosity for greater wind resistance and downproofness.

Another variable to porosity is the degree of heat set or *calendering* applied to the fabric during its manufacturing. Continuous filament nylon yarns, being smooth and slippery, resist compaction into a tight and stable weave. This problem is overcome by running the woven fabric across rollers at a temperature around 350° to 400°. This may be done once or several times. Calendering serves two purposes. First, it shrinks the fabric, thereby compacting the weave even further. Yardage that goes into the process at a 51" width may come out at 45" width. Calendering also permanently sets the fibers, giving dimensional stability and resistance to deformation. Once nylon or any other thermoplastic fiber has been heat set, it must be heated beyond the original temperature of calendering to be creased or textured differently. This explains why your windshirt that spent the day stuffed in a pack looks freshly ironed after a short wearing time. This same technique is used to make permanent press clothing. A thermoplastic synthetic fiber is blended with the primary fiber to make it wrinkle free and maintain the creases and pleats.

If you have had experience with washing permanent press clothing, you are aware that these garments lose some of their press or set through repeated laundering. This is true for all nylon items, such as down parkas and sleeping bags. Calendering, especially when overdone to make up for a sleezy weave, is decreased by laundering and abrasion. For this reason, your synthetic items should be washed as infrequently and as gently as possible.

Too much calendering is bad for fabrics. This process has been used to give some clothing the "shiny" look. The fabric is actually melted on its surface to form a sort of polymer crust. This is essentially over calenderizing and destroys a great deal of the fibers desirable strength. If function is to take precedence over fashion, avoid doing this.

Fabric porosity is technically measured by the number of cubic feet of air per minute that can pass through a prescribed area of the fabric. Porosity ratings are a very important functional design consideration of elemental equipments. Unfortunately, porosity ratings are not always available or listed. But, there are several things you can do to compare the relative porosity of fabrics. Blowing through the fabric and/or inspecting the amount of light that will pass through the weave can give you some idea of the porosity of the fabric. Fabrics may also be compared for sheen differences, which will indicate the relative amounts of calendering applied. The more a fabric is calendered the shinier and less porous it will be. Nylon fabrics are also sometimes treated with a silicon finish to add a degree of water repellency. This will also lower the porosity, but only slightly. If you have an old down-filled garment that is leaking its filling, you might remedy it with an application of the type of silicon spray coating that drys to a non-wet finish.

To be made totally waterproof, as opposed to water-repellent, a fabric must be coated completely with a sealer. Most nylon fabrics used for elemental equipment are coated with one or two applications of a urethane film. Coated fabrics, to retain effective waterproofness, must be treated with great care for two reasons. First, because the coatings further immobilize the movement of the threads in a fabric, the tear strength is lowered. Second, nylon fabrics are non-absorbant, or hydrophobic, and very smooth, making a difficult surface to bond to.

There has been a lot of talk in the equipment industry about the superiority of so called *polymer* coatings. This coating was originated as a variation of the Kenyon Piece Dyeworks, Inc. existing K-Kote, to increase the tear strength of light weight fabrics. Unfortunately, while the tear strength was improved, the adhesion of polymer coatings was not as good. Kenyon has since modified their K-Kote family, including their heavier Super K-Kote, so that the only appreciable difference of polymer coatings is a better drape or hang.

Most elemental equipment is made from nylon fabrics because it is strong and light weight. For example, the woven strength of nylon fabric may be more than three times that of a similar size cotton. This means that a seven pound nylon tent would have to weigh twenty-one pounds if made from cotton, to be of an equal strength. The ability to alter the characteristics of a nylon fabric also has contributed to its wide use.

One such current modification of nylon fibers has resulted in a new fabric, better suited for equipment that is subjected to rough use. *Cordura* is the trademark and development of Du Pont. It is made by cordurizing, or fuzzying, large denier fibers. The net effect is a fabric that has a slightly lower tensile strength, but has considerably more abrasion resistance. Cordura is now almost exclusively used in place of the incumbant nylon duck pack cloths.

All is not nylon, so listed here are some other generic types and their functional characteristics:

Polyesters

Dacron, also a child of Du Pont, is a polyester based fiber. Polyesters are hydrophobic and thermoplastic and somewhat similar to nylon with the exceptions of slightly less deterioration from sunlight, very little less tensile strength and, most important, close to half of the elasticity of nylon. The latter property makes dacron the peerless sail fabric. Polyester is also used for high strength sewing thread, eliminating stretch problems in sewing machine operation. Polyester fibers are also used in a crimped staple form for fiberfill insulations such as Eastman Fibers "Kodel" and Du Pont "Fiberfill II."

Rayon

Rayon was the first man-made fiber to be produced commercially in 1910 by the American Viscose Company. However, it is not a true synthetic. Rayon fibers are composed of regenerated cellulose extruded through a spinneret. Because rayon is a natural substance fiber it shares many of the same characteristics of cotton. It is highly absorbant and soft, and, because it is extruded like a synthetic, it may be modified for different sheens and textures. Like cotton, its principal uses are for clothing.

TABLE 1/SOME PHYSICAL PROPERTIES OF MAN-MADE FIBERS

| Fiber | Breaking Tenacity[1] (grams per denier) | |
	Standard	Wet
Acrylic (filament and staple)	2.0 to 3.5	1.8 to 3.3
Nylon		
nylon 66 (regular tenacity filament)	3.0 to 6.0	2.6 to 5.4
nylon 66 (high tenacity filament)	6.0 to 9.5	5.0 to 8.0
nylon 66 staple)	3.5 to 7.2	3.2 to 6.5
nylon 6 (filament)	6.0 to 9.5	5.0 to 8.0
nylon 6 (staple)	2.5	2.0
nylon H.T. Resistant		
(DP01) filament	4.8 to 5.8	3.8 to 4.8
(DP01) staple	3.0 to 4.0	2.0 to 3.0
Olefin (polypropylene) (filament and staple)	4.8 to 7.0	4.8 to 7.0
Polyester		
regular tenacity filament	4.0 to 5.0	4.0 to 5.0
high tenacity filament	6.3 to 9.5	6.2 to 9.4
regular tenacity staple	2.5 to 5.0	2.5 to 5.0
high tenacity staple	5.0 to 6.5	5.0 to 6.4
Rayon (filament and staple)		
regular tenacity	0.73 to 2.6	0.7 to 1.8
high tenacity	3.0 to 6.0	1.9 to 4.6

Acrylics

The first and the most well known is Du Pont "Orlon," which was developed to be totally resistant to deterioration from the ultraviolet rays of the sun. General characteristics are: lightweight, resilient, quick drying and reasonably strong. Acrylics may be made to resemble wool by bulking and shrinking. The resultant synthetic fabric has more than twice the strength and abrasion resistance of natural wool and, as an added plus, is not susceptible to moths and mildew. Socks and sweaters, made entirely of acrylic or a blend with wool, would be excellent durable clothing.

Olefin

Olefin fibers possess some interesting characteristics. Spun from a polypropylene base, olefin is the lightest of the synthetic fibers. Although it is a hydrophobic material (in fact it has the lowest moisture regain), these fibers have the best ability to wick moisture

Specific Gravity[2]	Standard Moisture Regain (%)[3]	Effects of Heat
1.14 to 1.19	1.3 to 2.5	Sticks at 450° to 497°F., depending on type.
1.14	4.0 to 4.5	Sticks at 445°F. Melts at about 500°F
1.14	4.0 to 4.5	Same as above.
1.14	4.0 to 4.5	Melts at 414° to 428°F.
1.14	4.5	Melts at 414° to 428°F.
1.14	4.5	Melts at 414° to 428°F.
1.38	5.0	Decomposes above 700°F.
1.38	5.0	Decomposes above 700°F.
.91	—	Melts at 325° to 335°F
1.22 or 1.38*	0.4 or 0.8*	Melts at 480° to 550°F.
1.22 or 1.38*	0.4 or 0.8*	Melts at 480° to 550°F.
1.22 or 1.38*	0.4 or 0.8*	Melts at 480° to 550°F.
1.22 or 1.38*	0.4 or 0.8*	Melts at 480° to 550°F.
1.50 to 1.53	13	Does not melt. Decomposes at 350° to 464°F.
1.50 to 1.53	13	Burns readily.

1. Breaking Tenacity: The stress at which a fiber breaks, expressed in terms of grams per denier.
2. Specific Gravity: The ratio of the weight of a given volume of fiber to an equal volume of water.
3. Standard Moisture Regain: The moisture regain of a fiber (expressed as a percentage of the moisture-free weight) at 70°F. and 65% relative humidity.

*Depending on type.

Note: Data given in ranges may fluctuate according to introduction of fiber modifications or additions and deletions of fiber types.

away from the skin, through the fibers and out onto the surface of the material. As a result of this, olefin has a particularly dry feel. Olefin is close behind polyesters and nylons in strength. The only currently popular application is in wick dry type socks.

Table 1, "Some Physical Properties of Man-Made Fibers," is partially reprinted here, courtesy of the Man-Made Fiber Producers Association, Inc. This organization also has educational materials and should be contacted by anyone who is interested in more information on synthetics engineering and manufacture. (See the sources appendix for their address.) This association can also supply you with the addresses of its member producers for information on particular fiber characteristics and applications.

The information in table 1 gives some of the characteristics of the raw, unprocessed fibers. Statistical data on ready to use, woven, and finished fabrics is not listed because of considerable variations from one to another, even of an identical weight, weave and type. Most reputable elemental equipment manufacturers and suppliers of fabrics print the performance data in their catalogues.

The technical information commonly proferred to the public includes such things as the fabric weight (in ounces per square yard), the finished width, the type, if any, of coatings, the thread count, and the denier. This information may be used to estimate porosity and strength. A few manufacturers, notably Recreational Equipment, Inc., commonly known as the Seattle Co-op, and Eastern Mountain Sports of Boston, also give the tear strengths of their fabrics. The tear or tongue strength of a fabric is measured as the force in pounds required to continue a rip in progress. Tear strength ratings are listed for the warp and fill directions on the fabric, respectively.

The tear strength in the warp and fill of a fabric should be reasonably close for maximum durability. A fabric with a considerably lower tear strength along one grain is only as strong as that weak link. A good example of a radical warp to fill tear strength discrepency is 60/40 cloth, cotton and nylon, respectively. The cottong fill is less than half as strong as the nylon warp threads. A stronger substitute for 60/40 cloth, with similar characteristics, would be a 50/50 cotton and nylon or polyester blend, where the strength of the synthetic is used to its maximum advantage in both the warp and fill directions of the fabric grain.

Two other strength ratings are *tensile strength* and *abrasion resistance*. Tensile strength measures the bursting point of a fabric and is usually referred to in pounds. This is similar to tenacity, as used in table 1, with the difference that tensile strength measures the finished fabric, whereas the tenacity commonly refers to the individual yarns. Tenacity is used in the context of individual filaments or yarns because it is also an indication of elasticity. For example, a high tenacity yarn is one that has been stretched and orientated more in manufacture to impart greater strength. A low or regular tenacity yarn is weaker, but more elastic.

Abrasion resistance is an important consideration for use in climbing packs, gaiters and other gear subject to rough use. Abrasion resistance is measured in *cycles to fail.* Cordura is the peerless fabric in this respect. Its abrasion resistance in a 9.7 oz. weight is 2900 cycles as compared to 18.2 oz. cotton duck (no. 8) at only 1020 cycles to fail. (These figures are for the cordura fiber cloth made by Howe & Bainbridge, Inc.) The relative abrasion resistance of cordura cloth depends on whether or not both the warp and the fill yarns are cordurized and on the tightness of the weave.

Make Your Own Camping Equipment

The equipment chapters in this book further discuss fabrics performance and characteristics for specific applications.

Table 2 gives some sources for the more popular fabrics. The availability of a fabric type from a certain supplier is listed by the weight as given in their catalogues. It must be noted that some of the weights listed for coated fabrics may not include the coating. The weights are listed simply to give you a better idea of who has what.

TABLE 2

FABRICS: WHO HAS WHAT BY WEIGHT (oz./sq. yd.)

				Suppliers			
	Blacks	EMS	Frost-line	Kelty	REI	Sierra Designs	Ski Hut
Uncoated ripstop	1.5	1.9	1.9	1.5 & 1.9	1.9	1.5 &	1.9
Coated ripstop		1.9		2.2		N.A.	2.3
Uncoated taffeta		2.3	2.4			2.2	1.6 & 2.5
Coated taffeta	4.0	3.5 & 2.5	3.7	2.7	3.1	2.7	2.3 & 3.5
Coated duck		7.8	7.5	7.8	8.5	7.5	7.8
Coated cordura		9.0		11.5	1	11.0	
60/40 cloth		5.0	4.5	5.0	2.5	5.0	4.0
Mosquito netting	N.A.	1.0	1.0	1.0	1.0	1.0	.75

N.A. — Weight not listed in catalogue.
See appendix for supplier's address.

Chapter 2

Insulations

The functional requirements of insulations for the self-propelled traveler are light weight, maximum loft or thickness, breathability and the ability to be compressed into a small space with full recovery of loft after repeated compressions. This basic criteria of portability has long maintained waterfowl down as the peerless insulator. Down has a loft to weight ration that is unmatched. It is almost completely resilient and may be compressed into a fraction of its lofted mass repeatedly, without ill effects. Down also ventilates or breathes to allow body moisture to escape. Down is also one of the most confusing and misrepresented substances, second only to Watergate, so it is here that our discussion of insulations begin.

There is no doubt as to the superiority of down as a lightweight and efficient insulator. There is, however, considerable confusion as to what down is, what kind is best and from where, what color is most efficient, what climates raise the best down, how it should be measured and rated, etc. The problem seems to stem from claims made by equipment manufacturers, most of whom are in disagreement. The contradictions reduce the process of selection to price shopping and guesswork. You can't even see the down you're buying, so the confusion is compounded. It is the intention of this chapter to clear up some of the myths about down and to enable the average person to compare one to another.

Down is officially described by the Federal Trade Commission as, ". . . the undercoating of waterfowl, consisting of clusters of light, fluffy filaments, i.e., barbs, growing from the quill point, but without any quill shafts." These down pods may range in size from a silver dollar for exceptional down, to a quarter for good down. Each pod has hundreds of light and fuzzy barbs, which entangle with one another and other pod tentacles to form minute pockets of trapped air. This is opposed to other things which may find their way into a coat or sleeping bag, such as crushed or curled feathers from a turkey vulture, rodent reminants and other substances officially called trash.

Trash is unacceptable insulation simply because it does not have the functional characteristics of down pods. Military testing on insulations proved that it is the thickness of the trapped air space and not its substance which determines effectiveness. If it were found that hogs hair displayed better lofting and compression than down, you would surely see labels stating, "This item made from prime grade AAA Northern European Hog!" Down as a substance does not have any mystical properties that make it warmer. It simply lofts well and is extremely lightweight.

One of the most absurd myths is the quasi-racist assumption that white down is better than grey or brown down. White down may be fashionably preferred with light color fabrics simply because it does not show through, but that's the only reason.

Perhaps the greatest controversy in the equipment industry is that of goose versus duck down. Some suppliers use both, and have presented the issue with refreshingly more objectivity, along with some really fine equipment to match it. The heart of the issue is what type of waterfowl produces the best down. Best in this case meaning largest and, hence, more efficient in terms of lofting power to weight. Ducks and geese both produce down pods that are functionally identical. Now everyone knows that a goose is a lot larger than any duck, and so it would seem logical that goose down is indeed larger and better than duck down.

Unfortunately, it isn't that simple. Due to the economics of poultry farming, ducks and geese raised for eating are harvested extremely young; from three to six months of age. As a result, a goose may or may not grow more than a duck, and the resulting down pods can be the same size.

Another sales pitch says that waterfowl raised in colder northern climates will produce down that is superior to that of fair-weather birds. In reality, however, poultry waterfowl don't do much flying and spend their time in coops and barns, not out in the snow. Besides, feather and down processors take their stock from many localities. For example, an equipment manufacturer here, might buy his down from a European processor who bought his stock from Asia as well as Europe. Ducks and geese from colder climates probably do grow larger and/or more numerous down pods, but these are invariably mixed by the processor with down from other origins in order to attain more consistency within their random quality categories.

The most annoying myth surrounding down fills, is provided by the naming and grading of down. Adjectives such as "prime," "northern," "European," grade AAA," "premium quality," and "super" are sales words that are arbitrarily applied by either the processor or the maker of a down filled article. These adjectives may be used to describe a maker's particular grade of down, but have not been standardized from one company to another, and are not recognized by the Federal Trade Commission (FTC).

(What the FTC does require is that items labeled "down" contain at least 80 percent down, plumules, and down fiber. The remaining 20 percent may contain feathers and feather fibers with a maximum of 2 percent "residue." If the label indicates that the filling material is goose or duck, an option to the manufacturer, the item must contain at least 90 percent of the designated species. Except for some other minor legal requirements such as cleanliness, this is about as tough as the FTC gets.

Many consumer groups and some of the more quality oriented manufacturers of elemental equipment have been pushing for qualitative rating methods. In short, down fill quality has nothing to do with the particulars of the bird. It is concerned with the lofting power of a prescribed weight of down. Several years back, a laboratory came up with a device for measuring this quality. It consists of a plexiglas cylinder with gradations on its side indicating volume in cubic inches. An ounce of down is weighed and put into the cylinder, compressed under a wood plunger, and the loft of the down is indicated by the level at which the plunger comes to rest.

Using this device, or a similar one, down fills could be rated, once and for all. The idea for the device is timely. Unfortunately, technical problems are preventing its being written into the law. A lack of repeatable results comes from slight variations in the temperature and humidity, problems with static electricity, how many times the down is stirred or fluffed, and slight variations in the volume from one cylinder to another. Work is under way to eliminate these problems and fairly soon there should be legal criteria for rating and labeling down. One elemental company, Eastern Mountain Sports, is already measuring the loft of the down it uses in this fashion, and is listing the ratings in their catalogue.

Even though poultry waterfowl is being harvested younger, with resulting smaller down pods, the feather and down processors are maintaining the quality by mixing their stocks and more completely separating the down from the feathers. Processors receive their stocks in bundles containing the down and feathers, and whatever else was crawling around the barnyard at the time. This trash, as it is called, is first washed and then separated through a process called *fractionalization.* The trash is placed in the bottom of a large vacuum tube and stirred, causing the lighter down pods to rise. When the desired separation is achieved, screens are inserted at the various quality levels, and the vacuum turned off. Although the present day down pods are smaller on the average, the efficiency of the filling mixture is being maintained by more thorough fractionalization.

So how does the average consumer gauge the quality of a down? Well, you don't have your own measuring devices and you still can't see the down. What you can do is compare the loft to weight of different manufacturers finished products as they list them in their catalogues. Once you think you have found an item with an efficient down fill, run on down to your local mountain shop and take a look at the item in fact. Even go so far as to compare several identical items by a single manufacturer to see if his quality is consistent. Bear in mind that a down item that has been stuffed is going to take some sitting and fluffing before it will match one that has been hanging on a rack. Simply eyeing a down product in this manner can tell you a lot about its quality. Needless to say, a product of poor quality down is going to be comparatively heavier and lay limp and lifeless on the floor.

FIBERFILLS

Polyester fiberfills are fast gaining acceptance by both industry and consumer. It is openly acknowledged that synthetic fiberfills are not as efficient as down, but they do have some characteristics that, in some cases, make them desirable. When down gets wet, it mats and clumps, thereby eliminating its ability to provide insulation. Fiberfills, on the other hand, are made from hydrophobic synthetics that retain their loft and thickness when wet, and their ability to insulate. A fiberfill coat or bag will also dry more quickly than one made of down.

The cost of fiberfills is considerably less than down. Being a man-made substance, it is not as susceptible to the fluctuations in price that result from increased demand and short supply; the situation with the price of down. Fiberfill is one of the best buys on the market compared to down.

The characteristics that maintain down as a more efficient insulator than polyester fiberfills are compactability and weight. It takes about 10 percent more space to stuff a sleeping bag made of fiberfill than one of an identical weight of down. However, weight is really the critical determination and there fiberfills have their greatest shortcomings. Eastern Mountain Sports, using their cylinder loft measuring device, has found that fiberfill has only half the lofting power of a good grade of down; 375 cubic inches versus 550 cubic inches for the down. Of course, the weight of the coat or bag is going to be almost half from the fabrics and hardware, so your average sleeping bag with two pounds of fill will only weigh about a pound more with fiberfill.

Regardless of the shortcomings of polyester fiberfills, they have been used successfully on extended duration winter trips where a wet bag that loses its loft is just plain dangerous. They are also being used for light summer bags where overall weight is not so critical. The fact remains though, down is lighter.

Regardless of the filling, if you end up with a sleeping bag that doesn't measure up to standards or that you feel was misrepresented, send it back to the manufacturer for replacement, refilling or a refund. Any equipment manufacturer with the slightest concern for a qualitative reputation is going to try to satisfy you. However, if you draw a blank here, you still may have recourse through the FTC or your appropriate state department regulating bedding fills. In California, it's the Department of Consumer Affairs, Bureau of Home Furnishings. They have a standard complaint form, reprinted here, which covers sleeping bags. In the event that such drastic action is necessary, a copy of the complaint form to the manufacturer might bring some action.

STATE OF CALIFORNIA—AGRICULTURE AND SERVICES AGENCY   RONALD REAGAN, Governor

DEPARTMENT OF
Consumer Affairs

BUREAU OF HOME FURNISHINGS
3401 LAGRANDE BLVD . SACRAMENTO, CALIF. 95823
TELEPHONE: 916—445-0796

COMPLAINT FORM
(Please print or type)

Name of firm complained about: _____

Address: _____

Sales person: _____ Date of transaction _____

Does complaint involve misrepresentations? _____ If so, were they:

     Advertized _____ , Oral _____ , Other _____

What kind of article or service was involved? _____

Was the article or service advertised? _____ When? _____ Where? _____

NOTE: Please attach copy of Ad if available.

Was a contract signed? _____ (If so attach a copy of the contract)

This complaint may be sent to company complained about: Yes _____ No _____

COMPLAINT IN DETAIL
(Use reverse side if necessary)

_____

_____

_____

_____

_____

_____

_____

_____

_____

_____

Your name _____ Phone number _____

Address _____

Signature _____ Dated _____

291-42 (rev 10-72)

GROUND SUPPORT INSULATIONS

Ground support insulations, specifically sleeping pads, are designed to resist compression and provide insulation under the weight of your body. Neither down nor fiberfill will support you enough to give adequate ground insulation, and one night out without a pad would convince you of this.

You spend the night turning over to warm the side that was down, and invariably you have an uncomfortable night on the hard ground. Sleeping pads are necessarily bulky in order to resist compression, but they need not be heavy. Following is a run-down on different types of pads, their compostions and characteristics:

Polyurethane foams

Poly-foams are perhaps the most widely used pad material. They are usually encased in a fabric sheath with a breathable top and waterproof bottom because they are open-celled and will soak up water otherwise. Poly-foams are the softest and most comfortable of the foam type pads, which accounts for their popularity.

Ensolite

Ensolite is a closed-cell foam. It compresses only about one third as much as poly-foam, so a much thinner layer is sufficient. It also weighs about one quarter less than poly-foam, on the average.

Volarafoam

Volarafoam is the trademark of an outfit called Volteck known for their super-light, closed-cell foam. Sometimes also called *blue-light* or *super-light*, it weighs almost half of the other foams. It is recognizable by its light blue color. This foam is flexible at extremely low temperatures, does not absorb water, and, having a greater proportion of trapped air cells, is an efficient insulator. The only drawback to Volarafoam is its strength. It is not very abrasion resistant and it dents easily. Nevertheless, it makes for a very light, if not real soft, sleeping pad and pack load. It is also very inexpensive when compared to poly-foams. Volarafoam has been used successfully for several years for the liners in Scott USA's super-light ski boots. These boots have gained a reputation as one of the warmest boots on the market.

Air Mattresses

Although not as bulky to pack, air mattresses weigh quite a bit more than foam pads. They are also not as durable as foam pads because of their tendancy to develop air leaks, usually at three in the morning. And try to blow one up at ten thousand feet elevation . . . instant hypoxia.

More specific information on heat maintenance and comfort may be found in the chapters on clothing and sleeping bags.

Make Your Own Camping Equipment

TABLE 3

INSULATIONS: WHO HAS WHAT

			Suppliers			
	EMS	Frost-line	Kelty	REI	Sierra Designs	Ski Hut
Goose down	X*	X		X	X	X
Duck down				X	X	
Ensolite	X		X	X		X
Volarafoam	X		X	X		

*EMS uses a blend of duck and goose (500-600 cubic inches per ounce filling power.)
See appendix for supplier's address.

Chapter 3

Hardware And All The Other Stuff

Often, the only difference between an okay piece of equipment and an excellent one, is the hardware and other trappings used on it. There is hardware that works, and then there is hardware that is stronger, lighter, and easier to operate. The difference in cost is usually very little. For the discount, "shove the stuff on the market in mass" producers, it may be just another way to make a few cents at the expense of the uninformed consumer. Armed with a little knowledge of what is available, and table 4 at the end of this chapter, there is no need to settle for second best hardware.

ZIPPERS

Gone are the days of zipper hassles. It used to be that all zippers had to be made out of aluminum, nickel alloy, or brass. To keep the weight down, these zippers would be used in their smaller sizes and consequently, would be more problem prone. They would very easily cut through light nylon fabrics that became snagged in them, or jam. The zippers now used in light weight elemental equipments are made from synthetic plastics. They are stronger, lighter, smoother operating and more jam-proof, they don't harm fabrics that become snagged, and they are easier to repair and work with. There is absolutely no reason to my thinking, why any equipment manufacturer should continue to use metal zippers when the newer synthetic ones are readily available. Yet, they are still found and, surprisingly, on some of the most expensive equipment on the market.

The most widely used, and in my estimation, the best of the new zippers, is the nylon *continuous coil* type. Each half of this zipper consists of a single large monofilament of nylon formed into a flattened coil and then stitched onto a nylon or cotton tape. Because all of the teeth are interconnected, one single tooth cannot break off, and stresses are distributed evenly through all the teeth and their collective tape attachment. ①

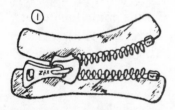
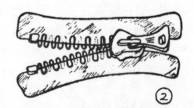

If a continuous coil zipper does come apart, it may be rejoined by simply backing the pull-slider over the separated section. This feature is unique to the coil-type zippers.

Another type of synthetic zipper, often confused with the preceding coil type, is the *continuous loop*. Like the coil, the teeth of this zipper are made from a continuous monofilament of nylon. It differs from the coil type as shown in illustration ②

The tape runs between the top and bottom connecting loops and is attached like the coil type by stitching over the monofilament on both sides of the tape.

The strength of continuous loop and coil zippers is beyond question. They have been in use for several years on packs such as the North Face Ruthsac that open with a zipper around three sides of the rear perimeter, holding in the entire load weight.

Another one of the new synthetic zippers is formed along the lines of a conventional metal zipper. So called *delrin* zippers are purportedly even stronger than the monofilament types. Delrin is an acetate resin from which the individual teeth of this zipper are made. The teeth are molded around a corded edged tape so the bonding is extra strong. Delrin teeth resemble those of the standard metal zippers but, unlike a metal zipper, the plastic material is unaffected by the freezing and fabric cutting problems. They are also lighter, so a larger and stronger size may be used. ③

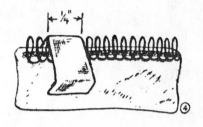

If you go with a delrin type zipper make sure the teeth are notched on top (see arrow in illustration 3). When the zipper is closed, these notches engage with the corded edges of the tapes to prevent inadvertant opening of the zipper from right angle stresses. Some molded plastic zippers don't have these notches.

My personal preference is the continuous coil zippers. I had a tooth break off due to the cold, on a delrin zipper used on a pair of gaiters, with very little provocation. Once a tooth breaks off one of these zippers, they will not stay closed satisfactorily. On the other hand, I have had nothing but good luck with coil type zippers.

Both the coil and loop and delrin type zippers may be found in fabric stores, in a variety of colors, in the smaller sizes and lengths used for clothing applications. The larger sizes and lengths for use in tent doors and sleeping bags, are available through the suppliers listed in table 4 at the end of this chapter. Coil and delrin type zippers may be bought by the yard and cut to size yourself for nonseparating uses. The pull-sliders, with either single or two sided tabs, are ordered separately. For the home-builder of elemental equipment, buying zippers in this fashion eliminates the necessity of perfect measurements for the zipper openings. It also makes possible custom applications of odd lengths. You simply cut off whatever you need, melt the ends together in a match flame, and sew it in.

Separating zippers to be used for coat fronts, gaiters, and sleeping bags, can be shortened at their top ends. They must be ordered in an approximately correct length, however, for the sake of the molded-on starter tabs on the bottom end. Stop tabs for the top ends, if not movable, can be made out of a one quarter inch strip off a tin can cut into two, one-half inch or so lengths. These are then bent over a bit at the edges and folded onto the zipper tape with a pair of pliers. ④

VELCRO

The stuff that sounds like a ripping crotch seam when separated is available through most equipment manufacturers and almost every fabric shop. Velcro comes in several widths and can be bought by the yard. Velcro is very handy for things like clothing wind flaps and cuffs because it can be operated while wearing gloves or mittens. It also makes for lightweight, easy operating accessory straps on packs.

SNAPS

When velcro won't work, use a snap. Most fabric stores stock different size snaps that come with a lightweight setting tool adequate for the installation. Or you can find a local establishment that will put snaps on for you. Larger ski and/or mountain shops usually have snaps and a setting tool in their service departments. Commercial laundries and saddle and tack shops might also have the goods.

WEBBING AND TAPES

Most of the webbing used in elemental equipment is the flat woven type, as opposed to the tubular or flattened sheath types used for climbing nut loops and runners. Three quarter inch, one inch, and two inch flat webbings are commonly used in pack suspension systems. The wider webbing is used for shoulder straps on daypacks and small rucksacs, with or without padding sewn to it. Flat webbing is stronger than strong, so don't overdo it. Some one inch flat webbings test out at over six thousand pounds breaking strength!

Nylon tapes are, essentially, lighter flat webbings. They can be distinguished from flat webbing by their herringbone weave. Sometimes a very thin one inch webbing will be sold as a tape. Nylon tapes are used for reinforcements, tent loops, accessory straps, and light pack harnesses. Both webbings and tapes should be cut with a hot knife, or have the ends melted in a flame to prevent them from unravelling.

BUCKLES

It is just plain common sense that there should not be one ounce of ferrous metal in lightweight equipment hardware. But almost every manufacturer in business today is still using heavy steel "D" rings on pack suspensions and lashing rings. For less than a dime, retail, you can get seamless aluminum "D" rings from Recreational Equipment, Inc. in Seattle. These come in one inch and one-half inch sizes.

Nearly half the hipbelts in existence use a buckle that weighs as much as an automobile seat belt buckle. If you plan on being in a wreck wearing your pack, buy this kind! Camp Trails, among some others, use a lightweight aluminum clincher type of buckle that is durable and easy to adjust.

There are two basic types of adjustable shoulder harness buckles; the double-bar buckle and the tablar buckle. To tighten either of them, you simply pull downwards on the loose end of the strap. To loosen them, you pull up on the finger tab, and the weight of the pack pulls the webbing through. ⑤

Make Your Own Camping Equipment

The double bar type is designed for use with medium to light flat webbings. The tablar buckle is made with more of a bend to hold light flat webbings and nylon tapes.

My personal preference is the tablar buckle with light flat webbing for pack harness applications. The strength seems most adequate and the weight is reasonable. The smaller size tablar buckles with nylon tape make good sleeping bag and accessory straps. Of course, your intended use may dictate differently.

Another type of buckle sometimes found on elemental equipment is the clincher type. This buckle has one or two rows of teeth, one on a sliding bar, that grips the webbing or tape, as it may be. ⑥

The pull of the webbing against this buckle tightens the grip of the teeth; the stronger the pull, the tighter the grip. Compared to the double-bar and tablar buckles, clinchers can be a headache. They are next to impossible to release when they are clinched tight. For a kite, kayak, or ski rack, where security is desired, clinchers will do the job. But don't forget the pliers, to get them undone.

GROMMETS

Yes, there are good grommets and there are bad grommets. The standard type brass grommet has sharp unfinished edges like a washer, that will easily cut into light, and even not so light nylon fabrics. What you want are *spur* grommets. These grommets have rolled edges that won't cut your fabric. They also have teeth, or spurs, on the female halves that go through the fabric and into the rolled edges of the male halves when flattened. The spurs prevent the grommet from rotating, which may further abraid the fabric, and give it a much better grip. Spur grommets are no harder to install than the standard type. The Frostline kit company sells spur type grommets in the no. 0 (5/16") size used most commonly for attaching packs to frames via clevis pins. Frostline also sells a setting tool for less than a dollar.

CLEVIS PINS

All that need be said about clevis pins is that they are used in both steel and aluminum versions. So don't neglect to check and be sure you're getting the light ones. Some equipment manufacturers forgo clevis pins entirely and use steel nuts and bolts in their place. These may look impressively strong, but they are ridiculously unnecessary.

RIVETS

Rivets are commonly used in flat webbing and leather stress patches on daypack and rucksack harnesses. The most commonly used rivet is the "Dot Speedy Rivet." Dots are available in a nickel, brown or black color and can be obtained from older, funky hardware stores. Dots are easily set with a hammer and go for about 40¢ a dozen in the large size.

The use of rivets at all, in anything but leather, is somewhat questionable. Climbing loops of webbing that are merely stitched together have proved to be far stronger than knotted webbing loops. The latter has the effect of localizing the stresses at only a portion of the webbings width. Rivets localize stresses at an even smaller area and do not have the ability to stretch as stitching does. While a stitched joint in a webbing loop may test to two thousand pounds, a riveted joint would probably only take two hundred pounds, if that. When rivets are used, it should be in conjunction with stitching, and reinforced with a leather or tape backing.

LEATHER

Leather is sometimes used for harness straps and commonly used for reinforcement on pack bottoms. Nylon webbing has pretty much replaced the leather used for pack and crampon straps and the like. The leather most often used for pack bottoms has a smooth, tanned surface. Several manufacturers are now using a rough-out or suede finish leather for cosmetic durability. The strengths of both are pretty much the same, though. The rough-out leather just doesn't show scratches.

Leather is ordered by animal type, finish, and weight, or thickness. Pack bottoms usually use the thicker cowhides. The weight is measured in ounces per square foot. Leather weighing five to six ounces per square foot will be about 3/32″ thick. This is approximately the weight that is used in pack bottoms. It is light enough to work with and still very durable. Any leather used on elemental equipment should be well treated with oils and preservatives to prevent it from stiffening and cracking.

The resurgence of interest in handcrafted products has brought with it many new leather shops. These shops will sell you leather and sew it for you if your machine can't handle it (see chapter 5 on sewing). Saddle and tack shops and some hardware stores, also sell leathers. If none of these are available, you can mail order your leather through the Tandy Leather Company (address in sources appendix). Tandy also sells leather working tools, if you want to be creative.

THREADS

The strongest threads for sewing synthetics are themselves synthetic. The two types most commonly used are twisted or bulked nylon, and cotton wrapped polyesters. To choose between these two, there are several considerations. Cotton wrapped polyesters are often shunned because the cotton is prone to rot and not very strong. On the other hand, the cotton wrap is advantageous for tent and rainwear applications. The cotton will swell when wet, to seal up the stitching holes and add another measure of water repellency. How long it would take for a cotton wrapped polyester thread to rot and deteriorate is hard to say. A more than adequately strong cotton and polyester thread may be had by using a slightly larger size. Because polyester does not stretch much, this thread is very easy to work with on a sewing machine.

Nylon threads have the advantage of greater strength, because they are not mixed with cotton or some other weaker fiber. The arguments against nylon threads are that they can cut through fabrics and their elasticity makes them difficult to work with at first. The former problem doesn't really exist. Threads that appear to be cutting through the fabric have been sewn with too much tension and a chisel tipped needle. This type of needle is sometimes used to minimize the problems caused by thread stretch on sewing machines. What it does is to actually cut some of the yarns in the fabric, as opposed to a ball point needle, which simply passes through the weave. Obviously, items that are sewn with a chisel needle are going to be considerably weaker and should be avoided. A close inspection of some of the stitching on a piece of equipment will reveal how it was sewn. Following the adjustment instructions in chapter 5 on sewing, you should not have any great problems with thread stretch, and a chisel tipped needle should not be required.

Thread sizes are measured numerically, backwards. Size 46 twisted nylon, a medium/heavy weight available through the outlets listed in table 4, is larger than a size 70 thread.

Threads for sewing leather should be heavy cotton wrapped polyester. Nylon thread will cut leather. Coats and Clark's button and carpet thread (size 13) does the job fine.

Table 4 shows who has what in some of the more commonly used hardware items. Often, much of this hardware is available locally from fabric stores, hardware stores, surplus shops, and other local merchants. For quality, though, the following suppliers have the best.

TABLE 4/HARDWARE: WHO HAS WHAT

			Suppliers			
	EMS	Frost-line	Kelty	REI	Sierra Designs	Ski Hut
Velcro		X	X	X	X	X
Delrin zippers	X*	X	X	X		
Coil zippers	X*				X	X
Loop zippers			X			
Grommets & Sets	X	X		X		
Rivets						X
Snaps	X	X		X		X
Webbing	X	X	X	X	X	X
Tapes	X	X				
Double-bar buckles	X	X		X		
Tablar buckles			X			
Clincher buckles	X	X				
"D" rings	X	X		X+		
Acc. strap patches	X	X	X			X
Thread	X[n]	X[p]	X[n]	X[p]		

*Zippers available by the yard.
+Seamless aluminum
[n]Nylon
[p]Polyester and Cotton
See appendix for supplier's address

SECTION TWO

CONSTRUCTION TECHNIQUES

CHAPTER 4

Making Your Own Patterns

Designing your own is a rewarding way to obtain perfectly suited gear of excellent quality. A great sense of satisfaction and self-sufficiency comes from having a unique product that fits and functions to your particular needs. And it's not that difficult. Working out all the angles and measurements for your own designs is relatively simple and quick.

The patterns and accompanying instructions in the equipment chapters, and the general assembly instructions in chapter 5 on sewing and assembly techniques, are complete and may be referred to as they apply to your own designs. Operations such as zippers, pockets, catenary seams, and reinforcements are all fairly basic with respect to construction techniques and processes.

Functional design considerations that are common to both home and ready-made equipment are also detailed in the above mentioned chapters. This information, as well, may be of some help to you during the conceptual stages of your project.

The first step towards production is some rough sketches of your planned item. These rough sketches should be used to work out the relative dimensions of your project.

The next step is to draw scale dimensioned profiles using graph paper. Quadrille paper, measuring 8½″ × 11″, that has quarter inch squares within bold line one inch squares is an easy paper to work with, and a standard stationary item. For medium size items such as packs and accessories, use a scale of one quarter inch to the inch. Larger items such as tents and sleeping bags will require a scale of four inches or more to each quarter inch square. If you plan on doing up several items, a draftsman's type ruler with a quarter inch scale is a handy tool. Your first dimensional profiles may not look like what you had in mind, so expect to modify them at this point. Remember, if you are making something such as a pack or tent using commercially made poles or frames, you are going to need their dimensions.

Using these profile drawings, figure out your pattern pieces and where your seams will go. Confused? Look at a comparable design in the equipment chapters. Maybe even a quick trip to your local mountain shop will help to see how other manufacturers put their equipment together. Bear in mind that the fewer pieces of fabric you use, the less seams you will have to sew. Some packs on the market are whacked right out of a single piece of fabric and simply folded together like a paper bag. Consideration must be given to the cutting layout for the particular width of fabric being used in order to avoid ending up with large wasted scraps. More on this shortly.

Draw the pattern pieces in scale using the same type of graph paper, and write in all the measurements. A drafting compass can be used for stepping out the length of compound curves where such a measurement is needed; such as between a tent and tunnel entrance, or the insertion of a sleeve on a coat. Set the compass to a scale inch division and simply walk it around the curve on your scale drawing. ⑦

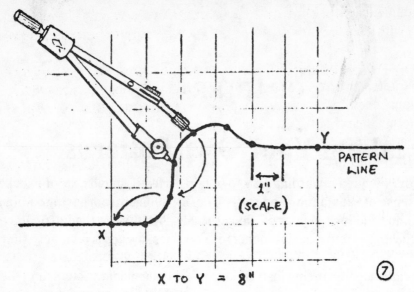

PATTERN LINE

1"
(SCALE)

X TO Y = 8"

(7)

Granted, this technique may not be as precise as using a pocket calculator, but it is functionally accurate, has the added romantic nostalgia of counting on your fingers, and allows you to design an item of limited symmetry and maximum function. Seam allowances should be included in these drawings. Usually an allowance of five-eighths inch or one half inch is adequate, but remember that some may require more for reinforcements or grommets.

If you are making a tent, be sure to include *catenary* seams as discussed in chapter 9 on tents. If your tent design is somewhat unconventional, consider making a scaled down model first, from some scrap material. Model pole structures may be quickly fabricated from coat hanger wire. The model may be useful for determining dimensional feasibility, locating stress points and panel reinforcement seams. Modifications and corrections may be more easily made to the scale pattern.

The next step is to transfer the scale pattern to full size pattern paper, available at larger fabric stores. This paper is dotted every square inch, making the transfer a simple matter of plotting the curves, angles, and lines from the scale drawing to the full size pattern paper. Like fabrics, pattern paper is bought off the roll, by the yard, so you won't end up lining your shelves with the excess. The full size pattern pieces are then cut out for transfer to your material. For extremely large or symmetrical pieces the pattern paper may be done away with and the piece measured right on the fabric. In this case, make sure that the fabric is laid out flat without any diagonal stretch. The corners of the fabric may be tacked down or held by some weight to be sure it remains square while you are marking it.

A cutting layout may be figured using the separate pattern pieces. Find some floor space in your house with a few existing boundries, such as the corner of a carpet or a linoleum floor with a symmetrical pattern. Lay out some books or a yardstick to mark off an area, the width of the fabric you intend to purchase. The pattern pieces may then be fit, jigsaw puzzle fashion, into the shortest area possible without overlap. Many fabrics are available in different widths, so you might have two possible layouts to work with in order to buy the least amount of fabric necessary for greatest economy. The resulting cutting layout will probably require far less fabric than you had anticipated. For example,

Make Your Own Camping Equipment

most full size, sophisticated packbags require less than two yards of 45" wide fabric. If you are working with a coated fabric, make sure your pattern pieces are laid out with the right sides up.

For making most of your general clothing items in the pants and shirt category, try a commercially marketed pattern that approximates what you want and then modify it. A variety of functional needs may be met by substituting different fabrics, changing closures, and altering the pockets and trappings.

Once your pattern is done, the rest is easy. The next steps in construction are marking and cutting. Marking your fabric may be done by simply outlining the pattern pieces with a dressmaker's pencil, tailor's chalk, or soft artist's pencil, in a contrasting color. Another method, commonly used with store bought patterns where the pieces are already arranged in the proper cutting layout, is to pin the pattern to the fabric and cut through the pattern.

There are two ways to cut nylon fabrics, either with conventional extremely sharp scissors or a hot-knife. Cut edges must be heat sealed to prevent their tendency to unravel. The usual method for the home-builder of elemental equipment is to sear the fabric edges lightly by passing them over a candle flame. Keep a close eye out for burning edges when you are doing this. Whereas the nylon itself will not burn, the dyes and finishes in many fabrics will ignite and spread into the fabric quite rapidly, if not immediately blown out. These techniques for heat setting are necessary only if the fabric is cut with scissors, or as is sometimes the case in commercial manufacture, with a specialized type of saw. Most kits on the market now require you to heat set the edges yourself. Do it!

Cutting thermoplastic synthetics, such as nylon, using a hot-knife, simultaneously heat sets the cut edges of the fabric. This method of cutting is much quicker and far less tedious. A hot-knife can be obtained from hobby shops in the form of a wood burning tool. It resembles a soldering pencil with a small blade that screws on the end. Cost is around six dollars. Another way to achieve this end is to heat an old table knife using a propane torch. A hot-knife will cut through fabrics, webbing and tapes like butter. The resulting edge is strong and usually straighter. Hot-knifing should be done with the fabric held flat with tacks or some weight, against a smooth flat surface.

The necessity for heat setting some edges may be avoided by making use, whenever possible, of the finished edges or *salvage* of the fabric. This can be especially time-saving on very large pieces of fabric, such as a tent wall or sleeping bag.

The final step before assembly, is to mark sewing reference points on the fabric edges to be joined. The purpose of these marks is to assure the proper mating and fit of the fabric pieces when sewing. These references are invaluable when sewing curved seams such as those found on sleeves, tent vents, sleeping bag baffles and the like. They are even more important when sewing with nylon fabrics because of the tendency of these fabrics to stretch considerably on the diagonal of the fabric's grainline. Reference marks may be made on the seam allowances by either cutting small notches or simply marking with your pencil.

The subsequent assembly and finishing of your particular project should be careful and well planned to avoid the necessity of ripping out any seams sewn incorrectly or out of order. The instructions and assembly orders listed for the projects in this book should help you plan your own assembly. Simple!

Chapter 5

Sewing And Assembly Techniques

The following information on sewing machine operation and adjustment is for the experienced sewer as well as the beginner. Sewing the synthetic fabrics used in light weight equipment presents some problems not usually encountered with standard clothing fabrics. Foreknowledge of the idiosyncracies of synthetic sewing will save you time and headaches during assembly.

The assembly techniques detailed in this chapter are common to many equipment items. The various seam types listed, their construction and purposes, are basic to all fabric construction operations. The different zipper assemblies listed may be used wherever this type of closure is called for. The reasons for using one assembly technique instead of another are detailed to give you a better working understanding of why a certain application may be necessary or better suited.

THE MACHINE

If you don't already have one, the first order of business is to get your hands on a sewing machine. Renting one from a sewing or rental shop is relatively inexpensive. By having all of your materials on hand and ready to go, even the longest projects can be completed within a week. This will keep your rental charge down to a minimum. Better yet, borrow a machine from a friend, if possible. This method has the added plus of having the owner give you a rundown on the idiosyncracies and operation of that particular machine. Even if you have never used a sewing machine, an hour or so should be sufficient time to learn. The operation manuals for sewing machines are written to be understood by almost anyone, and may be kept on hand for quick reference while soloing.

A special type of machine is not needed to complete the projects in this book or to do up your own designs. Commercial machines are great if you're a professional seamstress, but they operate far too quickly for the inexperienced to keep up with. The design prototypes for the projects in this book were made with an almost antique Singer portable described in its operations manual as ". . . especially designed for operation by electricity . . ."! All that is really necessary is a machine in good working order that produces a basic straight and even lockstitch. That includes treadle machines.

Nylon materials, because of their light weight, elasticity, and slipperiness, present demands not normally made of a sewing machine. The problems which are most likely to occur with these materials are in the fabric feed and dropping or skipping stitches.

Uneven material feed is just what the name implies. This problem is usually due to excessive pressure on the fabric from the presser foot. On most machines this adjustment is made by loosening a spring holding screw, directly above the presser foot shaft on top of the machine's sewing head. Do it. A very light setting is necessary for fabrics such as light ripstops and taffetas. Holding the fabric taut, front and rear evenly, is the best guarantee of keeping the layers of fabric mating evenly. Do not hold the fabric so tight that the feeding action is inhibited. Uneven feed and puckering are more apt to occur when sewing curves, so take particular care while twisting the fabric through the machine.

Skipping or dropping a stitch is another problem more likely to occur when using synthetic, especially nylon, fabrics. To understand how to alleviate this prolbem, it is necessary to know how a machine makes a lockstitch. It goes like this. Machine needles are grooved on one side from the eye up. ⑧

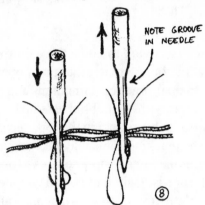

NOTE GROOVE IN NEEDLE

⑧

As the needle comes up and out of the fabric, it will bring with it the thread lying in the groove. The thread on the other side of the needle is held back by the greater friction of the fabric. This causes this latter thread to form a loop under the fabric for the bobbin hook to catch and pass around its spool, thereby forming the twist for the lockstitch. If this loop is not formed, a skip will result.

Several things may combine or act independently to cause skips. Because the fabrics we are concerned with are very slippery, the skip may be the result of insufficient friction against the needle and the loop forming thread. The use of nylon threads will amplify this situation because they are both slippery and elastic. The thread may stretch enough on the downstroke to cause it to spring back and initiate slippage on the upstroke. Slippage and the resulting skips and dropped stitches caused by nylon threads and/or fabrics may be minimized by using a larger size, fatter needle to increase the friction between the fabric and the loop forming thread. For light ripstops and taffetas, a size 14 needle should do the trick, although a standard size 12 will often times work. The same size needle should also work with heavier weight nylon fabrics, because their increased bulk will supply more resistance to the thread. The same is true for coated fabrics. If you still have trouble with the heavier materials, go ahead and try up to a size 16 needle.

Some other causes of skips are needles that are bent, incorrectly installed, and threaded backwards or from the wrong side. Using a needle made for another machine which is either too long or short will also cause problems.

When switching a machine over to sew synthetic fabrics, it is necessary to re-adjust the thread tensions on the machine. Improper adjustment will also cause skips. There are two adjustments, one for the needle thread and the other for the bobbin thread. How and where to make these adjustments should be in the operation manual for your machine. On a newer model, adjusting the top, needle thread tension to closely match the bobbin thread tension should suffice. The tensions are correctly set when they are synchronized and produce a stitch that is locked securely in the center of the fabric layers. If one tension setting is tighter than the other, it will cause the thread to lay flat on that side of the material.⑨

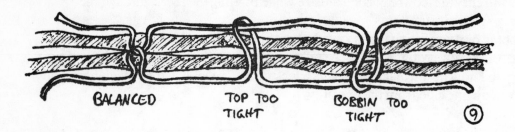

BALANCED   TOP TOO   BOBBIN TOO   ⑨
                   TIGHT   TIGHT

Because of the extreme elasticity of nylon threads, the uniformity of the thread tensions becomes more of a critical factor. A greater margin of operation can be obtained by loosening both thread tensions to their practical minimums and re-balancing them low to minimize the effects of stretch. Start with the bobbin tension by setting it so that it just slightly gives some resistance. Finish up by matching the top, needle thread tension by running some test scraps through the machine. This may take some time and a few rows of trial stitches, so be patient. If your machine simply refuses to operate reliably with nylon threads at both low and high speeds, switch to cotton wrapped polyester threads.

On the right side of the throat plate of your sewing machine, are reference lines marked in fractions of an inch. These lines serve as seam allowance guides. On all the projects in this book there is a seam allowance of one half inch, unless otherwise specified. A good trick for making straight seams is to watch the fabric at these reference lines while feeding it through the machine. The natural tendency for the beginning sewer is to watch the fabric at the needle. The result of this may be seams that wander back and forth in laze "S" curves. Try this while you are practicing different types of seams on the cutting scraps of your fabric. It works! This will also give you the chance to become more familiar with the operation of your machine and to test its reliability and consistency.

When beginning a seam, hold the two loose thread ends taut behind the machine until you are under way. This will prevent these loose ends from being dragged down into the bobbin case and making a bird's nest. This practice is absolutely necessary with nylon threads because of their elasticity.

To keep your seams from coming apart at their ends, they should be backstitched. Stop your machine after the first half inch or so and reverse stitch back to the start. Backstitching should be done to both the beginning and end of a seam. Otherwise it is very likely that your seams will start coming apart within a short period of use.

The stitch length should be around ten per inch. This adjustment is usually made with the same lever used to reverse the machine. Some newer machines have an independent reverse lever or knob, though. The stitch length adjustment device is marked with numbers indicating the amount of stitches per inch. Simple! Uneven length stitches mean uneven feed. Hold the fabric taut, front and rear, and/or adjust the presser foot tension. For sewing seams that are curved or on the bias (not with the fabric grain line), the stitch length should be shortened to around twelve to fifteen stitches per inch. This will provide added strength and stretchability, to compensate for the greater diagonal elasticity of nylon fabrics.

Make Your Own Camping Equipment

SEAMS

Following is a rundown on some of the most common seams used for our purposes and some of their applications. Note that most of these seams are usually made on the wrong side of the fabric, which is then turned to the inside for a more finished appearance. These instructions, as well as those for zipper assemblies, are referred to by name in the project directions in this book. They are detailed here to save space and repetition and may be referred to as needed, when called for in the projects.

Plain Seam

This seam is exactly what its name implies. The fabric pieces are placed right sides together and stitched up. A double row of stitches is a mark of quality and almost a necessity with light nylon fabrics to insure durability. Plain seams are almost always sewn with the work inside out for a finished appearance, with no exposed fabric edges. Where it is impossible to make the seam inside out, the exposed edges may be covered with some fabric strips or binding tape, as shown in illustration 10. Plain seams are found almost everywhere; in tent corners, pockets of all sorts, sleeves, and the like. ⑩

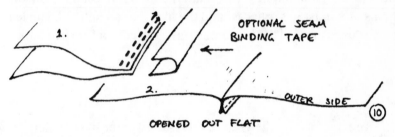

Top Stitched Seam

This seam is made by folding under a portion of the seam allowance of a piece of fabric or subassembly and stitching this down onto another piece. Top stitched seams are found most often on pockets. This seam is used when it is impossible to make a plain seam inside out. It is about the same, except for the exposed top stitches. ⑪

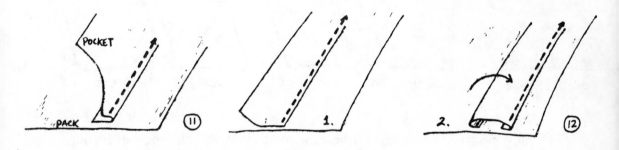

This seam may also be used for making drawcord tubes. The drawcord fabric strip is plain seamed on its wrong side, and then folded over and top stitched along its other side. ⑫

Hemmed Seam

This seam might also be called a folded or finished plain seam. Both layers of fabric to be joined are folded over once (rough) or twice, (finished) and then stitched together. ⑬

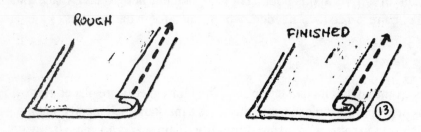

This seam is often used in the construction of down filled gear because it is more leak proof The down fill may pass through the stitches between the layers of fabric, but is stopped by the fold. As the name implies, this seam is commonly used for finishing the bottom edges or hems or windshirts, parkas, and **the** like. For an unlined, single layer parka, the hem seam is used around the bottom, to give the edge a finished look and to prevent unravelling.

Flat Felled Seam

Sometimes referred to as a lap felled seam, this is used extensively where two pieces of fabric are joined straight into each other. The flat felled seam is a plain seam with the remaining edges folded over once (rough) or twice, (finished) and then top stitched down with the two pieces of fabric being joined opened out flat. ⑭

For tent wall seams, for example, where the coated side wall joins the roof section, his seam is felled up on the inside to shed water like a shingle on the outside. When this seam is used on heavier fabrics, the inside layer of the felled edges may require trimming to half of its width to avoid excessive bulk.

That's it! For most elemental equipment you will only need the plain, top stitched, and flat felled seams. Most other seams are concerned primarily with a fashionable, finished appearance rather than functional considerations, and so are not listed here.

Make Your Own Camping Equipment

BASTING AND BLENDING

Basting is the process of fixing the layers of fabric to be joined in their desired position before sewing to insure a neat and accurate finished seam. Pin or stitch basting is often a necessity for very difficult seams or applications requiring absolutely correct placement, such as in the joining or curved pieces where the lengths may not come out evenly otherwise. Machine or stitched basting is a long length stitching that is easily removed by ripping it out, once the final seam is completed. This may be done on almost any sewing machine by setting the stitch length control lever or knob to the longest setting. Basting stitches may be removed by cutting the thread every four to six stitches on one side, and then ripping the thread off the other side.

Pin basting is used more often than stitch basting because it lends itself better to more difficult matings. Particularly tricky seams will usually require the slower and more deliberate process of pinning before sewing. Pins placed in the seam line at a right angle may be run through your sewing machine without any difficulty. At this angle, the sewing needle will roll off any directly encountered pins. ⑮

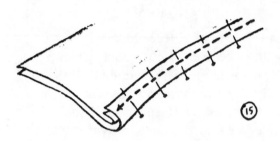
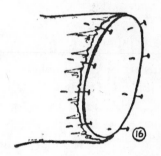

Basting is absolutely necessary for curved seams joining two pieces of fabric at a right angle. Examples are sleeve insertions, internal pack shelves, and collar and hood attachments. The unique problem in these applications is the even matching of the lengths or circumferences of the two pieces. More often than not, I find the inner piece wants to come out shorter than the outer piece as a result of its being tucked inside the outer piece. The real or projected excess material of the outer piece has to be gathered over the length of the seam so that your edges match up all the way around. This operation is called *easing*. First the fabric pieces are pinned together at one point or, in the case of only a portion of a full circle, at the ends. The existing fullness of the longer piece is then evenly distributed, or eased through the length of the seam, pinning as you go. ⑯

The full side of the seam should be on the bottom, when feeding the eased and basted assembly through your sewing machine. This will allow you to feed the curve down, up, and out of the machine.⑰

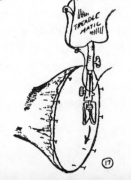

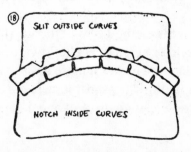

SLIT OUTSIDE CURVES

NOTCH INSIDE CURVES

Curved seams sometimes require *blending* the seam allowance, so that the finished seam will lie flat and unpuckered. This consists of notching or cutting the fabric in from the edge along the seam allowance. The allowance on the outside of a flat curve is slit every inch or so, as needed, to allow it to bend out and lie flat. The inner allowance of a curved seam is notched to allow it to gather together without wrinkles. (18)

Blending notches and slits are not absolute necessities with very light nylon fabrics and can cause unravelling if not very thoroughly heat sealed. For clothing applications, the resultant seam may be much neater in appearance. This may or may not be a worthwhile consideration to you. Blending may be done before or after a seam is made, so you still have the option if it looks desirable.

ZIPPER ASSEMBLIES

Like different seams, the following zipper assemblies are common to most clothing and equipment applications. These methods for construction are referred to by name in the projects in this book.

Slit Installation

This is the simplest way to install a zipper in the middle of a piece of fabric. Examples are on pack pockets, clothing pockets, and wherever a zipper must be placed without the aid of a seam to put it in. A slit is made in the fabric, with inverted arrows at the ends, angled out at about forty-five degrees. The depth of these end slits will determine the width of the finished opening. Their lengths should be included in the finished length measurement. The ends and the sides are folded under to provide for a finished edge on the zipper, which is sewn on underneath. (19)

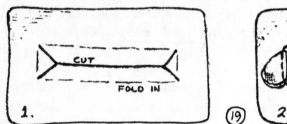
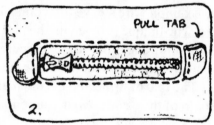

Rain and wind flaps may be added as desired. In the slit type installation, these are made of a separate strip of fabric that is folded once lengthwise for a finished exposed edge. The separate flap piece may be sewn directly to the zipper tape first, or may be sewn on along with the zipper in one operation. Slit applications may also be used to extend in from a finished fabric edge, such as a pant fly opening.

Full Width, Separate Flap Installation

This method is used for attached pockets on parkas and packs that are to zip all around or across a pocket's width and sides. The accessability provided by this type of application makes it more desirable than the slit type. Another common use for this type of opening is for separating parka and coat fronts. The reason for making the weather flap from a separate piece of material is for ease of design. Many full width applications are not in perfectly square sections of fabric. That is, the sides which the zipper opening butts into may not be at a ninety degree angle to the zipper opening.

If you make the weather flap from a separate piece of fabric, you don't have to consider it in the layout of the fabric section into which it will go. So, wherever you want to put a zipper, you have only to cut that piece in half, and the flap may be added to achieve the desired finished height. (20)

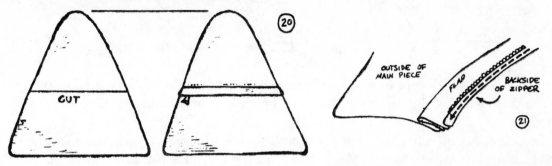

The top flap side of the opening is made first. The projects in this book use a flap two and one-half inches wide before folding a couple of inches longer than the expected opening. The flap is folded once length wise and matched to the edge of the main piece on its right side with the folded edge of the flap up. The zipper is placed facing down on top of these pieces with its lower edge lined up with the others. These three pieces are then stitched from the top at one quarter inch allowance. The flap may then be trimmed flush. (21)

The flap and the zipper are then folded down to their finished configuration. Pulling the main piece to keep it taut against the stitching, sew the assembly flat about one quarter inch up from the first seam. (22)

The bottom half of the zipper is attached in the same way, lining up the edge of the zipper tape with the bottom main piece with the zipper facing it, stitching once at one quarter inch, and then folding this out and stitching it flat. (23)

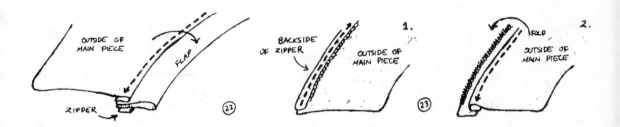

Full Width, Integral Flap Installation

For basically square piece installations, this method is easier to construct than the previous one. The rain or wind flap is made by folding back a sufficient amount of the main piece fabric. In order for the end product to be a prescribed height, one and one-half inches of extra length must be included in the main pattern piece for forming the flap. To make the top flap side of this opening, the zipper is lined up with the main piece edge, facing it as in the previous method. Once this is stitched, at the same allowance, a

Construction Techniques

reference line is drawn parallel to the edge and two inches up on the wrong side or inside of the fabric. The already joined zipper and fabric edge is then folded up to this line on the inner side and stitched down. ㉔

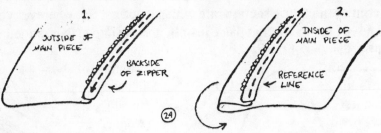

For a more finished appearance, stitch along the fold of the zipper flap so that it lays flat. The bottom half of the zipper is attached in the same manner as the previous method.

Another factor affecting the choice between these two applications is fabric quantity and the cutting layout possibilities. Making the flaps from separate pieces may provide for a more efficient cutting layout, requiring less fabric. This is one reason why the design in this book for a divided front opening pack sack uses a separate piece for the weather flap on the bottom compartment.

Seam Installation

In some cases it is desirable to have the zipper opening at the very top or seam edge of a pocket or pack. Examples are belt and daypack top openings. This installation is similar to the slit method with the exception of the end "V" cuts or inverted arrows. In this case the lower side end cuts are done away with. ㉕

The top half of the zipper is sewn in first with a separate flap piece which will line up with the seam line when finished. The same construction is used as for the separate flap installation with the exception of the ends, which are finished with the flap sewn under the folded back end cut. ㉖

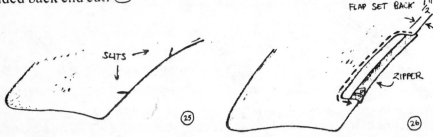

The bottom half of the zipper may then be sewn to the bottom main piece, or in the case of a pocket, the front piece, along with its entire seam. The pocket is then turned right side out through the zipper opening. This final seam, of course, requires that the zipper be closed. ㉗

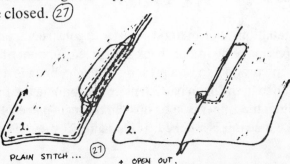

Make Your Own Camping Equipment

Curved Installation

This type of installation is constructed with the appropriate above mentioned techniques, but presents some unique problems of its own. First, you will encounter the same problems discussed under blending and basting with easing the fabric in a curved seam. The addition of a zipper assembly to a seam requiring easing necessitates very careful pin basting. This insures that the zipper will close completely, without puckering itself or the fabric around it. Second, the weather flap will have a tendency to stand out from the fabric at a ninety degree angle, as will the zipper itself. Essentially, you are trying to bend the zipper in a flat arch and it just doesn't want to work that way. To avoid these problems, be aware of them, and plan around their inevitability. Realize that the zipper is going to stand out from the fabric and plan for it by cutting the inside diameter of the installation curve larger. Where this is not possible, like for a cook hole in a tent floor where the opening is cut in a panel, careful easing and basting will work sufficiently. Don't expect perfection in these types of seams. Even professionally made seams of this sort come out a little on the ragged side. The finished product should look okay and be functional, if some care is taken. If so desired, the weather flap may be made to lie flatter against the installation by sewing some tucks into it. This will, however, make access to the zipper slightly more difficult. (28)

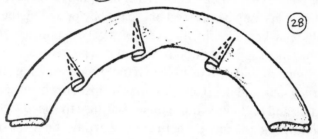

Curved zipper installations are used on the patterns for the top opening of the "A" shaped daypack (pattern 6), and the top compartment of the divided front opening pack sack (pattern 9).

With the exceptions of the above curved installations and some seam installations, it is not always necessary to perform each construction step with the zipper closed. I have found it to be easier and less expensive to work with the coil type zipper, which is sold by the yard. This allows you maximum freedom of length and can prevent potential goofs caused by cutting the opening too long. You simply match the amount of zipper needed, plus a couple of inches extra for the end seams, to match your openings. The end teeth where the seam will go are then removed and the few remaining end teeth are melted in a flame to seal them together. For most installations, it is easier to completely separate the two halves of the zipper, however this is entirely up to you. The sliders are relatively easy to thread onto the teeth and you also have the option of using two for either-side-access on larger applications.

LEATHER

Sewing leather on a home sewing machine, (even my comparatively gutless little portable with a slightly oversized rubber band drive) is feasible and easier than you think. Most machines, including mine, will stitch a reasonably thick, well tanned piece of leather. If not, the machine may be turned over by the handwheel. This still beats hand stitching by a mile.

Surprisingly enough, the tension settings for the presser foot and threads and the needle size are just about the same for leather as they are for the light synthetics. What this means is that you don't have to mess around with all your carefully balanced machine adjustments. The only change necessary is that of stitch length. This should be increased to about eight to ten stitches per inch or longer to avoid weakening the leather with an excess of holes.

If basting is necessary, it is best done with rubber cement or paper clips to avoid making a lot of holes in the leather. Pin basting may be employed if the pins are kept within the seam allowance where they will not show. Of course, this will be possible only on very thin leathers. Unlike fabrics, once you poke a hole in leather, it is there for good. For this reason, great care should be taken so that your first stitching is correct. An incorrect seam that must be ripped out will leave a permanent row of holes. The extra holes caused by backstitching the beginnings and ends of your seams may also be avoided by hand tying the remaining loose threads.

Because leather is considerably more substantial than fabric, blending the seam allowances may be a necessity. This and all other cutting may be done with a utility knife, or a single edged razor blade. Use a metal edged ruler as a guide to prevent the blade from wandering. The leather seams may be pressed or creased by pounding them with a rubber, wood, or rawhide mallet. The finished seams may be set open in the same manner or, better still, filled with the trappings of your pursuit and put to use.

Most sewing machines should also be able to handle wide webbing and quarter inch thick felt for making rucksack and daypack shoulder straps. However, care must be taken to prevent bending and breaking your needle. Because the needle enters the material at a higher point while the feeder teeth are still eating, it may be deflected backwards enough to miss its hole in the throat plate. Such a mechanical problem may be minimized by setting the stitch length as short as seems reasonable, this will limit the movement of the feeder teeth so that they eat slowly. With such good table manners, your sewing machine should be able to handle any situation.

That's just about it for the sewing department. Of course, there are lots of other little tricks in putting things together with a machine. As with all tools, be aware of possible difficulties. Most problems may be overcome with a little patience and ingenuity. One last trick and an example. If your machine simply refuses to feed evenly using coated fabric with the coated side down, it is because the sticky coating material is hanging up on the throat plate. To eliminate the friction problem, sew the assembly with a layer of light tissue paper on the bottom. When the seam is finished, the tissue paper will rip right off the seam. Seemingly impossible problems like this may be solved very simply.

In any case, expect to make mistakes. Sewing synthetics, in fact, sewing at all can be tricky and frustrating at times. If you don't already have one, it's a god idea to pick up a seam ripper for about fifty cents. This well designed little tool makes ripping out incorrect seams quick and easy, not that you're likely to feel good about it at the time! There really is a lot of room for minor errors when working with fabrics, so hang in there. With a minimum of effort, you will usually end up with an item that is equal to, if not better than, the store bought, more expensive equivalent.

One last note. Don't let your nylon or thermoplastic fabrics come in contact with the lamp on your sewing machine. It can get hot enough to melt a hole!

Make Your Own Camping Equipment

SECTION THREE

PATTERNS AND DESIGN CRITERIA

Chapter 6

Accessories And Beginning Projects

So you've decided to give it a go and make your own gear. If you have limited or no experience with a sewing machine, this is the place to start. The five projects in this chapter are all fairly quick and easy. Even the most complicated pattern, the book pack, can be completed in less than a day, if you have all the materials. Starting with these quickies, you can experiment and make the inevitable beginner's mistakes. In any case, the basic constructions are the same as the longer, more sophisticated designs and patterns.

Keep an open mind for modifications on all the patterns in this book. Variations can be achieved by substituting features from one pattern to another, or by changing dimensions. Design overlap and repetition has been minimized to give as much choice in equipment as possible in a workbook of limited size and complexity. For example, there are several different types and sizes of shoulder harness constructions. These can be substituted on different projects.

Because they are small, these beginning projects use very little fabric. Since most suppliers sell their fabrics by the yard, you are going to have quite a bit left over. So you can either make two or more small projects or practice making a bigger project. You might also want to consider working with a friend to make several of the same item. After the first one, the rest are quick and easy.

HOW TO USE THE PATTERNS

1. MATERIALS; gives all the hardware and fabric needs for the design as pictured and described. Material for options must be added.

2. CUTTING LAYOUTS; show how to fit the pieces on the indicated amounts of fabric. When altering the cutting layouts to add options, remember that there is a right and wrong side to many pieces, and they must be cut out rightside up as shown.

3. PIECE DIMENSIONS; include seam allowances. Round, square, and rectangular piece dimensions are written. All others are noted on the cutting layouts or illustrated.

4. ASSEMBLY; instructions tell you how and what types of seams to use as detailed in chapter 5.

5. ILLUSTRATIONS; the rightsides, or finished outer sides, are pictured as unshaded outlines. The wrong sides, or coated, finished insides, are shown shaded. The stitching described in each step is shown as a bold dotted line with an arrow showing the working direction. Light dotted lines represent previous steps stitching and are for orientation only.

6. SEAM ALLOWANCES; one half inch unless otherwise stated. A considerable amount of deviation from this is possible without consequence on all seams except as specifically noted.

Patterns and Design Criteria

PATTERN 1

STUFF-SACK

Stuff-sacks are easy to make and handy to have. They take only a few minutes to sew up and don't present any difficulties other than those you might initially have working with nylon fabrics. This pattern will make a stuff-sack measuring 18″ long with a circumference of 24″; just about the right size for a light, summer weight, down sleeping bag.

MATERIALS:

25″ × 23″—Coated nylon fabric.
40″—Drawcord or ¼″ nylon tape.

PIECE DIMENSIONS:

One piece, same as above measurement.

ASSEMBLY:

1. Make the drawstring tube along a longer edge; Fold in corners ½″ and stitch down. Fold towards wrong side, ½″ then 1″ and *top-stitch* twice to form tube. (29A)

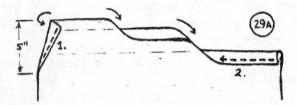

2. Place and center drawstring in the tube and stitch across the center of the tube to hold it fast. (29B)

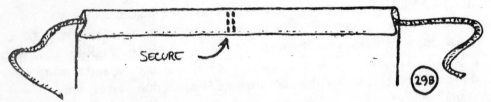

3. Fold rightsides together and stitch square. Do not stitch the drawstring tube closed. (29C)

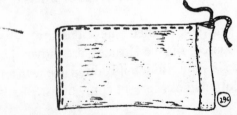

4. Stitch the bottom square; Flatten the sack with the lengthwise seam up and centered, and *plain stitch* 6½″ across corners. Trim off and heat seal triangular pieces. (30)

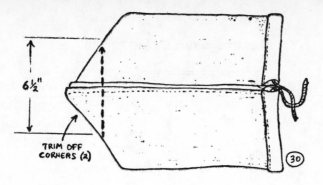

5. Turn the sack rightside out.

PATTERN 2

ROUND BOTTOM COMPRESSOR STUFF-SACK

Compressor stuff-sacks are designed to compact their contents in as small a space and bulk as possible. This can be a real convenience when weather necessitates taking a heavier sleeping bag of considerable bulk. You simply stuff your bag as usual, then cinch up on the drawcord lacing and tie it off. The dimensions given here will make a sack for a 2 to 2½ pound down bag; 18½" long with a 31" circumference, uncinched.

MATERIALS:

36" × 32" —coated nylon fabric.
42"—1" light nylon tape.
10'—drawcord.
9—no. "O" spur grommets.

CUTTING LAYOUT:

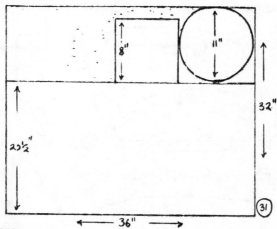

PIECE DIMENSIONS:

Body—36" × 20½".
Bottom—11" diameter circle.
Flap—8" square.

Patterns and Design Criteria

45

ASSEMBLY:

1. Fold body rightsides together and *plain stitch* as shown.

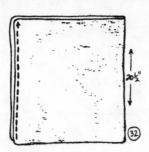

2. Turn body rightside-out. Flatten with the previous seam up and centered, and place two 20" length of 1" tape centered in the side folds. *Plain stitch* in as shown.

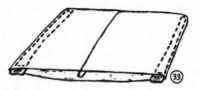

3. Stitch in 2" piece of 1" tape at indicated point and place one grommet centered in it to make the top drawstring hole.

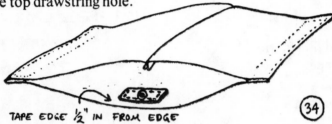

TAPE EDGE ½" IN FROM EDGE

4. Fold this end towards wrong side, ½" then 1" and *top-stitch* on inside to make drawstring tube. Grommet should now be on the outside edge.

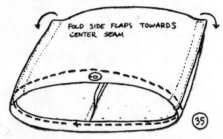

FOLD SIDE FLAPS TOWARDS CENTER SEAM

5. *Hem* edges of flap piece if desired and stitch in one corner over previous seam.

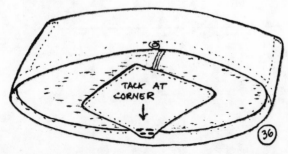

TACK AT CORNER

6. With assembly inside-out, ease, pin, and *plain stitch* bottom to body. (37)

7. Place four evenly spaced grommets in each side tab and lace with drawcord like a shoe. Cut off 3′ of drawcord and thread through top drawstring tube. Tie ends to secure. (38)

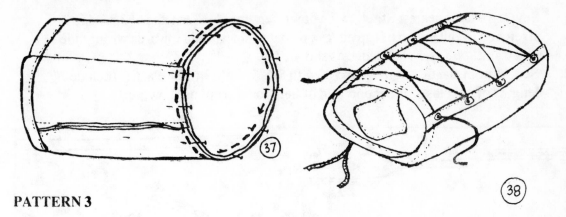

PATTERN 3

ANKLETS

These short gaiters may be used either as scree and snow guards on hiking boots, or as snow guards on cross-country ski boots. (For more elaborate, high gaiters, see chapter 10 on clothing.) These anklets have a top circumference of 13″, widening to 16″ around the boot and are 4½″ high. They are held in place by elastic hems and heavy elastic stirrups.

MATERIALS:

34″ × 7½″ or 17″ × 15″—coated nylon fabric (heavy) or 60/40.
32″—3/8″ elastic.
14″—¾″ heavy synthetic elastic.

CUTTING LAYOUT:

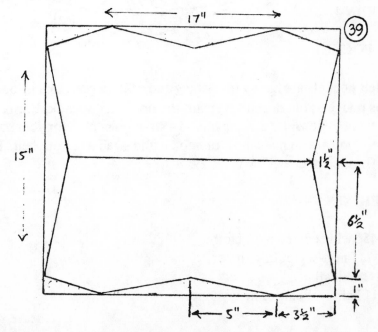

PIECE DIMENSIONS:

Two pieces, as shown in illustration 39.

ASSEMBLY:

1. Sew top elastic seams; Stitch twice down center of 7½″ lengths of 3/8″ elastic stretched to full length of top edges on coated sides. Fold towards wrong side ½″ twice and *top stitch* along edge as shown. ④⓪
2. Sew bottom elastic seams as above with 8½″ lengths of 3/8″ elastic. Include 7″ lengths of ¾″ elastic in second fold of hem for stirrups as shown. ④①

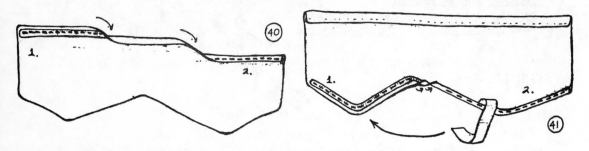

3. Sew anklets round with *plain* or *flat felled* seam on insides.

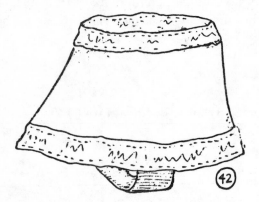

PATTERN 4

BELT POCKET

Belt pockets are handy for fishing and camera gear, that is too bulky for your clothes pockets, but doesn't warrant the use of a daypack. For backwoods use, you might want to consider making this as a strap on pocket for your packbag. When you get to where you are going, simply unhook it and strap it to your belt. The dimensions give you a finished pocket 9″ × 6″ × 2½″.

MATERIALS:

10″—45″ wide coated pack cloth.
One—11″ non-separating zipper.
12″ × 2″—leather.
7″—¾″ light webbing or heavy tape.

Make Your Own Camping Equipment

CUTTING LAYOUT:

Fabric
Leather

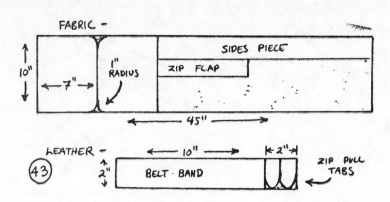

PIECE DIMENSIONS:

Front and back—as shown in illustration 43.
Sides piece—30″ × 3½″.
Zipper flap—12″ × 2″.
Leather—as shown in illustration 43.

ASSEMBLY:

1. Sew on leather back and belt loops to back and belt loops to back piece; Cut two 3½″ lengths of ¾″ webbing, include under top edge seam as shown, then fold over and include in bottom edge seam.

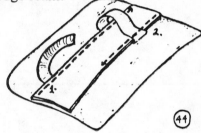

2. Sew in zipper with flap using the *seam installation* as detailed in chapter 5, "Sewing and Assembly Techniques." Center in the sides piece as shown, and include leather pull tabs at ends.

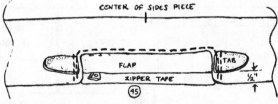

3. *Plain stitch* sides piece round on wrong side.

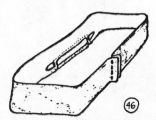

4 With assembly inside-out, ease, pin, and *plain stitch* front and back pieces to sides. Turn it right-side out through the zipper opening and you're done.

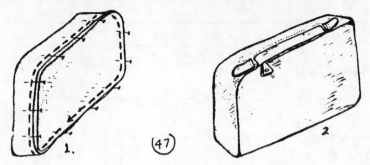

PATTERN 5

BOOK PACK

This mini-daypack is designed primarily for biking with books, although it may serve many other purposes. The shoulder straps are relatively short to keep the pack from shifting from side to side when bent over your handlebars. Consequently, a waist strap is not necessary. This bag can be made of any fairly heavy fabric, but pack weight nylon is recommended for durability. The finished dimensions are 13″ tall by 11″ wide with a 5″ depth. In addition to the zippered top flap pocket, there is a paper or map sleeve on the front and a side pencil sleeve. The top edge of the pack is kept under the flap via an elasticized hem.

MATERIALS:

21″—45″ wide coated pack cloth.
30″—2″ flat webbing.
51″—1″ medium/light flat webbing.
3—1″ tablar buckles.
One—11″ non-separating zipper.
4″—¾″ elastic.

CUTTING LAYOUT:

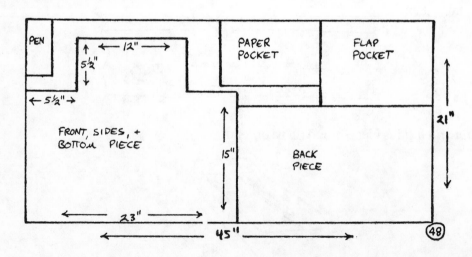

PIECE DIMENSIONS:

Front and sides piece—as shown in illustration 48.
Back—21″ × 12″.
Flap pocket—12″ × 9″.
Paper pocket—11″—11″ × 7″.
Pen pocket—6″ × 3″.

ASSEMBLY:

1. Sew zipper into flap piece at indicated position using the *full width, integral flap installation.*

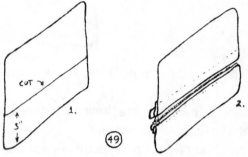

2. Place the flap pocket and the back pieces together, wrong sides up as shown, and *plain stitch* three outer edges. Include 6″ length of 1″ webbing looped through tablar buckle facing up on inside as shown. Turn rightside out and *top stitch* back edge to finish.

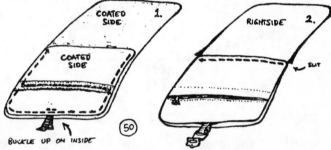

3. Taper the ends of the 30″ length of 2″ webbing as shown and sew on 6″ lengths of 1″ webbing looped through tablar buckles. Because 2″ webbing will be folded over, (see next step) buckles must be attached facing opposite sides of webbing. (51)

4. Fold 2″ webbing in center as shown and stitch to rightside of back piece, ½″ or so down from flap pocket edge. (52)

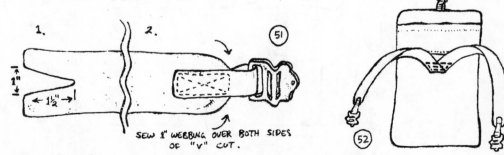

5. Make the top elastic hem on the front and sides piece; Stretch 4″ length of elastic to 7½″ and stitch down ½″ from edge on wrong side. Fold edge towards wrong side ½″ then 1″ over elastic and *top stitch* with elastic fully stretched. (53)

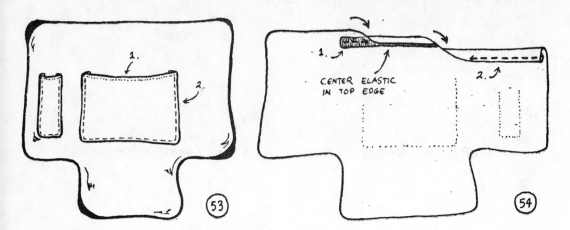

6. *Hem* the top edges of the pen and paper pockets, and *top stitch* to the front and sides piece as shown. (54)

7. Cut a 9″ piece of 1″ webbing and stitch end down ½″ or so, and centered above paper pocket for the top flap hold-down strap.

8. Join the halves; Ease, pin, and *plain stitch* together inside-out. Include two 12″ lengths of 1″ webbing for lower shoulder straps inside as shown. Double or triple stitch entire seam with bar-tacks at ends and five or six passes over straps.

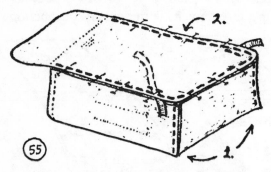

9. Turn the pack rightside out and inspect the seams. Hook up the harness and you're ready to go!

Chapter 7

Softpacks

You would think that softpacks, rucksacks, daypacks and the like, would be the simplest of elemental equipment from the standpoint of design. After all, what you have is basically a bag with a suspension system hooked to it. However, functional and efficient softpacks are much more complicated in their design than is apparent.

The idea behind softpacks is to keep the load close to your back and to the center of gravity, in order to give you maximum balance and mobility. To do this, a softpack must be engineered so that it will shadow your anatomy and maintain a narrow profile for a minimum back overhang. Softpacks that do not meet this design criteria will fit poorly against your back and usually take on a round, barrel shape when stuffed full; just like a loaded grocery bag.

Many softpacks employ built-in frames of either contoured aluminum or fiberglass. While these frames will insure a close fit to your anatomy, they do not maintain the shape of the pack itself. The bag may still take on a barrel shape and give you an upset balance. And the larger the capacity, the worse this problem will be.

The key to controlling both the fit and the profile of a softpack, without the necessity for elaborate solid framing, is the *monocoque* structure. This utilizes the stressed walls of an assembly to achieve rigidity. Such a structure may be effected in any softpack by simply adding one or more vertical or horizontal dividers inside the bag. Like an airplane wing, the dividers and the sides of the pack combine to work like ribs, while the outside skin of the pack holds them in place. When the pack is stuffed full, it becomes rigid.

An obvious shortcoming of the purely monocoque design softpack, that is, one without any framing, is that it will only be rigid when it is stuffed full. Consequently, a load-bearing hipbelt, which requires rigidity to support the pack from the bottom, will not always be functional. A solution to this is to design a monocoque softpack that has some solid framing as well. But then again, a partially filled softpack isn't always so heavy as to make only shoulder strap suspension objectionable. My preference is for the pure monocoque design. I like the pack to be able to move with me when I twist and bend, and I dislike the occasional poking you get from aluminum batten frames, even when they're encased in sleeves.

To work really well, your softpack should be tailored just like any other piece of attire, to fit your anatomy. The monocoque structure principal lends itself to this. By cutting the sides and dividers of a softpack in a contour, you can make the pack assume any shape. Thus, it is possible to make a pack that fits your back like a mold and keeps a thin, flat back profile as well. The result is an optimum center of gravity with a load carried anywhere but the top of your head.

Naturally, when a softpack becomes this sophisticated in its tailoring, size becomes a variable. Consequently, most of the better commercially made softpacks, and the monocoque design (pattern 7) in this chapter, come in four or five different sizes. The proper fit is indicated by shoulder straps that extend back almost horizontally from your shoulders. This is measured with the pack on and loaded, and with the hipbelt on at the most comfortable spot.

Any large softpack that extends more than a few inches above your shoulders should be fitted with *lift straps*. These are separate adjustable lengths of harness webbing which are attached between the padded sections of the shoulder straps and the top back corners of the pack.

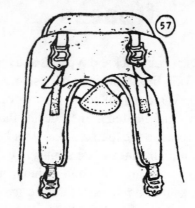

By adjusting the lengths of the lift straps, the top portion of the pack can be kept in a close and comfortable over-the-shoulders position. This keeps more of the load over your center of gravity and prevents an uncomfortable backward pull on the shoulder straps.

Other features for pockets, openings, and such on softpacks are options which should not affect the basic design for contour and fit. These trimmings are up to you, so they are not discussed here. What you want in the way of these features will depend on your needs.

PATTERN 6

DAYPACK

This pattern is for a standard "A" shaped daypack. It is just a shade larger than most of the commercially made versions. The height is 21" up your back and 18" up the front of the sack. The width is 14" at the bottom, tapering to a 4" radius curved top. The depth is 6" at the bottom and tapers to 1½" at the top. The pack has an upper and lower compartment, each opening with a 16" zipper protected by weather flaps, and angled 20° up toward your back to keep the load in close.

The plans and materials list here calls for shoulder straps made from 2" webbing with felt pads sewn to it. The felt padding can be purchased from a surplus, hardware, or saddle and tack shop. If padded shoulder straps are desired, use the pattern and assembly instructions for those listed for the "standard rucksack" (pattern 8). The materials list here also calls for a bottom and sidewalls reinforcement of leather. The addition of the leather can cost you as much as $4 more (much more expensive than the meat, but at least it lasts longer!) The leather bottom is also extra work but I recommend it highly for the durability it adds. You might also want to consider vinyl or another heavier fabric for the bottom. The reinforcement should at least be made of a double layer of fabric, in which case you must add the appropriate extra amount of fabric to your order to make the two bottom pieces.

This pack may easily be modified as a roomy, single compartment daypack by eliminating the shelf piece and one zipper and flap, and cutting the upper and lower front pieces as one. None of the measurements need be changed to do this because the lower compartment opening uses a separate flap zipper installation. The top opening should be made a good 17" or so longer to give you an ample, drop flap type opening. Simply extend the side cuts for the top zipper further down the sides to suit, and cut a flap to fit.

MATERIALS:

33" × 34" or 22½" × 45"—coated nylon fabric.
9'—1" medium/light flat webbing.
3'—2" flat webbing.
2'—2" × ½" to ¼" felt padding.
Two—16" non-separating zippers or 3' #5 zipper and 2 pullsliders.
6½" × 3"—leather (zip pull tabs and harness patch).
23¾" × 2½" and 14" × 8¾"—leather (bottom reinforcement).
3—accessory strap patches.
2—1" double-bar buckles.
3—1" "D" rings.
1—1" snap hook.
1—1" slider.

CUTTING LAYOUT:

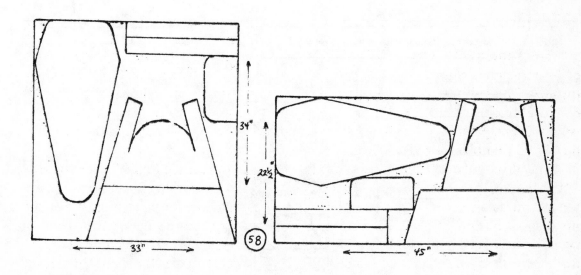

35" × 34"   or   22½" × 45"

PIECE DIMENSIONS:

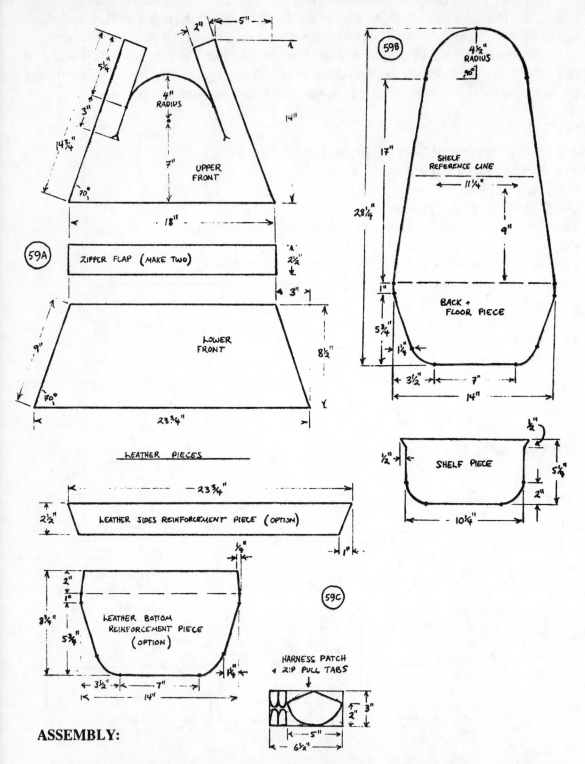

ASSEMBLY:

1. (A) Cut out and heat seal all edges; Make the curves with a compass or string and pencil (as in illustration 77 for "monocoque rucksack", pattern 7) from indicated radius points. On top front piece, extend zipper slits 3″ down from where circle hits 2″, 90° from fabric edge as shown. Make end **"V"** slits as shown. ⓺⓪

(B) Mark a reference line across the wrong side of the back piece, 15¾″ up from bottom edge, for latter placement of shelf. ⑥⑦

2. Sew on bottom reinforcement pieces; Match up long piece of leather with bottom of lower with bottom of lower front piece, and stitch along top edge. Match up larger leather piece with bottom of back and floor piece, and stitch along top edge as shown. ⑥②

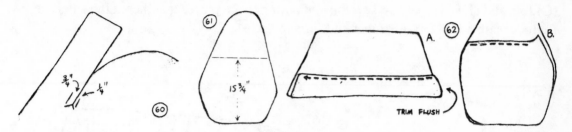

3. Place three accessory strap patches as shown. ⑥③

4. Join top sides; *Plain stitch* at standard allowance with top front piece folded right sides together. ⑥④

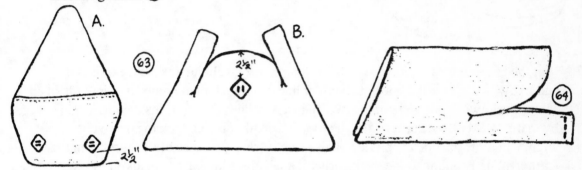

5. (A) Install top zipper using a combination *separate flap* and *slit installation*; Use the instructions in chapter 5 on sewing for the *full width, separate flap installation*, but stop the first seam short of the ends to allow the flap to be tucked under the slit ends. Ease and pin first to assure proper mating. ⑥⑤

(B) Fold over and finish top half of zipper per *separate flap installation* instructions. Do not sew across ends yet.

(C) Close zipper, fold the edge of the lower half fabric under ¼″, and ease and pin lower half of zipper. *Top stitch* on and continue across ends now, with the flap tucked under and the leather pull tabs in place, as shown. ⑥⑥

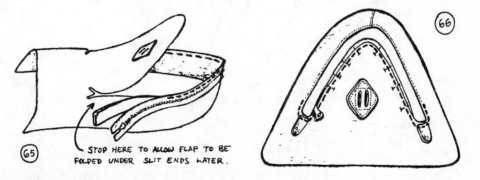

STOP HERE TO ALLOW FLAP TO BE FOLDED UNDER SLIT ENDS LATER.

6. (A) Install bottom compartment zipper; Use the *full width, separate flap installation.* Include shelf in top half of zipper installation by pinning and easing it on top of the assembly, rightside up. Center the shelf so that a ½″ allowance will remain along its back edge. Start stitching from the right side so the curved assembly may be fed down and out of your machine. ⑥⑦

(B) Center the lower half of the zipper on the bottom front piece and stitch on per same installation instructions.

(C) Join and close zipper and sew top and bottom front pieces together at the sides. Include leather pull tabs at zipper ends as shown. ⑥⑧

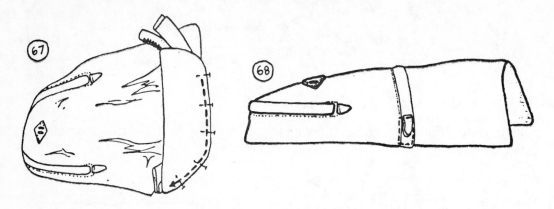

7. Join the back and front pieces; Cut a 10″ length of 1″ webbing for the ice-axe loop and two 4″ length for the bottom shoulder harness attachment points, and include in seam, as shown. Ease and pin the two main assemblies together, inside out. Begin by mating the bottom corners and the top. The leather is too thick to pin, so check alignment after the body is pinned. This seam is tricky because of the corners in the leather. When coming to the back corners, angle the stitching out to about ⅛″ allowance and push enough of the front piece leather (on top of the assembly on the machine) back to make the proper angle. Don't forget to include the webbing and "D" rings above these corner points. When everything is together, *plain stitch* all around this seam a second and third time to make a straight and even seam of extra strength. Being an inside seam, a perfect job isn't necessary, so be patient with the leather, correcting any crooked seams with the final passes.

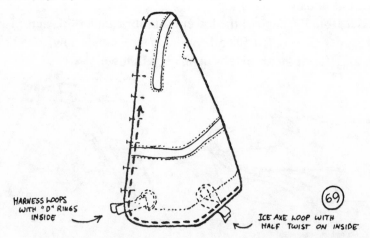

HARNESS LOOPS
WITH "D" RINGS
INSIDE

ICE AXE LOOP WITH
HALF TWIST ON INSIDE

⑥⑨

8. Turn the pack rightside out through the top compartment zipper opening. Open the bottom compartment and *top stitch* the shelf to the back piece along the reference line. ⑦⓪

9. (A) Make and attach the shoulder straps; Cut two 18" lengths of 2" webbing and stitch a 12" length of felt on each. Stitch slowly with the felt up in your machine.⑦①

   (B) Taper the longer ends of the straps and stitch on a double-bar buckle in a 6" loop of 1" webbing on each, as shown. The front, or flat side of the buckles should face away from the felt sides of the straps. ⑦②

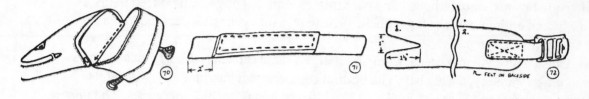

   (C) Center the leather shoulder strap reinforcement patch on the rightside of the back piece, 1" down from the top seam, and stitch around the lower perimeter with the top front pack opening pulled back out of the way. Cut a 12" length of 1" webbing for the hauling loop and place under the leather with the shoulder straps and stitch fast around upper perimeter of leather. Finish with stitching pattern shown. ⑦③

10. Cut the remaining 1" webbing in the lengths shown. Sew lower shoulder straps and waistbelt to "D" rings and hook up the hardware. You now own one of the better daypacks around. ⑦④

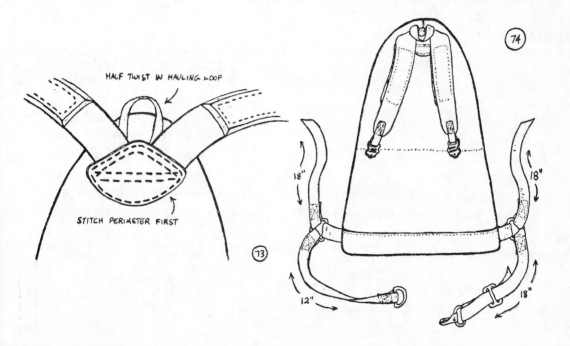

PATTERN 7

MONOCOQUE RUCKSACK

This rucksack has no aluminum battens or fiberglass inserts. It depends on its shape and compartmentalization for rigidity, enabling a good deal of the weight to be supported from the bottom by a hipbelt. It has also been engineered to take maximum advantage of the rucksack principal of keeping the weight and center of gravity close to your body. The side profile forms the shallow "S" curve of your back, while the width also curves around you. The top section of the pack angles back and away from your head to allow full vision upwards, something many packframes inhibit. The pattern is sized to insure a good fit and optimum use of the hipbelt. How to measure your fit is detailed in the assembly instructions.

These plans will make a pack with a relatively large capacity, though not as large as the average frame type pack bag. The bottom compartment measures 15" wide at its bottom, tapering to 12" at its top. This 12" width continues up the upper tubes. The upper half of the top compartments are cut to curve in, over your shoulders, 3". This contour is maintained when the pack is full, through the use of lift straps between the shoulder pads and the top flap. The average depth is 7". The side pockets measure 10" × 4" × 3". The top pocket measures 10" × 6" × 3" at its base and angles back away from your head to 10" × 2½". The incorporation of removable side pockets and the drawstring top closure are intended to give the pack a greater workable load range.

Two possible modifications worth considering are constructing the back piece of a breathable cotton canvas or corduroy, and/or adding an ensolite pad in a sleeve on the back, for increased comfort. The suspension may also be altered through the use of an ensolite padded hipbelt in place of the 2" webbing belt called for in the plans.

MATERIALS:

2 yds.—45" wide coated nylon fabric.
6½" × 6½"—leather (zip pull tabs and harness patch).
4"—¾" elastic.
13'—1" medium/light flat webbing.
32"—2" webbing.
2'—¾" flat webbing.
3 yds.—drawcord.
11" × 10"—3/8" ensolite (shoulder straps).
4—2" ¶ 5" leather accessory strap/pocket patches.

1—accessory strap patch.
10—1"—1" tablar buckles.
2—1" double-bar buckles.
1—2" waist belt buckle.
2—½" "D" rings.
9—no. "O" spur grommets.
1—fixlock
1—8" non-separating zipper.
2—10" non-separating zipper.

1—21" non-separating zipper.
or
1½ yds.—#5 coil zipper and 5 pullsliders.

CUTTING LAYOUT:

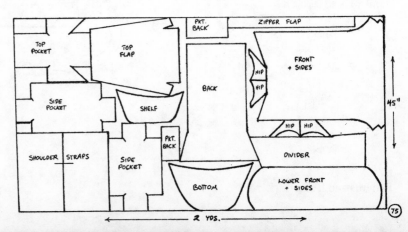

60

PIECE DIMENSIONS:

Shoulder strap pieces (2)—17″ × 6½″.
Side pocket backs (2)—11″ × 5″.
Zipper flap—24″ × 2½″.

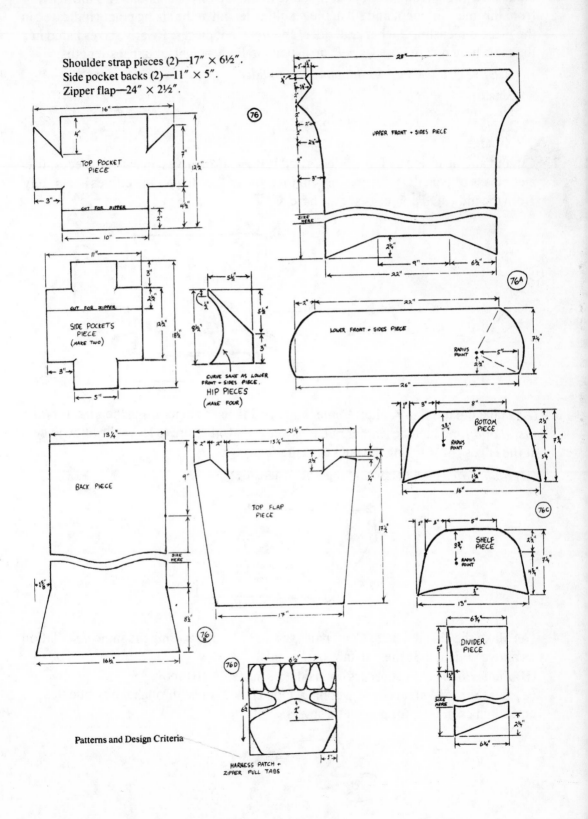

Patterns and Design Criteria

ASSEMBLY:

1. Measure a straight line from your hipbone to the top of your shoulder. Subtract 10″ from this measurement and fill in the resulting length at the sizing points indicated in the piece dimensions on back, divider, and top front pieces. Relative sizes listed in the table here do not necessarily correspond to body heights, but back lengths.

Relative size	hipbone to shoulder	pattern length
Small	16½″	6½″
Medium	18½″	8½″
Large	20½″	10½″
X-Large	22½″	12½″

2. Cut out and heat seal all fabric pieces and leather. For curves on pattern pieces, use a compass or pencil on a string the length of the radius, to plot the curves accurately from the indicated points as shown here. (77)

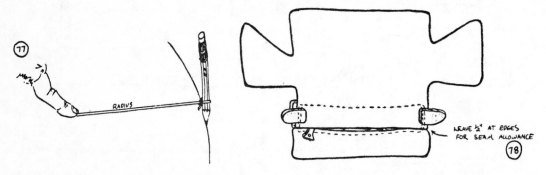

3. (A) Make the top flap pocket; Center and sew in the 8″ zipper using the *integral flap installation* and include leather pull tabs at the ends (be sure to leave the allowance at the edges for stitching the pocket to the flap.) (78)

   (B) *Plain stitch* pocket corners together on inside.

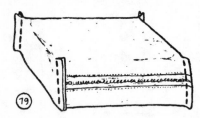

4. (A) Make the side pockets; Center and sew in 10″ zippers using the same installation as above and include the pull tabs at the ends.

   (B) *Plain stitch* pocket corners on insides as in step 3. (B) above.

   (C) Cut four 15″ lengths of 1″ webbing, loop back 2″ or so through tablar buckles and stitch each fast, for pocket tie straps.

(D) Stitch two tie straps to wrong side of each pocket back piece, 1″ from top and bottom edges with fabric sides folded under ½″ and tablar buckles at sides facing up.

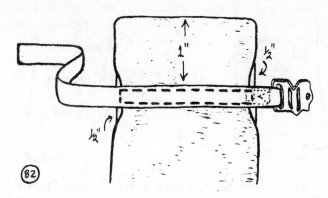

(E) Pin, ease, and *top stitch* side pockets to back pieces with the latter folded in ½″ all around as above.

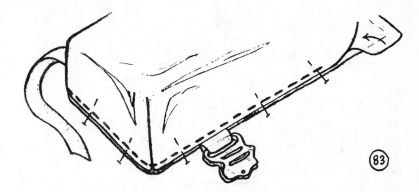

5. (A) Prepare top front piece; *Hem* top edge for drawstring grommets. Fold down towards wrong side, ½″ then 1″ and stitch as shown. Place seven grommets every 3″ from one centered in hem. ⑧④

(B) Sew on leather 2″ × 5″ accessory strap/pocket patches on sides of top front as shown. ⑧⑤

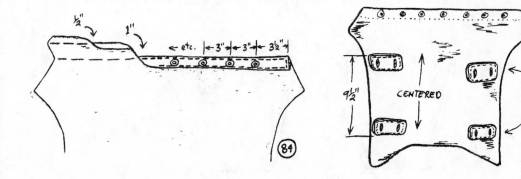

(C) Cut two 6″ lengths of ¾″ webbing and loop evenly through ½″ "D" rings. Stitch down next to pocket patches, 1″ up from bottom edge of fabric.

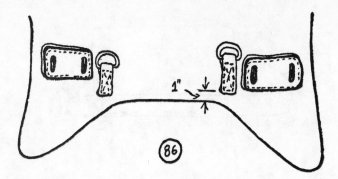

6. (A) Prepare top flap piece; *Hem* bottom edge with 4″ length of elastic in center. Stretch elastic to 7½″ or so and stitch on ½″ up from bottom edge. Then turn bottom edge towards wrong side, ½″ then 1″ over elastic and stitch fast with the elastic fully stretched. Do not stitch over elastic on hem seam.

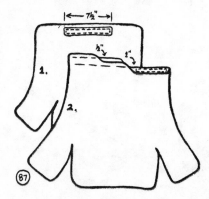

(B) Make the top flap drawstring / tie down tubes; Fold sides ½″ then 1″ towards wrong side and <u>top stitch</u> as shown in illustration ⑧⑧

(C) Cut two 24″ lengths of drawcord and thread into side tubes. Stitch fast across the upper ends with eight or ten passes. Make this bar-tack extra strong, as the ties will support the pull from the lift straps.

(D) Cut two 6″ lengths of 1″ webbing and loop evenly through tablar buckles and stitch, as shown, to the rightside of the flap piece for the upper ends of the lift straps. ⑧⑨

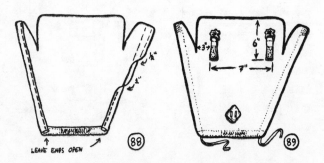

(E) Center top flap pocket 3½" down from top edge of flap and *top stitch* on with the angled side up. Leave the lift strap buckles and ½" or so of the webbing out.

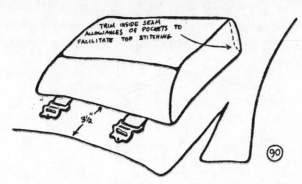

(F) Place one accessory strap patch centered below flap pocket, as shown in illustration 89.

7. Prepare the hipbelt flaps; Pair up the four halves and stitch as shown, rightsides together. Turn rightsides out and *top stitch* sides.

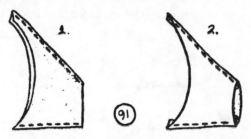

8. (A) Install bottom compartment zipper; Use the *full width, separate flap installation* with the 21" zipper. Include shelf in top half of zipper installation by pinning and easing it on top of the assembly, rightside up. Center the shelf so that a ½" allowance will remain along its back edge. Start stitching from the right side so the curved assembly may be fed down and out of your machine. ⑨²

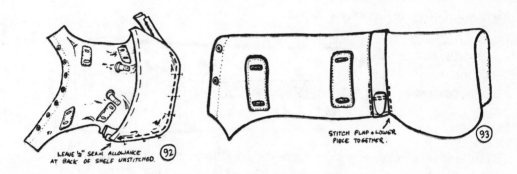

(B) Center the lower half of the zipper on the bottom front piece and stitch on per installation instructions.

(C) Join and close zipper and sew top and bottom front pieces together at the sides. Include leather pull tabs at zipper ends, as shown. ⑨³

9. *Top stitch* the divider to the inside of the front assembly; First *hem* top edge with two ¼" folds to one side, then pin and stitch along center of top front piece, and then to center of shelf. Leave ½" unstitched at back of divider and shelf piece for seam allowance to back. Bar tack at seam ends. For extra strength, a small scrap of leather may be sewn to the rightside of the top front piece first, as an anchor point for the top corner of the divider.

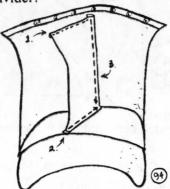

10. Stitch bottom reinforcement material to bottom piece and sidewall reinforcement to bottom front piece. ⑨⑤

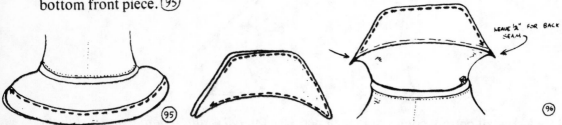

11. *Plain stitch* several times on inside, after pinning and easing bottom piece to lower front piece, rightsides together. Leave ½" unstitched at back corners for seam allowance to back piece. Turn rightside out. ⑨⑥

12. (A) Make the shoulder straps; Cut two 10" lengths of 1" webbing and stitch down to right sides of strap pieces, as shown.

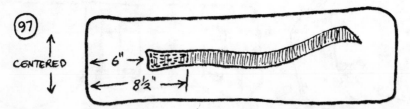

(B) Fold strap pieces, rightsides together, lengthwise and stitch twice at ¼" allowance. Be careful not to stitch over the webbing inside.

(C) Turn rightsides out. Cut four 11″ × 2½″ pieces of 3/8″ ensolite, poke loop of thread or string through ends and pull into strap tubes to the indicated points. Remove pullstrings.

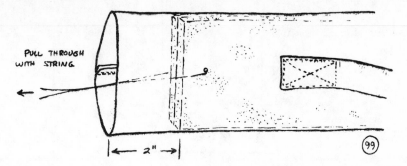

(D) Cut two 5″ lengths of 1″ webbing, loop evenly through double-bar buckles and insert into 2″ ends of strap tubes. Fold fabric end under ¼″ or so, and fold sides over towards seam side and stitch fast as shown.

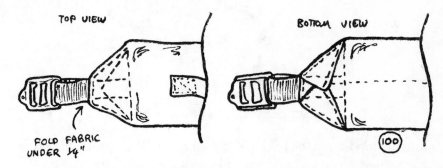

(E) Sew tops of shoulder straps closed.

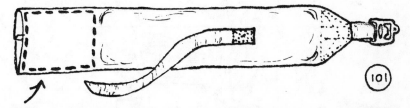

13. (A) Prepare back piece; Cut a 12″ length of 1″ webbing for the hauling loop, fold lengthwise and stitch center 5″ or so. Stitch down behind shoulder straps, under leather reinforcement patch, centered and 1½″ down from the top edge of the back piece. Stitch around bottom perimeter of patch first, then insert straps and loop and stitch top perimeter to hold. Finish with stitch pattern shown.

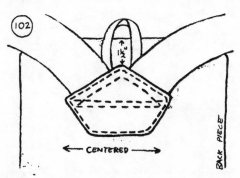

(B) Cut two 19″ lengths of 1″ webbing and stitch, as shown, to wrong side of back piece for lower shoulder straps. Leave ¾″ at edge unstitched for allowance.

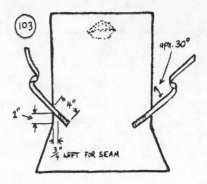

(C) Pin, ease, and *plain stitch* the two hipbelt assemblies to the rightside, bottom of the back piece, with the flat sides of the hipbelt flaps down and ½″ up from the bottom edge.

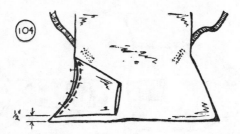

(D) Join the top flap to the back piece with a *flatfelled seam.* Stitch first with rightsides together, then open flat and finish.

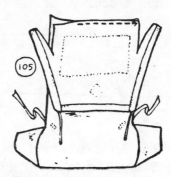

(E) With the assembly out flat and rightside up, fold over corners of flap as shown and *plain stitch* closed. Turn rightside out when done.

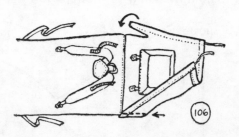

Make Your Own Camping Equipment

14. **(A)** Join the halves; Mark two reference lines on the wrong side of the back piece, as shown. *Top stitch* shelf, and then divider to the lines.

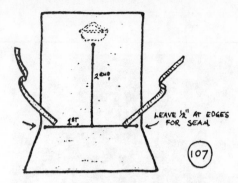

(B) Pin the back and front assemblies together for *top stitching* all around. Begin by pinning the corners, the bottom, and then up the sides. Adjust until all corners except angled top of front piece mate evenly. Stitch it up strong. (Blending notches will help eliminate wrinkles between the front piece and the hipbelt flaps) (108)

(C) *Plain stitch* on insides, angled top edges of front piece on top of top flap corner seam as shown in step 13. (E). Trim off excess fabric for perfect mating. (109)

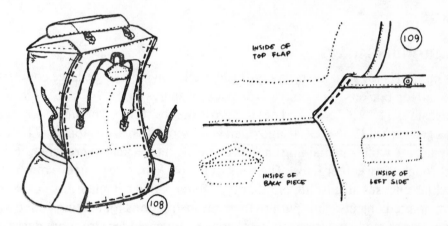

15. Install hipbelt; Cut two lengths of 2" webbing to fit your waist. Loop one piece 3" back through the waist belt buckle and stitch fast. Insert the buckled webbing into the left hipbelt flap and the other piece in the right flap, fold under fabric edge ¼" or so and stitch fast as shown.

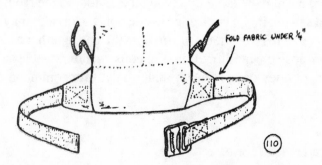

16. Hook up the shoulder straps and the lift straps. Thread the remaining 3' of drawcord through the top compartment drawstring grommets and install fixlock as shown. Load it up and try it on!

PATTERN 8

STANDARD RUCKSACK

This pattern is for your everyday type rucksack, having a single large compartment with side and top pockets. The body of the pack measures 20" × 14" × 6". The top flap pocket measures 11" × 6" × 3" and opens across the front side. The side pockets measure a generous 12" × 4" × 4" and open via diagonally placed zippers. These afford maximum access while maintaining enough angle off the vertical to prevent rain from seeping through the weather flaps. The back of the pack includes a sleeve of breathable cotton, which encases an ensolite or other type foam pad to eliminate any poking in the back from pointed objects. This pattern includes instructions for making your own shoulder straps of medium weight. If extra heavy, super padded straps are desired, use the instructions and dimensions for the straps in chapter 7.

Being shaped essentially like an oversized grocery bag, careful loading is necessary to prevent the pack from assuming a barrel shape with an excessive back overhang. If the expanse and roominess of a single large compartment isn't needed, add a vertical divider up the center of the bag. This may be done by sewing the divider to the front piece, assembling the bag, then sewing in the back edge inside. Or, the divider may be put in by stitching in both sides, front and rear, then *top stitching* the bag together as is done in the previous design. Another possible modification is to construct removable side pockets, as in the previous design, or ones sewn along the sides only, to accommodate skis.

MATERIALS:

1½ yds.—45" wide coated nylon fabric.
17" × 15"—medium/heavy cotton duck or corduroy.

8″ × 4″—leather (zip pull tabs and harness patch).

25″ × 2½″ and 15″ × 8½″—leather (bottom reinforcement).

8′—1″ flat webbing.

2′—¾″ flat webbing.

4″—¾″ elastic.

9′—drawcord.

15″ × 14″—3/8″ ensolite or volarafoam.

1—10″ non-separating zipper.

2—12″ non-separating zippers.

3—1″ "D" rings.

2—½″ "D" rings.

1—accessory strap patch.

2—double-bar buckles.

7—no. "O" spur grommets.

1—fixlock

1—1″ snap hook.

1—1″ slider.

CUTTING LAYOUT:

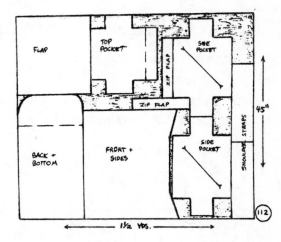

PIECE DIMENSIONS:

Shoulder strap pieces (2)—17″ × 5″

Zipper flaps (2)—13″ × 2″

Cotton back sleeve—17″ × 15″

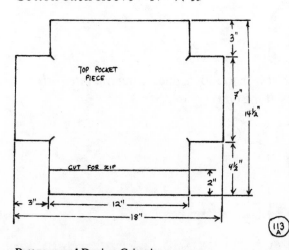

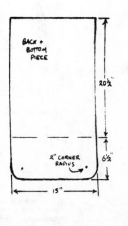

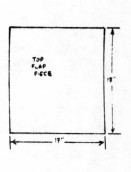

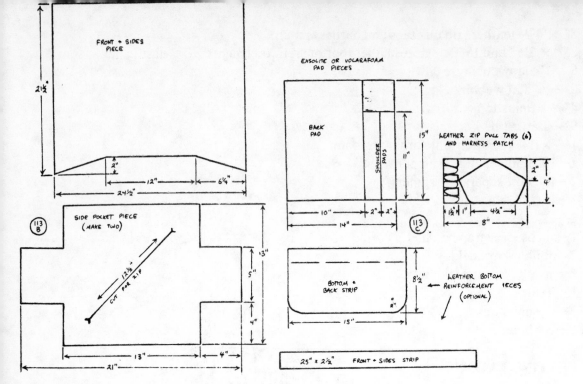

ASSEMBLY:

1. (A) Make the side pockets; Use the 12″ zippers with separate flap pieces and the *slit installation*. Make a right and left pocket as shown with the pullsliders at the tops when closed.

(B) *Plain stitch* pocket corners together on insides.

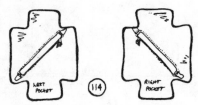

2. (A) Make the top flap pocket; Center and sew in the 10″ zipper using the *integral flap installation*. Include leather pull tabs at the ends.

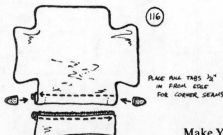

PLACE PULL TABS ½″ IN FROM EDGE FOR CORNER SEAMS

Make Your Own Camping Equipment

(B) *Plain stitch* pocket corners together on inside.

3. Prepare the top flap piece; *Hem* the bottom with the 4″ length of elastic, make the side drawstring tie down tubes, *top stitch* the flap pocket on, and the accessory strap patch, as shown. Construct in the order given here using the assembly instructions for the flap piece in the previous design (6. (A) through (F), pattern 7) with the location measurements given here. (117)

4. Make the shoulder straps; Use the assembly instructions for the shoulder straps in the previous design (12. (B) through (E), pattern 7.) (118)

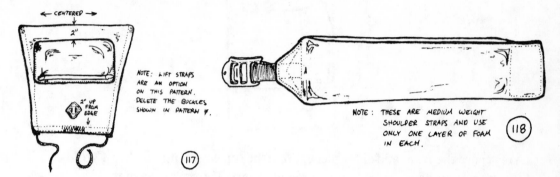

5. Stitch bottom reinforcement material to bottom of the back and floor piece, and sidewall reinforcement to bottom of the front and sides piece.

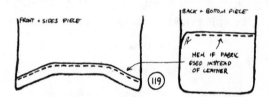

6. (A) Prepare back piece; Cut a 12″ length of 1″ webbing for the hauling loop, fold lengthwise, and stitch center 5″ or so. Stitch down behind shoulder straps under leather reinforcement patch, centered and 1½″ down from the top edge of the back piece. Stitch around bottom perimeter of the patch first, then insert straps and loop and stitch top perimeter to hold. Finish with stitch pattern shown.

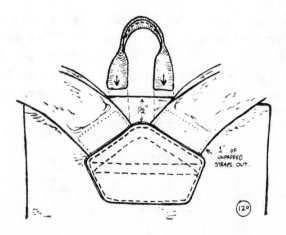

(B) Sew on the cotton back pad sleeve; *Hem* a shorter, top edge with a couple of ¼"
folds. Pin the sleeve on the back piece with the bottom edge just short of the bottom
reinforcement piece and the top edge 3½" down or level with the widest part of the
leather shoulder patch. *Top stitch* on with the bottom folded under the standard ½"
allowance. Leave the top open with a 1" fold to the inside to trap the padding when
in place. (Making the pad removable allows its use for sitting and sleeping as well.)

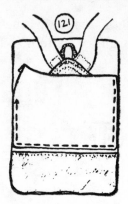

7. (A) Prepare the front and sides piece; *Hem* the top edge with ½" then 1" folds
    towards wrong side. Place seven grommets every 3" from one centered.
    (B) Ease, pin, and *top stitch* side pockets on, 1½" from the side edges and centered
    vertically.
    (C) Cut two six inch lengths of ¾" webbing, loop evenly through ½" "D" rings, and
    stitch down right next to the side pockets, level with their bottoms.

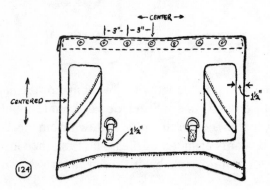

8. Join the front and back assemblies; Pin the assemblies together evenly for plain
    stitching inside out. Include as shown, two 4" lengths of 1" webbing looped evenly
    through 1" "D" rings for bottom harness attachment points, and one 10" length of
    ¾" webbing looped evenly with a half twist for the ice axe loop. Run several rows of
    stitching all around and bar tack over webbings for extra strength.

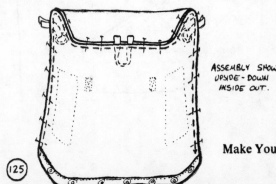

ASSEMBLY SHOWN
UPSIDE-DOWN +
INSIDE OUT.

Make Your Own Camping Equipment

9   Sew on the top flap; Line up the back and flap piece edges, rightsides together, and stitch across a couple of times. Fold the assembly out flat and fell the allowance down with another line of stitching from the inside.

10.   Stitch on the harness webbing and hardware as shown.

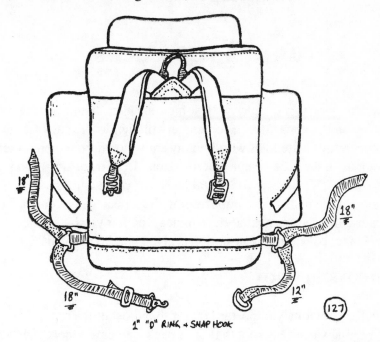

11.   Thread the remaining drawcord through the top perimeter grommets and secure with the fixlock, as shown in the previous design instructions. Trim and insert the foam pad into the back sleeve, with the top tucked under the 1″ fold in the sleeve. Check for loose and unclipped threads. It's done.

Chapter 8

Frame Type Packs

It would be nice to open this chapter with something like, "Gone are the days of the wooden Trapper Nelson Packboard!" Unfortunately though, while pack frames are now made from aluminum alloys instead of wood, many show no improvement in terms of comfort. If you took an old wooden chair, cut the back off, and put straps on it, you would probably have a pack frame as comfortable as many contemporary versions.

While the design of the pack bag is important with respect to convenience of access and load management, it is the frame that determines whether you have a good trip or break your back. Hence, considerable attention is given here to frame design.

STRENGTH AND CONSTRUCTION

Strength is such an obviously important factor that most of the reputable manufacturers have long since seen to it that their pack frames are more than strong enough to withstand rough use. Still, many models might better be classified as "collapsible" or "disposable."

The most common point of failure on a frame is at the joints. There are two types of joints; welded and coupled. The welded type are either brazed, a technique akin to soldering, or gas-arc welded. In the latter case, the alloy is actually melted together to form a joint that is potentially as strong as the tubing itself. This is by far, the strongest and most reliable welded type joint. It can be recognized by its hand-made appearance. The brazed type joints are usually mass-produced on machines which leave a smaller, symmetrical bead. They are only half as strong as the arc welded joints.

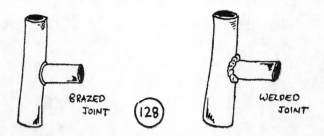

BRAZED JOINT   (128)   WELDED JOINT

In the coupled category are joints of machined or cast metal, or Lexan, a polycarbonate synthetic developed by Du Pont. Lexan joints have been used, so far exclusively, by Alpine Designs on their frames. I have had one since they first came out and have had no trouble with the joints. Lexan is not affected by temperature extremes and is advertised as being stronger than a welded joint. Take note that the soft nylon bushing used in the arthritic joints of "discount" frames are not made of Lexan and are notoriously weak. The metal type frame couplings are used by Himalaya, Eddie Bauer, Jan Sport, and Gerry.

A major advantage of coupled frames is their adjustability, making them ideally studied for growing kids and lending to friends. This also guarantees a perfect fit. Another advantage is that any one piece of the frame, or the joint itself, may be replaced if damaged.

There is a tremendous difference in strengths between various aluminum alloys used in pack frames. The discount frames are almost always made of a soft, inexpensive aluminum which is easily broken. For maximum strength and durability with a minimum of weight, a good frame should be made from a 6000 or 7000 series aluminum alloy. A commonly used alloy is 6061-T6, with a maximum tensile strength of 45,000 pounds per square inch. The newer Gerry frames use 7011-T6 which has a maximum tensile strength of around 83,000 pounds per square inch. Both of these alloys are commonly used in aircraft construction and the 6061-T6 for hang glider spars. Both are stronger than strong! If you want to spend money for a frame only once, go with one made from these alloys.

CONTOUR AND FIT

The best design frames are those which keep the load as close to your back and center of gravity as possible. This requires that the frame be contoured to shadow the shallow "S" curve of your profile. It is in this contouring that many frames are totally inadequate.

The degree of "S" curve in a frame is not the only factor determining a proper contour. The fit also depends on the depth of the bend around your back of the lower horizontal crossbars. The deeper this bend is, the more radical the "S" contour must be to keep the upper half of the frame over your shoulders.

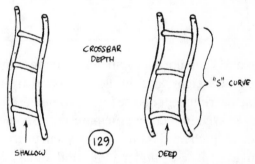

A very small amount of variation in the "S" curve and the crossbar depth, along with your own unique profile, can easily combine to make the best frame unsuitable. Consequently, you can't simply go out and buy the strongest frame made and have a good fit.

The type of backband used on a frame will also affect the fit. A full surface backband will stretch flat across the back of the frame, having the same effect as a shallow horizontal crossbar depth. A partial backband at a higher level will allow full use of the lower crossbar depth to wrap the load in close and consequently, will require a greater "S" contour to bring the upper load in over your shoulders. My personal preference is for a ten inch high partial backband constructed of a breathable mesh panel held by wide, two inch webbing at its top and bottom edges. This allows the backband panel to form a sort of pouch, which conforms to the bend around the shoulder blades.

The lower section of the frame is then allowed to ride in close to the center of gravity where it is padded via a full circle hipbelt, discussion of which is forthcoming.

Like good quality rucksacks, the fit of the frame and its contour should be checked with the pack on and loaded. Put it on and look at your profile in a mirror. With the suspension properly adjusted to the most comfortable position, the back of the pack should curve in over your shoulders rather than hanging back any.

Some pack frames are impossible to fit correctly in the contour because of the placement of the top horizontal crossbar directly behind your head. This necessitates moving the upper load back, and away from your head, thereby increasing the backwards pull of the load on your shoulders and disturbing your already marginal center of gravity. This problem is neither limited to, nor exclusive of, cheaper frames, so buyer beware! You will receive continuous bumps to precisely the same point (literally) on the back of your head when travelling the most slightly ascending trails, or when looking up towards the hill and sky you came to see! This problem is taken care of by the more intelligent manufacturers, such as Trailwise and Camp Trails, by employing a "V" truss instead of a straight spar for the upper frame cross-support.

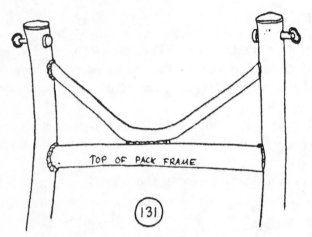

TOP OF PACK FRAME

(131)

SUSPENSION

The suspension system is a major factor in determining comfort. Quality wise, all materials should be of a good weight, and should be properly reinforced at stress points with bar tacks and double or triple stitched seams. Grommets and other hardware should be up to the standards discussed in section I on materials. Shoulder and hipbelt padding should be of at least one half inch hard foam. It may seem uncomfortably stiff, but it will quickly mold to conform to your body under a load and retain its padding ability, whereas a softer foam will collapse and concentrate the load through a thin strip of fabric. The shoulder adjustment straps should be supple enough to slide through their buckles easily. Otherwise, on-the-go adjustments are a hassle.

There are two types of shoulder harnesses. The common type, is attached directly to the frames' upper crossbar. A relatively newer type, the *load-spreading harness*, differs from the standard type in its top attachment. The pads of the load-spreading harness continue down the backs of your shoulders and attach via adjustable straps to a lower horizontal crossbar. These behind-the-back straps cross each other or are joined to keep the pads up and centered on your shoulders. The pack is held in towards your body at the top by separate adjustable straps between the tops of the pads and an upper horizontal crossbar. (132)

Make Your Own Camping Equipment

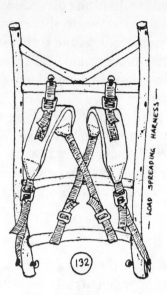

These straps function the same as the lift straps discussed in chapter 7. The net effect is to give a very even pressure distribution over your shoulders. The vertical adjustability of this system also makes frame sizing less critical. Three applications of this type of harness can be found on the frame suspensions by Trailwise and Mountain Master and on the North Face Ruthsac. Functionally, the only argument I have heard against this type of harness is that it causes the load to ride farther away from your back. This just isn't true if it is properly adjusted. *Wilderness* authors Colin Fletcher and Robert Wood have both used and praised this system and I concur. Pattern 11 shows you how to make your own.

The most significant advance in pack frame rigging is the development of the full circle, padded hipbelt. Previously, this consisted simply of two pieces of webbing connected to the bottom sides of the frame. Their only function was to keep the pack from swinging from side to side. In contrast, the hipbelt today is amply padded with ensolite and has been redesigned to completely circle the hips and carry all or a portion of the load weight. I consider this piece of rigging as the single most important item short of the frame itself, and would not even consider using a pack and frame without one.

Presently, Camp Trails makes the only hipbelt equally suited for both on and off trail use. One very important feature found almost exclusively on their hipbelts is the long (4″) tabs that connect the belt to the frame. These tabs connect to the belt at its top edge, so the downward pressure from the frame is distributed over the full five inch height of the belt. On other designs of full circle hipbelts without the long suspension tabs, the frame will hold the belt away from the hips, leaving gaps at the point of attachment.

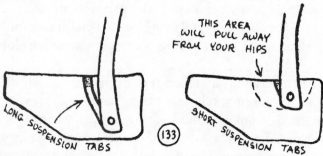

The advantage of the long suspension tabs is that they allow the hipbelt to stay in its correct and snug position while cinching up the load to your shoulders to rest your hips, or when bending forward to rest or to step over logs and such on the trail. The long tabs allow the frame to swing up and/or out, without resulting in a binding at and between the shoulder harness and the hipbelt. The resulting freedom of movement saves unnecessary fatigue and fidgeting with strap adjustments.

For off trail use, the Camp Trails design hipbelt has two light webbing straps sewn to its back that will attach to a frame's lower horizontal crossbar. When secured, these straps lock the frame tight to the hipbelt to eliminate sway and instability. The Camp Trails design hipbelt, as well as other riggings, may be purchased separately and adapted to fit most frames. They come in different sizes to allow padding all around.

WRAP-AROUND FRAMES

Out of the development of the full circle hipbelt has come several new frame designs called wrap-arounds. These frames are intended to make maximum use of the hipbelt. The lower frame side shafts or additional spars are extended in around your hips, and attach to the hipbelt at your sides and directly over your center of gravity.

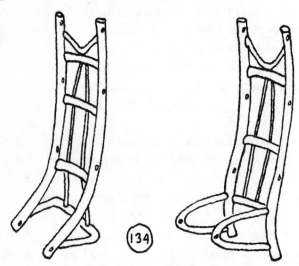

The wrap-around frame concept has just recently been revived from scrapped military testing and, in a matter of a few years, has become widespread. Among those companies offering this design are Alpenlite, Universal Field Equipment, Adventure, Sun Bird, and Jan Sport. The unique function of the wrap-around style frame is its ability to fix the load securely to your body for a minimum of load shifting and balance problems, while still allowing full fore and aft body movement. This is made possible by attaching the frame to the hipbelt at the center of your axis. Essentially, the frame becomes co-ordinated with your anatomy, allowing you to bend at the waist, as opposed to a standard "S" type frame which can act like a body splint when the hipbelt is locked to the frame.

An advantage claimed of wrap-around frames is the placement of the load weight directly over your hips and center of gravity. One thing this does is prevent the hipbelt from slipping down in back, a common problem with many insubstantial or poorly designed hipbelts. A well designed hipbelt of frusta-conical shape with long suspension

Make Your Own Camping Equipment

tabs will not have this problem. The suspension tabs are only two or so inches back from the center of each side. The difference in attachment points between the standard type of a good design and the wrap-around hipbelt is significant, but it is not the black and white issue most often presented by salesman/advocates and advertising. As for placing the weight over your center of gravity, the wrap-around frame does not in fact alter the center of gravity of you or your pack. This can be done only by moving the actual load mass in or away from your back.

There are many arguments for and against the wrap-around frame concept; some are based on experience, many more are theoretical. Some people swear by them while others find them claustrophobic and complain of bumped elbows. The fit is also more critical on the wrap-arounds. They must be the right width and depth for your hips, as well close in the profile contour. The best way to find out which design you prefer is to rent and use what you think is the best of each. Most mountaineering stores will deduct a few days rental fee from the purchase price of a related item, so it shouldn't cost you too much to find out for sure.

PACKBAG DESIGN AND CONSTRUCTION

Although most packbags are of excellent design and construction, there are some that should be avoided. The packbags typically found in our monuments of false economy, the warehouse "discount" stores, are usually the same quality as the torpid music they play. Vulnerable seams are not reinforced, there are no bar-tacks at stress points, and the lines of stitching end without any backstitching to prevent them from coming apart. Some of these "mistakes" can be found on more expensive packbags as well. You should give careful attention to the relevant strengths of all packbags, regardless of their price.

Interior access is an important variable to be aware of. Most of the different basic bag designs offer the potential for nearly equal access, but some are considerably better than others. A good example is of the opening for the bottom compartments on divided bags. Maximum access here can be had by running the zipper around the sides of the bag as well as across the front. In the case where full length side pockets are used and this is not possible, a curved, flap type opening may be used on the back panel alone and still provide ample access. However, many bags on the market provide access to this lower compartment by a short, straight zipper across the front of the bag only . . . even though they don't use full length side pockets! Access to all pockets and compartments should be as generous as the particular design allows.

PATTERN 9

FRONT OPENING DIVIDED BAG

This pattern is for a drop flap, front opening packbag. Rather than reaching the top compartment's contents through a conventional flap top, access on this bag is through a toilet seat shaped panel that zips 30″ around the front side perimeter. Although not essential, the top compartment may be fitted with a hold-open bar without any modifications to the pattern. It makes loading a little easier. The bottom compartment and the four side pockets zip open all around the sides for maximum accessibility. All of the zipper openings are protected by weather flaps.

This pattern will make you a packbag with a comfortably larger than average capacity. The body of the pack proper measures 14½" wide by 24" high with a 9" depth at the top tapering down to 7" at the bottom to compensate for the curvature of a frame, and to maintain the back at a vertical angle. Lighter and smaller loads can be controlled by cinching up on the built in lash-on straps at the top and bottom of the bag. The lower side pockets measure 7" × 6" × 3" and the upper side pockets a generous 12" × 6" × 3". There is also a sleeve type map pocket located at the back top of the bag. This may be reached easily behind your head with the pack on.

The dimensions given for this pattern will make you a packbag to fit any size of the Camp Trails frames. However, any other frame with an outside width of 14¼" to 14¾" will work by simply locating the attachment grommets to match the frame's clevis pin holes. Other frames that will fit include the Kelty Mountaineer, the Gerry "K" frame, and the Eastern Mountain Sports Heliomaster, all in their small and medium sizes, and all of the Denali Company Mountain Master frames.

As with all of the pack patterns, the use of leather or webbing zipper pull tabs, and the number and placement of accessory strap patches is entirely up to you. The patterns call for placements common to most ready made packs. The lower front pocket listed in the optional pattern pieces of the following design (pattern 10) may also be used on this pack. Ski sleeve and/or removable side pockets may be incorporated by using the assembly instructions from the "monocoque rucksack" (pattern 7) in the previous chapter.

MATERIALS:

2 yds.—45" wide coated nylon fabric.
11"—1" medium/light flat webbing.
4—1" tablar buckles.
1—accessory strap patch.
6 or 8—no. "O" spur grommets.
1—12" tall × 15" wide hold-open bar (optional).
1—29" non-separating zipper.
1—25" non-separating zipper.
4—10" non-separating zipper.

or

3 yds.—#5 coil zipper.
8—#5 single pull-sliders.

CUTTING LAYOUT:

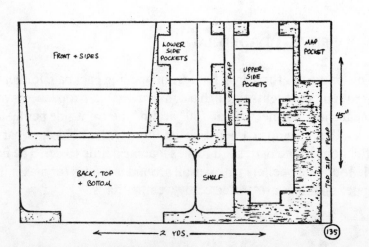

82

PIECE DIMENSIONS:

Bottom compartment zip flap—29" × 2½".
Top compartment zip flap—31" × 2½".
Map sleeve—13" × 7".

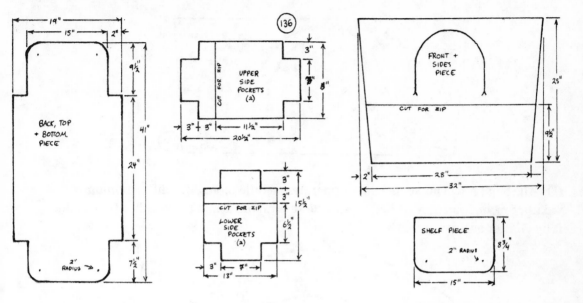

ASSEMBLY:

1. Cut and heat-seal all fabric pieces; Cut the front piece across, as shown for the bottom compartment zipper. Cut the curved opening in the top front piece for the 29" zipper, as shown here.

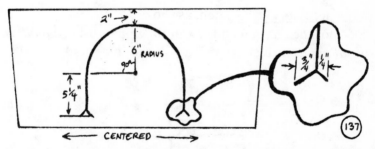

2. (A) Install the top compartment zipper using a combination *separate flap* and *slit installation*; Start with the outer perimeter as the top and use the *full width, separate flap* installation but stop short of the ends to allow the weather flap to be tucked under the end slits when all else is done. Ease and pin to assure proper mating.

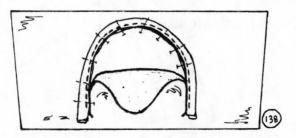

(B) Fold over and finish top half of zipper per instructions. Do not sew across the ends yet.

(C) Close the zipper, fold the edge of the lower half fabric under ¼″ and ease and pin on top of lower zipper half. *Top stitch* on and continue across ends with the flap and the slit ends folded under. (Add pull tabs if desired.)

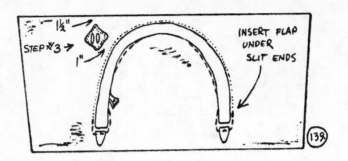

(D) Although it will make the zipper operation a little more difficult, maximum weather protection may be had by sewing several tucks into the weather flap so that it lies flatter against the surface.

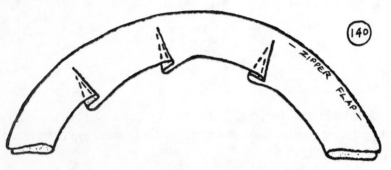

3. Sew on the leather accessory strap patch, as shown.
4. **(A)** Make the side pockets; Center and sew in 10″ zippers using the *full width, integral flap installation* and include pull tabs at ends if desired.

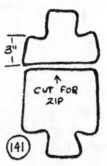

'B) *Plain stitch* pocket corners on insides.

5. **(A)** Prepare back piece; Cut four 24" lengths of 1" webbing and stitch to back piece, as shown.

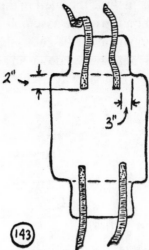

(B) Cut four 6" lengths of 1" webbing, loop evenly through tablar buckles, and stitch down to wrong side of back piece as shown, with fabric edges folded under ½" as shown, and buckles rightside up.

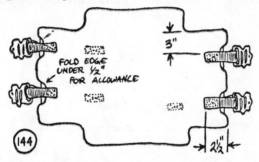

(C) *Hem* one long edge of map sleeve piece with two ¼" folds to wrong side. *Top stitch* to rightside of back piece as shown with hemmed edge open.

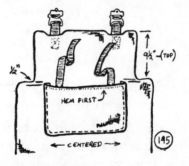

6. Pin and *top stitch* side pockets to front pieces, as shown.

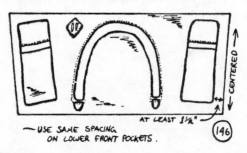

7. (A) Install 25″ bottom compartment zipper along with the shelf piece; Using the *full width, separate flap installation,* include the shelf in the top half of the zipper opening by pinning and easing it on top of the assembly, rightside up. Center the shelf so that an allowance will remain along its back edge. Start stitching from the right side so the curved assembly may be fed down and out of your machine. Turn rightside out and finish, with shelf pulled away to the side for the second, finishing top half seam.

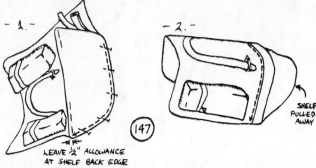

- 1. -

- 2. -

SHELF
PULLED
AWAY

147

LEAVE ½″ ALLOWANCE
AT SHELF BACK EDGE

(B) Sew on lower half of zipper per same instructions, close zipper, and sew lower and upper front pieces together at zipper ends with pull tabs, if desired.

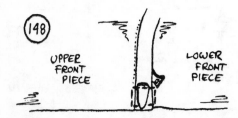

148

UPPER
FRONT
PIECE

LOWER
FRONT
PIECE

8. Sew the shelf piece to the back; Mark a reference line 15″ down as shown. Stitch on shelf with allowance angled up or top stitch.

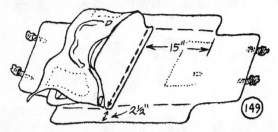

15″

2½″

149

9. Ease, pin and *top stitch* the top and bottom of the back piece to the front assembly. Check the side, grommet seam allowances for proper lengths and alignment before stitching. Start the top seam from the right corner and the bottom from the left corner, so the assembly may be fed down and out of your machine. Include 12″ length of webbing for ice axe loop.

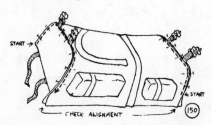

START →

← START

CHECK ALIGNMENT

150

Make Your Own Camping Equipment

10. Make the side, grommet flaps joining the front and back assemblies; Fold the back piece edge ¼" then 1" over the front piece edges. Pin and stitch along the outer edges first, then fold under the ¼" and stitch down with as many rows of stitching as you have time for. Fold ends under.

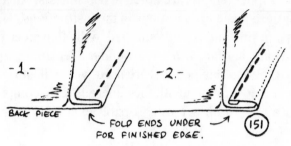

11. Hold the pack up to your frame and mark and install the mounting grommets in the side flaps.

12. The optional hold-open bar may be added by melting two very small holes next to the grommet flaps. Bar dimensions should be 15" wide and as long as necessary to reach bag mounting clevis pins. If packbag attaching wires are used to secure the clevis pins instead of split rings, the hold-open bar ends may be bent 90° and threaded onto the attaching wires. Pretty nice packbag, isn't it!

PATTERN 10

FLAP TOP DIVIDED BAG

Like the preceding "front opening" design on which this is based, this packbag will accommodate very large loads as well as lighter, on-the-way-out loads. The load in the top compartment is compressed and secured via a top perimeter drawstring, which is covered by a conventional top flap with an elasticized bottom hem for a snug and weatherproof fit. The bottom of the bag is made with lash-on straps sewn into its seam to carry your pad, bag, or whatever, or to compress the bottom compartment.

All the other features and dimensions of this bag are the same as the preceding design (pattern 9) with the exception of 9" instead of 12" tall upper side pockets to accommodate the flap and drawstring top closure. This pack will also fit the same frames listed in the preceding pattern.

Shown with the piece dimensions following, are several optional pockets. Materials for these are not included in the materials list. All these pockets use an *integral flap installation* for their zippers. Zipper lengths are noted in parenthesis. All are top stitched on during the appropriate pattern piece preparations in the instructions. The bellows type flap pocket zips along one seam side and is *plain* stitched to the flap piece by its lower zipper half. Then it is folded back and *top stitched* around the remaining three sides. If both back pockets and one of the top flap pockets are used, you will have a pack with no less than seven exterior pockets. Combined with the generous main compartment capacities, this will give you all the room you will probably ever need. It makes packing and in-use access a whole lot easier.

MATERIALS:

2 yds.—45″ wide coated nylon fabric.
6′—1″ medium/light flat webbing.
9′—drawcord.
2—1″ tablar buckles.
2—1″ "D" rings.
1—fixlock.
2—accessory strap patches.
15—no. "O" spur grommets.
4″—¾″ elastic.
1—25″ non-separating zipper.
4—10″ non-separating zipper.

or

2¼ yds.—#5 coil zipper.
6—#5 single pull-sliders.

CUTTING LAYOUT:

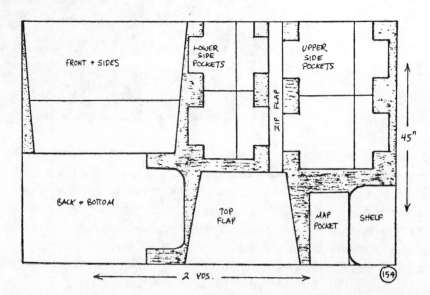

PIECE DIMENSIONS:

Zipper flap—29″ × 2½″.
Map sleeve—13″ × 7″.

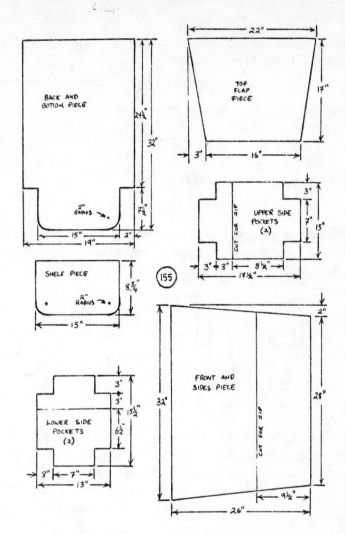

OPTIONAL POCKET PIECE DIMENSIONS:

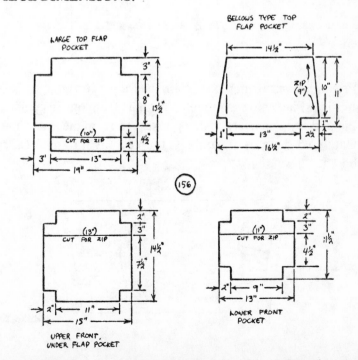

ASSEMBLY:

1. (A) Make the pockets; Center and sew in 10″ zippers using the *integral flap installation*. (Pull tabs are optional.)

   (B) *Plain stitch* pocket corners on insides.

2. (A) Prepare back piece; Cut two 24″ lengths of webbing and stitch to rightside on lower half of back piece as shown. ⑤⑨

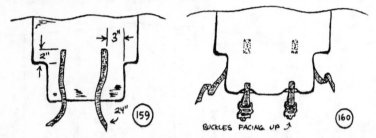

BUCKLES FACING UP

   (B) Cut two 6″ lengths of webbing, loop evenly through tablar buckles, and stitch down to wrong side of back piece as shown with fabric edges folded under ½″ towards wrong side and buckles rightsides up. ⑯⓪
   (C) *Hem* one long edge of the map sleeve piece with two ¼″ folds to the wrong side. *Top stitch* to rightside of back piece as shown, with hemmed edge up and open.

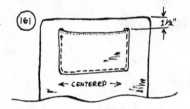

← CENTERED →

3. (A) Prepare upper front piece; *Hem* the longer top edge with ½″ then 1″ folds to wrong side. Place nine grommets, 3″ apart from one in center.
   (B) Pin and *top stitch* larger side pockets to front piece as shown.
   (C) Cut two 6″ lengths of webbing, loop evenly through "D" rings, and stitch down as shown.

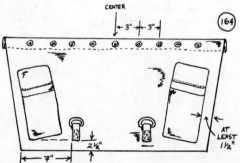

CENTER

AT LEAST 1½″

Make Your Own Camping Equipment

4. Prepare lower front piece; Pin and *top stitch* the lower side pockets as shown, then stitch on one accessory strap patch in center.

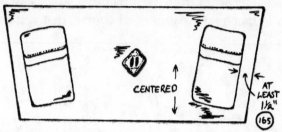

5. (A) Prepare top flap piece; *Hem* bottom edge with 4″ length of elastic in center. Stretch elastic to 7½″ length and stitch on ½″ up from bottom fabric edge. Then turn bottom edge up towards wrong side ½″, then 1″ over elastic and stitch top edge with elastic fully stretched.

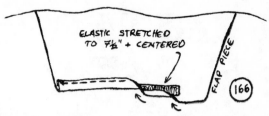

(B) Make the side drawstring tie down tubes; Fold towards wrong side ½″, then 1″ and stitch on inside edge. Then cut two 24″ lengths of drawcord, thread into tubes until flush with top ends and stitch fast at tops.

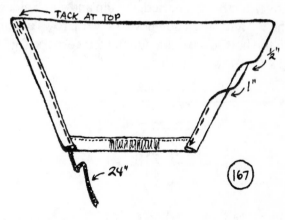

(C) Stitch on one accessory strap patch centered on flap and 4″ up from elastic hemmed edge.

6. (A) Install 25″ bottom compartment zipper along with the shelf piece; Using the *full width, separate flap installation,* include the shelf in the top half of the zipper opening by pinning and easing it on top of the first seam assembly, rightside up. Center the shelf so that an allowance will remain along its back edge. Start stitching from the right side so that the curved assembly may be fed down and out of your machine. Turn rightside out and finish top half seam with the shelf pulled away.
(B) Sew on lower half of zipper per same installation. Then close zipper and sew lower and upper pieces together at ends.

7. Sew shelf piece to back piece; Mark a reference line 15″ down as shown. Stitch with shelf allowance angled up.

8. Ease, pin, and *top stitch* the bottom of the back piece to the front piece assembly. Check the side grommet tab seam allowances for proper lengths and alignment before stitching. Start the seam from the left corner so the assembly may be fed down and out of your machine (assuming, of course, that you have a right handed sewing machine!)

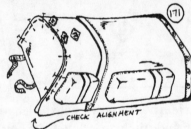

CHECK ALIGNMENT

9. Sew the top flap piece; Place pieces rightsides together and stitch several times along center 14″ only, as shown.

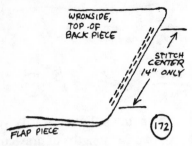

WRONSIDE, TOP OF BACK PIECE

STITCH CENTER 14″ ONLY

FLAP PIECE

10. Make the side grommet flaps joining the front and back assemblies; Fold the back piece ¼″ then 1″ over the front piece edges. Pin and stitch along the outer edge first, then fold under the ¼″ and stitch down with several rows of stitching. Fold the ends under ¼″ or so on the bottom corners. On the top corners, fold the flap corners under ¼″ and *top stitch* down in the second side seam.

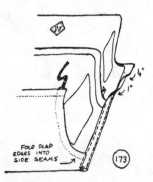

FOLD FLAP EDGES INTO SIDE SEAMS

11. Thread the remaining drawcord through the top compartment grommets, knot at ends, and place fixlock at center as shown.

KNOT ENDS

Make Your Own Camping Equipment

12. Hold the pack to your frame, mark, and install bag mounting grommets in side flaps. That's all folks!

PATTERN 11

LOAD-SPREADING SHOULDER HARNESS

This harness arrangement is easy to construct and a pleasure to use. Follow the assembly instructions for the shoulder straps from pattern 7, "monocoque rucksack," in the previous chapter, adding the back webbing straps in the same manner as the front adjustment straps are connected there.

MATERIALS:

4—11" × 2½" pieces of ¼" or 3/8" ensolite.
2—16" × 6½" pieces of fabric (try 60/40 cloth for naked comfort).
11½'—1" medium weight flat webbing.
4—1" tablar buckles.
2—1" sliders.
2—no. "O" spur grommets.
2 more—no. "O" spur grommets or 2 "U" rings for the attachment of the bottom front shoulder straps to the lower frame side rails. (see illustration)

ASSEMBLY:

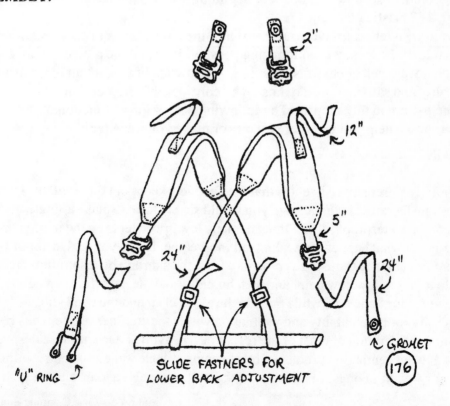

"U" RING   SLIDE FASTNERS FOR
                LOWER BACK ADJUSTMENT

Chapter 9

Tents

Several years back some friends and I were caught in an all night hailstorm without any sort of tent or shelter, save a mulberry tree. This particular tree, along with some spirits and a campfire, were doing a fair job of minimizing the weather. But, while breaking the barrage of the hail, our mulberry tree was also divesting itself of an entire cold and hungry population of ticks. This became apparent when we found that the reason for my numb thumb was a particularly glutinous tick dining on my brachial artery! Fortunately, I was with good friends who performed first-aid with such comments as, "We'd better lance it!," and "Burning it out might be quicker!!" A very informative discussion ensued on the neurological effects of Rocky Mountain Tick Fever—how it caused impotency, insanity, and the loss of all teeth and hair!!! Sometimes you learn about things the hard way!

A well designed, light weight tent does more than protect you from things that go bump in the night. It is an essential tool for making wilderness travel possible in inclement seasons. Beyond protecting you from the rain and snow, a tent keeps you out of the wind and considerably warmer. However, tents are not found in most people's equipage. A good lightweight tent costs upwards of $100. Spending less usually means getting very little more than a $2 plastic tube tent.

Making your own tent can save you almost half the cost of an equivalent retail model. This is one of the greatest economizing possibilities of all the projects in this book. Although not a quick or easy task, making your own lightweight tent is rewarding in terms of quality and satisfaction. To those who consider this project, I highly recommend the pattern in this chapter. The following discussion of functional considerations should help you whether you buy or make your own tent.

BASIC DESIGN

The obvious requirement of a tent is that it effectively keeps out the weather. If this were the only consideration in tent design you would simply have to make a single walled structure of coated waterproof fabric. Indeed, many low priced tents on the market are so constructed. But what happens in sealing out the weather is that you seal in about 1½ pints of water per person, exhausted as moisture from the skin and by respiration during the night. Add to this, a low dew point and high humidity and the net effect can be a cloudburst inside your "shelter" while outside the sky is clear and the wind still!

The necessity for breathability and ventilation within the confines of a tent has been the paramount consideration of most of the recent design hybrids. One of these designs attempts to solve the ventilation problem while keeping a single walled structure, either for simplicity or weight savings. In this design, the wall material is a foam and urethane

Make Your Own Camping Equipment

coated nylon. The idea is that the porous foam material will absorb the moisture in the air, keeping it off your sleeping bag and gear, while also adding a greater degree of insulation. The drawbacks to this design are an obvious lack of fresh air—with the open venting kept to a minimum to take any advantage of the foam's insulating ability—and a soggy tent in the morning that weighs considerably more due to retained moisture in the fabric. With this type of tent, as with any single walled coated tent and plastic tube tents, effective ventilation must be provided by independent vents and openings.

One of the advantages of a tent is its ability to provide added warmth by virtue of its stilled inner air. A major factor in heat loss is *convective transfer* in moving air. As is the case with the single wall design, all of the ventilation must be provided by large open vents. This causes increased air movement and consequently lower temperatures on the inside.

The classic answer to this design dilemma of breathability vs. weatherproofness is to construct the tent proper of a breathable fabric with a separate waterproof roof called a *rain fly*. The fly pitches three or four inches above the breathable tent wall to allow ventilation without the aid of large, direct vent openings. Thus the interior air movement is kept to a near standstill, and convective heat loss kept to its greatest possible minimum. In really heavy weather the rain fly may be pitched independently of the tent proper, save for its contacts at the pole tops. This allows the fly to take the major force of the wind without causing a lot of movement of the tent walls, which may also contribute to convective heat loss.

Vent openings are a necessity on even the most porous walled tents. They provide for additional fresh air on still nights and for inside cooking when necessary. (Any cooking done within the confines of a tent should be kept to a minimum. When you do cook inside, open up everything. Carbon monoxide poisoning comes on quickly and without perceivable warning.) A functional tent has vents both front and rear. All the vents should be located high up in the end walls for two reasons. First, warm and moist air will rise. Secondly, locating the vents high allows them weather protection from the fly.

Keeping the vents high is the reason zippered doorways are made to open from the top on better tents. Rather than simply running a zipper down the center of the front end, two zippers are used extending down the side seams to make a triangular doorway. In this fashion, the top of the door panel may be left open to provide the exact amount of ventilation desired. Backing up this type of opening with a similarly installed one of mosquito netting allows you to make adjustments to the outer "door," without having to completely zip open the netting, which would be the case if the netting were zipped down the middle. Constructing the netting doorway in this same fashion also allows it to be sewn along its bottom edge, thereby sealing out hungry bugs.

Another type of vent is the *tunnel* type which consists of a tube of fabric sewn into a hole, high on the end walls. Closure is by a drawstring on the outside end which is in turn covered by a circle of netting. The purpose behind this configuration is weatherproofness. When hanging limp, the tunnel vent approximates an upside down stove chimney. In a wind, the vent will point away from the weather to keep out the wet while still allowing full ventilation. And when a tunnel vent is angled away from the wind, a low pressure area is created at the opening which effectively draws the interior air out.

Like the vents, *tunnel entrances* are designed for weather-proofness. They allow entrance to the tent without admitting the weather and also work as a sort of mud room in which you can sit to clean off and remove your shoes. For people who travel in groups, two tents may be joined by their tunnel entrances to make a human sized hamster cage. And because they close via drawstrings, there is no problem with iced up zippers and doorway snow drifts. When a tunnel entrance is left open, it is held out of the way by tie straps fixed around its exterior perimeter. Your tunnel entrance should be backed up by netting with a similar drawstring type closure.

Some tents are made with both a zippered and a tunnel entrance at opposite ends. While this gives you the convenience of both types, you pay for it in added weight. Much of the writing on tents with both types of entrances justifies such extravagance as a safety feature . . . if your zippers jam or freeze up, and/or your tent is buried under a massive snow drift, you still have an escape route. Well, I haven't heard of anybody perishing because they couldn't get out of their tent. I think it should be either/or. Lightweight means freedom and two doors, you don't need!

While the side walls of the tent proper should be made from a breathable material, the end walls need not. By making the end walls of the same coated material as the floor, the rain fly doesn't have to extend way out over each end and have an access zipper. This design feature saves on weight and bulk and is found on the best tents. Of course, not all tents are made in the classic double "A" pole style, and will not lend themselves to this.

Probably the most important basic design feature of the lightweight tent is the application of *catenary* contouring to the seams and overall geometry. A catenary is the curve assumed by a line suspended from its ends. This is most apparent along the ridgeline of a tent. Even when tightly pitched, the weight of the fabric will tend to pull the ridgeline down in a catenary sag, resulting in loose and wrinkled side walls. To eliminate this problem, the ridgeline seam of the tent is sewn in a catenary curve. The result is a tight pitching tent without any wrinkles to catch the wind. And the tighter a tent pitches, the warmer it will be in windy weather because wall movement and subsequent convective heat loss is minimized. The accuracy and degree of catenary sewn into a tent ridgeline is a major determinant of function and quality. You won't find this feature on inexpensive tents. You will, however, find many high priced tents with ineffective geometry. Fortunately, you can easily spot a bad one by its wrinkles.

Catenary seams may also be used on a tent to compensate for the diagonal stretchability of nylon fabrics. Nylon fabrics have very little stretch along the grainlines and a great deal along the diagonal to the weave. For this reason, it is necessary to analyze a tent design for expected diagonal stresses and to compensate accordingly with reinforcement and/or catenary seams. The "A" pole tents made by Sierra Designs are a good example of a tightly engineered tent.

Sidewall *pullout* tabs may also be used to offset the diagonal stretch in the roof

Make Your Own Camping Equipment

panels of a tent. They also add considerably to the usable interior space by creating short vertical sidewalls.

Another notable feature of a well engineered tent is the *tub floor*. The floor material is folded up around the edges to form a sort of tub or rectangular pan. This eliminates the necessity for ground level seams at the tent's bottom perimeter, adding an extra margin of weatherproofness.

— TUB FLOOR —

This type of floor construction limits the ground level seams to the corners and down the center of the floor, where two pieces of fabric must necessarily be joined. All ground level seams should be treated with seam sealer to prevent leakage. This usually is not done on retail tents because it detracts from their clean appearance and takes some time to apply. Seam sealer in small, four ounce bottles is available from most of the sources listed in this book and I strongly recommend its use from the start.

For the classic "A" pole design tent, internal area is increased considerably through the addition of a *vestibule extension* on one or both ends. The extra added fabric weight is minimal in light of the interior space gained. The vestibule, or alcove, is simply a triangular end extension, sloping down from the pole tops and held by one or two additional stakes. It may be an actual part of the tent, or a porch like affair without a floor. In the latter case, you get a great cooking area but you're not really adding anything to the closed interior area, which is where a lot of time can be spent in bad weather.

WINTER

With the addition of a few more features, the same double "A" pole tent that you use in the fair seasons can be used for snow camping as well. Where temperatures are low enough for dry snow, a rain fly isn't always necessary. The condensation problem becomes one of falling ice crystals instead! Hence, the *frost-liner*. Frost-liners are made of very light cotton or a cotton and polyester blend and fit on the inside of the tent. Cut to shadow the inside contours of the roof, they may be either tied or snapped in by short tabs to hang an inch or so below the tent roof. Frostliners are made from cotton so they can absorb and hold the ice crystals which form when the rising, warm and moist air hits the cold outer walls. While the cotton is not very strong and can not be expected to last, the fabric is relatively inexpensive and a new liner can always be made using the old one as a pattern. Because it is not a structural part of the tent proper, its construction can be as hasty and simple as you care to make it.

Another feature of the winter equipped tent is *snow flaps*. These consist of fabric panels attached along the bottom edges of the tent. By covering them with snow or rocks, you effectively anchor the tent down. Snow flaps provide a firmer mounting and prevent the wind from getting under the tent, where it can have enough leverage to blow you over. While snow flaps are essential at a high camp, way up the side of a mountain, they are not necessary in lower areas where protective wind dikes can be built from snow and some protection is afforded by other natural features. Illustrated here is my own version of a sort of removable snow flap. The exact configuration is not really important as long as they work like a deadman. (A deadman is a large object, such as a log or a stuff sack full of snow, that may be buried in the snow and used as an anchor for guy lines, belays, etc.)

PROTECT EDGE OF TENT FROM WIND WITH SNOW PIKES.

SECURE WITH STICK OR TIE OFF.

BURY IN SNOW AND/OR ROCKS.

179

By making these snow flaps removable, you can save a bit more all-important weight, while trucking your way through the fair weather seasons. Making them removable also makes them expendable. After an extended camp in one place, you may find your snow flaps securely locked into blocks of ice. Needless to say, for this reason, the snow flaps should be made from a waterproof fabric, preferably coated on both sides. This design also eliminates full length ground level seams, necessary with sewn on snow flaps.

Bad weather means cooking indoors. To keep the kitchen off the vulnerable nylon floor, the winter tent should be equipped with a built in *cook hole*. Cook holes consist of a semi-circle opened via a single synthetic zipper backed on the bottom by a flap. The cook hole should be positioned in the floor under one of the highest peaks of the roof, with a vent directly above to protect the roof fabric from heat damage. While the heat from your stove might not actually burn the fabric, it can cause significant deterioration and subsequent weakening of the fibers. (Being directly on the floor, the cook hole zipper is very susceptible to freezing. An ample application of silicon and/or beeswax to all zippers prior to each winter trip can help to remedy this problem.)

MATERIALS

Most manufacturers use 1.9 ounce ripstop nylon for tent walls. When used in a well engineered tent, this weight has proven to be both light and strong enough to withstand high winds. However, some manufacturers of dubious character may make their tents from the same low porosity, downproof fabric that they use for other equipment. In this manner they can buy their fabrics in larger quantities and subsequently at lower prices. Forewarned is forearmed! Either their down products will leak their filling or their tents will be stuffy.

The most abused and vulnerable piece of the tent is the floor. It must stand up under traffic on ground that is often rugged, and still remain waterproof. The major strength consideration here is puncture resistance rather than tear strength. The floor fabric should be, at the very least of 2 ounce taffeta nylon, with a double coating of urethane or super k-kote. The coated side of the fabric should be up on the inside of the tent. This protects the coating from excessive wear and prevents your sleeping bag and pad from sliding down the, more often than not, inclined ground.

Make Your Own Camping Equipment

Rain flys are now being made from coated ripstop fabrics weighing as little as 1.4 ounce. This is, in part, possible because of the new developments in fabric coatings which do not decrease the tear strengths of the fabrics. The Kenyon Piece Dyeworks' "Temper Kote" is such a coating. When using a fabric this light, it is extremely important that the stress points be amply reinforced with fabric patches and even taped seams.

The poles must be considered as a very important component since they hold the whole thing up. Most of the better commercially made tents use 5/8″ thin wall aluminum tubing. But there is a vast difference in strengths among aluminums of various alloys and tempers. Whereas a medium grade, relatively inexpensive aluminum might be fine for summer camping, 6061-T6 should be considered a must for anything else. The weight is not a consideration. 6061-T6 × 5/8″ O.D. × .035 weighs in at a mere .0763 pounds per linear foot, or less than one pound per twelve foot length! A good guide to the quality of the poles is in the price. Strong aluminum alloys cost proportionately more by strength. So naturally, a cheaper tent is going to have weaker poles.

The number and type of joints in a tent pole is also worth considering. Not only are the joints prone to damage and breaking, they add considerable weight. Your best poles will have a minimum of joints. Most commercially made poles break down into thirteen inch or so lengths, generally four sections per pole. These are usually joined by lengths of shock cord to prevent loss and facilitate assembly. If you intend to build your own tent, or the one you presently own has a broken pole, consider making your own. My idea of the perfect pole setup is only one joint per pole and color matching instead of shock cords to save on weight. The longer pole sections could easily be carried on the outside of your pack via accessory straps. The resulting poles would be lighter, more rigid, and less prone to damage.

Many of the newer design tents of dome geometry, as well as some expeditionary type "A" pole tents, use fiberglass wands for either added support or all of it. Because fiberglass is flexible, the tents which rely completely on wands are not as rigid. The chief advantage of the wands is that they bend, allowing interesting curved designs with improved headroom. For fair weather tents this is great. However, I'm not sure that I would want one in much of a wind. Fiberglass wands can be added as mid-wall ribs to a standard double "A" pole tent to make a tent of ultimate strength. The Gerry Himalayan Tent is constructed in this fashion and has been proven on countless expeditions. If you're interested in working with wands, Eastern Mountain Sports sells the same type that Gerry uses. Eleven inch sections sell for a half dollar each and have metal couplings. The top fixtures are the same price.

CONSTRUCTION

The quality of the stitching is one of the best indicators of a manufacturer's worth. On tents, the stitching is critical because of the stresses it must take. Seams that wander in lazy "S" curves will localize stresses and cause tent destruction sooner than one of similar materials and superior workmanship. A tent's worst enemy is the wind. It can easily rip out a corner seam with a single heavy gust. The canopy is momentarily caved in by the gust then released to snap back, imposing a strong and quick load on the seams.

Beyond the straight seams of a reputable manufacturer, there are several other construction details that determine quality·

1. Every seam found on the tent and fly, and the frost-liner too, should be of the flat felled type.
2. The seams joining the lower sidewalls with the roof panels should be felled up on the inside to shed the rain like a shingle.
3. The sidewall pullouts should be sewn completely into the sidewall seams and should be of a large enough area to avoid localizing stresses.
4. The apexes and corners of the tent should be reinforced with patches of fabric at least equal to the fabric used throughout the tent. These should be stitched in around their perimeters.
5. A very heavy load is imposed on the corner seams at the top ends of the pole sleeves. In a gust cave in, this is where the seams will usually begin to rip out. The stresses at this point may be lessened either by curving the sleeve out deeper at its top and/or by cutting the top ends of the sleeves on the diagonal. The result of the latter is to cause an offset in the sleeve halves where they enter the corner seams.

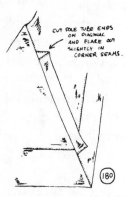

PATTERN 12

MOUNTAIN TENT

This pattern is for your basic two man, double "A" pole tent with a built in vestibule extending 30″ back. The main, rectangular floor area measures 5′ wide by 7′ 11″ long; comparable to most larger and more expensive high altitude tents of this basic design. While giving a lot more interior "roominess" (a term somewhat stretched when applied to any two man tent) the small amount of added fabric does not significantly affect the overall weight. The interior height at the poles is 43″ reduced to 31″ at the center by a 12″ catenary in the ridgeline. While this comparatively extreme catenary cuts down on the interior height, it is a key ingredient in making this a tight and wrinkle free tent, capable of withstanding high winds.

This pattern includes instructions for a frostliner. A tunnel entrance which is normally found on the winter tent is not included. The reason is simply to cut down on weight. Entrance is at one end only via a triangular panel of fabric backed by one of netting. Both zip down their sides from the apex. A tunnel entrance may be added after the tent is completed, so the option remains open if you decide to add one. You might want to consider making a tunnel entrance in place of the zippered doorway. The tunnels are much easier to construct than the zippered type doors. If you go this route, use the construction techniques detailed for the tunnel vents, two of which are called for in this pattern, and add the necessary extra fabric to the materials list.

Make Your Own Camping Equipment

The prototype of this pattern was made using the lightest possible materials without sacrificing strength. For the floor, I used a 3.1 ounce polymer coated taffeta. The roof panels are of 1.9 ounce ripstop. These fabrics, along with the ready made poles, came from Recreational Equipment, Inc. The rain fly is made of coated 1.9 ounce ripstop. (I wanted 1.4 ounce but couldn't find it. You might be able to get it by special request through a manufacturer who uses it.) This and the #5 coil zippers used for the door were bought from Eastern Mountain Sports. The frost-liner was made of extremely light weight cotton lining material from a local yardgoods store. Using these materials, the finished tent, including guy lines and eight S.M.C. channel stakes (1.3 ounce each, heavy as stakes go) weighed in at a good five pounds. The fly weighs in at just under 1½ pounds. This gives a combined fly, pole, stake, and tent weight of under 6½ pounds, right in there with commercially made tents with similar features. Weight was saved in the fly sheet by constructing the tent end walls of the coated floor fabric, save for the upper quarters which are of breathable 1.9 ounce ripstop to increase ventilation. Hence, the fly sheet does not extend far beyond the tent ends. The finished frost-liner weighs only ½ pound, giving a total winter travel weight of 5½ pounds!

This pattern may be used to make a tent with as few or as many features as your needs dictate. Essentially, what you have here is a basic set of dimensions for an "A" pole tent. These can be used to make either a lightweight summer tent with large netting panels or a high strength mountain tent. You might also want to consider making it into a super light two man tent by tapering the roof to the rear, eliminating the vestibule, and using a single "I" pole in back. Then again, you might find that the pattern will suit your needs as is.

MATERIALS:

Basic Tent

9⅓ yds.—45" wide, double coated lighted taffeta (floor).
6⅓ yds.—45" wide, breathable 1.9 oz. ripstop (roof).
4—56" long poles with top connectors and bottom spikes. (prototype uses P-56 pole set from Recreation Equipment, Inc.)
1 yd.—45" wide, mosquito netting.
4—43" zippers, separating one end, double pull sliders.
10—no. "O" spur grommets.
4" × 3"—leather.
6" × 6"—heavy nylon fabric (for grommet reinforcements).
10'—¾" nylon tape (stake loops).
10½'—¼" nylon tape or ribbon (frost-liner tabs and vent closures).
40'—guyline cord.
8 to 11—tent stakes.
1—small bottle seam sealer.

Rain Fly

6⅔ yds.—extra light coated ripstop fabric.
10—no. "O" spur grommets.

6″ × 4½″—heavy nylon fabric (grommet reinforcements).
40′—guyline and extra stakes if fly is to be pitched independently.

Frost-liner

6 yds.—very light cotton or cotton/polyester, 36″ wide.
13′—¼″ light nylon tape or ribbon.

CUTTING LAYOUT:

Basic Tent

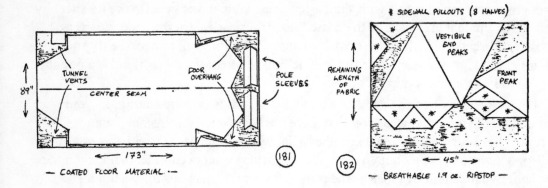

The floor material is 9⅓ yards of 45″ wide fabric cut in half and sewn together lengthwise. The roof panels of 1.9 oz. ripstop (not shown) are cut from two 96″ lengths of 45″ wide fabric. The layout shown is done on the remaining length of fabric for the end wall peaks and pullouts. The appropriate fabric scraps from these layouts are used to make the corner, apex, and stake loop reinforcement patches.

Rain Fly

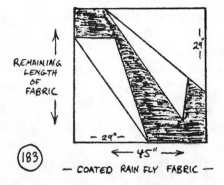

Cut two 96″ lengths for the roof pieces, then cut the overhangs from the remainder, as shown. Again, use the scraps for the reinforcements.

Frost-liner

Nest the two vestibule roof overhang pieces as a square to fit them into the material allotment.

PIECE DIMENSIONS:

Basic Tent

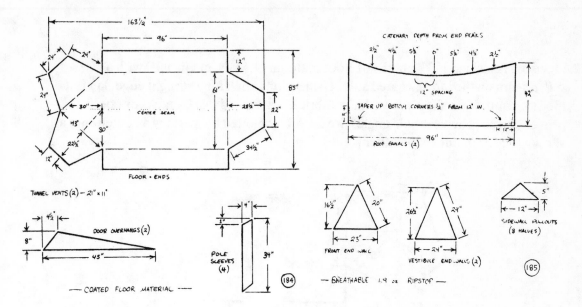

All other pieces (netting and reinforcements), cut to fit during the assembly. (Note: Cutting a six inch catenary in each roof panel results in a one foot finished depth.)

Rain Fly

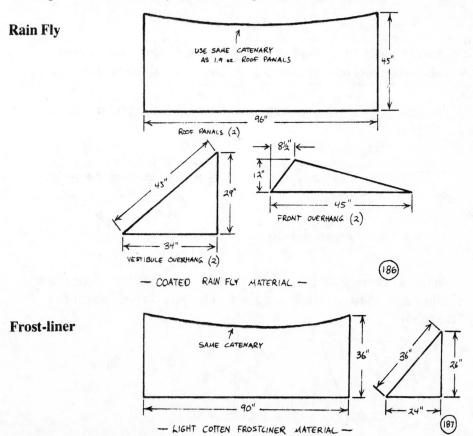

Frost-liner

The frost-liner and rain fly roof pieces use the same catenary dimensions as those shown for the basic tent walls.

ASSEMBLY:

Basic Tent

1. Piece together two 173″ lengths of floor material (9⅓ yds. cut in half) with a *flat felled* seam on the inner, coated side. Using a long stick for a straight edge, lay out the floor and sidewalls piece with the fabric corners held fast by tacks or books to prevent error. The vestibule angles are correctly plotted by marking a center line, as shown here. Cut out all the other pieces.

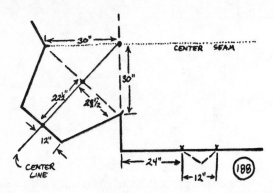

2. Mark the sidewall pullout tab locations (4), as shown above.

3. (A) Make the sidewall pullout tabs; *Plain stitch* together at ¼″ along outer edges with one heavy fabric grommet reinforcement patch, as shown stitched on top of each pair. (189)

   (B) Turn rightside out and *top stitch* all around edges and reinforcement patches. Trim, as shown. (190)

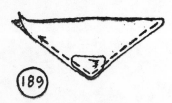

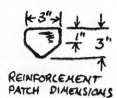

REINFORCEMENT PATCH DIMENSIONS

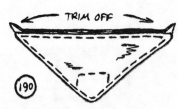

4 (A) Make the two tunnel vents; Fold the pieces, rightsides together and *plain stitch* at standard ½″ allowance. Turn rightsides out and finish with a *flat felled* seam on the insides of the tubes.

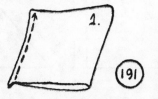

(B) Cut a 1¼″ slit at the opposite sides of the tubes from the previous seam and stitch down, folded back to the inner side, to make the drawstring openings.

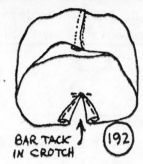

BAR TACK
IN CROTCH

(C) With the tubes again inside-out, fold the slit ends towards the wrong side, ½″ then 1″ and *top stitch* around the edge. Leave the slits open for the drawstrings.

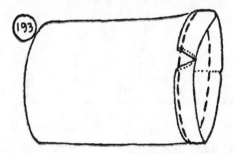

(D) Cut out two 7½″ diameter circles of netting from the corners of the netting piece, indicated below. *Top stitch* the netting around the inside of the tube at the outer edges of the drawstring tubes. Work with the tubes rightsides out.

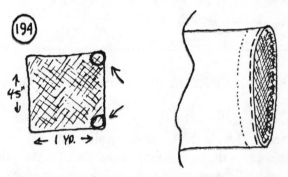

45″

← 1 YD. →

(E) Thread a 30″ length of ¼″ tape or ribbon into each of the drawtubes and secure the ends as shown with a ¾″ × 1½″ piece of leather, slit as shown.

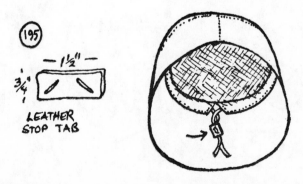

— 1½″ —

¾″

LEATHER
STOP TAB

5. If a cookhole is desired, add it now. Use a *curved slit installation* with a flap on the underside in whatever size you desire. The cookhole should be positioned directly under the vestibule end apex. (Note: The coated side goes up, right!

6. Sew on peg loop reinforcement patches cut from matching fabric scraps. Cut the patches to extend 4½" around and up each panel section and seam and *top stitch* onto the inside of the floor piece with the edges folded under. Make the two midwall patches from 4" × 8" rectangles.

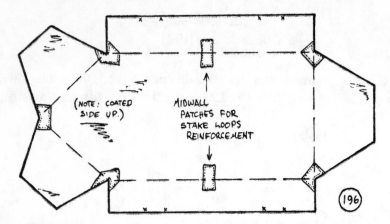

7. Cut two 16" lengths of ¾" tape, fold in half with a half twist in the loops, and stitch across 3½" down from the loop end. Stitch 4" of the resulting free ends to the center wall patches, as shown.

8. Sew the ripstop upper end walls to the floor piece ends with *flat felled* seams felled up on the inside.

9. Cut a 6" diameter hole in each vestibule upper end wall, 5" up or so and centered from the previous seam. Cut eight 3/8" blending slits outward around each hole, as shown. Pin the tunnel vents through the holes, ¼" or so beyond the edges of the wall fabric. *Plain stitch* around each from the inside. (Vent fabric up in your machine.) Then fold the vent fabric edges twice, out and over the blended wall edges and *top stitch* from the outside for a finished seam.

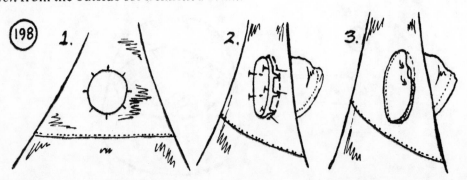

Make Your Own Camping Equipment

10. Sew the two ripstop roof pieces to the sidewalls of the floor piece, including the side pullout tabs at the reference marks. Use *flat felled* seams, felled up on the insides. (199)

11. Sew on the sidewall frost-liner tabs; Cut Thirteen lengths of ¼" tape or ribbon, 5" long each. Stitch down as loops, four in each roof panel seam, 24" apart, as shown. (200)

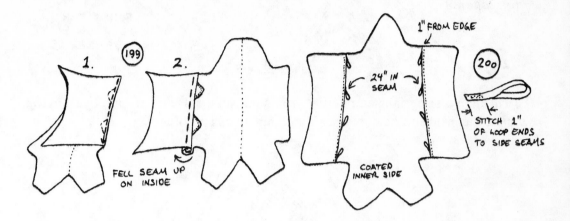

12. (A) Make the front zippered door; Mark two cutting lines 3" from the side edges and extending 43" down each side of the front panel. Before cutting on these lines for a *slit installation* of the door zippers, use them as a template to cut the netting door panel. Allow an inch or so extra across the bottom of the netting for stitching it to the wall later. (The weave of the netting may be fit on the diagonal without any consequences.) Mark reference lines and cut in end "V" slits, as shown.

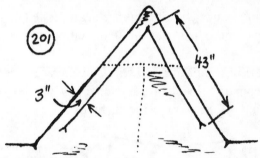

(B) Proceed with the zipper installation per the *slit type assembly* instructions in the sewing chapter. Sew on two zippers on each outer side. The inner zippers are for the netting door. (Note: Because you are sewing on the diagonal on a narrow 3" strip, fabric stretch is extreme! To insure a reasonably even mating within functional limits, pin the assembly every two inches, checking against the reference marks for match. That takes a lot of pins and some extra time but is well worth the effort. Considerable stretch and puckering of the fabric may still occur between the pins. Don't let it bother you. As long as the seam is properly mated and pinned, the finished doorway will pitch tight and wrinkle free.)

(C) Pin the outer zipper half to the fabric door flap and, with the mating checked, sew it on up. Use the same installation instructions.

(D) Pin the mosquito netting to the inner zippers and *top stitch* on with several rows of stitching, then *top stitch* the bottom edge of the netting across the bottom of the doorway.

(E) Finish the apex of the doorway with a 3″ length of ¾″ tape folded up around the top, as shown. The zipper tape ends should be folded under themselves at the ends.

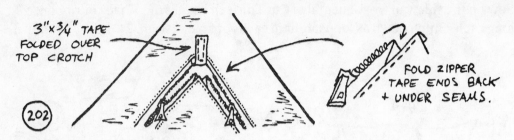

(F) Cut an oversize triangle of netting from your scraps. Hem the long edge and *top stitch* to the inside of the door apex for complete bug proofness.

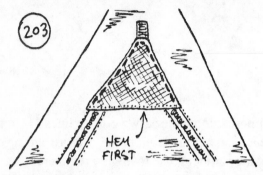

13. If a vestibule end tunnel door is desired, it is most easily added now. Use your own dimensions (It need not be round) and install it in the same manner as the tunnel vents.

14. Sew up the roof ridgeline seam; Use a *flat felled* seam, felled up on the inside. Stitch on four frost-liner loops on the inside of the seam with the same spacing found on the sidewall loops.

15. Cut out from similar fabric scraps and *top stitch* on apex reinforcements extending 5″ down and in each seam line. Place one at each end wall apex (3) and one at each end of the ridgeline seam (2). Sew on inside surfaces.

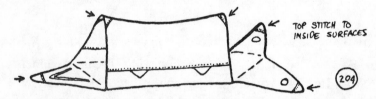

16. Cut one 14″ length of ¾″ tape, fold in half with a half twist in the loop, and stitch across 3½″ down from the loop end. Stitch one of the free ends to the reinforcement patch at the bottom of the vestibule floor apex on the outside.

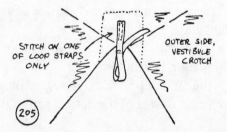

17. Sew up the vestibule end walls; Pin the two halves rightsides together with the ends lined up. Mark a shallow 2″ deep catenary on the sewing side and *plain stitch* along this line. Trim off the excess and finish with a *flat felled* seam. (The accuracy of the catenary is not critical here.)

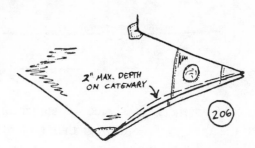

18. Stitch on the top end of the vestibule floor apex stake loop and stitch in the remaining frost-liner loop, 25″ down from the top of the previous seam and right in it.

19. Prepare the pole sleeve; *Hem* the ends to the wrong sides with two ½″ folds. Stitch together lengthwise to form the tubes. (This is not absolutely necessary but it makes the next assembly easier.) The diagonally cut ends of the sleeves should come out offset, as shown, to distribute pitching stresses.

20. Sew up the vestibule end corner seams; Pin both corners rightsides together to insure the even mating of the apexes and bottom corners. Include the pole sleeves, inserted between the two fabric layers, 10″ from the top and 9″ from the bottom. Inside pockets to hold small items may be made from netting scraps and included in the corner seams. *Plain stitch* both sides, trim, then *fell* the seam towards the center of the tent. (Be careful not to stitch over the pole sleeves on the finishing seam. If you have any doubts about the fit of the poles, check the assembly before felling the seam to facilitate correction).

21. Sew up the front corner seams with its pole sleeves, as above.

22. Cut four 17″ lengths of ¾″ tape, fold in half with a half twist in the loop, and stitch across 3½″ down from the loop end. Stitch onto the corners like the other stake loops with one free end sewn to the bottom and the other up the seam.

23. With the help of a friend, insert the poles into the sleeves, join them at the top, and pull an end wall tight. With the friend holding the top and one corner, mark the location for the pole end spike grommets in the corner tape pole/stake loops. Go for a snug fit without putting excessive strain on the corner seams. If all is going as planned, the grommets will probably be best placed 2″ or so out the tapes from the tent corners. Place these four corner grommets along with one in each of the four sidewall pullouts, and one at the front and rear canopy apexes. (209)

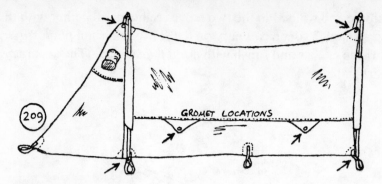

24. Cut two oversized washers from the 4″ × 3″ piece of leather that you've been wondering about. Insert the apex guylines through their grommets and these washers and secure with a couple of bulky knots.

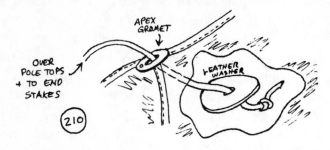

That's it. If you have employed a bit of care in the assembly, you now have yourself a tight and clean pitching tent. Go pitch it and have a beer.

Rain Fly

1. Sew up the ridgeline. (All seams are flat felled)
2. Sew up the front and rear overhang center seams as shown.

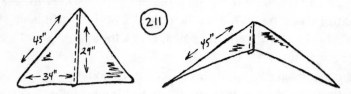

3. Cut out and stitch on apex reinforcement patches. Make similar fabric patches to extend 5″ out each seamline.

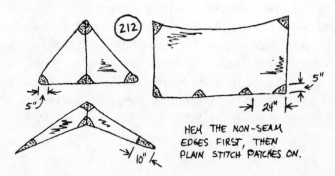

HEM THE NON-SEAM EDGES FIRST, THEN PLAIN STITCH PATCHES ON.

Make Your Own Camping Equipment

4. Sew the overhangs to the roof assembly.
5. *Hem* around all the edges with two folds to the coated side.
6. Place the ten grommets at the pullout points; Four on each side and one at each overhang end.
7. Pitch the fly on the tent inside out and mark depths for diagonal stress catenary seams, as shown. Triple *plain stitch* these seams and coat all of them with seam sealer.

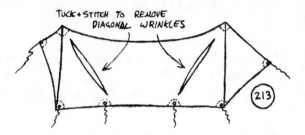

Frost-liner

1. Sew up the ridgeline. (Again, all seams are *flat felled.*)
2. Sew up the vestibule overhang along the shorter, 24″ edges.
3. Sew the overhang to the body.
4. *Hem* around all the edges with two ¼″ folds.
5. Cut thirteen 12″ lengths of ¼″ tape for the ties. Fold in half and stitch to the liner on the folds at the appropriate locations to match the loops sewn into the tent proper.

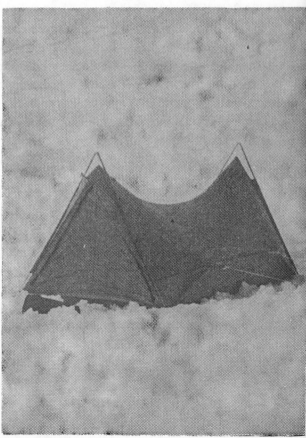

Chapter 10

Clothing

Charlie Snutz stands at the top of the mountain, toasty warm and comfortable in a lofty down filled parka of the latest fashion. "Gosh," he thinks to himself, "that sales clerk at Megalopoland Sports really did me right with this coat, even if it did cost seventy-nine, ninty-nine!"

Others with Charlie, not so well-equipped, are swinging their torsos and stomping their feet to fight the cool crisp air of the Sawtooth Mountains. Looking like jumpin' jack flash, Snutz screams at the top of his lungs and "points 'em downhill." (Lookout!)

By the time he reaches the bottom of the lift, Snutz is sweating enough to raise the humidity level ten feet around him. Ripping frantically at the zippers, he tears off the parka and—extracting a chain and lock from one of the eight inside pockets—secures the coat to a tree. Still pouring out sweat, Snutz flops onto the chairlift where for the ensuing fifteen minutes, he gets colder than he has ever been in his life.

To avoid the problems of Charlie Snutz is to have an understanding of wilderness clothing design and a basic working knowledge of body heat production and regulation.

METABOLISM

Metabolic rate is the major determinant and measure of internal heat production. While some body heat does come from external radiant sources, the majority in cold weather, which is what we are concerned with, is self generated. In the process of turning food into energy, your metabolism creates a proportionate amount of heat and some water. Your metabolic rate and heat production vary considerably, depending on your activity level, caloric intake, environment, and emotional state. Table 5 shows the metabolic variation for different levels of activity.

TABLE 5
GENERAL LEVELS OF ACTIVITY

Condition or activity (young man, average rather than at peak training)	Total Metabolism (Including basal)
	$\frac{kg\ cal}{m^2\ hr}$
Sleeping, post digestive	36
Lying quietly, post digestive	40
(Average for day, including digestion)	
Sitting	50
Standing	60
Strolling, 1½-mph	90
Level walk, 3-mph	155
Level run, 10-mph	500

Sprint (cannot be sustained for an hour, only for a few seconds)	2000
Light activity	60-100
Work, light	100-180
Work, moderate	180-280
Work, heavy	280-380
Work, exhausting	Over 380

U.S. Army, Natick Laboratories. *The Comfort and Function of Clothing,* technical report 69-74-CE.

The water produced as a result of metabolism is expelled through respiratory evaporation and *insensible perspiration*; the continual drying out of your skin surfaces. While evaporation of this water takes some of the produced heat with it, the major portion of your heat production is regulated through *homeostasis*.

HOMEOSTASIS

Homeostasis defined, is the autonomic process employed by the human body to maintain a reasonably stable and functional temperature. There are several things that happen when you are either too hot or too cold. Specifically, *vaso-constriction* or *dilation*, sweating, shivering, and goosebumps.

The primary homeostatic control system of your body works through the regulation of the blood supply to your skin surfaces and extremities. *Vaso-dilation* occurs when you have an excess of heat. It is the opening up, or dilation of the blood vessels in your arms, legs, hands, and feet. This increases the blood flow to your extremities and allows them to work like radiators to dissipate the unnecessary heat. Conversely, when your internal organs and body become too cool, *vaso-constriction* takes place. The blood vessels constrict to a smaller size in your extremities to concentrate your store of heat where it is needed most.

It is important to note that the blood vessels in your head do not constrict or dilate. Because your head is comparatively overexposed most of the time, it becomes a major avenue of heat loss. It should also be noted that nicotine and alcohol affect the otherwise autonomic operations of vaso-constriction and vaso-dilation. Nicotine will cause some vaso-constriction and can make already cold fingers and feet even colder. Alcohol, on the other hand, will cause some vaso-dilation. While it may warm you for a short time, it can result in an abnormal loss of body heat ultimately.

Sweating is another homeostatic control which begins if vaso-dilation doesn't do the cooling off job. Sweating in a hot environment is great, but in the cold it should be avoided. The cooling effect of sweating under clothing in cold weather is severe. When you begin to sewat, you lose the heat that was initially required to raise the sweated moisture to body temperature. Once on your skin, this moisture cools and draws more heat from your skin during evaporation. The evaporating moisture passes out through your inner layers of clothing until it condenses in a cooler layer (the dew point.) Here it cools even more, releasing its remaining heat out into the atmosphere, and then begins to wick back towards your body through your clothing. At this point, even further cooling of your body will result from another cycle of evaporative cooling at the skin, and an increased conduction of cold due to the moistened clothing. This is exactly what happened to Charlie Snutz, with the exception that Snutz took off his coat when he needed it most; while sitting on the chairlift with a lowered metabolism and heat generation. Needless to say, sweating in a cold environment can be disasterous ιo your comfort.

Shivering and goose-bumps are also autonomic homeostatic reactions to an excessive cooling of your body. Shivering serves to increase your metabolic rate and, hence, your heat production. Goose-bumps seek to increase the thickness of "dead" insulating air next to your skin by erecting your body hairs.

INSULATION

When the temperature drops and your homeostatic controls and metabolism are not sufficient to keep you warm, external insulation in the form of clothing and "dead" air becomes necessary. Exhaustive research on insulation requirements has been carried out by the U.S. Army Natick Laboratories. One of the outcomes of this research is data determining the insulation thickness requirements of a person in various states of activity and at different temperatures. Table 6 and 7 may be used to find the thickness of insulation needed to maintain a heat steady state.

Actual temperatures with the following wind chill chart. For example, with an actual temperature of 30°F. and a wind speed of 20 mph, the effective temperature will be 4°F.

TABLE 6
WIND CHILL CHART
Actual Temperature (°F.)

Wind Speed (mph)	40	30	20	10	0	−10	−20	−30
			Effective Temperature (°F.)					
10	28	16	4	−9	−21	−33	−46	−58
20	18	4	−10	−25	−39	−53	−67	−82
30	13	−2	−18	−33	−48	−63	−79	−94
40	10	−6	−21	−37	−53	−69	−85	−100

TABLE 7
INSULATION THICKNESS TABLE

Effective Temperature (°F.)	Required for Comfort (in inches)		
	Sleeping	Light Work	Heavy Work
40°F.	1.5"	.8"	.20"
20	2.0	1.0	.27
0	2.5	1.3	.35
−20	3.0	1.6	.40
−40	3.5	1.9	.48
−60	4.0	2.1	.52

The values in the thickness table, number 7, derive from this general equation for insulation:

$$Clo = \frac{3.09}{H_d} \ (t_s - t_a)$$

Clo = a unit of insulation used to characterize clothing and sleeping bag systems.

H_d = the metabolic rate of the individual corresponding to different activity levels expressed as Kcal/m² /hr.

Make Your Own Camping Equipment

t_s = skin temperature (°F.)

t_a = air temperature (°F.)

You can compute an insulation thickness requirement by using the metabolic values listed in table 5, General Levels of Activity. Skin temperature is assumed to be 95°F. So, at a metabolic rate of 36 Kcal/m²/hr, that of a post digestive sleeping state, and with an effective temperature of 40°F., Clo will be approximately 4.5.

$$\text{Clo} = \frac{3.09}{36} \ (95 - 40)$$

$$\text{Clo} = 4.5$$

Clo may be converted t the required thickness in inches by dividing by three. Hence, the above conditions would require 1.5" of insulation to remain in a heat steady state.

The thickness data here is a good reference for a person of average size and in fair condition. Physical or emotional fatigue, altitude, relative humidity, caloric intake and digestive activity, and the types of foods eaten, are all variables that can affect these recommendations.

CLOTHING FOR THE ELEMENTS

In order to maintain a reasonably stable and comfortable state, clothing for elemental activities must interact with the physiology of your body. The key word here is activity. Hiking, climbing, and skiing all involve periods of high activity and metabolic rates, combined with periods of rest and lower metabolic rates. Add to this the temperature and wind variations that occur throughout the day and at different altitudes and you have a highly variable range of insulation needs. For elemental clothing to be functional, it must allow you to extend your comfort margin beyond that which is provided by homeostatic controls.

An extreme example of the variation in insulation requirements, and a challenging comfort problem, is that of alpine or downhill skiing via chairlifts. The day is divided between periods of extreme activity followed by quiet sitting on the ride back up the mountain. Whereas an insulation thickness of only ½" may be necessary during the downhill run, 1½" of thickness might be called for during the ride up. As Charlie Snutz found out, you can't simply dress for the ride up and be comfortable all day long.

One way to solve this problem is to use the *layer technique* of clothing. Instead of wearing one massive down filled parka, you combine thermal underwear, a turtleneck, a sweater, and a down vest, all topped with a wind shell type parka. In this manner, you can peel off excess layers as needed to maintain a comfortable amount of insulation. The idea behind the layer technique should be applied to your extremities and head as well. Because your head has no homeostatic controls, it should be the first point of voluntary heat control. The use of a hat and/or hood can add immeasureably to your workable comfort margin. The extremities are next in importance. If they remain covered during over-heating and vaso-dilation, the result will be the same as a car with a clogged radiator. If Snutz had been aware of this, he would have skied down wearing an unzipped 60/40 parka or wind shell with a hat in his pocket (instead of a lock) for the ride back up.

It follows that clothing for wilderness pursuits should be designed for maximum possible ventilation. Cuffs should close with snaps or velcro. The knit cuffs, common on fashion oriented clothing, allow no ventilation adjustment. Coat front zippers should be of the double slider type to allow both upper and lower ventilation when it's needed. These zippers should also be fitted with draft flaps. This enables you to leave the zipper completely undone and close up the front by the flap alone for partial ventilation, and a greater usuable comfort margin. High collars, hoods, and drawstring hems also add to the ventilation capabilities of a coat.

Pants should be considered for ventilation capabilities. Insulated and shell type pants should ideally be fitted with full length side zippers. This also allows their donning or removal without having to take off a bulky pair of boots, and skis too for that matter. Getting stuck in too warm weather with a pair of warmup pants that can't be ventilated is a bummer. Your only recourse is to remove everything else possible to vent your excess heat which, if you're in inclement weather requiring warmups in the first place, might be impractical. When donning your shell or warmup pants in the morning, bear in mind that this increased insulation will reduce the necessary thickness around your torso. If elastic hemmed snow cuffs are used, they should be made from a breathable material to allow some extra margin of lower leg ventilation. They need not be made of a coated, waterproof fabric to serve their function.

Whatever the application, the possibilities for ventilation should be a primary consideration in buying or designing functional clothing for elemental activities.

A further comfort margin may be obtained by considering the ample cooling effects of the wind. As is evident from the wind chill chart, table 6, the effect is considerable. In many elemental pursuits, increased activity and metabolism means movement. The breeze produced on your body by this movement may be used to keep you cool. Thus, any fabrics or clothing which will allow some wind penetration will also provide some automatic cooling without conscious adjustment of clothing. Down parkas and vests with sewn through baffle constructions work well to this effect by allowing some wind passage through their seamlines. Corduroy fabrics will also function this way. In a still air, or under a protective wind shell, the wales of a corduroy fabric provide insulation by trapping and deadening some surface air. Even in a light breeze, corduroy gives some warmth (insulation) by breaking-up the air flow over its surface. (The same as a wind gradient caused by trees and buildings, but on a much smaller scale.) Corduroy pants are also excellent for use in dry snow conditions. While providing good insulation combined with excellent ventilation, they also serve to hold any falling or blown snow on the surface where it may be brushed off before melting from your body heat.

So you can see that maintaining comfort requires more than simply maintaining warmth. Versatility in a comfort margin must be provided through the use of the layer technique, adequate ventilation possibilities, attention to your head and extremities as avenues of heat loss (in that order), and fabrics which both ventilate and insulate. In this manner, clothing for the elements works in harmony with your metabolic and homeostatic systems.

CLOTHING FOR THE STORM

High winds, rain, and wet snow require outer shell protection to maintain dry and effective insulation. While a 60/40 shell parka may do the job in light rains, keeping out

Make Your Own Camping Equipment

heavy rains presents problems of insufficient ventilation of insensible perspiration. Keeping dry in a downpour requires an outer shell of coated, waterproof fabric. The problem is, that in keeping out the rain, you're also sealing in your own body moisture, which during periods of high activity might be considerable.

The most comfortable means of staying dry in such weather, short of staying in your tent, is under a very loose fitting poncho or cagoule. These garments are intentionally made to fit very, very loosly in order to allow air circulation and ventilation from below. Unless absolutely necessary for complete mobility, waterproof jackets and pants should be avoided. Even with breathable linings to cut down on a bit of the inside condensation, waterproof clothing is a sort of Hobson's choice (damned if you do, damned if you don't.) You either get wet with rain or cooked in your own perspiration! In either case, you should plan increased insulation to counteract the conductive cooling caused by wet clothing. (Like tent floors, rainwear should have its seams coated with a sealer for increased protection.)

FIT

As was discussed in chapter two on insulations, it is not the material around you that keeps you warm, but the thickness of "dead" air. Thus, to get the maximum insulation from a garment, while maintaining a comfort margin, you need a proper fit.

Obviously, a coat which is too tight is not going to allow much thickness and insulation, or ventilation. Too loose a garment, on the other hand, will allow excessive air movement and subsequent convective heat loss. The ideal fit is loose, but not too loose, with drawstrings which will allow you to tighten it up when desired.

All your garments—vest, down parka, and wind shell—should not be cut the same size unless they are to be worn separately, in which case they won't be as effective with the layer technique. An exception to this can be a vest or parka that is used in a larger size for better ventilation and relies on an outer wind shell to eliminate the excess room.

In any case, the fit should be comfortable and should not interfere with freedom of movement. This means sleeves that don't pull at the shoulders when your arms are extended, hoods that don't choke you when you turn your head, and enough length to keep the bottom hem below your waist when you bend over.

MAKING YOUR OWN

The following patterns represent some of the more popular basics. They may be made to "spec" as detailed or altered in a number of ways to fit your physique and needs. Pockets, closures, and hardware may be whatever variety you prefer. As for fit, lengths and contours are tailorable. The sleeves in the patterns are cut on the long side and may be shortened, if necessary. The side body seams may be tailored as well for tapers or bulges of your own. For example, ladies in the smaller sizes may cut the coat bottoms on the large side to accommodate wider hips. The emphasis is on a custom fit.

Consider commercial patterns (shirts, pants) and conversions of existing garments for your elemental clothing. For example, you can make a really fine pair of knickers by chopping the lower legs off a pair of old wool or corduroy pants.

With a minimum of effort, and a lot of enjoyment, you can come up with some fine and functional clothing at a fraction of what it would cost new.

Patterns and Design Criteria

LINED HIGH GAITERS

For deep snow, high gaiters are a necessary luxury. They keep you dry, are functional, and add a good deal of insulation to a usually overexposed part of your body. Like a kid exploring the puddles in his first pair of rubber rain boots, high gaiters can open up the winter for you.

These gaiters are lined with light taffeta or ripstop to add an extra measure of weatherproofness and warmth. The tall uppers are made from 60/40 cloth for ventilation, while the lower ankle sections are made from a coated pack cloth. Closure is by a flap covered zipper up the front with a heel strap at the bottom and a drawstring at the top. The bottoms of these gaiters are shaped like spats to fit snugly over and around your boots. Provision is made for a lace hook on the bottom fronts for securing them to your boot lacing. The uppers are also contoured to fit well around your calfs. The finished dimensions are 17½" tall with a 15½" circumference at the ankles. This circumference will give a good fit around most cross-country and hiking boots. For alpine ski boots, measure the upper boot circumference and increase the width of the ankle pieces to suit. Alpine skiing use will also call for some leather or vinyl edge protectors on the insides of the lowers to prevent them from being cut up by your ski edges.

MATERIALS:

19" × 45"—60/40 cloth.
25" × 45"—light taffeta or ripstop.
6½" × 45"—coated pack cloth or Cordura.
2—16" zippers, single pull-slider, separating.
6—no. "O" spur grommets.
8 or 10—heavy snaps.
40"—drawcord.

CUTTING LAYOUT:

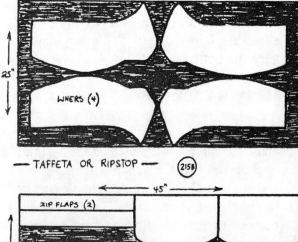

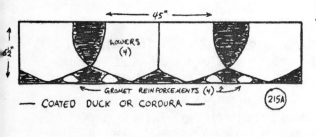

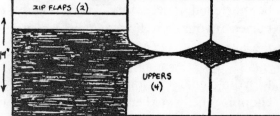

PIECE DIMENSIONS:

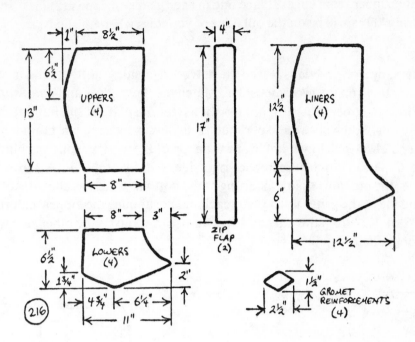

ASSEMBLY:

1. Cut out and heat seal all pieces. Note that the liners are cut 1″ shorter than the outers due to the absence of a cross seam in the centers of the liners. To assure accuracy, fold the fabric for cutting curved sections, paper doll fashion, and use the first cutting as a template.

2. Join the lowers, uppers, and liner halves. *Plain stitch* on wrong sides at standard allowance. (217)

3. Join the outer uppers and lowers. Use a *flat felled seam*, felled up on the insides. (218)

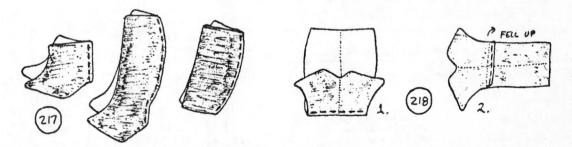

4. Fold and stitch along edges and ends of flaps, tucking in the ends ½″ for a finished edge.

5. Place a top drawstring grommet in each of the outers, 1″ down from the upper edges, 1½″ from the zipper seam edges. Place one in each gaiter on opposite sides, so that the drawstring knots will be on the outsides of your legs when finished.

6. Join the liners, outers, and flaps. Place the halves, rightsides together, and insert the flaps between them on the grommet sides. Match the three edges and *plain stitch* at standard allowance, being careful not to stitch over the ends of the flaps at the upper and lower seams. Stitch all around perimeters, as shown, placing one grommet reinforcing patch at each lower ankle apex, on top of the work in your machine. (221)

7. Sew on the zippers; Turn the assemblies rightsides out. Place the zipper tapes about halfway over the previous seams. Starting at the bottom corner, as shown, stitch up with the outside of the gaiter up in your machine, positioning the zipper underneath as you go. Stop 1½″ from the top and stitch across, then down the other side with the other zipper half. (222)

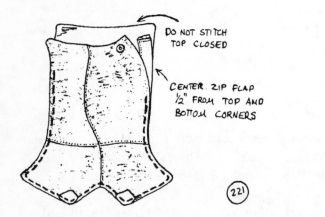

DO NOT STITCH TOP CLOSED

CENTER ZIP FLAP ½″ FROM TOP AND BOTTOM CORNERS

(221)

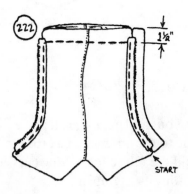

(222)

1½″

START

8. (A) Place a 20″ length of drawcord through each top grommet and fold the top edges of the outers and liners together ½″ to form the drawstring tube. Pin this secure, including one to hold the drawcord at the closed end.

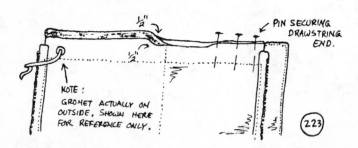

½″

½″

PIN SECURING DRAWSTRING END.

NOTE: GROMET ACTUALLY ON OUTSIDE, SHOWN HERE FOR REFERENCE ONLY.

(223)

(B) The last seam! Starting at the bottom corner indicated, *top stitch* across the bottom. Continue this seam up the sides at ¼″ or so, next to, but not on top of, the existing stitching, then across the top at ⅛″ or so, to close up the drawstring tube. Turning the top corner to stitch down to the starting point, catch the end of the drawstring to hold it in with a couple of backstitchings. (224)

120   Make Your Own Camping Equipment

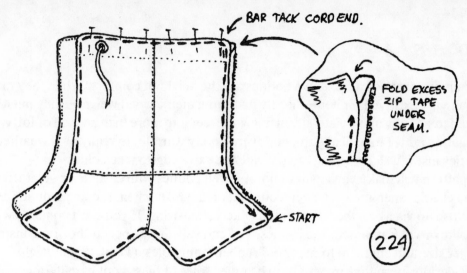

9. Place the flap snaps and heel cord grommets. Zip gaiters together and mark locations for four or five evenly spaced snaps on the flaps. Place the heel cord grommets as shown, through the reinforcing patches inside.

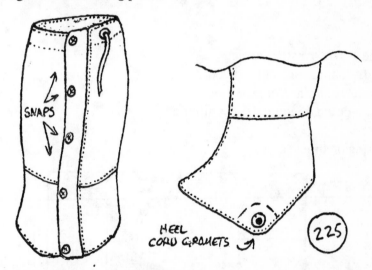

10. The finishing step requires the services of a boot and shoe repair shop. Have these people place a heavy duty lace hook on the bottom of each flap.

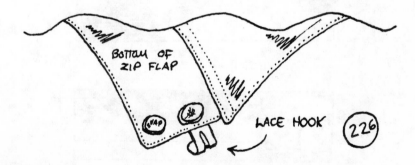

There you are. Super gaiters! They work equally well for hiking, or hang-gliding in star thistle and fox tail weeds!

PATTERN 14

DOWN BOOTIES

For lounging around camp, down booties are the height of comfort. While they may seem like a really extravagant item—hardly justifying their carried weight—they must be experienced to be fully appreciated. Stuffing your feet into more than an inch of lofty down insulation adds fantastically to your overall body warmth. In really cold weather, down booties inside a sleeping bag can provide the extra edge on the cold.

This pattern will make you a pair of non-baffled booties with ensolite or volarafoam insoles and elastic inner ankles to keep your feet on the pads when trucking around camp. The tops close up via a drawhem, very much like a shoestring. If you can't come up with some ensolite or volarafoam for the insoles, you can substitute Spenco shoe type insoles (buy a larger size and cut them to fit) or old rubber thong soles. (Think "lightweight," when considering alternative materials.) The outer soles of these booties call for coated pack cloth or Cordura and include 1½" high sidewalls. The pattern includes dimensions for four sizes for a perfect fit for anybody.

MATERIALS:

1 yd.—45" wide 1.9 oz. ripstop fabric.
⅓ yd.—45" wide coated pack cloth or Cordura.
12" × 8"—ensolite or volarafoam.
1½" to 2½" oz.—down or equivalent synthetic fill.
20"—½" elastic.
40"—heavy string or shoe lacing.

CUTTING LAYOUT:

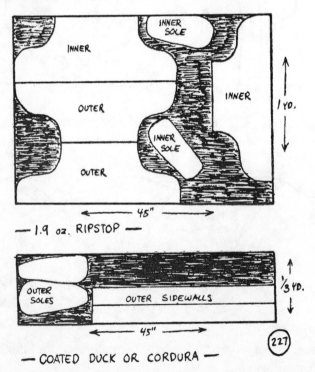

Make Your Own Camping Equipment

PIECE DIMENSIONS:

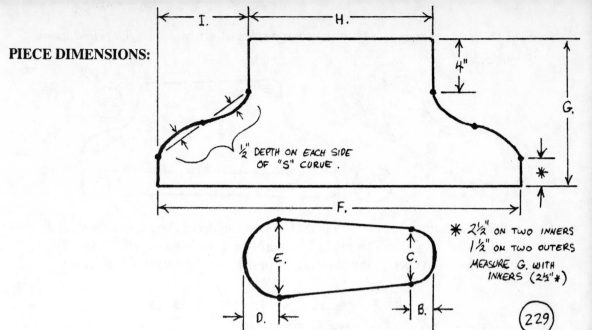

1/2" DEPTH ON EACH SIDE OF "S" CURVE.

* 2½" ON TWO INNERS
1½" ON TWO OUTERS
MEASURE G. WITH INNERS (2½"*)

229

Sidewalls (2)—2½" × F.

Soles: make two from ripstop and two from coated pack cloth. The centers of lines C. and E. on soles are radius points for the end curves.

DIMENSIONS TABLE

		Size		
	Small	Medium	Large	X-Large
A.	10"	11"	12"	13"
B.	2	2	2¼	2¼
C.	4	4	4½	4½
D.	2½	2½	2¾	2¾
E.	5	5	5½	5½
F.	24³⁄₈	26³⁄₈	28⁷⁄₈	30⁷⁄₈
G.	11	11	12	12
H.	14½	15½	16	16½
I.	5	5½	6½	7¼

The dimension marked by an asterisk are 2½" on the two inners and 1½" on the two outers.

ASSEMBLY:

1. Measure your foot length, with or without socks, as you prefer. The dimensions for the different sizes are;

   sm.—9" long × 9" high.
   med.—10" long × 9" high.
   lg.—11" long × 10" high.
   x-lg.—12" long × 10" high.

2. Make the soles; Cut two foam sole pads, ½" smaller all around than the fabric sole pieces. Sandwich the pads between one coated and one ripstop sole piece (coated side in) and stitch around perimeter at a ⅛" allowance. 230

3. Join the shorter, outer uppers with the coated sidewall strips. Use a *flat felled seam*, felled up on the insides. (231)

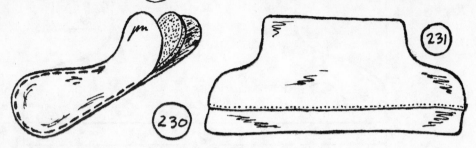

4 Sew the ankle elastic to the inner uppers; Cut two lengths of elastic, each just long enough to go around your ankle plus 1" for allowance. Holding the elastic stretched taut, *plain stitch* it to each of the taller, inner uppers, on the wrong side and, as shown.

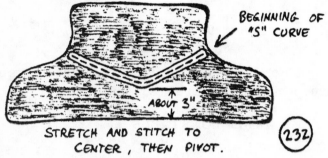

BEGINNING OF "S" CURVE

ABOUT 3"

STRETCH AND STITCH TO CENTER, THEN PIVOT. (232)

5. Fold each of the upper pieces rightsides together and *plain stitch*, as shown. (Elastic side of inner uppers goes out.) Leave 1" at tops unstitched, as indicated.

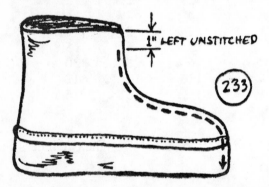

1" LEFT UNSTITCHED

(233)

6. Sew the outer uppers to the sole assemblies; With the pieces inside-out, insert the soles into the uppers and pin all around evenly for stitching at ¼" or so, or just inside of the existing sole stitching. *Plain stitch* all around with the sole material up in your machine.

INSIDE OF SOLE

(234)

7. (A) Sew the inner uppers to the remaining allowances of the above seams; With the outer assembly in the above pictured configuration, pin the inner uppers allowance on top of the sole fabric side, edges matched. (This should look like two shoes put soles together.) *Plain stitch* all around with the inner uppers in your machine. Do not sew further in than the previous steps seamline at ¼". (235)

    (B) Turn the outer uppers rightsides out. The inner upper will now be inside where it belongs and the sole seams hidden between the upper shells as shown. (236)

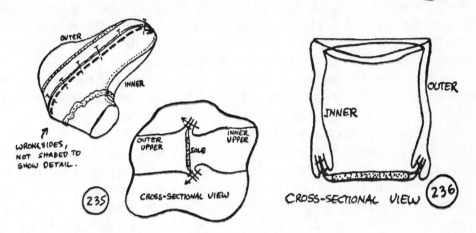

8. Make the opening for the top hem drawstring tube. Mate the upper corners of the inner and outer uppers that were left unstitched in step #5. Roll each side outwards (towards the right sides) and stitch, as shown, to make a "V" shaped opening at the top of each bootie. (237)

9. Fill each bootie with about one ounce of down and pin the tops closed with a ½", then 1" fold to the outside. With a 20" length of shoestring in each, stitch around the bottom edge of the drawhem to close up the tops and make the drawtube. (238)

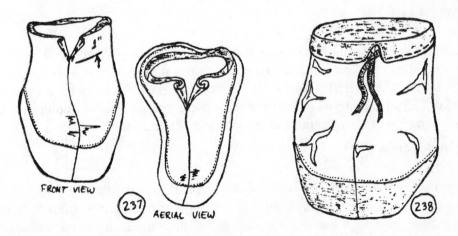

10. Wearing nothing but your jocky shorts and down booties, grab a beer, kick back, and turn on the game!

PATTERN 15

RAIN OR POWDER PANTS

Considerable effort was spent trying to come up with a sizable pattern for these shell pants. This effort revealed the complexity of a good, satisfactory fit for everybody within the confines of simple small, medium, and large sizing. While a pattern of this type would work, the much desired quality of the fit would be no better than the cheapest commercially made shell pants which look more like baggy GI fatigues.

Consider the vast amount of sizes in which pants are sold. Both the waist sizes and inseam lengths are specified. There must be a hundred different sizes made to fit everyone satisfactorily. Simply buying a new pair of jeans can be a chore, trying to guess the degree of shrinkage in relation to the length, width, girth, etc.

So . . . this project is designed to make use of your best fitting pair of jeans as a pattern. (Of course, without ripping them apart!) This way you will get the desired fit. The finished shell pants will fit you far better than any ready made ones in a standard sizing, and if done carefully, the resulting pants will fit you perfectly.

You will be making your own basic pattern and materials requirement so the features you build into the pants are entirely up to you. The following assembly instructions detail procedures for putting in side zippers, pockets, snow cuffs, and edge protectors (for downhill skiing use) as well as covering the basic assembly techniques. Note, that if the full length side zippers are used, the snow cuffs must be either omitted or fitted with their own velcro or snap closures.

MATERIALS:

Most sizes may be fit into under 1½ yards of fabric. To make the pants with all the details covered in the assembly instructions, you will need: one no. "O" spur grommet, about 40" of drawcord (for the waist), some scraps of heavy pack cloth or Cordura cloth, some scraps of uncoated ripstop for the snow cuffs, one spring cord lock or fixlock, 16" or so of elastic, and the side zippers. Of course, this is all up to you.

CUTTING LAYOUT:

You will have four pant sections, plus whatever add-ons you choose. The four pant sections should be layed out parallel to one another, noting that there is a right and wrong side with the coated material. Consider fitting the pieces widthwise or lengthwise on either 45" or 55" wide material to arrive at the most economical fabric requirement. (Refer back to chapter 4 on design and layout for more on this.

PIECE DIMENSIONS:

Illustrated here are the basic outline of a front and back pant quarter, with the necessary dimension locations indicated. (These happen to be bell bottoms or flairs.) Lay out your pattern jeans on a flat surface and take the appropriate measurements. Use the fabric grainlines on your pattern pants to measure the depth of curved sections. Note that the crotch length on the front section is shorter than that on the back section. This discrepancy is corrected by either cutting the legs 3" to 4" longer than necessary and hemming them straight and at the proper length when done (easier). Add ½" to each edge for the seam allowances. The top edges should get a 1½" seam allowance for a drawstring or elastic top hem.

Depending on the fit of your pattern pants, and what you intend to wear under the finished shell pants, an extra margin of roominess should be added to the outside leg seams. The pants I used for my pattern and the project prototype, fit loosely and comfortably. Consequently, I added only ½" to each outer leg seam to get 1" of extra girth in each leg and 2" of extra girth around the tops and hips. If in doubt, add more and take it in later. You can't make them larger once they're cut!

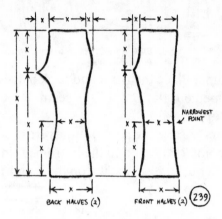

BACK HALVES (2)   FRONT HALVES (2)   (239)

Note: back leg widths are usually larger than the fronts.

ASSEMBLY:

1. Sew the front and back halves together at the crotch seams with *flat felled seams*, felled on the coated insides. Place the halves rightsides together, *plain stitch* at ½", then open out flat and fell them.

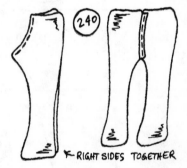

(240)

← RIGHT SIDES TOGETHER

2. Sew on pockets if desired. Pockets may be either flat patch types or bellows type. (See 60/40 pattern, #18, for construction of the latter)

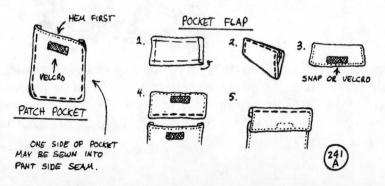

HEM FIRST

POCKET FLAP

VELCRO

1.   2.   3.

SNAP OR VELCRO

PATCH POCKET

4.   5.

ONE SIDE OF POCKET
MAY BE SEWN INTO
PANT SIDE SEAM.

(241 A)

127

3. If outside seam zippers are desired, first hem the tops of the pants (see step 8. **(A)** for details.) Use the *full width installation*, including a weather flap on the front halves if desired. (Make it it short.) No zippers? Go to step 4.

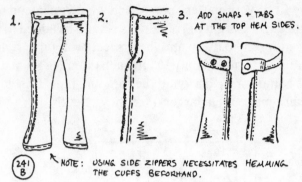

3. ADD SNAPS + TABS AT THE TOP HEM SIDES.

241 B

NOTE: USING SIDE ZIPPERS NECESSITATES HEMMING THE CUFFS BEFORHAND.

4. Stitch up the outer leg seams; Place the front and back halves rightsides together, *plain stitch* up one side, open out flat and *fell* the seam. Repeat on the other side, felling the seam from the inside.

5. If you want edge protectors to save the pant bottoms from your ski edges, now is the time. These may extend completely around the bottom perimeters, (useful for making the pants longer if you made a mistake on the length) or just on the insides of the legs. 242

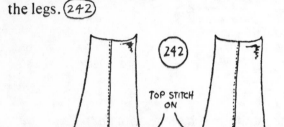

242

TOP STITCH ON

OUTSIDE LEG SEAMS

243

PANTS WRONGSIDES OUT

6. **(A)** Stitch up the inseam; Lay the pants flat, inside-out again, pin, and *plain stitch* it up with a couple of rows of stitching. 243

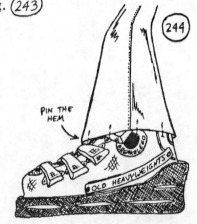

244

PIN THE HEM

OLD HEAVYWEIGHTS

(B) Turn them rightsides out and try them on wearing whatever is expected underneath. Too loose? . . . Sew up the inseam again, ¼″ or so in from the last stitching as needed. Mark the top and bottoms for hemming. (If these are to be worn for alpine skiing, put on your ski boots. This will change the optimum location for the bottom hems.) 244

Make Your Own Camping Equipment

7. (A) While they cut down on ventilation, snow cuffs are great for powder skiing. Cut two 5½″ wide strips of breathable ripstop fabric, long enough to go around the bottom leg perimeters, plus ½″ allowance on each end. Cut two lengths of ¾″ or so wide elastic to one long side of the strips, matched up with the edges and fully stretched. Fold this under with a couple of folds and stitch fast.

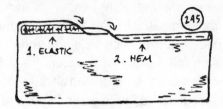

(B) Fold the strips rightsides together and sew into donuts with *flat felled* seams. If the side zippers are used, make this a velcro or snap closure instead.

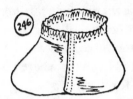

(C) Place the cuffs inside the leg bottoms, pin, and *top stitch* in around the perimeters.

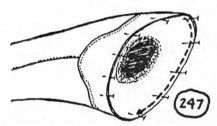

8. (A) Hem the waistline; If side zippers are used, the waist must be held by elastic in the back hem and/or adjustable side snap closures by the zipper tops.
(B) No side zippers? . . . Hem the waistline to make a drawstring tube. (The drawstring closure is better than elastic because it will not stretch open in a nose dive, and let snow in.) First, place a grommet 2½″ down from the unfinished edge in the front seam. Fold the top edge down ½″ then 1″ and top stitch to make the tube. Thread in a drawcord and secure it with a fixlock or similar device.

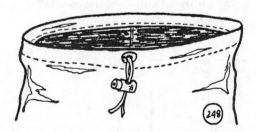

For $2.50 or so, it's pretty fine pair of shell pants!

PATTERN 16

DOWN VEST

This pattern is for the ultimate down vest. The tailoring basics have been carefully engineered to eliminate the most common problems in many of the commercially made models. Large gaping armholes are eliminated by the accurate angling of the shoulder seams and under arm curve depths. Different neck sizes and underclothings are accomodated by an adjustable down filled collar with a generous 4" height. The vest is cut long enough to stay below the waist and is fitted with an adjustable drawstring to eliminate lower drafts. The vest is finished off with down filled handwarmer pockets and a down filled zipper draft flap extending all the way up through the collar. Velcro is called for in place of snaps to allow easy, gloved hands operation.

By making it yourself, the loft may be whatever you please. (Bearing in mind that it is limited, to a certain extent, by the sewn through baffling construction.) Most ready made vests average around 4 ounces of down fill. I recommend 5 ounces or more and up to 8 ounces for the extra large size. Of course, this will depend on the quality of down used. The extra loft is most appreciated in a vest where your uncovered limbs act as radiators and must rely on torso heat for warmth.

	Pattern Size				
	X-Small	Small	Medium	Large	X-Large
Zipper (two-way, separating)	18"	20"	22"	24"	26"
1.9 oz. ripstop (downproof) 45" wide	2⅓	2⅓	2½	3	3

5 to 8 oz. – down
5' – drawcord
9½" – ¾" velcro tape
1 – no. "O" spur grommet

MATERIALS:

CUTTING LAYOUT:

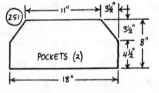

PIECE DIMENSIONS:

Find your size using the instructions in step 1 of the assembly. Use the appropriate measurements from the alphabetically keyed sizing table below.

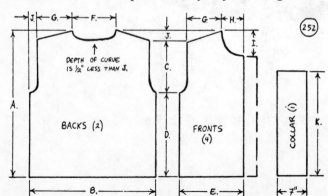

Make Your Own Camping Equipment

DIMENSIONS TABLE

	X-Small	Small	Medium	Large	X-Large
			Size		
A.	25"	27"	29"	31"	33"
B.	20	22	24	26	28
C.	7½	8½	9	9¾	10½
D.	16	17	18	19	20
E.	10½	11½	12½	13½	14½
F.	6	6½	7	7½	8
G.	5½	6	6½	4¼	4½
H.	3½	3¾	4	4¼	3½
I.	2½	2¾	3	3¼	3½
J.	1½	1¾	2	2¼	2½
K.	19¾	21¼	22¾	24¼	25¾

Note: Shown above is a right front piece (rightside up). On the two left front pieces, add 2½" to the zipper seam for the zipper draft flap (indicated by dotted line above and in cutting layout).

ASSEMBLY:

1. Measure yourself for size; Measure around your chest or stomach, whichever is larger, and find your size in the table below.

	Your Chest Measurement (in inches)				
	28-32	32-36	36-40	40-44	44-48
Pattern size	x-sm.	sm.	med.	lg.	x-lg.
Finished Girth (may be reduced by tailoring)	38"	42"	46"	50"	54"

As you can see from the above sizing table, a person with a 36" chest measurement could wear either a small or a medium. In this case, the small would give 6" of extra girth while the medium would give 10" of clearance. I recommend the larger, for an ideal finished girth of at least 8". This may be accomplished in the above case by using the medium size pattern and tailoring the side body seams, 1" on each side. While this kind of custom sizing is possible, it is by no means a necessity for a decent, store bought quality fit.

2. *Plain stitch* each back piece to two front pieces across the shoulders and sides to make an inner and outer shell. When the assembly to be the outer shell is turned rightside out, (seam edges in) the front pieces will be switched, left for right, so sew on the wider flap front pieces on opposite sides in each assembly, as shown.

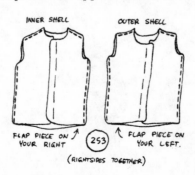

Patterns and Design Criteria

3. (A) Make the collar; Fold it lengthwise and *plain stitch* across the ends at ½"
   allowance. Check the length when turned rightside out with the body neckholes and
   adjust, if necessary. With the collar rightside out, (end stitching inside) stitch across
   the bottom at ¼", leaving 5" or so, open for filling.

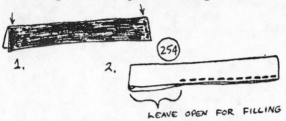

1.   2.

LEAVE OPEN FOR FILLING

   (B) Fill the collar with down, pin, and stitch closed.

4. Turn the inner shell assembly inside-out (seam edges in) and place inside the
   inside-out outer assembly. *Plain stitch* the shells together along the zipper seams at
   the standard ½" allowance.

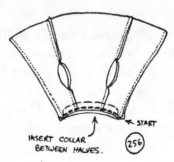

OUTER

INNER

FLAP PIECES ON YOUR LEFT

5. Open this assembly out flat, in the same configuration as above, insert and center
   the collar between the two halves. Pin, and *plain stitch* in.

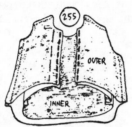

INSERT COLLAR
BETWEEN HALVES.   START

6. Sew up the armholes; Turn the assembly rightsides out with the fronts folded
   together. Cut *blending* slits around the armhole edges, fold in ½", and pin for *top
   stitching*. Stitch two rows, working from the insides of the armholes, with the liner
   fabric up in your machine.

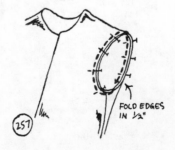

FOLD EDGES
IN ½"

7. With the assembly still rightsides out, reach inside the layers, locate, and pull out the seam edges of the shoulders from both the inner and outer shells. *Plain stitch* these edges together at ¼″ or so to create vertical, side baffles. Repeat this step with the seam allowances of the side body seams. Stitch from close to the existing seam ends.

8. Place the drawstring grommet at the bottom of the nonflap right front pieces, 1″ up from the bottom edge and 4″ over from the zipper seam edge, through both inner and outer shell layers. (Note: at this point the vest is reversible. Make sure that the longer flap side is on the wearer's left)

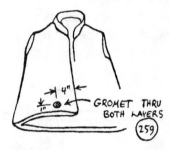

9. Fill the vest with down; Pin across the bottom edges, up about 3½″, leaving sections open for filling the fronts and back. Fill, pin closed, and pat the down to distribute it evenly and check for proper fill. Without any baffles yet, the down should loft the vest 4″ or so. Be sure to leave three or four handfuls of down for the pockets.

10. Make the drawstring tube; Fold the bottom edges up to the inside ½″ then 1″. (This will place the grommet on the inside of this hem.) Begin stitching from the inside on the flap side. Stop after 4″ or so, and pin the drawstring at the end. Continue across with the drawstring exiting through the grommet. Use a zipper foot on your machine to get by the grommet.

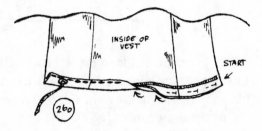

11. **(A)** Sew the three baffle lines; Mark along the seams at 6 to 7″ intervals for quilt lines, as shown by heavy dots below.

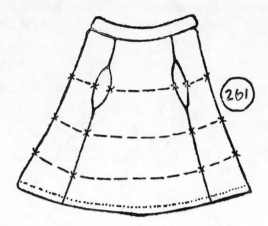

(B) Distribute the down evenly through the vest by patting it. **Pin** the shells together along the center baffle line, pushing the down out of the intended seamline. Stitch this baffle from the outside, all around the vest. Caution: The down between the fabric layers is very slippery and can cause unplanned tucks and folds. Work slowly, holding the fabric taut, front and rear, and checking for sideways slippage as well.
(C) Stitch across the bottom and top quilt lines in the same manner and with the same careful attention to fabric slippage.

12. **(A)** Install the zipper; separate the zipper halves and stitch in the right front half, right along the fabric edge. Work from the top side, from the neck down. Run two rows of stitching, ¼″ apart, with bar tacks and bottom. (262)

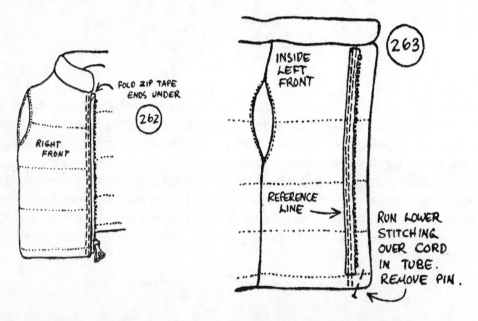

(B) Mark a reference line 2½″ in on the inside of the left front (flap) piece. Stitch in the left zipper half with the zipper tape edge on the reference line after checking for proper mating. Stitch with two rows as on the right side and continue down to the drawhem to tack in the end of the drawcord. (263)

13.	Cut five 1″ lengths of velcro and one 2½″ length. Stitch on as shown with the fuzzy "pile" sides on the right side of the vest. (Note: If your machine has zig-zag, use it to tack on the velcro squares with two stitch lines as shown below.)

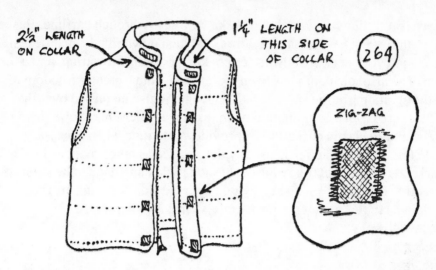

14.	(A) Make the pockets; Fold together and *plain stitch*, as shown. ⑳⑤
	(B) Turn rightsides out, fill with down, and *plain stitch* closed at ¼″. Stitch on 1″ pieces of velcro "hooks," as shown. ⑳⑥

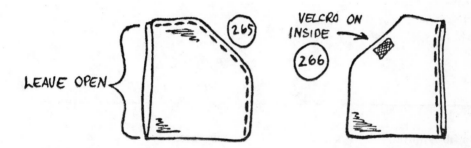

15.	*Top stitch* the pockets to the vest front with the plain seamed edge turned under, 2″ or so from the zipper stitch lines and lined up with the bottom hem seam. (If you're very close or right on the hem seam, you'll need the zipper foot again to get by the grommet.) Bar-tack 1 to ½″ short of the angled pocket openings, or as required for a snug hand entrance. Stitch on velcro "piles" at appropriate points with the pocket openings pulled back. That's it!

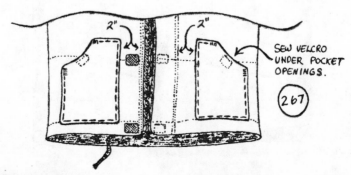

DOWN SWEATER/PARKA

This pattern is for your standard down parka with sewn through baffling. Based on the vest pattern, this parka has the same features; 4″ high down filled collar designed to be adjustable around your neck, handwarmer pockets, bottom drawstring, and a down filled draft flap. The armhole depth has been increased to allow greater freedom of movement without binding at the shoulders. The length is also increased over that of the vest. The cuff closure is via a combination of snaps and elastic. This allows them to function like a standard elastic cuff and still provide ventilation when necessary.

Like most clothing, satisfaction is usually determined as much by fit as by design. Hence this parka, as well as the following 60/40 shell parka, are made to be tailored down to fit you perfectly. This is accomplished by taking in the side body and arm seams (see assembly for detail.) In this manner, a perfect fit is virtually guaranteed.

MATERIALS:

7 to 11 oz.—down.
9½″—¾″ velcro.
5′—drawcord.
1—no. "O" spur grommet.
8″—½″ elastic.
4—male snap halves.
2—female snap halves.

	Pattern Size				
	x-small	small	medium	large	x-large
zipper (two way, separating)	20"	22"	24"	26"	28"
1.9 oz. ripstop (downproof) 45" wide	3²⁄₃	4	(in yards) 4⅓	4²⁄₃	5

CUTTING LAYOUT:

Use the same layouts shown for the vest pattern, #16, with the below illustrated sleeve piece layout added.

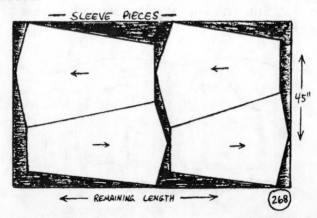

— SLEEVE PIECES —

45"

← REMAINING LENGTH → (268)

PIECE DIMENSIONS:

Find your size using the directions in step 1 of the vest assembly instructions. The arm lengths are cut correspondingly long to be shortened during assembly if required. Use the same piece dimensions shown for your size in the vest pattern with the exceptions listed here for dimensions A. and C.

	Size				
	x-small	*small*	*medium*	*large*	*x-large*
A.	27"	29"	31"	33"	35"
C.	9½	10¼	11	11¾	12½

The sleeve pieces are cut straight sided for layout ease. Dotted lines show a tailoring possibility for normal to slim arms. If your arms are atypically long, add an inch or so to measurements M. and O.

SLEEVES – DIMENSION TABLE

	Size				
	x-small	*small*	*medium*	*large*	*x-large*
L.	12½"	13"	14"	15"	15½"
M.	26½	27½	28	28½	29¼
N.	22	24	26	28	29
O.	25¾	26	26⅓	26¾	27
P.	2	2¼	2½	2¾	3

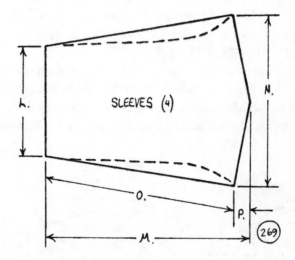

ASSEMBLY:

1. *Plain stitch* each back piece to two front pieces, rightsides together, across the shoulders to make an inner and outer shell. When the assembly which is to be the outer shell is turned rightside out, the front pieces will be switched right for left, so sew on the wider flap panels on opposite sides, as shown. (The finished coat has the flap on the left side.) ②⑦⓪

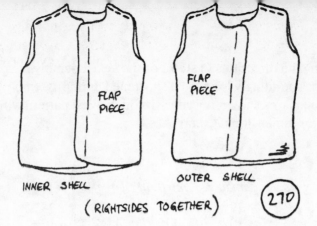

INNER SHELL   OUTER SHELL

(RIGHTSIDES TOGETHER)   270

2. Sew one sleeve piece to each of the four shell armholes, rightsides together. Begin *plain stitching* from the center of each sleeve and shell shoulder seam, or pin to match and stitch it pit to pit. (The sleeves are cut longer than necessary to insure a complete fit in this seam; the excess is trimmed later.)

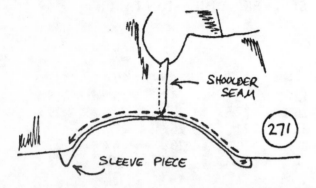

SHOULDER SEAM

SLEEVE PIECE   271

3. Turn the inner shell inside out (seam edges in) and place inside the wrong side out, outer shell. *Plain stitch* the shells together along the zipper seams. (See illustration 255 for step 4 in the vest pattern.)
4. Make and install the collar using the instructions for such in the vest pattern.
5. With the assembly rightside out, locate, pull out, and *plain stitch* together, the shoulder and armhole seam edges of the outer and inner shells to create inside baffles. Stitch from close to the seam ends, along the cut edges of the seam allowances.

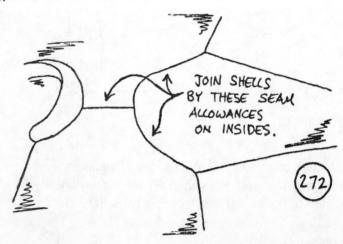

JOIN SHELLS BY THESE SEAM ALLOWANCES ON INSIDES.   272

6. Still rightsides out, *plain stitch* at ¼" along the below indicated edges to join the shell halves. Mark three or four baffle lines on the sleeves, as shown, and stitch them up. (Note: At this point the assembly will look ten sizes too big! Don't let it bother you. When all the seam allowances are eliminated and the down put in, it will change.)

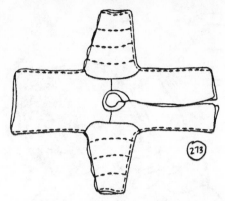

7. Fill with down through the remaining openings and pin shut. Stitch at ¼" along the remaining edges to hold the down in and remove the pins.
8. (A) Sew up the arm and side body seams. Fold the parka rightsides together as shown, pin, and *plain stitch*. Round off the stitching around the arm pit corners.

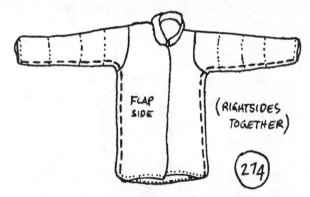

FLAP
SIDE

(RIGHTSIDES
TOGETHER)

274

(B) The parka should now be tried on for proper fit in the body and arm girths. Try it on wearing different amounts of clothing. The body and the sleeves, especially the latter, are intentionally cut large to allow custom tailoring and to accomodate meatier humans. Play around with different arm and body girths by pinching in the previous seam. When the desired fit is decided on, mark and restitch the previous arm and side body seams. Trim off any excess seam allowance and heat seal the edges. If the unfinished edges on the insides are objectionable to you, they may be covered with bias binding tape.

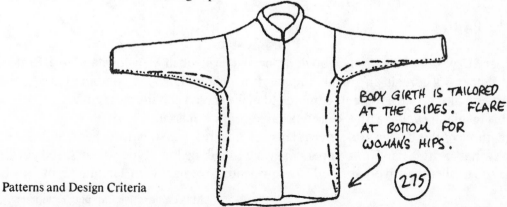

BODY GIRTH IS TAILORED
AT THE SIDES. FLARE
AT BOTTOM FOR
WOMAN'S HIPS.

275

9. (A) Make the cuffs; if necessary, mark for a shorter length (be generous) and add 1″ seam allowances. Cut two 4″ lengths of ½″ elastic. Stitch one end of elastic on inside of cuffs at the seam. Stitch the other end 6″ from the arm seam on the back side of the arms.

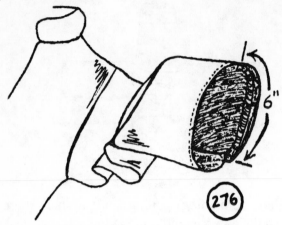

(B) Fold the cuff edges in ½″ twice and stitch around from the inside to envelop the elastic and make a finished cuff hem. Pull the inner fabric folds taut when making this seam to prevent puckering on the outer layer. Place one female and two male snaps in each cuff hem as shown.

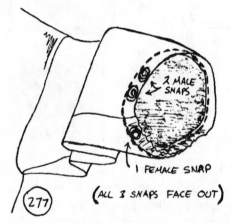

(ALL 3 SNAPS FACE OUT)

10. Finish your parka using the instructions in the vest assembly. Go to step 8, skip 9, and continue from step 10 through the finish.

PATTERN 18

60/40 SHELL PARKA

At under $15 worth of materials, you don't need a desk job in Megalopaland to afford this parka! It does not contain any insulating or lofting material, but the combination of wind-proofness, along with a full cut, combine to make this a versatile garment of considerable insulating value with a wide workable comfort margin.

The features of this design are: velcro flap cuff closures, waist, bottom hem, and hood drawstrings, a draft flap front zipper cover, gusseted, bellows type pockets, full cut shoulders, and a taller than average hood to allow head movement with a minimum of binding. The pockets are all protected by flaps. The bottom pocket flaps are an integral part of their pockets. When they are folded down, the pocket tops also fold to make a secure and snow proof closure.

The common inside pockets, and a large "backpack" pocket in the rear, have both been left out of this pattern. I do not feel that the added cost and construction time justifies their presence. First, any undergarments, shirt or parka, usually have ample pockets. As for the "backpack" pocket, I think a daypack does a better job. Still, if you want either of these, it is simple enough to add them during the assembly.

Like the down parka pattern, this one may also be tailored during construction for the desired fit. While this pattern uses the same sizing table detailed in step 1 of the vest assembly, bear in mind that the more you want to wear underneath, the larger the shell should be. You might want to consider making this coat a full size larger and then tailoring it down if needed. However, this should not be the case unless you are already a borderline case between sizes. The patterns are cut quite full to begin with, for the layer technique.

A few tips for the assembly . . . First, cut out the 60/40 cloth pieces and use them as templates for the liner material cuts. Second, during the assembly operations, sew up the liner first. This way if you make any mistakes they won't be seen and you can tune up for the same steps on the outer shell.

About fabrics . . . Although more expensive, you might want to consider making the liner or the entire coat out of British "Ventile" cloth. This is an extremely tightly woven, long fiber cotton with excellent water-repellency and wind-proofness combined with the comfort of cotton. As far as I know, Sierra Designs is the only outfit that retails it. (They line their 60/40 Mountain Parka with it.)

MATERIALS:

			Pattern Size			
	x-small	small	medium	large	x-large	massive
zipper (two way, separating)	22"	24"	26"	28"	30"	32"
drawcord	9½'	10'	10½' (in yards)	11'	11½'	12½'
60/40 cloth 45" wide	2¼	2½	3	3½	4	4½
ripstop or taffeta (liner) 45" wide	1¾	2	2½	3	3½	4

10" — ¾" velcro or
10 — snaps
11½" — 1" velcro
2 — no. "O" spur grommets or eyelets

CUTTING LAYOUT:

Due to the fact that each size parka requires a totally different cutting layout for maximum economy—in both the 60/40 and liner materials—they are not all illustrated here. Use your paper pattern or a scale one to figure your layout. (See chapter 4 on design and layout for details.) The fabric requirements listed above are minimums. The cutting layouts for the small size are shown here to give you some idea of what I mean by "minimum" and to give you some nesting ideas.

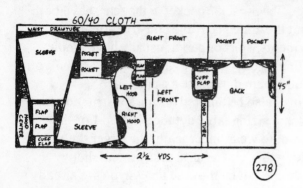

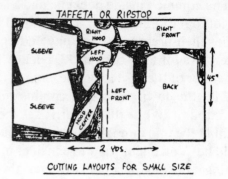

CUTTING LAYOUTS FOR SMALL SIZE

PIECE DIMENSIONS:

Find your size using the sizing table listed in step 1 of the vest pattern assembly instructions (pattern 16). Use the appropriate measurements from the alphabetically keyed dimension tables following.

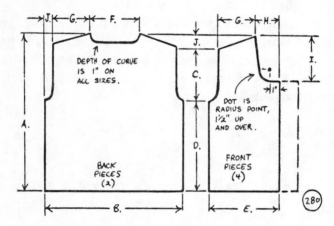

BODY – DIMENSIONS TABLE

	Size					
	x-small	small	medium	large	x-large	massive
A.	30"	32"	34"	36"	38"	40"
B.	20	22	24	26	28	30
C.	10	10½	11	11½	12	12½
D.	18½	19¾	21	22¼	23½	24¾
E.	10½	11½	12½	13½	14½	15
F.	5½	5½	6	6	7	7
G.	5¾	6½	7	7¾	8	8¾
H.	3¼	3¼	3½	3½	4	4¼
I.	6½	6½	7½	7½	8½	8½
J.	1½	1¾	2	2¼	2½	2¾

Note· Shown above is a right front piece (rightside up). On the two left front pieces (one liner and one shell), add 2½" to the zipper seam for the zipper draft flap (indicated by dotted lines above and in cutting layout illustration).

142   Make Your Own Camping Equipment

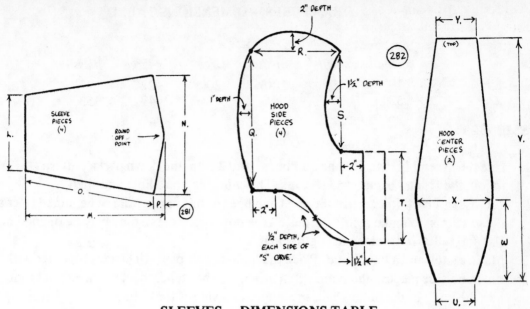

SLEEVES – DIMENSIONS TABLE

| | *Size* | | | | | |
	x-small	*small*	*medium*	*large*	*x-large*	*massive*
L.	11"	12"	13"	14"	14½"	15"
M.	24½	25¼	26	27	27¾	28½
N.	22	24	26	28	29	31
O.	22½	23½	24½	25½	26½	26¾
P.	1¾	2	2¼	2½	2¾	3

HOOD – DIMENSIONS TABLE

| | *Size* | | |
	x-small & small	*medium & large*	*x-large & massive*
Q.	10½"	11½"	12½"
R.	7½	8½	9½
S.	7	7½	8
T.	8¼	9	10
U.	4	4	5
V.	19½	20½	23
W.	6¾	7½	8¾
X.	7½	7½	8
Y.	3½	4	4½

Pocket Pieces: (two of each)

Top – 10½" X 7"   Flap – 6½" X 5"
Bottom – 12" X 12"   Flap – 8" X 6"

Cuff Flap Pieces: (two) 8" × 3".
Hood Drawtube Piece: (one) 2" × K.
Waist Drawtube Piece: (one) 2" × Z.

	Size					
	x-small	small	medium	large	x-large	massive
K.	19"	19"	20½"	20½"	22"	22"
Z.	33	37	41	45	**49**	53

ASSEMBLY:

1. Use the assembly instructions numbers 1 and 2 from the down parka pattern (# 17) to join the fronts, backs, and sleeves. This will give you a liner and shell sub-assembly. (Note: Since the shell and liner of this parka will not be joined later at these seams (to make inside baffles on the down garments), they may be opened out flat and felled for greater strength. Do it.)

2. Make a shell and a liner hood; Place the hood center piece rightsides together with the hood side pieces, and plain stitch around at the standard allowance. Note that, like the body of the outer shell, the longer flap side of the outer shell hood must be assembled on the wearer's right side so that it will be on the left when turned rightside out. Open the seams out flat and fell towards the middle. If trimming is necessary on the ends, do it now. You should come out with two separate hood sub-assemblies.

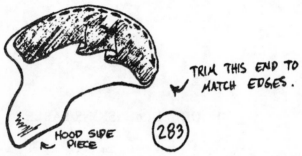

TRIM THIS END TO MATCH EDGES.

HOOD SIDE PIECE

(283)

3. Place each hood assembly rightsides together with its respective fabric shell assembly. Match and pin the hood edges with the body neckline and *plain stitch.* Open out flat, and *fell* the seams up.

4. (A) Sew up the sleeve and body side seams; Fold each assembly rightsides together as shown. Pin, and *plain stitch* from the bottom to the pit and down the sleeve. Round off the stitching around the armpit corners. You should still have two separate assemblies. Mating will proceed after a little more foreplay.

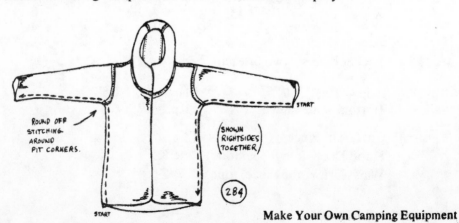

ROUND OFF STITCHING AROUND PIT CORNERS.

START

(SHOWN RIGHTSIDES TOGETHER)

(284)

START

(B) Try the outer shell on for fit. Refer to step 8 (A) in the previous pattern's assembly instructions for details on tailoring. Tailor the liner to match the outer shell modifications. (Accuracy here is required only at the sleeve ends, which must be the same circumference).

5. **(A)** Make the pockets; Fold each pocket piece in half and mark a reference line 1″ on both sides from the center fold. Open out flat, reference lines down. Fold one side in at reference line, then back at center crease. Repeat on other side to make the illustrated bellows. *Hem* one top edge of each with two ¼″ or so folds in.

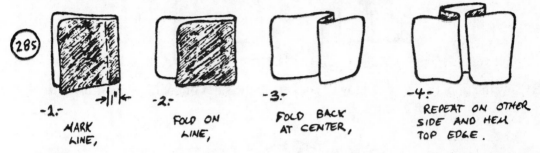

(B) Place a male snap or 1″ patch of ¾″ velcro on the center front of the pockets, 1″ down from the hemmed edge on the small upper pockets and 3″ down on the lower pockets.

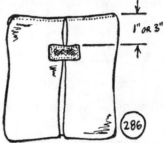

(C) Make the flaps; Fold in half and stitch as shown, trim corners off, turn rightsides out, and *top stitch* along edges.

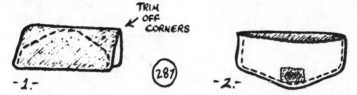

(D) Place a female snap or 1″ patch of velcro on flap, as shown above.

6. Top stitch the pockets to the outer shell, as shown. Leave the upper 1½″ of the lower pocket sides unstitched. Stitch the top pockets all the way up their sides.

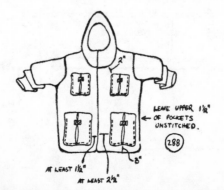

7. (A) Sew on the lower pocket flaps; Fold the upper 1½" of the lower pockets down and out of the way and *plain stitch* the flaps, placed as shown. Then turn down the flaps and *top stitch* to cover rough edges of flaps.

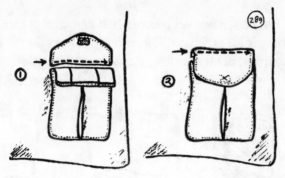

(B) Sew the upper sides of the lower pockets to the sides of the flaps, as shown, to make the storm proof closure.

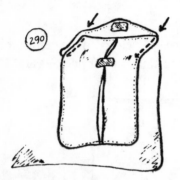

8. *Top stitch* the upper pockets flaps on in the same fashion, as above, without the storm flap feature.

9. (A) Install the waist drawtube and cord; *Hem* both ends of the drawtube piece after checking it for correct length. (It should be 3" short of the front zipper seam edges.) Cut a length of cord, 5" longer than the tube piece. Fold the drawtube around the cord with the ends matched, and stitch, as shown, to secure the cord in the tube.

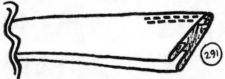

(B) Mark a reference line for the drawcord on the inside of the outer shell, 1" above the top stitching lines of the lower pockets. *Plain stitch* the drawtube and cord in with a couple of rows of stitching with the rough edges of the drawtube up.

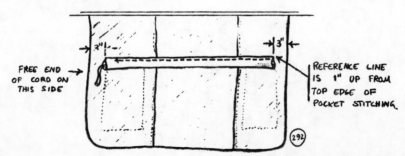

Make Your Own Camping Equipment

10. *Hem* the ends of the hood drawtube piece with a couple of ¼" folds to one side.

11. Join the outer shell, liner, and hood drawtube; Place the outer shell inside the liner, both rightsides out, as shown. (Seam edges out.) Pin together at the zipper seams and around the hood edges with the hood drawtube folded lengthwise, rightside out, and inserted between the layers and centered. *Plain stitch* from the bottom of flap side, up and around the hood, and back down the other side.

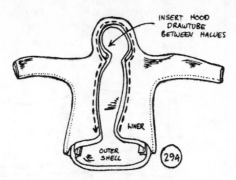

12. Turn the assembly rightside out through the bottom. Beginning again at the bottom of the left flap side, and with the outer shell up, *top stitch* up and around the hood and back down the other side. Do this seam with a zipper foot on your machine and include the right side zipper, as shown, with the excess tape on the top end folded under. Continue top stitching down this edge, securing the zipper as you go. (Don't forget to backstitch over the zipper ends to secure them.)

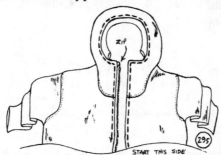

13. Run a second row of stitching ⅛" in from the previous seam, over the right zipper half to doubly secure it.

14. Sew in the flap side of the zipper; Mark a reference line 2½" in from the fabric edge on the liner. With the top excess zipper tape folded under and the mating of the coat front checked, stitch in this left zipper half, keeping the inside edge of the tape liner up with the reference line. Run a second row of stitching, as was done on the other side.

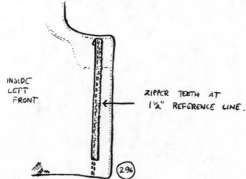

15. (A) Place the drawstring grommets; Put one through the liner for the waist drawstring. Put the other through both inner and outer layers, 1½" up from the bottom edge and about the same distance in as the waist grommet. (297)

(B) Reach inside and thread the waist drawcord through its grommet. Knot to secure it.

16. *Hem* the bottom; Fold both layers to the liner side with two 1" folds and a drawcord inserted, exiting at its grommet. *Plain stitch* the tube closed, then stitch the end of the cord secure at the other end. A zipper foot will be necessary to make the hem by the grommet. (298)

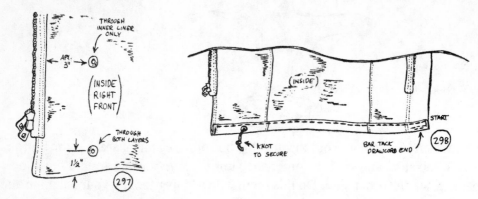

17. Insert the remaining drawcord through the hood drawtube. Knot the ends to secure and stitch fast at the top center of the drawtube.
18. Make the cuff flaps; Fold and *top stitch*, as shown. Cut a 1¾" length of 1" velcro "hooks" and stitch on the flap end.

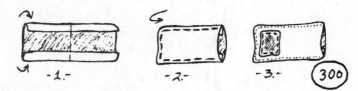

19. The cuffs . . . Trim to desired length and *hem* with two ½" folds to the inside.
20. Stitch the cuff flaps to the cuffs at the sleeve seams, with the velcro facing forward. *Plain stitch*, fold over, and *top stitch*. (see illustration below)
21. Cut two 4" lengths of 1" velcro "pile" and stitch around the cuffs, about 1" in from the cuff edges. Place the strips so that the cuffs may be secured either loose or tight.
22. Finish up by placing six snaps or 1" patches of ¾" velcro for the front weather flap, as shown.

Make Your Own Camping Equipment

Chapter 11

Sleeping Bags

A functional lightweight sleeping bag is essential for enjoyable back country camping. It is an expensive necessity, and not having one is a major deterrent to most would-be backpackers. Without good lightweight equipment, the usual alternative is lugging along a super heavy, car camping type sleeping bag. In this case, your woman must be an accomplished masseuse and your best friend a chiropractor! This is, of course, assuming that you can fit such a bag into a pack in the first place.

This chapter will give you the basics of what makes a good and efficient lightweight sleeping bag. If you're short on money, or if you enjoy doing things yourself—which I would expect and hope if you've come this far—the pattern in this chapter will do you right.

BASIC DESIGN

The first functional criterion of the light and portable sleeping bag is shape. There are several standard shapes; *rectangular, barrel,* and *mummy*. While the shape determines the size and interior roominess, it also affects the bag's insulation capabilities. The most efficient bag is the smaller mummy style because it concentrates the loft and insulation around your body. Thus, it requires less overall bulk and weight to sustain a given warmth than the larger rectangular bag. The latter is both heavier and colder. Besides having to carry the extra weight, more of your body heat is required to warm the extra internal air space. When considering space for comfort, bear in mind that you pay for it in weight and that no functional sleeping bag is going to match your queen-sized waterbed for roominess.

A head flap or hood extension on the top end of a bag will add considerably to the usuable temperature range of a sleeping bag. Because it has no homeostatic controls, a cold head can lead to cold feet by causing vaso-constriction in your extremities. Hence the saying, "if your feet are cold, cover your head." A hood can make the difference between a good sleep and a long miserable night of shivering. (If you have a bag with no hood, it is simple enough to make one that will snap on. Just make a semi-circular pie of ripstop and down with a drawstring around the curved portion, and snaps or velcro tape along the straight edge for attachment to the bag.)

Another feature of the functional sleeping bag is a *boxed foot section*; one that is built to stand up around your feet as opposed to a flat foot area that is made by simply folding the bag over at the foot end. As the coldest part of your body, your feet require ample insulation. The boxed type foot section provides this insulation because it is engineered to fit your anatomy. Hence, your feet do not have to push the fabric out at the toes, which can result in a cold spot on a non-boxed foot section. The result of the boxed foot is greater insulation effectiveness and more freedom of movement, which is at a premium in a mummy or barrel shaped bag .

A lightweight sleeping bag may be made more versatile as well as lighter by having less down fill in the bottom half. Because it compresses under your body weight anyway, making a foam sleeping pad necessary, there is no sense in putting a lot of down in the bottom half of the bag. The usable temperature range is increased by this as well. In warmer climes, you can sleep with the bag upside-down. This is beginning to catch on with the better bag manufacturers.

BAFFLES AND OTHERS INSIDE

Being as loose as the air around it, down requires baffling to keep it evenly distributed and inside the bag where it belongs. There are several types of baffle configurations commonly used, the three most functional and common are illustrated here.

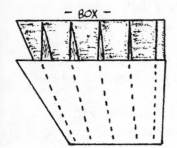
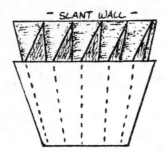
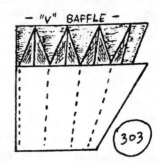

These are cross baffles and run horizontal to the bag. The most efficient baffles are those which maintain an even loft without allowing thin, cold spots. The *box baffle* is the least effective of the above, because the down can fall away from the baffle walls and allow the shells to collapse together to form cold spots. The *slant wall baffle* construction beats this problem by maintaining an even thickness of down between the baffles and the shell layers. The *"V" tube* construction shown is essentially a double slant wall design. While it provides for a greater control of the down, it uses twice as much fabric for the baffles and is that much heavier. One manufacturer claims that the "V" tube construction requires more down fill to achieve an equal loft than a slant wall type, because it takes more down to fill each chamber right up to the narrow apex of each and to support the added weight of the baffles. My own preference is the slant wall design. I have used a bag of this construction for years and have experienced no problems with cold spots. I have also been quite impressed with the loft to fill of this bag, compared to other more expensive models in the "V" tube category.

The efficiency of any of the above baffle types will vary by their spacing. This may be anywhere between 10″ to 3″ on commercially made bags. The average baffle width, or spacing, runs about 6″. Naturally, the closer they are spaced, the more the down is controlled and the chances for cold spots eliminated.

In order to keep the down from shifting from the top to the bottom of the bag, a *block baffle* may be sewn into the side seams and to the cross baffles from the head to the foot of the bag. Many bags do not have a block baffle and will require a periodic re-distribution of the down by opening the bag out flat and patting it. For lighter weight summer bags, a block baffle is not essential. In fact, its absence will allow you to alter the down distribution to suit the evening's temperature. If a bag does have a block baffle, it should be at least 3″ wide, preferably more.

Sleeping bag baffles may be made from either a lighter nylon fabric, nylon mosquito netting, or light nylon tricot netting. The latter two, being very porous, will trap some of the down in their weave, further preventing cold spots that may be caused by the down falling away from the baffles and an uneven distribution of the filling. Nylon tricot is probably the best baffling material because of its elasticity. When a stress is put on a baffle, the baffles will absorb some of the force. However, while this sounds very good, it is pretty theoretical that such stresses will ever be encountered. The North Face switched to tricot just recently, for reasons of construction simplicity (the tricot need not be heat set when cut). They previously made their bags with a mosquito netting type material and claim to have had complete success with it. I have heard of some bags with cotton baffles. This might be the case with some of the cheaper imports. For sure, if you find a bag with cotton baffles, tell all your friends so that they can avoid it. A bag with cotton baffles could not be expected to last any longer than a pair of cotton socks. You can get a good idea of what kind of material is used for the baffling in a bag by feeling and pulling it between the shell layers and at the seams. Netting will have a rough texture, tricot will stretch, and nylon fabric will be slippery.

No matter how a bag is baffled, it must be filled with the proper amount of down in relation to its dimensions and construction in order to work efficiently. Too much down will result in a bag that is heavier than necessary and not any warmer. Because the volume of the baffle chambers is set by the baffle widths and heights, any excess down will not have room to loft, and hence, will not provide any more insulation. Conversely, too little down fill will allow empty cold spots to develop. The proper amount of down for a particular baffle chamber is slightly more than will freely loft to that given capacity. The extra is required to support the weight of the surrounding fabrics.

To prevent a cold seam along the zipper, a *draft tube* should be fitted to the bag. This lengthwise external baffle, as it is, should be top stitched to the upper liner and zipper seam as shown below. Some bags have the draft tube sewn with both edges at the zipper seam and are not as effective. The draft tube should extend beyond the foot end of the zipper to prevent a cold spot at your feet.

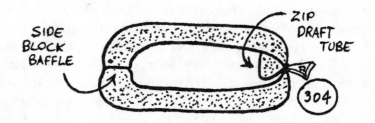

SIDE BLOCK BAFFLE

ZIP DRAFT TUBE

304

DIFFERENTIAL VERSUS EQUAL SHELL SIZE CONSTRUCTION

Along with all the verbiage and sales pitches about down quality, are arguments and claims about *differential* versus *equal shell size* construction. The differentially cut bag has a smaller circumference liner and a larger outer shell to create what has been dubbed a "thermos bottle" type structure. The equal shell size construction, also called "the space filler cut" and "shell parity", is just what the name implies. Both the liners and the shells are the same size.

DIFFERENTIAL CUT (305) EQUAL SIZE CUT

Purveyors of the differential type construction, presently in the majority, claim that; 1) the down is allowed to loft easier, 2) the outer shell of the bag remains smoother, thus giving up less heat through convection, 3) you can't press your elbow into the side of the bag to collapse the shells and cause cold spots, and 4) the liner does not drape so tightly around your body as to cut off ventilation and inhibit movement inside the bag. In the other corner, wearing the dark trunks made with the equal shell size construction, we have claims that the larger, or equal size liner will; 1) allow more internal room and freedom of movement, and 2) drape around your body, thus eliminating excess air pockets that must be heated. The dark trunks further assert that 3) a differentially cut bag, being made of soft and flexible materials, will not prevent your elbows and knees from pushing the shell and liner together to create cold spots.

In my opinion, from experiences with both types, the difference is negligible. Everything that both have to say is true, to a degree. My personal preference slides towards the differential construction. First, I like to have some ventilation around my body. I get claustrophobic otherwise. Secondly, I feel that a sleeping bag which is engineered to develop a certain amount of loft will achieve that thickness more readily and with less filling material. As for the differentially cut bag having less internal volume, that is a variable which has no logical place here, being a controllable design factor. While you will take it into consideration, the question of differential versus equal size shell construction should not be *the* deciding factor in the selection of a sleeping bag design.

DIFFERENT APPROACHES

If the down under your body is compressed beyond being functional insulation, why bother with it at all? Several companies are turning out efficient, lightweight sleeping bags with removalbe foam pads built into the bottom of the bag. The only objection I have heard to this is that all your tossing and turning inside the bag must be done carefully in order to remain rightside up and on top of the pad. When I move in a sleeping bag, I usually roll the bag with me. With a separate pad underneath, I can stay on top of things without too much trouble. Honestly though, I've never tried this type of bag and the weight saved may very easily justify modifying your outback sleeping habits.

Another new deviation from the standard bag design comes from the Snow Lion Company. They call it "recessed contour baffling." What they have done is to make the top half of the bag wider than the bottom so that the side block baffle and zipper seams are almost at ground level. They have also contoured the upper cross baffles to give a greater loft directly over your body.

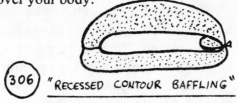

(306) "RECESSED CONTOUR BAFFLING"

The reason for the lowered side seams is to prevent the down fill on the lower half of the bag from falling down and away from the side seams, which would create cold spots. The increased depth of the upper half cross baffles is a logical design progression from the theory that the down you carry on your back might as well be concentrated where it is needed most. Again though, this type of design detailing in a sleeping bag will require sound and still sleeping to keep things where they belong.

POLYESTER BAGS

Sleeping bags for wet environments, those made from hydrophobic fiberfills such as Polarguard from the Celanese Corporation and Fiberfill II from Du Pont, require different construction techniques. Totally unlike down, most fiberfills come in rolls of batting. While its edges must be secured and stabilized by stitching, it does not require any baffling structure to keep it in place. The usual method of securing fiberfills in sleeping bags is to stitch through both the shell and liner. This is the common construction found on car camping type bags and is not suitable for use by the self-propelled traveler concerned with maximum insulation and minimum weight. The stitching lines are "cold seams."

The most efficient fiberfill bag construction at present comes from the North Face Company. They sew in batts of fiberfill similar to the way in which slant wall baffles are installed. This gives excellent stabilization of the fill and a double layer of the batting throughout the bag. I endorse the North Face fiberfill bags whole-heartedly. I haven't seen any others that match theirs either in design or construction quality.

Fiberfill bags also differ from down filled ones in their fabirc requirements. Naturally, fabrics for fiberfills need not be downproof. Hence, a more porous fabric which will more readily ventilate your insensible perspiration may be used instead. For camping in humid climes, this along with the fiberfills hydrophobic, works-when-wet properties, makes for a very real and sometimes necessary advantage.

ACCESSORIES

Many manufacturers offer their bags with snap tabs inside which will hold in a light cotton liner. For extended trips where your bag might get pretty gooey, and when you care to take along some non-essential weight, a liner can be a good thing to have. However, they do make movement in a bag more difficult and will foul up with very little provocation. Restless sleepers beware!

Bivouac bags, or "bivis", are sleeping bag size envelopes with a coated fabric bottom and a breathable top, some with zippers down the side. Slipping your sleeping bag into a bivi-bag can add considerably to your insulation. Their weight is justified in the absence of a tent as a groundcloth and, when necessary, shelter.

BUYING A BAG

Before you even look at a bag, you should decide just how much insulation you really need. Try to satisfy the majority of weather conditions in which you camp, rather than buying a bag for the coldest trip anticipated. The latter may always be accomplished by combining clothing with your bag for that extra warmth or by renting a heavier one. If you do go for the really thick bag, you may find yourself the not-so-proud owner of a backwoods sauna bath. Two pounds of down or so is a pretty good compromise . . . sometimes. Use the insulation thickness table (#7) in the previous chapter for a reference and take into consideration the use of a tent and other variables listed there. Also take into consideration the desired shape and size of the bag. The smaller the bag, the warmer you will be.

For specific details on the filling and construction quality, see the appropriate chapters in **the first** section of the book.

PATTERN 19

DOWN SLEEPING BAG

While the large amount of stitching in any sleeping bag makes for a lengthly project, it is by no means as tricky as you may fear. The most difficult seams are in the installation of the end foot box pieces, and these are simply pinned and plain stitched in. And for about $60 you'll have a bag comparable to ready made ones costing more than $100.

I chose a mummy shaped bag for this pattern because of its insulation to weight efficiency. I've given it a 2¼ lb. to 2½ lb. down fill capacity, depending on the quality of down fill used, to make it suitable for cooler, high mountain conditions. The pattern can be modified to make a lighter bag if desired by cutting the baffles narrower. The cross baffles are at 5″ spacings in a slant wall configuration with a minimum of 3″ overlaps. The cross baffles are sewn in with a *tuck stitch* (see assembly, step 7) to eliminate surface level threads. The bag opens down one side via a 70″ zipper, which may be placed on the right or left side (so two can be zipped together), and is backed by a 10″ draft flap. The plans call for strips of interfacing stiffener sewn inside along the zipper on the bottom liner and draft flap to eliminate the problem of jamming the zipper in the fabric. The bag is also designed with a boxed foot section, differential cut, and a head flap that closes up to form a hood with a drawstring closure.

The prototype bag for this pattern required roughly 2¼ lbs. of grey goose down from Recreational Equipment, Inc. ($9- per ½ lb.) and was underfilled on the bottom by 25% or so. This produced a surprising 9″ to 10″ of total loft (honest!) . . . more than enough for winter camping with a tent. The overall weight came out somewhere between 3½ to 3¾ lbs., exceptionally light for this class of bag. This was using 1.9 ounce ripstop for the shells and liners with 1 ounce mosquito netting for the baffles. The finished bag measures 6′ long inside with a 62″ girth at the top.

MATERIALS:

7½ yds.—45″ wide 1.9 oz. ripstop, downproof.
2¼ to 2½ lbs.—down.
1—70″ zipper, two way, double sliders, separating.

80"—drawcord or ¼" nylon tape.
1—fixlock or spring cord lock.
2"—¾"velcro tape
2—3" × 75" interfacing strips, medium/light weight.
Baffling material—one of the below;

4⅓ yds.—64" wide netting
5½ yds.—55" wide netting
6⅓ yds.—45" wide netting
7⅔ yds—36" wide netting

CUTTING LAYOUT AND PIECE DIMENSIONS:

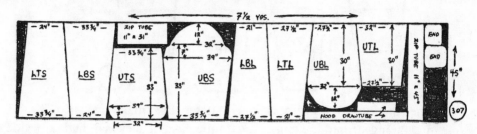

(Illustration 307)

End foot boxes—11½" × 11½" & 13½" × 13½", both have curved corners 4" radius.
Hood drawtube—3" × 80", pieced together.
Zipper draft tube—11" × 75", pieced together.

Label the liner and shell halves along their seam allowances during the layout, with the below initials, to avoid piecing incorrectly;

LTS—lower top shell
lbs—lower bottom shell
UTS—upper top shell
UBS—upper bottom shell

LTL—lower top liner
LBL—lower bottom liner
UTL—upper top liner
UBL—upper bottom liner

(ie.; to make the top outer shell you would join LTS with UTS)

Piecing the shell and liner pieces uses ⅓ less material than would be required if the four bag layers were each cut as one. The curved head pieces should match, but the particular curve angle is not critical.

Baffling—Cut the netting into 9" wide strips. Cut one side block baffle piece, 8" × 79".

ASSEMBLY:

1. Piece together the hood drawtube and the zipper draft tube pieces with a *felled seam*.

2. Piece together the 9″ wide strips of netting to make one continuous length about 27½ yds. long. Use *felled seams.* (The baffles are cut to length as they are sewn in.) Cut the 8″ × 79″ side block baffle from the remainder.

3. Piece together the shell and liner halves with a single *plain stitching* on the wrong sides at ½″ allowance. (The remaining seam edges will be used for a cross baffle seam, so do not fell these.)

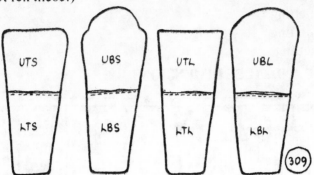

4. Piece together the interfacing (zipper fabric stiffener) to make two strips 3″ × 75″.

5. Sew one interfacing strip to the zipper draft tube piece, edges matched (any side.) Sew the other interfacing strip to the wrongside of the bottom liner, matched with the edge on which side the zipper will be (decide that now.) *Plain stitch* interfacing strips with three rows of stitching, done in the numbered order below.

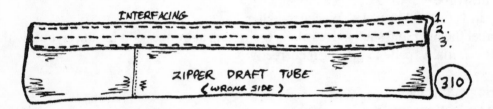

6. Beginning ½″ from the foot ends, mark cross baffle reference lines every 5″ on the wrong sides of all four liner and shell pieces. (14 lines on the top shell and liner, and 16 lines on the bottom pieces with the head flap.) The four main piece cross seams should measure out to be one baffle line each.

7. Sew the cross baffle material to the two outer shells. Cut it off as you go so that the baffles are flush with the fabric edges on the zipper sides and extend ½″ or so beyond the block baffle side edges. Use the *tuck stitch* shown here; fold the shell rightsides togehter at the reference lines, lay the baffle on top with its edge slightly beyond the fold, and stitch at ⅓″ or so from the folded fabric edge. Work from the foot end up.

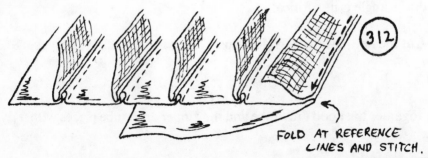

FOLD AT REFERENCE LINES AND STITCH.

8. (A) Sew in the end foot box pieces; Lay the liners rightsides together (cross baffle reference lines out) and *plain stitch* side edges together, from the foot end up 1". Lay the outer shells in the same configuration, rightsides together and cross baffles out, and stitch edges from foot end up 4½".

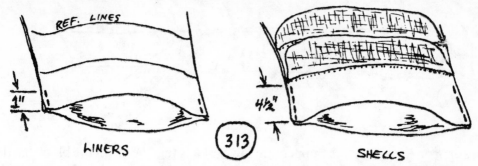

(B) Cut a foot baffle, as shown below, from the remaining 9" wide cross baffle material. Ease, pin, and *plain stitch*, the smaller end foot box piece into the liner end with the short side of the foot baffle strip. Place the latter on top of the foot piece so that its ends are on the zipper side, and leave ½" of these ends unstitched and overlapped. (The down is inserted later at this baffle's ends, upon which it will be sewn shut.)

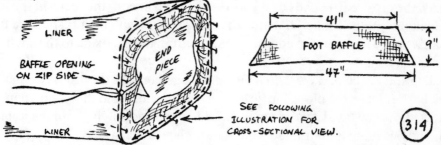

(C) *Plain stitch* the larger, outer end foot box piece into the wrongside out shell's foot end, along with the longer edge of the above foot baffle. (Make sure that the shells and liners will jibe right when the outer is turned rightside out over the liners.) ③15

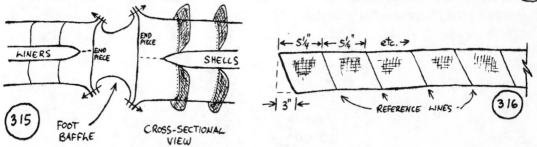

9. When the previous step is done, the outer shell baffles are *tuck stitched* to the liners from the foot end up, until the shells and liners are joined by the cross baffles. *Plain stitch* the upper shell and liner together at a ¼" allowance across their top edges when all the upper baffles are in.

10. Cut one end of the 8" wide block baffle piece on the diagonal as shown and mark the baffle every 5¼" with reference lines. ③16

11. Sew in the block baffle; begin at the first cross baffle at the foot end of the upper shell and liner. *Plain stitch* the diagonally cut end of the block baffle to this cross

baffle, then continue towards the head end of the bag with the below illustrated *tuck stitch*; fold the block baffle at the reference line and stitch with the cross baffle ends inside the folds, at ¼" or so from the folded edges.

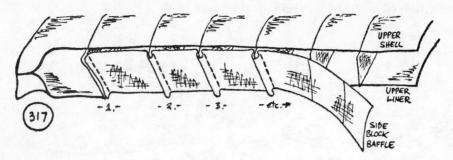

12. *Plain stitch* on the insides, the upper and lower shells together with the block baffle; Turn the bag inside out and match up the shell edges with the block baffle. Beginning on the foot end stitching made in step 8. (A), continue *plain stitching* up to the head end of the shorter, upper shell. Keep the cross baffles and the block baffle tucks pulled out of this seam as much as possible. Trim the block baffle at the head end and tuck any remaining excess inside. Use the cross baffle seam lines for reference marks to insure a reasonably accurate mating here.
13. *Plain stitch* the cross baffle ends of the lower shell and liner to the tucks in the block baffle. Beginning at the foot end, match the cross baffles with their respective tucks on the block baffle, pull out the edges, and stitch from the liner side to the shells seam inside.
14. With the bag still inside out, *top stitch* the liners together with the last free edge of the block baffle. Place the block baffle edge inside the liner fold that is down in your machine as shown below. Lay the top liner fold on top and stitch. As in the joining of the shells, this seam is continued from the stitching done in step 8. (A). (The alternative to top stitching this seam is to plain stitch the liners and block baffle together, and then cover the rough edges with bias tape. I found top stitching to be quicker and satisfactory, if you are careful to keep the block baffle well inside the liner fold and thus, well secured by the stitching.) Go on to the next step without removing the material from your machine.

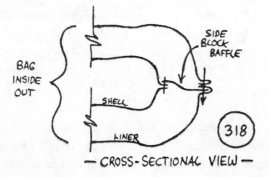

— CROSS-SECTIONAL VIEW —

15. Make a transition from the above *top stitching* at the head end, to *plain stitch* the lower shell and liner together around the hood. Stop stitching this seam just past half way around the hood to leave room for the down filling. ③⑲

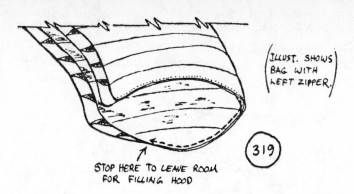

(ILLUST. SHOWS BAG WITH LEFT ZIPPER.)

STOP HERE TO LEAVE ROOM
FOR FILLING HOOD

319

16. Fill the square, end foot box with down through the opening at the foot baffle ends,
    then *plain stitch* this closed on the baffling. Be careful not to stitch the baffling here,
    with too much of an allowance, or a tuck may result in the circumference of the end
    foot box seams.

17. Fill the rest of the bag with down, pinning the chambers closed with the fabric mated
    evenly as you go. Put less down in the bottom of the bag where a pad will provide
    most of the necessary insulation. Continuing from the seam at the hood, *plain stitch*
    the bottom half of the bag closed at a ¼" allowance. At the foot end of the bag, the
    stitching done in step 8. (A) should match up on the shells and liners. If they don't,
    rip one seam until they do. Continue plain stitching at ¼", up the top half of the shell
    and liner to complete the closure. Double check for proper down fill and
    distribution. If you muffed it, rip open where necessary to correct. Be sure to leave
    enough down aside to fill the zipper draft tube later. About five hand fulls will be
    needed.

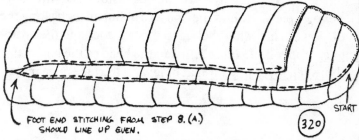

FOOT END STITCHING FROM STEP 8. (A.)
SHOULD LINE UP EVEN.

START

320

18. Trim off any protruding pieces of baffling material left in the previous seam.

19. Sew on the top half of the zipper, along with the stiffened edge of the draft tube
    piece. Begin at the head end with the zipper tape and draft tube piece matched up
    with the top fabric edge. *Plain stitch* as shown with the three edges mated. Stop
    stitching 4½" from the foot end crotch and leave the assembly in your machine.

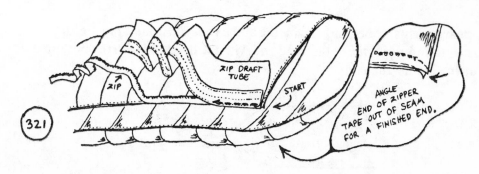

ZIP DRAFT
TUBE

ZIP

START

ANGLE
END OF ZIPPER
TAPE OUT OF SEAM
FOR A FINISHED END.

321

20. Cut from your scraps, a 4″ × 10″ diamond for the zipper foot end cover. (A bellows in the crotch.) Fold in half and insert, as shown, between the zipper and the draft tube piece. Continue stitching as above, stopping right at the end of the crotch of the upper and lower bag halves.

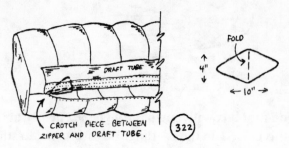

21. With the rightside top of the bag up in your machine, and starting at the head end again, fold the zipper and draft flap out, as shown, and *top stitch*. Stop ¼″ beyond the end crotch.

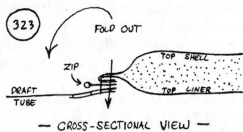

22. Stitch in the bottom half of the zipper; Turn the bag inside out at the foot and *plain stitch* the crotch bellows piece around the end and about an inch along the bottom bag edge. Insert the lower zipper half between the bag edge and the crotch so that it mates with the upper zipper half. *Plain stitch* to the head of the bag with the zipper on top of the bottom shell layer in your machine, and the tape edge mated with the fabric edge.

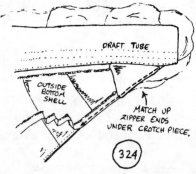

23. Turn the bag rightside out and, beginning at the foot end again, fold the zipper tape to the inside and *top stitch* to the head end with the head end with the bottom outside shell up in your machine.

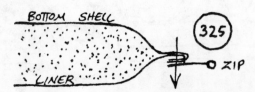

25. Mark a reference line for the inside draft tube seam, 4″ in from the zipper seam, curved in to 2″ from the seam at the head end and curved in all the way to the zipper seam at the foot end. Beginning at the head end, fold the bag's liner along the reference line and *top stitch* the draft tube edge to this tuck. The foot end of the draft tube should extend beyond the zipper end, all the way to the foot of the bag.

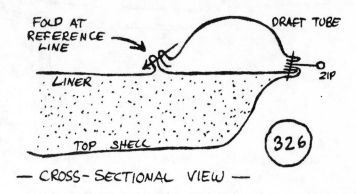

FOLD AT REFERENCE LINE

DRAFT TUBE

ZIP

· LINER ·

TOP SHELL

326

— CROSS-SECTIONAL VIEW —

25. Fold the edges of the draft tube together at the foot end and *top stitch* closed.

26. Fill the draft tube with down through the opening in the top and stitch closed, as shown.

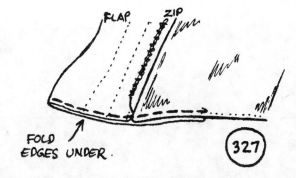

FLAP

ZIP

FOLD EDGES UNDER.

327

27. (A) Sew on the hood drawtube; *Plain stitch* it on, beginning at the lower zipper end with the drawtube piece rightside against the lower liner, edges matched.

(B) Cut a 1¼″ slit in the drawtube at the bag's side seam. Roll the edges to the wrong side and stitch fast, as shown, to make the drawstring opening.

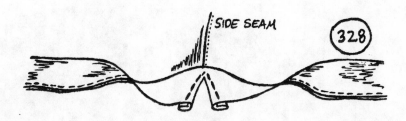

SIDE SEAM

328

(C) Trim the drawtube piece to extend 2½" beyond the upper zipper end. Fold this end in ½", then fold the tube over, as shown, and *top stitch* all around the hood to make the drawtube.

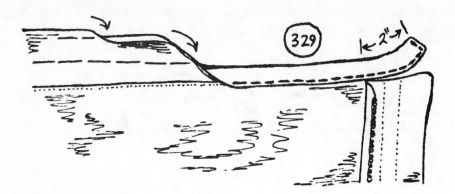

28. Stitch on the 2" pieces of velcro . . . "hooks" on the outside of the 2" drawtube end tab, shown above, "piles" on the inside of the lower drawtube end. The velcro halves should mate to make a continuous circle hood drawtube.
29. Thread in the drawcord and stitch it fast at the velcro ends to secure. Fasten at the side seam opening with the fixlock or spring cord lock. Melt the cord ends to prevent unraveling.
   Make yourself a stuff sack for it and you're ready for the trip you've been thinking about.

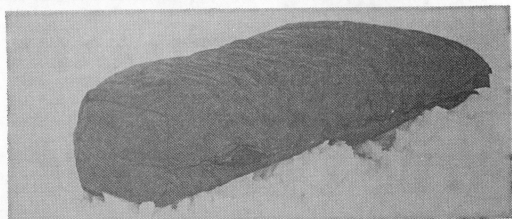

Chapter 12

Repairs and Maintenance

With a little respect and care, your equipment should last for a good many years of use. Unlike skis, kayaks, and hang-gliders, your basic elemental equipment does not demand constant attention. But there is that occasional cleaning, rip in the fabric, or abraiding of threads that should be taken care of before it develops into a major problem.

FABRICS

It is a good idea to carry some thread and a needle and some ripstop repair **tape** with you in the outbacks. A hole in a down garment or sleeping bag could be a real problem otherwise.

Ripstop repair tape will plug the hole temporily, but it will eventually loose its grip and peel off. And if you leave one of these patches on for very long, the glue works its way into the fabric where it will forever after attract dust and grime. The only permanent solution is a stitched on patch. On single layer items such as tents and ponchos, the patching job is a simple matter of *top stitching* on, a swatch of fabric cut out in an appropriate configuration. But on double layer, baffled items such as sleeping bags and garments, a *tuck stitched* patch is required. This is made by folding the fabric layer to be repaired along the patch seamlines and stitching along the edges of these tucks. The resulting patch seams will stick up a bit, but the finished patch is both permanent and secure.

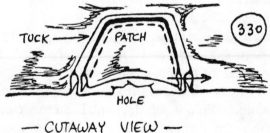

— CUTAWAY VIEW —

Some items just can't be repaired on a sewing machine and will require hand stitching. You can do these jobs right on the trail.

HARDWARE

Unless they are of really poor quality, your zippers shouldn't blow apart. Replacing them can be difficult. Usually, they are sewn in, in the midst of an assembly so that replacing them in the same manner would require disassembling the item. The exception is parka zippers which go on last. These can be simply replaced by ripping out the old one and sewing in a new one. When this is not possible, it is far easier to *tuck* or *top stitch* on a new zipper than it is to rebuild the item. If you are in a real hurry, you can simply cut the old zipper off and sew another over the remaining zipper tape. If none of this sounds acceptable to you, Eastern Mountain Sports does repair work at a reasonable cost. Before ripping out an inoperative zipper, make sure it is beyond repair. End stops and pullsliders are usually replaceable. The stitching that holds coil type zippers to their tapes can also be restitched. Use a good, beefy hand needle with Coats & Clarks Button and Carpet Thread.

Snaps, grommets, and velcro can usually be replaced without much ado. Whenever any item fails, fabric or hardware, consider replacing it one of extra strength to avoid another failure.

CARE AND CLEANING OF DOWN

No matter how careful you are with your down gear—sleeping bag, parka, and down booties—it's going to need cleaning periodically. Eventually, the accumulated insensible perspiration, body oils, and grime will reach an objectionable level and begin to reduce the lofting effectiveness of the down. When your down fill does get this dirty, it will attract more dirt and this can cause a premature deterioration of the down.

Many manufacturers of elemental equipments recommend that you have your down filled gear dry-cleaned. While this is not the best method (it is hard on the down and removes water-repellent treatments from the fabric), it is the safest if you don't know how to do it yourself or haven't the time. If you do opt for dry-cleaning, find a reputable establishment, experienced with down cleaning. These people will use *Stoddard's Solvent*; a mild petroleum based fluid which is not too harsh. Most general item dry-cleaning is done with a solvent called "perk", or Per-Chlorethlene, which is used over and over again. This stuff is as harsh as the name sounds and will ruin your bag by stripping the natural oils from the down. Imagine what would happen to your hair if you washed it with gasoline! That's what will happen to your bag if you let just any cleaner handle it.

If you do have your bag dry-cleaned, air it out afterwards until all traces of the solvent are gone. The residual fumes are toxic to both you and the down. This might take some time, a week or two even, so be patient.

With a little time and care, you can clean your own down gear in your bathtub. Clean the tub first and clear out the rubber ducks and other "bathing aids." The object is to get the down clean without removing the natural oils necessary to its existence. So, use a non-detergent soap like Ivory flakes or one of the special soaps designed especially for cleaning down. Both Recreational Equipment, Inc. and Eastern Mountain Sports stock special soap for this. Soak the item in about a half tub of lukewarm water for a half hour or so with the soap well dissolved first. Occasionally give the item a gentle kneading to push the soapy water through it and turn it over WITHOUT lifting it out of the water! Down absorbs a whole lot of water. Lifting a heavy, soaking wet sleeping bag can damage both the down and the internal construction. When the water has turned brown with the dirt and you think the item is as clean as it will get, drain the water from the tub and leave the item layed out flat for another half hour or so to let as much water drain as possible. Do two or more rinse cycles in the tub. Use the same care as in the washing and again, do not lift the bag out of the water. Make sure you get all the soap out or the down will matt and clump together, and attract even more dirt than before. Let the rinsed item drain for a half hour again and then VERY GENTLY press out as much remaining water as possible without pressing too hard. DO NOT wring or twist the water out!

Now comes the drying, and if you've never had a down item get wet, you're going to find out just what the fiberfill advocates are talking about when they say it is "difficult" to dry a down filled piece of gear. It takes forever! Because of this, some manufacturers recommend placing the item in a large dryer set for low or no heat along with a pair of tennis shoes to fluff it up. I think this is just fine, *IF* you let the item air dry for a day beforehand. Even after pushing out most of the water, a quick yank on a sleeping bag can rip out all of the baffles. While a down filled parka with sewn through seam construction (no internal baffles) would probably fare okay, you're gambling against heavy odds with any baffled structure item. So . . . lift the bag or garment out of the tub, handling it like a baby, and lay it out on a couple of beach towels or a clothesline. Give the thing a turn every now and then to speed the airing process. Do not be surprised to find that after a full day outside, the down is still almost soaking wet and clumped together in baseball size wads. Even if you completely line dry the item, which can take anywhere from three days to a week, you should put it through a dryer cycle to fluff up the down to its original loft. Again, the dryer must be set on very low or no heat, or you'll be out one used-to-be piece of elemental equipment!

Needless to say, if you attempt to clean a down filled item in a washing machine, you're taking a big chance on destroying it. While the odds are not too bad on a sewn through baffle construction, such as a vest or sweater, it should never be attempted with a sleeping bag.

So now that you know what the cleaning involves, here are a few ways to keep the down in good shape, and put off the need for cleaning as long as possible. First, air your bag out thoroughly every morning and for a day or so after each trip. Down, like cotton and other organic fibers, will deteriorate if left wet for long. If the airing out is done on a hot day, lay the bag out in the shade if it is to be left for any length of time. Overexposure to the sun's heat, or a dryer that is too hot, can burn off some of the oils in the down, thus reducing its effectiveness. Secondly, never store your down items in their stuff sacks. The natural form of the fibers is straight. Storing them loosely will prolong the resiliency of the fibers and allow them to air continuously. Keeping your down gear clean is common sense practice. You don't crawl into your sleeping bag after a liberal application of bug juice and expect it to stay clean. If the bug problem is very bad, or if you're just the sort who goes nuts when you hear a mosquito going for your inner ear at a hundred decibels, try packing along a yard or so of mosquito netting to tent over the head of your bag. And there is no excuse for not having a ground cloth. Inexpensive and lightweight plastic paint drop cloths can be purchased for a song and discarded when worn out . . . IN A CARBAGE CAN! (I've been considering packing a gun for the next time I find a sheet of plastic left behind.) With a little care, you should be able to go a year or so between cleanings.

SOURCES APPENDIX

Listed here are manufacturers of the kinds of elemental equipment this book has dealt with. Note that, while many of these companies are involved in retail operations, their common factor is manufacturing. Even with about fifty-five companies listed here, I am sure that I have missed a few and to these people I apologize. Most of these companies will be happy to send you detailed product information on request. Those preceded by a capital "M" sell raw materials for making your own gear. Those preceded by a capital "K" make do-it-yourself kits.

Adventure 16, Inc., 656s Front St., El Cagon, Ca. 92020
Alpenlite Products, 115 South Spring St., Claremont, Ca. 91711
Alpine Designs, P.O. Box 3407, Boulder, Colo. 80303
Alti-Wear, 129 West Water St., Santa Fe, N.M. 07501
Altra Inc., Group 50, 3645 Pearl St., Boulder, Colo. 80301
Appalachian Outfitters, Box 4, Oakton, Va. 22124
Appalachian Designs, P.O. Box 11252, Chattanooga, Tenn. 37401
Ascente, P.O. Box 2028, Fresno, Ca. 93718
Bergans Janoy, Inc., 2000 East Center Circle, Minneapolis, Minn. 55441
(M) Black's, 930 Ford St., Ogdensburg, N.Y. 13669
Browning, Dept. C-21, Box 500, Morgan, Utah 84050
Bugaboo Mountaineering, 170 Central Ave., Pacific Grove, Ca. 93950
Camp Trails, 4111 West Clarendon Ave., Phoenix, Az. 85019
Camp 7, 802 South Sherman, Longmont, Colo. 80501
Caribou Mountaineering, 217 Main St., Chico, Ca. 95926
Chouinard (Great Pacific Iron Works), P.O. Box 150, Ventura, Ca. 93001
Chuck Roast Equipment, P.O. Box 224, Conway, N.H. 03818
Class 5, 2010 Seventh St., Berkeley, Ca. 94710
Columbia Sportswear, 6600 North Baltimore, Portland, Ore. 97203
Comfy, 310 First Ave. South, Seattle, Wash. 98104
Co-op Wilderness Supply, 1432 University Ave., Berkeley, Ca. 94702
CDC (Coworkers Development Corp.), 108 Lawrence St., Brooklyn, N.Y. 11201
Denali Company (Mountain-Master), 2402 Ventura, Fresno, Ca. 93721
(M,K) EMS (Eastern Mountain Sports), 1041 Commonwealth Ave., Boston, Mass. 02215
Eureka Tent & Awning Co., 625 Conklin Rd., binghamton, N.Y. 13902
Forrest Mountaineering, 5050-M Fox St., Denver, Colo. 80216
(M,K) Frostline, Inc., P.O. Box 589, Broomfield, Colo. 80020 Gerry, 5450 North Valley Highway, Denver, Colo. 80216
Great World, 250 Farms Rd., W. Simbury, Ct. 06092
High & Light, 139½ East 16th St., Costa Mesa, Ca. 92627
High Touring, 1251 E. 2100 S., # 2, Salt Lake City, Utah 84106
Himalayan Industries, P.O. Box 5668, Pine Bluff, Ark. 71601
(K) Holubar, Box 7, Boulder, Colo. 80302
Jan Sport, Vashon Island, Wash. 98070
Kelmore Industries, 409 West Fremont St., Stockton, Ca. 95203
(M) Kelty, 1801 Victory Blvd., Glendale, Ca. 91201
Kreeger & Son, 30 West 46th St., New York, N.Y. 10036
Laacke and Joys Co., 1432 North Water St., Milwaukee, Wisc. 53202

Lowe Alpine Systems, P.O. Box 151, Louisville, Colo. 80027
Maran, P.O. Box 931, Kent, Wash. 98031
Moor & Mountain, Main St., Concord, Mass. 01742
(K) Mountain Adventure Kits, P.O. Box 571 Whittier, Ca. 90608
Mountain Paraphernalia, Box 4536, Modesto, Ca. 95352
MPC (Mountain Products Corp.), 123 South Wenatchee Ave., Wenatchee, Wash. 98801
Mountain Traders, 1702 Grove St., Berkeley, Ca. 94709
The North Face, Box 2399, Station A, Berkeley, Ca. 94702
Ocate Products, P.O. Box 1631, Santa Fe, N.M. 87501
The Pinnacle, Box 4214, Mountain View, Ca. 94040
(M) REI (Recreational Eauipment, Inc., also known as the Seattle co-op), 1525 - 11th Ave., Seattle, Wash. 98122
Ridge Line, Anglo Traders, Ltd., 1315 Davenport Rd., Toronto 4, Ontario, Canada
Rivendale Mountain Works, P.O. Box 198, Victor, Id. 93455
(M) Sierra Designs, 4th & Addison Sts., Berkeley, Ca. 94710
(M) Ski Hut (Trailwise), 1615 University Ave., Berkeley, Ca. 94703
Snow Lion (formerly Snowline), P.O. Box 9056, Berkeley, Ca. 94709
Stephenson's Warm-Lite, 23206 Hatteras St., Woodland Hills, Ca. 91364
Strawberry Mountain Co., 1405 Cypress Ln., Davis, Ca. 95616
Sunbird Industries, Inc., 5368 Sterling Center Dr., Industrial Center, West Lake, Ca. 91360
Universal Field Equipment, Mira Loma Space Center, Bldg. 811-A, Mira Loma, Ca. 91752
Washington Quilt Co., 2320 First Ave., Seattle, Wash. 98121
White Stag, 5203 S.E. Johnson Creek Blvd., Portland, Ore. 97203
Wilderness Experience, 9408 Irondale Ave., Chatsworth, Ca. 91311
Woods Bag and Canvas Co., 89 River St., Ogdensburg, N.Y. 13669
Woolrich Inc., Woolrich, Pa. 17779

TECHNICAL SOURCES

The Aluminum Association 402 P Lexington Ave. New York, N.Y. 10017
Celanese Corporation. P.O. box 1414, Charlotte, N.C. 28201 (manufacturers of Polarguard)
Eastman Chemical Products, Inc., 1133 Avenue of the Americas, New York, N.Y. 10036 (manufacturers of Kodel)
E.I. Du Pont de Nemours & Co., 308 East Lancaster Ave., Wynnwood, Pa. 19096 (Fiberfill Marketing Division, manufacturers of Fiberfill II)
&
Textile Fibers Dept., 1007 Market St., Wilmington, Delaware 19898
Feather and Down Producers Association, Inc., 257 West 38th St., New York, N.Y. 10018
Howe & Bainbridge, Inc., 816 Production Place, Newport Beach, Ca. 92660 (fabric finishers)
The Kenyon Piece Dyeworks, Inc., Kenyon, R.I. 02836 (fabric Finishers)
Man-Made Fiber Producers Association, Inc., 1150 - 17th St. N.W., Washington, D.C. 20036
U.S. Army Natick Laboratories, Natick, Mass. 01760

HOW TO SURVIVE IN THE WILDERNESS

DRAKE PUBLISHERS INC.
NEW YORK · LONDON

CONTENTS

Published in 1975 by
Drake Publishers Inc.
381 Park Avenue South
New York, N.Y. 10016

ISBN: 0-8473-1116-3
LC: 75-10705

Printed in The United States of Ameri

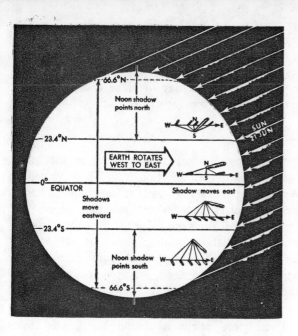

GENERAL SURVIVAL

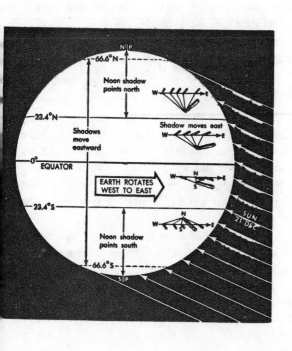

HEALTH AND HYGIENE

Your general state of health has much to do with resisting or recovering from the effects of disease or injury. A well-nourished human being, in good physical and mental condition, can tolerate a great deal before becoming incapacitated, and can recover satisfactorily from relatively severe disease or injury.

Water is most important in the survival situation. Since most body processes involve the use of water, an adequate supply of purified water is mandatory. Even at rest in good health, your body requires some two to three quarts of water daily. With fever, exercise, or hot weather, much larger amounts are required.

Food contributes to morale and replaces body substances burned to provide energy for the hard work of survival. However, if you are well-motivated and previously well-nourished, you can survive a relatively long time using resources stored within your body.

Salt is essential to health and may be replaced in the system by using salt tablets contained in survival kits, from the meat and blood of animals consumed, and from salt found in water. Salt tablets should be used as a 0.1 percent solution (two tablets per canteen of water) to minimize nausea. Never administer salt as a concentrated solution because this causes nausea and vomiting. Salt should not be taken unless your water supply is ample. If the blood of animals is to be consumed, it should be thoroughly cooked (as should be the meat) to prevent infection with disease-producing organisms. Cooking must be ruled out under certain conditions, but it is an ideal toward which you should strive.

Vitamins and other essential elements are found in vegetable and animal food, frequently in the less palatable and often discarded portions. Green and yellow vegetables are normally good sources of vitamins. Citrus fruits have long been recognized as a good source of vitamin C. Vitamin K (which is important in blood clotting) is found in uncooked leafy green vegetables. The livers of most animals are rich in vitamins A and D, which increase resistance to infection and aid in wound healing. You should eat as varied a diet as possible, discarding none of the food available to you.

Keeping well is especially important when you are stranded on your own. Your physical condition will have a lot to do with your coming out safely. Protection against heat and cold and knowledge of how to find water and food are important to your health, but there are more rules you should follow.

Save your strength. Avoid fatigue. Get enough sleep. Even if you can't sleep at first, lie down, relax, loosen up. Stop worrying. Learn to take

it easy. If you are doing hard work or walking, rest for 10 minutes each hour. Stop traveling early enough in the day to make a comfortable camp. The rest you get will pay off.

Cleanliness

Cleanliness is more than a virtue in survival —it is essential, if infection is to be prevented. Washing, particularly your face, hands, and feet, minimizes chances for infection of small scratches and abrasions. Soap, although an aid, is not essential to keeping clean. A substitute for soap can be improvised from ashes and animal fat. Ashes, sand, loamy soil, and other expedients may be used in cleaning the body and the utensils used in cooking and eating.

Even more attention should be devoted to field sanitation and safety than is usual in the normal military situation. In survival, the least incapacity can initiate a chain of events leading to major disaster because of the lack of outside assistance, including medical care.

Dump garbage in a pit or in a spot away from camp where it can not blow about. Dig a latrine or designate a latrine area away from the camp and water supply.

Burn all garbage, papers, cans, cartons, etc., before covering your garbage pit. If this is not done, animals can uncover the pit and spread the refuse about the grounds.

In hostile territory, all signs which would indicate that you are in the area must be obliterated.

Care of Feet

Take care of your feet if you anticipate doing a lot of walking. Prepare in advance. Be sure your feet and footgear are in good condition. Break in your shoes slowly.

Feet should be kept clean. Toenails should be cut straight across. Bathe and massage the feet daily.

Remove clots of wool from socks. Keep your socks clean and change them frequently, if possible.

Inspect the inside of your shoes and the inside and outside of socks for possible sources of friction. Improvised insoles may reduce friction inside shoes.

2

If you have boots which have not been broken in, and the climate permits, there is a shortcut to breaking them in. Soak them thoroughly by walking in shallow water. Then, walk the boots dry.

Air shoes at night by putting them on small stakes. This keeps inside of shoes dry and eliminates danger of scorpions, centipedes, and other crawling vermin.

Examine your feet when you first stop, to see if there are any red spots or blisters. Apply adhesive smoothly on your skin where shoes rub. If you have a blister, it is best to leave it intact. This decreases the chances of infection. If it is broken or punctured, do not remove the protective skin. Apply a sterile dressing.

Care of Skin and Nails

Guard against skin infection. Your skin is the first line of defense against infection. Use an antiseptic on even the smallest scratch, cut, or insect bite. Keep your fingernails cut short to prevent infection from scratching. Cuts and scratches are apt to get seriously infected, especially in the tropics. A bad infection may hurt your chance of coming out safely.

Guard Against Intestinal Sickness

Diarrhea and other intestinal sicknesses may be caused by change of water and food, contaminated water or spoiled food, fatigue, overeating in hot weather, or using dirty dishes. Purify all water used for drinking, either by using chemicals or by boiling for at least one minute plus one additional minute for each 1,000 feet of elevation above sea level. Cook the plants you eat, or wash them carefully with purified water. Make a habit of personal cleanliness; wash your hands with soap and water, if possible, before eating.

If one member of your group gets diarrhea, take special care to enforce measures for proper disposal of human waste and to insure cleanliness in handling food and water. Make sure feces are buried. Don't let affected members handle food and cooking utensils.

Field treatment of diarrhea is necessarily limited. Rest and fast—except for drinking water

—for 24 hours; then take only liquid foods such as soup and tea, and avoid sugars and starches. Keep up a large intake of water, with salt tablets. Eat several meals instead of one or two large ones. Overeating of fruit, especially green fruit, may cause a temporary diarrhea. Eliminating fruit from the diet, temporarily, relieves this condition.

Don't worry about lack of bowel movement; this will take care of itself in a few days, provided you have an adequate daily supply of water.

TREATMENT OF INJURY AND ILLNESS

Control of Bleeding

The control of bleeding is extremely important under all conditions. In the survival situation, it is of even greater importance since transfusions are not possible and may not be feasible for some time to come.

When bleeding is coupled with cessation of breathing, a critical situation is present which requires the most expeditious action. This is because oxygen is being denied to the system for lack of an airway. Even when your action correcting the airway deficiency begins to take effect, the loss of blood will still be robbing the body of its ability to provide the vital organs with the oxygen reaching the lungs. Remember that blood is the vehicle which transports life-giving oxygen. Under this combination of conditions, concurrent actions must be taken to insure that breathing is resumed and bleeding is stopped.

Immediate steps should be taken to stop the flow of blood, whatever its source. *The method used should be commensurate with the type and degree of bleeding.* Simple pressure over the bleeding point, with or without a dressing, suffices in most cases, especially when the bleeding is of the venous or capillary type. Minor arterial bleeding may also be controlled with local pressure. Extremity wounds should be elevated above the heart, along with the application of pressure. More serious bleeding of the arterial type can be temporarily controlled by compressing an artery against a bone that the artery crosses in

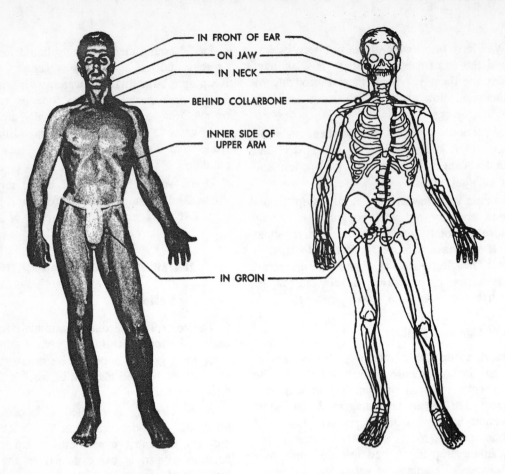

Figure 2-12. Pressure Points for Control of Bleeding

its normal course through the body. The location of standard "pressure-points" are shown in figure 2-12.

Pressure with the fingers is difficult to maintain for prolonged periods and must be replaced by a tourniquet.

The tourniquet, when required and properly used, will save life. If improperly used, it may cost the life, certainly the limb of the survivor. Although basic characteristics of a tourniquet and the standard methods of its use are well covered in standard first aid texts, certain points need emphasis in the survival situation.

Every aircrewman should clearly understand the correct improvisation and use of the tourniquet, on himself and others. This is particularly important in survival situations, because assistance may not be available. Never apply a

tourniquet unless it is the only way to stop the flow of blood from an injured extremity. Once applied, leave the tourniquet on *until the bleeding vessel can actually be tied off*. The old method of frequent loosening is now known to add little to the vitality of the extremity, but it does cause loss of great amounts of blood with resulting shock and death. Apply the tourniquet as near the site of the arterial bleeding (between the wound and the heart) as possible. This reduces the amount of tissue lost if the limb must be sacrificed to save the life.

Tourniquets can accomplish more than stopping hemorrhage. Properly applied, they amount to what may be called "physiological amputation," and may delay spread of infection and poisons from damaged extremities to the rest of the body. If left permanently in place, actual amputation will occur as tissues beyond the tourniquet die from lack of blood. When using

4

the tourniquet in this manner, you are risking a limb for a life.

Effort should be made to locate the bleeding artery so that it may be tied off, permitting release of the tourniquet. This is frequently very difficult. If the artery is completely severed, its ends may retract so as to be invisible in the wound proper. Further, the identification of the many structures in a severe wound is difficult. Relaxation of the tourniquet, to assist in locating the vessel as it begins to bleed again, is loaded with the danger of loss of more blood; just what you are trying to prevent. Clean the wound with sterile (boiled) water and gently explore with a clean finger under direct vision in an effort to find the severed vessel. This is the *one* emergency reason for touching an open wound. If you have a grasping instrument, such as needle-nosed pliers, it will help you locate and hold the bleeding vessel.

Once you locate the bleeding vessel, tie it securely with thread or a fine string such as the nylon cord pulled from the suspension lines of the chute. Make sure that there is not more than one major bleeding vessel. When reasonably sure that the bleeding vessel is tied, cautiously relax the tourniquet and watch for resumption of serious bleeding. If more bleeding is noted, immediately tighten the tourniquet and proceed as before. If reasonably sure that the bleeding vessel is in a given bit of tissue, the entire area can be tied off to stop the bleeding. This can be done by passing a large threaded needle into the tissue and around the suspected bleeding site and tying the entire mass securely. This is not as good as finding and tying the vessel itself but may have to suffice under survival conditions.

Locating and tying the ruptured vessel is far superior to leaving the tourniquet in place. The tourniquet stops the flow of all blood into the extremity; the tie, only that of the vessel which is tied off. Generally, unless the single major blood supply of an extremity is involved, a sufficient blood supply is available from other vessels to maintain the life of the limb. Regardless of these probabilities, one is still trading a limb for a life.

Cessation of Breathing

Cessation of breathing is a dire emergency, and treatment consists of immediate removal of any obstruction that might be present and application of effective artificial respiration.

The most frequent causes of asphyxiation are (1) blockage of the upper air passages caused by face and neck injuries, (2) drowning, (3) choking, or (4) inflammation and spasm of the upper air passages from inhalation of smoke, flame, or other irritants. Other causes are insufficient oxygen in the air, inability of the blood to carry oxygen, and compression of the chest.

Lack of oxygen may be the result of hiding in poorly ventilated areas. The inability of the blood to carry oxygen is most frequently due to inhalation of carbon monoxide produced by fires burning in poorly ventilated shelters. Compression of the body (chest) results from being caught beneath heavy aircraft wreckage, or as a result of avalanches or cave-ins.

The first and most important step in restoration of breathing is the establishment of an open airway. Unless this is done, artificial respiration is fruitless. In favorable cases, just restoration of the airway may permit the subject to begin breathing on his own. The mouth should be explored with a finger to remove any foreign material and to insure that the tongue is not obstructing the breathing passages. Placing the patient on his abdomen with his head lowered also assists in ridding the throat of foreign material, as well as preventing closure of the airway. The most favorable position of the upper respiratory passages for breathing is with the lower jaw held well forward and the neck extended (head held slightly back).

In some cases of asphyxia (i.e., injuries of the face and neck or inflammation and spasm of the upper passages), an artificial airway must be established to save life. Creation of an opening to bypass the problem can and sometimes must be done by unskilled nonmedical personnel. Place the unconscious patient on his back with shoulders elevated so that the neck is extended and in a straight line. Between the

Adam's apple and the smaller projection just below it is the desired point of incision. Using a sharp knife, make a deep cut in the exact midline, down to and into the trachea. With the end of the finger, this structure can be identified as "gristle." With this technique, no significant bleeding is encountered. Holding the trachea open, insert a small section of pencil-sized rigid tubing and anchor it into place with ties around the neck. The tube used may be any part of the fuel or hydraulic lines of the aircraft or even a section of fountain pen. The tube should be clean to avoid introduction of infection into the neck wound.

The important point is immediate restoration of the airway, all other considerations being secondary. The type of emergency procedure outlined here tends to cause constriction of the larynx and should be discontinued as soon as the normal airway becomes open.

Mouth-to-Mouth Respiration

The preferred method in artificial respiration is the so-called "mouth-to-mouth" procedure. This is the only method which guarantees enough air exchange to revive the patient, while letting the operator insure that the airway is open. The method is much better demonstrated than described, and it should be practiced, as the proper technique is not so simple as many think.

With the patient on his back, the operator holds the jaw well forward with one hand bending the head back. The nose of the patient is held closed with the other hand. The operator places his mouth over that of the patient and exhales. If the airway is open, the patient's chest and abdomen are noted to expand. The operator then removes his mouth and permits the patient to exhale passively. This process is repeated at a rate of approximately 16 breaths per minute, and the operator must be sure that he does not over-breathe himself.

With a tube in place following the surgical method outlined above, the method becomes "mouth-to-tube." The operator exhales into the tube rather than the patient's mouth. This requires some ingenuity, but it can be done.

Manual Heart Compression

If the heart has stopped beating (absence of pulse and heartbeat), manual heart compression or external cardiac massage can be used in conjunction with mouth-to-mouth resuscitation.

Pain and Shock

The control of the pain accompanying disease or injury under survival conditions is both difficult and essential. In addition to its morale-breaking discomfort, pain contributes to shock and makes the survivor more vulnerable to survival problems and enemy influences. Ideally, pain should be eliminated by elimination of its cause. Since this is not always immediately possible, measures for the control of pain are next best.

The part of the body that is hurting should be put at rest, or at least its activity restricted to the maximum degree possible. The position selected should be the one giving maximum comfort, and should be the easiest position to maintain. Splints and/or bandages may be necessary to maintain immobilization. Elevation of the injured part, along with immobilization, is particularly beneficial in the case of throbbing pain. Open wounds should be cleansed, foreign bodies removed, and a clean dressing applied to protect the wound from the air and accidental contacts with objects. Generally, the application of warmth reduces pain (e.g., toothache, bursitis). However, for some conditions, application of cold has the same effect (e.g., strains and sprains). Warmth or cold is best applied by using water because of its high specific heat. You should try both hot and cold water to determine which is the most beneficial.

Drugs are very effective in reducing pain but are not usually available in the survival situation. Aspirin is generally used to combat the discomforts of colds and upper respiratory diseases, and at best will just take the edge off severe pain. To be really effective in control of pain, stronger narcotic drugs such as codeine and morphine are required. During hostilities, morphine may be available in aircraft and individual first aid kits.

Like the tourniquet, morphine, if used properly, can be lifesaving. Reserve morphine for the most

6

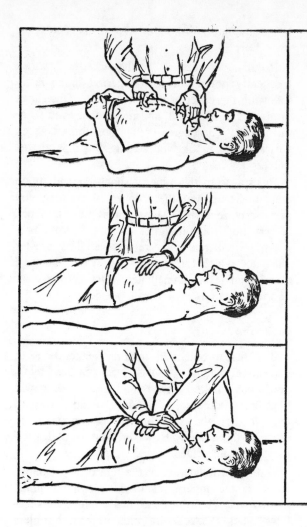

1. The patient should be flat on his back on a firm, level surface. Place yourself on his right.

2. Place the heel of one hand on the lower third of the patient's breastbone (sternum) pointing across the chest and away from you.

3. Place the other hand on top of the first hand, fingers pointing toward the patient's chin. Apply firm pressure vertically, downward, approximately once per second. The breastbone should move 1½ to 2 inches toward the spine.

4. At the end of each stroke, lift your hands to permit full recoil expansion of the chest.

5. Cardiac massage and mouth-to-mouth resuscitation should be carried out together. If you have no one to help you, interrupt massage every 15-30 seconds; fill the lungs with air two or three times; return to massage for another 15-30 seconds; and so on.

Figure 2-13. Manual Heart Compression

severe types of pain which do not respond to lesser measures. *Morphine should not be used on a patient who is unconscious; in deep shock; wounded in the chest and having breathing difficulties; suffering from a broken neck or head injuries. Morphine should never be given within 2 hours of a previous morphine injection.* You should inject morphine into the large muscle areas of the body following the instructions contained on the Syrette.

The danger of multiple doses of morphine in a patient who is cold and in shock is that as he becomes warm and his circulation improves, an overdose may suddenly be absorbed into the system. One further precaution: Morphine converts a "walking wounded" into a "litter case";

i.e., reduces the mobility of the patient and his capability for caring for his own needs. The impact of this situation on survival is obvious. You should provide survival needs before giving a morphine injection. You must have water, security, and shelter from the elements.

Shock of some degree accompanies all injuries to the body and frequently is the most serious consequence of the injury. Shock is a reaction of the body as a whole to an injury or emotional disturbance. While the circulatory changes initially favor body resistance to the injury by insuring adequate blood supply to vital structures, they may progress to the point of circulatory failure and death. You should be familiar with the signs and symptoms of shock so that the condition may be anticipated, recognized, and dealt with effectively. However, the best approach is to treat all patients suffering moderate and severe injuries for shock. No harm will be done, and the patient's recovery will be expedited.

All signs of shock are due to the disturbance of the normal blood circulation. The pulse is weak and rapid. Breathing is shallow, rapid, and irregular. The skin is pale, and feels cold and moist; "cold sweat" is quite characteristic. The eyes appear vacant, and the pupils may be dilated. The patient feels weak, faint, or dizzy, and may be very restless, frightened, and anxious. Thirst and nausea are common complaints. As shock deepens, the patient becomes quieter and may become unconscious.

Act! Don't wait! You should not wait for these signs and symptoms before treating shock. Anticipate shock in every serious injury and take care of it along with treatment of the specific injury. In many emergency situations, the most helpful thing that can be done is to begin treatment of shock. The patient should be made as comfortable as possible. The best body position is one favoring adequate blood supply to the brain with the head lowered. However, a person with a head injury should be kept flat on his back with his head slightly raised.

The injured person should be kept warm but not hot. Too much heat causes further loss in circulating body fluid through sweating, and brings the blood closer to the body surface and away from the vital parts. In the survival situation, injured personnel must be shielded from the elements and kept warm.

In the normal medical situation, giving fluids by mouth in the treatment of shock following severe injury is not recommended, as fluids may interfere with later administration of anesthetic. The situation is quite different in survival medicine, since the treatment given is often the final treatment. A man cannot be deprived of water for long periods just because he has been injured, since his recovery depends upon adequate hydration. Small amounts of warm water, tea, or coffee given early in the shock incident are beneficial if the patient is conscious, can swallow, and has no internal injuries. In later shock, fluids by mouth are less effective as they are not absorbed from the intestines. Burns particularly require

large amounts of water to replace the fluids lost from burned areas.

Peculiar to survival is the emotional shock frequently noted during the period immediately following the onset of the emergency. This shock originates in the mind, and may occur even without injury. The degree of this post-impact shock varies widely among individuals, but it is almost universal.

Resistance to this type of shock depends upon your make-up and the amount of training you previously received. Management of this shock is very important in order to keep it from progressing into more severe shock. The greater efficiency which follows the period of time used to relax and rest immediately after getting clear of the aircraft is well worth the delay.

Snakebite

The first problem in treating snakebite is to determine whether it has been caused by a poisonous snake. Many harmless snakes will bite in self-defense. The only reliable way to tell whether the snakebite is poisonous is to identify the snake. However, the wound itself may give some clues.

One good indication of the bite of a poisonous snake is the intense pain which results almost immediately (but not invariably). Numbness follows quickly. A severe bite from a harmless snake hurts no more than a wound made with any sharp instrument. The bite of a viper causes immediate swelling. A cobra bite may have no local symptoms except for an intense burning pain in the area of the wound.

The appearance of the wound gives additional clues. Vipers do not really "bite." They stab with their fangs. The wound usually consists of two small punctures, generally half an inch or more apart. Sometimes there may be only one puncture, if the snake partially misses or has one fang missing. Coral snakes, cobras, mambas, and kraits often hang on and chew; the result may be one, two, or more puncture marks. Harmless snakes usually have several teeth so that a bite may consist of several punctures formed in a semicircle. However, it is not always easy to distinguish for certain between the bites of a harmless and a poisonous snake.

FOLLOW THIS PROCEDURE IF YOU ARE BITTEN:

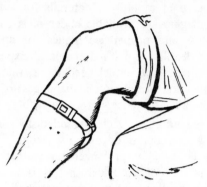

1. Avoid undue exertion. If circumstances allow it, lie down and remain quiet. A snug tourniquet (tight enough to impede the venous return of blood to the trunk, yet loose enough to allow arterial supply to the extremity) will further delay systemic absorption of the poison. Place the tourniquet between the bite and the heart, about two inches above the bite.

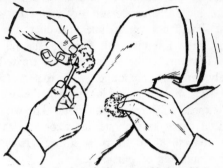

2. Daub the knife or razor blade and fang marks with antiseptic, if you have it.

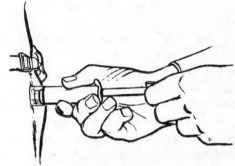

4. Apply suction. Suction can best be applied by mouth, but not if there are open oral lesions present. In this case, some other means of applying suction must be found. After 30 to 60 minutes, suction is of little benefit.

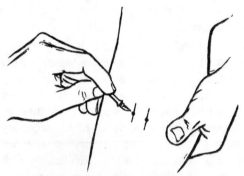

3. Make a small but deep cut over each fang mark (deep enough, ¼ inch or more, to penetrate the skin). Orient each cut parallel to vital structures (generally parallel to the long axis of the limb).

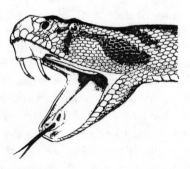

5. Immobilize and splint the injured member. This step is important in limiting the spread of toxin. Local cooling by application of cold wet packs will help relieve pain and reduce the spread of toxin.

6. A possible exception to steps 2 and 3 is in the case of snakebites sustained in the warm, moist tropics where any skin wound bears a high risk of infection. In this case, make no cut. Mouth suction, aided by deep massage with the teeth can be used in this case. Generally mouth suction is much more effective than devices contained in snakebite kits.

7. Use the antibiotics from the medical kit if you have one.

Figure 2-14. Snakebite

What you do in the first minute after being bitten by a poisonous snake will determine the effectiveness of the treatment. Unless you have a snakebite kit on your person or within easy reach, you should not waste time and energy in going after one. Exercise can quicken the circulation. However, snakebite should be treated immediately, and all personnel who expect to be flying over snake-infested areas, whether or not they expect to have a snakebite kit with them, should carry several sterile razor blades. They are convenient to carry and are always useful for a number of purposes.

In a survival situation you cannot be certain that you will have a snakebite kit handy, but you can be fairly certain that you won't have a medical officer to treat you. Therefore, you must act quickly and wisely. In such a case, undertake first aid measures immediately; speed is essential! (See figure 2-14).

Don't get excited. The mortality rate from snakebite, properly treated, is less than 1 percent. The rate is only 10% to 15% without any treatment—hence the fame of such useless remedies as kerosene, gunpowder, potassium permanganate, freshly killed chickens, whisky, etc.

Avoid doing anything which increases the circulation. Don't take alcohol, or start running back to camp. Sit right where you are and carry out the first part of this treatment. Don't do more harm to yourself than the bite would have done if you hadn't treated it, particularly if you are not sure you have been bitten by a poisonous snake. Don't overdo the use of the knife, and don't tie the lymph constrictor too tight or leave it on too long.

Injuries to Bones and Joints

Proper immobilization of fractures, dislocations, and sprains is even more important in survival situations than it is under more normal conditions. Under survival conditions, the initial immobilization is part of the ultimate treatment rather than a temporary measure to prevent further injury during transport to medical attention. Immobilization in proper position hastens healing and improves the chances of using the injured part. Under survival conditions, immobilization must suffice for a relatively long period and at the same time permit the patient to maintain a high degree of mobility. Materials for splinting and bandaging are available under most survival conditions, and proper techniques for applying them are detailed in first aid manuals. Experience has shown that personnel need more training in the application of splints and bandages to themselves should assistance not be available.

The reduction of fractures and dislocations is normally considered beyond the scope of first aid; however, in the prolonged survival situation, the correction of bone deformities is necessary to hasten healing and make it possible for the injured to carry out necessary tasks. The best time to reduce a fracture is in the period immediately following the injury, before painful muscle spasm sets in. Apply traction until overriding fragments of bone are brought into line (check by the other limb); then firmly immobilize the extremity. It is advantageous to continue traction after reduction to insure the proper alignment of the bones.

An immobilization device is necessary, and may be improvised by using several parallel pliable willow branches woven together with vines or parachute suspension lines. The extremity must not be constricted when the swelling starts. In survival situations, it is often necessary to preserve the mobility of the survivor after reduction of a fracture. This is particularly difficult in cases of fractures of the lower extremity. Improvised litters may be used when a group of survivors is involved, or crutches may be improvised from the limbs of trees so that the injured party may be more independent.

Reduction of dislocated joints is accomplished in a manner similar to that of fractures. Gentle, but firm, traction is applied, and the extremity is manipulated until it "snaps" back into place. Should you be alone, the problem is complicated but not impossible. Traction can still be applied by using gravity. The wrist or ankle end of the extremity is tied to or wedged into the fork of a tree or similar point. The weight of the body is then allowed to exert the necessary counter-traction, with the joint being manipulated until the dislocation is reduced. This sample expedient can be applied in the reduction of fractures. However, before beginning the procedure, necessary splinting materials should be collected and be readily available.

Wounds

All wounds should be promptly cleaned. Water is the most universally available and most commonly used cleaning agent, and should be clean, preferably sterile. Irrigation of the wound proper is preferred to hard scrubbing, as irrigation will minimize additional damage to the tissue. Foreign material should be washed *away* from the wound to remove sources of infection, and the skin adjacent to wound washed thoroughly before bandaging.

While soap is not essential to wound cleaning, a bar of medicated soap (containing phisohex, etc.) helps such cleaning. If you have a bar of medicated soap in the survival kit, use it routinely, and it will accomplish much in preventing infection. External antiseptics (benzalkonium chloride tincture, etc.) are best used for cleaning abrasions, scratches, and the skin areas adjacent to lacerations. Used in deep, large wounds, antiseptics produce further tissue damage.

The "open treatment" method is the only safe way to manage survival wounds. No effort should be made to close lacerations or other wounds. In fact, it may be necessary to open the wound even more to avoid entrapment of infection and to promote drainage. The term "open" does not mean that dressings should not be used.

A notable exception to "open treatment" is the early closure of facial wounds which interfere with breathing, eating or drinking.

Wounds, left open, heal by the formation of infection-resistant granulation tissue (proud flesh). This tissue is easily recognized by its moist red granular appearance, a good sign in any wound.

After cleaning, all wounds should be covered with a clean dressing. Although the dressing should be sterile, in the survival situation any clean cloth may be used to protect the wound from further infection. A proper bandage should then be applied to anchor the dressing to the wound and afford further protection. Bandages should be snug enough to prevent dressing slip-page, yet not constrict circulation of blood. Slight pressure reduces discomfort in most wounds and aids in the control of bleeding. Once in place, dressings should not be changed frequently unless required. External soiling does not reduce the effectiveness of a dressing, and there is certain to be pain and tissue damage associated with removing it, as well as the ever-present danger of admitting infection during changing.

You will have little control over the amount and type of infectious material introduced at the time of injury. However, you can exercise some control by insuring that your clothing is clean and properly worn. Care must be exercised to prevent introduction of additional sources of infection into wounds. Wounds, regardless of type or severity, should not be touched with the fingers or nonsterile instruments. One exception to the rule is the essential control of arterial bleeding, described earlier. Clothing should be cut away from wounds so as not to rub infection into the wound from surrounding skin areas.

Despite all precautions, some degree of infection is almost universal in survival wounds. This is the primary reason for the "open" treatment advocated above. The human body has a tremendous capacity for resisting infections, if it is permitted to do so. Proper rest and nutrition are important in healing wounds and controlling infection.

The injury should be immobilized in a position favoring adequate circulation to and from the wound. Constrictive clothing or bandages should be avoided. Application of heat to an infected wound further aids in the local mobilization of body defense measures. Lukewarm "salt soaks" are particularly good in counteracting local infections, and in promoting the drainage of body fluids from the wound thus removing toxic products. Poultice, made of clean clay, shredded bark of most trees, ground grass seed, etc. accomplish the same purpose.

Adequate drainage of infected areas promotes healing. Generally, this can be done without the use of wicks or drains. Occasionally, it may be advantageous to open an accumulation of pus (abscess) and insert light, loose packing to insure continuous drainage. The knife or other instrument used in making the incision for drainage must be sterilized, even though the area is already infected, to avoid introduction of other types of organisms. The best means of sterilization in the field is with dry or moist heat.

Take antibiotics, when they are available, for the control of infection. The drug should be of the so-called "broad spectrum type" to be effective against many microorganisms, for example Chloromycetin or Terramycin. If an antibiotic is included in the kit, a sufficient amount should be provided for adequate dosages. The exact amount to be included varies with the drug and the basic assumptions as to the number and types of infections to be expected. Antibiotics are potency-dated items (shelf-life about 4 years), and their inclusion in survival kits makes periodic kit inspections mandatory so that drugs nearing their expiration dates can be replaced from medical stocks.

Debridement of severe wounds may be necessary to minimize infection and to reduce secondary shock. Debridement is the removal of foreign material and dead or dying tissue. The procedure requires skill and should be done only in case of dire survival emergency. If it is to be done, the following general rules should be followed:

1. Although skin is very important in closure of wounds, nonvital skin must be cut away.

2. Muscle may be trimmed back to a point where bleeding starts and gross discoloration ceases.

3. Seriously damaged fat tends to die and should be cut away.

4. Bone and nerve tissue should be conserved wherever possible and protected from further damage.

5. Ample drainage of the potentially infected wound must be provided.

Amputation is a radical type of debridement, wherein all or part of an extremity is cut away from the body. Amputation is indicated when massive damage to the limb poses the threat of overwhelming infection or shock. In deciding to amputate, you are trading a limb for a life, and the decision should not be made lightly. Although all dead tissue must be removed, an emergency amputation should be done at the lowest possible level of live tissue, and the stump left open. If the amputation involves intact bone, some sort of saw is needed. If none is available, consideration should be given to disarticulation (amputation through a joint.) The flexible "wire saw" contained in some survival kits may be used in dividing the bone during amputation.

Only one type of emergency amputation is recommended—the open circular type. Make the incision through the skin and the underlying tissue connecting skin and muscle at the lowest apparently living level, and allow the skin to retract. Then sever the muscles at the new skin line. The muscle will promptly retract, leaving the bone exposed. Then cut the bone, dividing the limb. A tourniquet is normally required to control bleeding if the amputation is done (as it should be) through living tissue. As blood vessels are exposed, grasp and tie them, preferably before they are cut. Leave the stump open to allow for drainage. Apply a light bandage to protect the stump from infection without interfering with drainage. Apply some sort of protective splint, extending it well below the level of the stump.

Lacerations (cuts) are best left open because of the probability of infection. They should be cleaned thoroughly, foreign material removed, and a protective dressing applied. Immobilization will hasten the healing of major lacerations. Occasionally, it may be necessary to close the wound, despite the danger of infection, in order to control bleeding or to increase the mobility of the patient. If you have a needle, thread may be procured from parachute lines, fabric or clothing, and the wound closed by "suturing." If this is done, the stitches should be placed individually, and far enough apart to permit drainage of underlying parts. In scalp wounds, the hair may be used for closure after wound cleaning; infections is of less danger in this area because of the rich blood supply.

Injuries to the head pose problems directly related to brain damage as well as interferences with breathing and eating. If the patient is unconscious, he must be watched closely and kept still. Even in the face of mild or impending shock, the head should be kept level or even slightly elevated if there is reason to suspect brain damage. Give no fluids or morphine to unconscious persons.

Wounds in the abdomen area are also particularly serious. Such wounds have an extremely high mortality rate, and render the patient totally unable to care for himself. If gut is not already coming out of the wound, a secure bandage should be applied to keep this from occurring. If gut is extruded, it is best not to replace it but to cover it with a large dressing which is kept wet with any water that has been purified, as for drinking, if at all possible. The patient should lie on his back and avoid any motions that might extrude more gut. If movement is necessary, the patient must be moved on a litter.

Injuries of the chest are common, painful, and disabling. Severe bruises of the chest or fractures of the ribs require that the chest be immobilized. Apply the bandage while the patient exhales deeply. To wrap your own chest is difficult, but it can be done by attaching one end of a long bandage (parachute cloth) to a tree or other fixed object, holding the other end in your hand, and slowly spinning your body toward the tree, keeping enough counter-pressure on the bandage to insure a tight fit.

Sucking chest wounds are easily recognized by the sucking noise, appearance of foam or bubbles in the wound, and the severity of shock. These wounds must be closed immediately before serious respiratory and circulatory complications occur. The patient should exhale while holding his mouth and nose closed (valsalva maneuver) as the wound is closed. This decreases the chest expansion and reduces the amount of air trapped in the chest cavity; the lung is thereby allowed to expand more freely.

Burns

Burns pose serious problems and are frequently encountered in aircraft accidents or at some time during most survival episodes. Burns cause severe pain and are very susceptible to shock and infection. In addition, they cause an exceptional loss of body fluid and salts. The initial treatment is to relieve the pain and prevent infection.

Covering the wound with a clean dressing of any type reduces the pain and the chances for infection. Such protection enhances mobility and provides a better capability for performing other vital survival functions. Suspensions of bark (such as oak and maple) in water are used to soothe and protect burns. This is due to the effects of the tannic acid content of the bark used.

Maintenance of body fluids and salt is essential to recovery from burns. The only method for administering fluids in the survival situation is by mouth. The casualty should therefore drink a lot of water in the early period following the burn damage. The restoration of salts may require the use of the blood of animals if salt tablets are not available. Better would be the ingestion of solutions of salt and sodium bicarbonate. Small envelopes containing 3 grams of salt and 1.5 grams of sodium bicarbonate to be mixed with 1 quart of water should be included in individual survival kits. In burns about the face and neck, take care to insure an open airway. If necessary, an artificial airway should be established before the patient develops extreme difficulties. Burns of the face and hands are particularly serious in the survival situation, since they interfere with the accomplishment of survival tasks.

Exposure

HEAT. In certain climates, you will be exposed to excessive heat and must safeguard yourself from its effects. While the body will adjust to heat, the process takes time, and you must be especially careful during the first week of your exposure.

Three specific types of heat illness are heat cramps, heat exhaustion, and heat stroke.

Heat cramps are due to excessive losses of salt from the body. There is painful cramping of the muscles of the extremities and abdomen, but the body temperature remains normal. Treatment involves replacement of the salt that the body has dissipated. Recovery is rapid.

Heat exhaustion is a form of shock and is due to excessive losses of both salt and water from the body. The symptoms include headaches, dizziness, confusion, drowsiness, and weakness after exposure to heat. The skin is cool, pale, and wet with perspiration. Treatment is the same as for any other type of shock, plus replacement of salt and water.

Heat stroke is a serious medical emergency, and if not treated immediately and forcibly, the patient will die. In heat stroke, body heat loss is inadequate, the body temperature rises, and the heat regulating center in the brain is damaged and ceases to function. The skin is dry, hot, and flushed; this symptom is followed by collapse of the patient in a very sudden manner. The body temperature must be lowered immediately by whatever means possible. In the survival situation, the most adequate treatment may be stripping off all clothing, pouring water on the patient, and fanning him to promote evaporative cooling. Heat illnesses are much better prevented than treated.

COLD. In other climatic extremes, the problem of cold injury becomes proportionately important. The body attempts to prevent excessive loss of heat in vital parts by decreasing blood flow to superficial tissues. Blood vessels constrict until blood flow is inadequate to maintain tissue health.

When the entire body is exposed to extreme cold, as in immersion following over-water emergencies, there is a significant drop in body temperature until vital functions cease. The patient must be rewarmed immediately if he is to survive. He should be exposed to temperature of approximately 110°F. This may be accomplished by using warmed water which will feel warm to skin of forearm, or by putting the patient in a warmed room.

Frostbite is a term used to describe local tissue death from exposure to cold below freezing (usually below 10°F) for relatively brief periods of only a few hours. The part should be rewarmed and protected with a dry dressing.

Superficial frostbite (frost nip) involves surface skin only. Body heat may be used for rewarming. The hands can be used to warm face, ears, nose, and wrist. The groin, armpit, or belly area can be used for rewarming hands or a companions feet. Deep frostbite involves complete freezing of body tissues including blood vessels and bone. Rapid rewarming is required and is most easily accomplished in a water bath of between 105° and 110°F (at 105°F water feels "lukewarm"

when tested with a part of the body normally protected from the cold, e.g., the elbow). The frozen part should not be rubbed. Thawing should be attempted only when it is certain that refreezing can be prevented. Perhaps it is better to continue with the frozen part as it is than to risk refreezing which makes loss of the part a certainty. Once thawed, the part should be immobilized.

Trench (or immersion) foot is local tissue death from exposure to cold above the freezing temperature (usually 32°-40°) and to dampness for longer periods of time (48 hours or longer). Constricting clothing must be removed and the part rewarmed to between 70 and 80 degrees. If water is used, it should feel slightly cool to the forearm. The injured part should be protected with dry dressings and the patient treated as a litter case if at all possible. The aim is to prevent further damage and infection.

As in the case of heat injury, cold injury is much better prevented than treated. Avoid wind and moisture to the maximum extent. The buddy system aids in detecting frostbite in its early stage. Tight constricting clothing and footgear are dangerous. Keep your feet and socks dry, and your feet and toes exercised. Periodic elevation of the feet aids in maintenance of adequate circulation.

MEDICAL EQUIPMENT AND SUPPLIES

Equipment and supplies to be included in your survival kit represent a compromise between predicted requirements and certain very real limitations. You probably have your own personal idea as to the proper components of a survival kit.

When considering the proper medical components for an individual survival kit, you must consider the types of illnesses and injuries likely to be encountered; your capability to use the equipment provided; weight and space requirements of the material; the stability under storage conditions of the recommended items; and least of all, cost.

A stimulant drug, such as Dextroamphafamine tablets, may be used to reduce the "shock" of the immediate post impact period, and to delay the onset of fatigue symptoms in hostile situations. One of the antimotion-sickness drugs, such as Dramamine, Bonine, Marezine, and Campazine is indicated even though aircrew are selected for low susceptibility to motion sickness. Seasickness is disastrous to a survivor afloat in a life raft or preserver, and immunity to airsickness is no guarantee of resistance to seasickness.

Aspirin is commonly carried and is beneficial for the control of fever and minor discomforts. Like any other medical items, its presence in the kit may tempt you to open and cannibalize your kit for uses other than that for which it is intended. This tendency is better controlled by training and indoctrination than by removal of the items from the kit.

Salt replacement is essential to well-being in hot climates and in the prevention and treatment of the adverse effects of heat. Further, salt (plus water) is beneficial in replacing salts lost in vomiting, from diarrhea, or from burned areas. For this reason, the inclusion of salt tablets and standard envelopes of salt and soda (4.5 grams) is also recommended.

The broad utility of adhesive tape makes inclusion of a small roll highly desirable since, with tape available, even the least trained individual can apply a workable dressing. "Band-aids" are valuable for the protection of small wounds, abrasions, and blisters, and should be included in the kit.

A few medium-sized safety pins are also valuable. Like adhesive tape, safety pins permit the untrained survivor to apply a better dressing with less material. Also, safety pins have uses other than strictly medical—temporary repair of clothing, fabrication of packs, etc.

A large needle, either straight or curved, with a cutting edge should be included. The standard "autopsy" needle which has a straight shank but a slightly curved tip is very good. The needle discussed here should be in addition to needles provided for other survival sewing.

One highly desirable item, either in the first aid kit or contained elsewhere in the survival gear, is a pair of needle-nosed pliers with wire cutting jaws. This small, light piece of equipment has high utility, and is valuable in the prevention as well as treatment of injury.

In addition to items contained in standardized or base augmented first aid kits, you may desire to add specific items which are peculiar to your own needs. An example might be the addition of antihistamine tablets, if you are susceptible to hay fever or allergic to insect stings. Psychologically, such additions are helpful, as they make the kit very personal, and you will take better care of it.

The packaging of the first aid kit deserves consideration. Certain items may be required immediately upon entering into survival, such as salt tablets, chloroquine, antiseptic soap, water purification tablets, and possibly the Dexedrine. Other items may be needed only for specific emergencies. To reduce the loss of valuable items, the first aid packet should be sectionalized to provide a means of separating the routinely-used items from the emergency items. Size, weight, accessibility, retention during ejection or bailout, and utility should also be considered. The pint-sized, closable, vinyl plastic bag is well-suited for this purpose. This bag will hold the recommended items, fits well into the lower leg pocket of a flight suit, and can be used as a canteen after removal of the items.

Without good technique, you cannot make the best use of your equipment, nor exploit the environment in which you find yourself. Training in survival medicine should be applied training rather than purely academic training. The classroom may provide a point of departure but cannot replace actual practice under supervision of experienced personnel.

Practice of survival medicine procedures should be included in all survival training concurrently with other subjects, as isolation of the subject destroys the all-important perspective. You should realize that mastery of survival medicine techniques is something that you can and must achieve.

Survival medicine training should teach what can be done, rather than be a continuous warning against what cannot be done.

CLOTHING

Never discard any clothing. Clothing used properly can keep you cool as well as warm. Clothing also protects you against sunburn, insects, pests, and scratches, and it can be used for barter.

Try to keep your clothing clean and in repair. Clean clothes are better insulators than dirty clothes and they last longer. Also, if your clothing, as well as your body, is clean, you will feel better and keep free from skin infections and body parasites. (Examine each other for external parasites.)

Try to keep your clothing and shoes dry; use a drying rack in front of a fire. Don't put your wet shoes too close to the fire or they will stiffen and crack. Drying your clothes in the smoke of the fire helps get rid of insects. Turn clothes inside out.

Select your clothing wisely, maintain it conscientiously, and protect it carefully.

Select clothing to conform with the area being overflown, because it is extremely important to *wear* clothing that will protect you during survival. Emergencies happen fast, and space to don clothing, especially in high-performance ejection seat aircraft, is very limited. *The only practical means of insuring that clothing is available during survival is to wear it.*

One method of insuring that clothing will be worn is to keep temperature at a low point in the aircraft so that survival-type clothing will be comfortable when worn during flight.

SHELTERS

Shelter is defined as "something that covers, protects, or defends"; that it is a "place affording protection, as from the elements." To arbitrarily assume that a "place affording protection from the elements" can *only* be construed as being a framework, built to certain specifications and covered by parachute material is incorrect. Instead, every survivor, faced with the problem of

protecting himself from the elements or the enemy, *must* consider using every conceivable *place* already existing in his immediate area or using every available material at hand, to improvise a place that *will afford protection* that is needed. This statement does not rule out man-made framework constructions using parachute cloth or other materials; it merely enlarges the scope of *what* can be used as a shelter in a survival/evasion situation.

When deciding what type of shelter to build, the survivor must first consider what the shelter is to protect him from, i.e., rain, cold, insects, heat. As an example, when in hot arid areas, protection from the sun during the day and low temperatures during the night may be the prime consideration. In frigid areas extreme cold, aggravated by high winds, or, in some seasons, swarms of insects may be the factors that dictate what type of protection the survivor must seek. An evader must protect himself from enemy observation as well as from the natural elements facing him.

In addition to protection from natural elements and conditions, an adequate shelter also provides the survivor-evader that psychological well-being so necessary for sound rest. Adequate rest is extremely important if the survivor-evader is to make sound decisions and the need for rest becomes more critical as time passes and rescue prolonged. Some *rest* contributes to mental and physical health, and adequate *shelter* contributes to sound rest. Because of all these factors adequate shelters must be placed high on the priority list if survival is to be successful.

Actually, only two requisites must be satisfied when selecting the site in which the shelter is to be improvised or constructed—an area large enough and level enough for one to lie down comfortably, and materials available to improvise or construct whatever type shelter is needed. Being near water and fuel is desirable only if the situation permits these luxuries.

The general rule to remember when using parachute cloth is that "pitch and tightness"

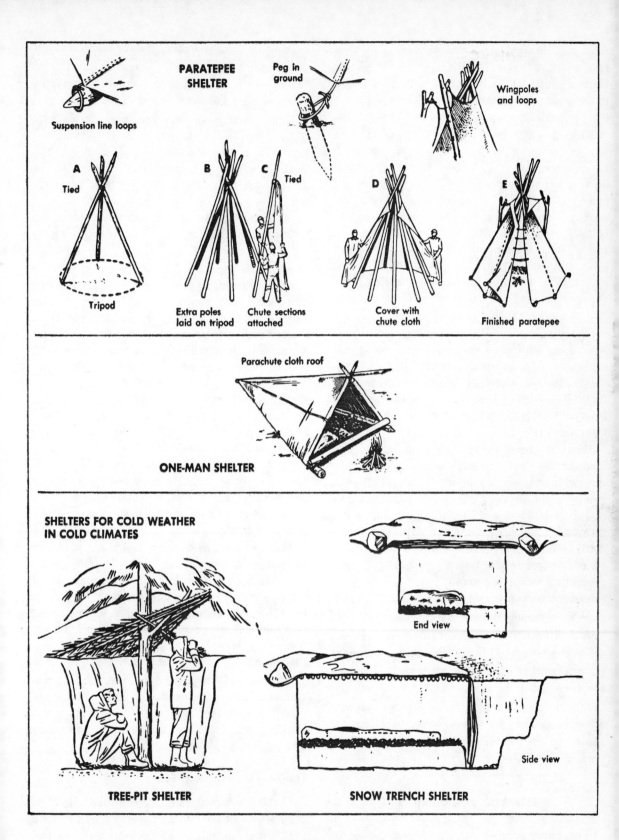

Figure 2-15. General Purpose Shelters

must be adherred to if the shelter is to shed rain or snow. Limiting the size of the shelter becomes important only if cold, lack of materials, or the enemy is a consideration. Otherwise, make the shelter large enough to be fully comfortable.

Shelters which are to have fires inside must have a ventilation system that will provide fresh air as it evacuates smoke and carbon-monoxide. Such a system is necessary whether or not the fire creates smoke. If possible, it is better to have the shelter opening placed at 90 degrees to the prevailing winds if the survivor intends to use a fire in front of the shelter doorway. Such positioning discourages the possibility of sparks and smoke being blown into the shelter even though the wind may reverse its direction each morning and evening.

The survivor-evader need not concern himself with *exact* shelter dimensions. He need only remember that he needs shelter, that he must decide to use existing shelters, improvise on natural shelters or construct a shelter, and that regardless of type each must provide his needed protection.

When it comes to building shelters, the survivor-evader must consider the amount of energy that will be expended in the building. Foolish indeed is the person who spends great amounts of energy building a shelter if nearby nature has provided a natural shelter that would satisfy his needs. Another shelter possibility that must not be overlooked is the fuselage interiors of some present high-altitude aircraft. Such aircraft have extremely well insulated interiors which aircraft of WW II vintage did not have.

A well known fact is that certain type shelters are best adapted to certain climatic conditions of the world. How these shelters are built, why they are best suited for certain climates, areas, and situations are illustrated in following chapters. Study them and, if the need arises, use them as shown or use them as pilot-types from which you can improvise.

FIRE AND FIRE-MAKING

The importance of fire in survival cannot be overemphasized. You need fire for warmth, for keeping dry, for signaling, for cooking, and for purifying water by boiling.

Fire can supplement your limited food supply by providing an external source of heat (calories).

Don't build your fire too big. Small fires require less fuel and are easier to control, and their heat can be concentrated. In cold weather, small fires arranged in a circle around an individual are much more effective than one large fire.

In friendly areas, a fire provides distinct advantages, and the proper use of fires is highly recommended.

In hostile areas, a fire or the smoke from a fire will announce your presence faster than any other survival practice. A fire can be seen for many miles at night, and a fire inside a parachute shelter becomes a veritable beacon. In hostile areas, you should insure that your fire is built so that an unwanted observer will not notice it until he is right on top of it. A very small fire built in a carefully selected site can usually be used in remote hostile areas. If you move in very close to it, a small fire provides as much usable heat as a larger fire.

In the daytime, the smoke from a fire can be seen for broad distances, particularly if the combustible material is not chosen wisely and the fire is located in an area where smoke would be very obvious.

Fuels which are dry and contain a minimum of resin or pitch put out very little smoke—and more heat. Select fuels from deciduous growth rather than evergreens. If possible, the smoke from the fire should blend with some existing condition of fog or mist or, best of all, be obscured by very bad weather. Remember also, that smoke can be smelled by anyone in the area.

The use of fire should be restricted to circumstances of extreme need. The ultimate decision of whether to build a fire in hostile territory will fall on you and must depend on your appraisal of the situation.

Tinder, Kindling, and Fuel

Combustible materials normally fall into three categories. In the order in which they are used, they are: (1) tinder, (2) kindling, and (3) fuel.

Tinder is that type of material which ignites

with a minimum of heat—even a spark. In this category may be found:

- Birch bark
- Shredded inner bark from cedar trees
- Fine, dry wood shavings
- Dry straw
- Sawdust
- Very fine pitch-wood scrapings
- Waxed paper
- Bird down (fine feathers)
- Seed down (milk weed, cattails)
- Charred cloth
- Lint from pockets and seams

Kindling is usually considered to be readily combustible fuel that is added to tinder as soon as sufficient flame to ignite it has become available. Kindling is used to bring the burning temperature up to the point where larger and perhaps less combustible fuel can be added. In the kindling category are found:

- Small twigs
- Split wood
- Heavy cardboard
- Pieces of wood removed from the inside of larger pieces
- Wood that has been soaked in or doused with highly flammable materials; i.e., gasoline, oil, wax .

Tinder and kindling must be kept dry. Other larger fuels can be used even though they are not completely dry as long as sufficient kindling is used to bring the burning temperature up to the point where they will ignite. *Gasoline or other highly flammable material should not be poured on a fire that has already started.* Even a smoldering fire can explode and cause serious burns.

Fuels:

- Dry standing dead wood and dry dead branches. Dead wood is easy to split and break—pound it on a rock.
- The inside of fallen tree trunks and large branches. These may be dry even if the outside is wet; use the heart of the wood.
- Almost anywhere you can find green wood that can be made to burn, especially if finely split.

- In treeless areas, you can find other natural fuels, such as dry grass which you can twist into bunches, peat dry enough to burn (found at the top of undercut banks), dried animal dung, animal fats, and sometimes even coal, oil shale, or oil sand lying on the surface.
- If you have no natural fuels but if you are with the aircraft, you can burn gasoline and lubricating oil or a mixture of both (see figure 2-17.)

Preparing Fireplace

Prepare the location of your fire carefully. To get the most warmth and to protect fire from wind, build it against a rock or wall of logs which will serve as a reflector to direct the heat into your shelter. Cooking fires may be walled in by logs or stones but only to provide a platform for your cooking pot. *Beware of wet or porous rocks—they may explode when heated.*

Clear away leaves, twigs, moss, and dry grass, so that you don't start a grass or forest fire. If the ground is dry, scrape down to bare dirt. If the fire must be built on snow, ice, or wet ground, build a platform of logs or flat stones.

After preparing your fireplace, get all your materials together before you start the fire. Make sure your matches, kindling, and fuel are dry. Have enough fuel on hand to keep fire going. Light it in a place sheltered from the wind.

Fire-Making With Matches (or Lighter)

Arrange a small amount of kindling in low pyramid, close enough together so flames can lick from one piece to another. Leave a small opening for lighting and air circulation.

Save matches by using a "shave stick," or make a fagot of thin, dry twigs, tied loosely. Shield match from wind, and light fagot or shave stick. Apply this to lower windward side of kindling, shielding it from wind as you do so.

Small pieces of wood or other fuel can be laid gently on kindling before lighting or can be added after kindling begins to burn. Lay on smaller pieces first, adding larger pieces of fuel as fire begins to burn. Don't smother fire by crushing down kindling with heavy wood. Don't make the fire too big. Don't waste fuel.

Waterproof matchbox

FLINT AND STEEL

This is the easiest and most reliable way of making a fire without matches. Use the flint fastened to the bottom of your waterproof match case. If you have no flint, look for a piece of hard rock from which you can strike sparks. If no sparks fly when it is struck with steel, find another. Hold your hands close over the dry tinder; strike flat with a knife blade or other small piece of steel with a sharp, scraping, downward motion so that the sparks fall in the center of the tinder. The addition of a few drops of gasoline before striking the flint will make the tinder flame up — FOR SAFETY, KEEP YOUR HEAD TO ONE SIDE. When tinder begins to smolder, fan or blow it gently into a flame. Then transfer blazing tinder to your kindling pile or add kindling gradually to the tinder.

One way to start a fire is with flint and lint ball.

1. Imbed a ¼-inch piece of lighter flint (pyrophoric alloy-large size) in a ½" X ¼" X 2" piece of soft wood or plastic. Flint should be imbedded close to one end and centered.

2. Wind 2- to 3-feet of 8-strand flax (linen) harness maker's thread at the end opposite the flint.

3. To use, unwind about 1 inch of linen, and on a smooth dry surface, scrape the strands of linen into a ball of lint using the sharp edge of a knife.

4. Place lint ball in contact with flint. With the sharp edge of the knife, use pressure and strike a spark directly into the lint ball. Lint will quickly blaze.

One of the distinct advantages of this piece of equipment is its usefulness, even after complete immersion in water. The linen dries very quickly and 5 minutes of air drying after a thorough wetting is sufficient to make it usable.

BURNING GLASS

A convex lens can be used in bright sunlight to concentrate the sun's rays on the tinder. A 2-inch lens will start a fire most any time the sun is shining. Smaller lenses will work if the sun is high and the air clear.

ELECTRIC SPARK

If you have a live storage battery, direct a spark onto the tinder by scatching the ends of wires together, to produce an arc.

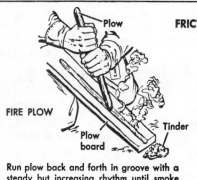

FRICTION

FIRE PLOW

Run plow back and forth in groove with a steady but increasing rhythm until smoke in tinder indicates a spark.

BOW AND DRILL

Tinder and wood dust

Hand holding drill socket is braced against left shin. Wood dust piles on tinder as drill spins.

FIRE THONG

Use a thong of dry rattan or other long, strong fiber, and rub with a steady but increasing rhythm.

FIRE SAW

Fibrous tinder

Notch

NOTE:

Split bamboo or soft wood makes a good fire saw. Dry sheath of coconut flower is a good base wood.

Figure 2-16. Fire Making Without Matches

Fire-Making Without Matches

First, find or prepare one of the following kinds of tinder: very dry powdered wood, finely shredded dry bark, or the shredded pith of a dead palm frond; lint from unravelled cloth, cotton, twine, rope, or first aid gauze bandage, fuzzy or wooly material scraped from plants; fine bird feathers or birds' nests; field-mouse nests; or fine wood dust produced by insects, often under bark of dead trees. Tinder must be bone-dry. You can make it burn more easily by adding a few drops of gasoline or by mixing in with powder taken from a cartridge. Once tinder is prepared, put some in a waterproof container for future use.

Fire-Making With Special Equipment

You can use the night end of the Mark 13 Mod O day-night flare as a fire starter. This means, however, having to balance getting your fire started against the loss of one of your night flares.

Some emergency kits contain small fire starters, cans of special fuels, windproof matches, and other aids.

The white plastic spoon packed in various inflight rations may be of the type that burns readily. Push the handle into the ground enough to support the spoon in an upright position. Light the tip of the spoon. It will burn for approximately 10 minutes, long enough to dry out and ignite small tinder and kindling.

If you have a candle, use it to start your fire and thus prevent the use of more than one match. As soon as the fire is well started, put the candle out and save it for future emergency use.

Burning Aircraft Fuel

You can improvise a stove to burn fuel, lubricating oil, or a mixture of both. Place 1 or 2 inches of sand or fine gravel in the bottom of a can or other container and add gasoline. *Be careful when lighting; the gas may explode at first.* Make slots at the top of the can to let flame and smoke out, and punch holes just above the level of the sand to provide a draft. To make a fire burn longer, mix gasoline with oil. If you have no can, simply dig a hole in

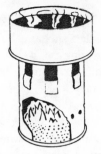

USING AVIATION FUEL   USING WICK TO BURN OIL OR ANIMAL FAT

Figure 2-17. Improvised Stoves

the ground, fill it with sand, pour on gasoline, and light; *take care to protect your face and hands.* Do not allow the fuel to collect in puddles.

You can burn lubricating oil as fuel by using a wick arrangement. Make the wick of string, rope, rag, sphagnum moss, or even a cigarette, and rest it on the edge of a receptacle filled with oil. You can also soak rags, paper, wood, or other fuel in oil and throw them on your fire.

You can make a stove of any empty waxed ration carton by cutting off one end and punching a hole in each side near the unopened end. Stand the carton on the closed end; stuff an empty sack loosely inside the carton, leaving an end hanging over top; light this end—the stove will burn from the top down and will boil more than a pint of water.

Useful Hints

Don't waste your matches by trying to light a poorly prepared fire. Don't use matches for lighting cigarettes; get a light from your fire or use a burning lens. Don't build unnecessary fires; save your fuel. Practice primitive methods of making fires before all of your matches are gone.

Carry some dry tinder with you in a waterproof container. Expose it to the sun on dry days. Adding a little powdered charcoal will improve it. Collect good tinder wherever you find it. Cotton cloth is good tinder, especially if scorched or charred. Works well with burning glass or flint and steel.

Collect kindling along trail before you make camp. Keep firewood dry under shelter. Dry damp wood near fire so you can use it later. Save some of your best kindling and fuel for quick fire-making in the morning.

To split logs, whittle hardwood wedges and drive them into cracks in the log with a rock or club; split wood burns more easily. Never swing an axe toward your foot or other parts of your body.

To make a fire last overnight, place large logs over it so that the fire will burn into the heart of the logs. When a good bed of coals has been formed, cover it lightly, first with ashes and then dry earth. In the morning, the fire will still be smoldering.

Fire can be carried from one place to another in the form of a lighted punk, smoldering coconut husk, or slow-burning coals. When you want a new fire, add tinder or small fuel and fan or blow the smoldering material into flame.

Don't waste fire-making materials. Use only what is necessary to start a fire and to keep it going for the purpose needed. When you leave the camp site, put out the fire with water and mineral soil. Mix it well until you can insert your hand.

SPECIAL EQUIPMENT

Weapons

Several types of survival weapons are available for inclusion in survival kits: the M4 and MA-1 caliber .22 Hornet rifles and the M6 over-and-under .410-.22 Hornet weapon.

The M4 and MA-1 are .22 clip-fed rifles chambered to use the Hornet cartridge. This cartridge has a longer and heavier slug than the .22 "plinking" load, and the cartridge case is enlarged to contain a heavier powder load. The cartridge was originally designed for varmint hunting (woodchucks, porcupines, gophers) but can be used on larger animals. This is a very accurate cartridge, with a high muzzle velocity and extremely flat trajectory. However, it should be used carefully on very small animals, such as squirrels or cottontail rabbits, because its high velocity and comparatively heavy slug usually causes extreme damage to the meat.

The M6 .410-.22 is a weapon which combines a small-gage shotgun and a caliber .22 rifle chambered for the Hornet cartridge. The rifle is mounted above the shotgun barrel. The shotgun is used for birds, squirrels, and rabbits. The rifle is used for shots at small game which are out of range of the shotgun.

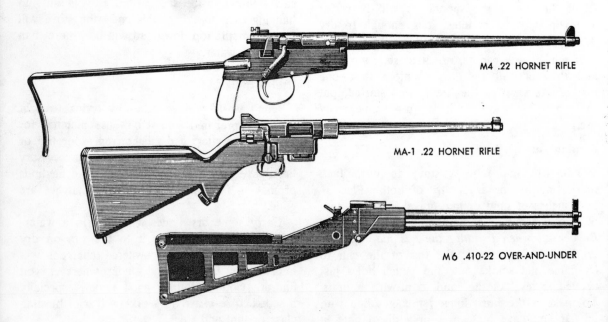

M4 .22 HORNET RIFLE

MA-1 .22 HORNET RIFLE

M6 .410-22 OVER-AND-UNDER

Figure 2-18. Survival Weapons

Figure 2-19. Using the Axe

The shotgun load has an effective range of 20-25 yards against birds and an effective range of 15 to 20 yards against small animals. Don't waste ammunition on long shots, especially long wing shots.

The survival rifle can kill at ranges over 200 yards, but your chances of hitting game in a vital spot at ranges over 100 yards are very slight.

Remember, most big game is actually killed at ranges under 60 yards. Unless it is impossible to secure a clean kill by closer stalking, never attempt to kill by shooting over 100 yards. Make sure of your first shot, for it may be your last one at that particular animal—and your ammunition supply is only what you are carrying with you.

Your survival weapons are built to withstand survival conditions, but they do require care if they are to function when you need them.

Keep your weapon clean. If possible, cover it when not in use. Keep the action, receiver walls, bolt and assembly, and especially the barrel, clean and free from oil, dirt, snow, or mud. If the barrel is obstructed by mud, snow, or any foreign substance, clean it out before shooting. *Never try to shoot out an obstruction. The barrel will burst.*

Your weapon is a precision-made instrument on which your life may depend. Don't use it as a club, hammer, or pry bar.

Don't over-oil your weapon. Only a few drops

on moving parts are needed. In extreme cold, use no oil.

A piece of cloth on a string pulled through the barrel is a handy substitute for a ramrod and cleaning patch.

If you must give the barrel a thorough cleaning and have no powder solvent, pour boiling water through it from the breech. Mop up the excess water by pulling a cloth on a string through the barrel, and the hot barrel will dry itself.

Axes and Knives

Your cutting tools are important aids to survival in any environment. For best results, use and care for them properly.

When you use an axe, don't try to cut through a tree with one blow. Rhythm and aim are more important than force. Too much power behind a swing interferes with your aim. When the axe is swung properly, its weight provides all the power you need.

Before doing any chopping, clear away all obstructions. A branch, vine, or bush can deflect an axe onto your foot or leg. Remember, an axe can be a wicked weapon. Figure 2-19 shows how to use it safely. Figure 2-20 shows how to maintain and repair an axe or knife.

A broken handle is difficult to remove from the head of the axe. Usually the most convenient way is to burn it out. For a single-bit axe, bury

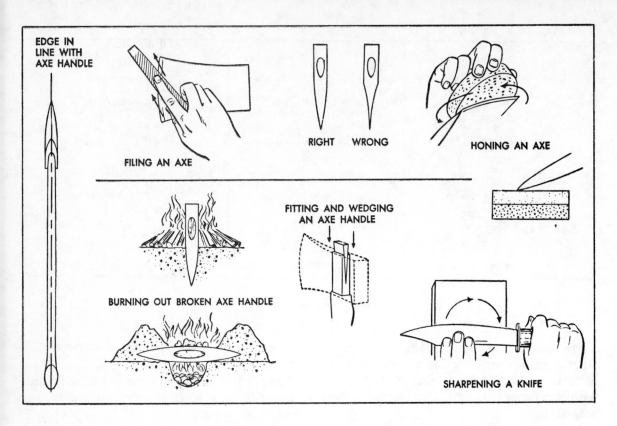

EDGE IN LINE WITH AXE HANDLE

FILING AN AXE

RIGHT   WRONG

HONING AN AXE

BURNING OUT BROKEN AXE HANDLE

FITTING AND WEDGING AN AXE HANDLE

SHARPENING A KNIFE

Figure 2-20. Repairing Axes and Knives

the blade in the ground up to the handle, and build a fire over it. For a double-bit, dig a little trench, lay the middle of the axe over it, cover both bits with earth, and build the fire. The covering of earth keeps the flame from the cutting edge of the axe and saves its temper. A little water added to the earth will further insure this protection.

If you have to improvise a new handle, save time and trouble by making a straight handle instead of a curved one like the original. Use a young, straight hardwood without knots. Whittle it roughly into shape and finish it by shaving. Split the end of the handle that fits into the axe head. After it is fitted, pound a thin, dry wooden wedge into the split. Use the axe awhile, pound the wedge in again, then trim it off flush with the axe. Scrape the handle smooth to remove splinters. The new handle can also be seasoned to prevent shrinkage by "scorching" it in the fire.

Your survival kit may include a file or a whetstone. If you haven't a sharpening tool,

look for a natural whetstone. You will need it to sharpen your knives and axes.

Any sandstone will sharpen tools, but a gray, somewhat clayey sandstone gives better results. Avoid using quartz. You can recognize quartz instantly by scratching your knife blade with it —quartz is the only common mineral that bites into steel.

If you don't find sandstone, look for granite or any glittering, crystalline rock except marble. If you use granite, rub two pieces of the stone together until they are smooth before you use one as a grindstone.

Axes can be sharpened best by using both file and whetstone, but a stone alone will keep the axe usable. Use the file every few days, the whetstone after each using. Always push the file away from the blade.

Put a finer edge on your axe with the whetstone. Wet the stone and move it in a circular motion from the middle of the blade to the edge.

A snow knife can be sharpened with file alone.

Other knives are sharpened with the whetstone alone. Hold the blade at a slight angle to the stone. Push the blade away from you. Sharpen the blade alternately. You can get a keener edge by gradually decreasing the pressure on the blade.

Sharpen a machete as you would a knife.

One of the most valuable items in any survival situation is a knife, since it has an extremely large number of uses. Unless the knife is kept sharp, however, it will fall far short of its potential.

A knife should be sharpened only with a stone. Repeated use of a file rapidly removes steel from the blade. In some cases, it may be necessary to use a file to remove plating from the blade before using the stone. A circular motion of the blade on the stone used on alternate sides will put a good cutting edge on the knife.

Section D — Water and Food

WATER

Water is one of your first and most important needs. Start looking for it immediately. *You may get along for weeks without food, but you can't live long without water,* especially in hot areas where you lose large quantities of water through sweating.

Even in cold areas, your body needs 2 quarts of water a day to maintain efficiency. Any lower intake results in loss of efficiency. If you delay drinking, you have to make it up later on.

Purify all water before drinking, either (1) by boiling for at least 1 minute plus 1 additional minute for each 1,000 feet above sea level; or (2) by using as directed the water purification tablets in your first aid kit; or (3) by adding 8 drops of 2% solution of iodine to a quart (canteenful) of water and letting it stand for 10 minutes before drinking. Rainwater collected directly in clean containers or in plants is generally safe to drink without purifying. Boiling is the surest and best purification method.

Don't drink urine. It contains too much body waste to be healthful.

Follow animal trails. Animals usually go to water at dawn and dark.

When no surface water is available, you may want to tap the earth's supply of ground water. Access to this water supply depends upon the kind of ground—whether it is rock or some loose material like clay, gravel, or sand.

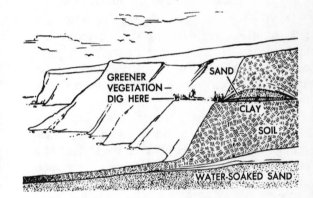

Figure 2-21. Perched Water

In rocky ground, look for springs and seepages. Limestone and lavas have more and larger springs than any other rocks.

Limestones are soluble; and ground water etches out caverns in them—some large enough for you to explore and many just cracks, an inch or so high, that the water has enlarged. Look in these caverns, large and small, for springs. If you go into a large one beyond sight of the entrance, *be careful—don't get lost.* Travel with a string or cord tied to a solid object at the entrance. Lacking a cord, mark your route every few feet on wall or floor.

Most lava rocks contain millions of bubble-holes; ground water may seep through them. Look for springs along the walls of valleys that cross the lava flow. Some flows have no bubbles but do have "organ pipe" joints—vertical cracks that

25

part the rocks into columns a foot or more thick and 20 feet or more high. At the foot of these joints you may find water creeping out as seepage or pouring out in springs.

Look for seepage where a dry canyon cuts through a layer of porous sandstone.

Most common rocks, like granite, contain water only in irregular cracks. Look over the hillsides to see where the grass is lush and green. Then dig your ditch at the base of the green zone and wait for water to seep into it.

Water is more abundant and easier to find in loose sediments than in rocks. Look for springs along valley floors or down along their sloping sides. The flat benches or terraces of land above river valleys usually yield springs or seepages along their bases, even when the stream is dry.

Don't waste your time digging for water unless you have some sign that water is there. Dig in the floor of a valley under a steep slope, especially if the bluff is cut in a terrace, or dig out a lush green spot where a spring has been during the wet season.

Water moves slowly through clay, but many clays contain strips of sand which may yield springs. Look for a wet place on the surface of a clay bluff and try digging it out. Try wet spots at the foot of the bluff.

Along coasts you may find water in the dunes above the beach or even in the beach itself, well back from the high-tide line. Look in the hollows between sand dunes for visible water—dig, if the sand seems moist.

FOOD

You should be able to find something to eat wherever you are. One of the best places to find food is along the sea coast, between the high and low water mark. Other likely spots are the area between the beach and a coral reef; the marshes, mud flats, or mangrove swamps where a river flows into the ocean or into a larger river; river banks, inland water holes, shores of ponds and lakes; margins of forests, natural meadows, protected mountain slopes, abandoned cultivated fields.

The food in your survival kit has been especially developed to provide you with proper sus-

tenance in survival emergencies. When you eat it as directed on the package, it will keep you at maximum efficiency. Save it for emergency use if you can find enough other food at hand.

Take stock of your available food and water. Estimate the time that you expect to be on your own. The conditions under which you are being forced to survive must be considered. Pickup may vary from a few hours to several months, depending on the environment, operational commitments, and availability of rescue facilities in the area. Available food and water must be allotted according to the time that will elapse before you are able to supplement your supply from the land. If you are able to move at will, you should probably divide your food into thirds; allow two-thirds for the first half of your estimated time before rescue, and save one-third for the second half.

If you have regrouped after the emergency and decide to divide your party, give each man traveling out to get help about twice as much food as you give each man remaining with the airplane. In this way, the men resting at the aircraft and those walking out will stay in about the same physical condition for about the same length of time, and the safety and rescue prospects of all will be increased.

If you have less than a quart of water daily, avoid dry, starchy, and highly flavored foods and meat. Keep in mind that eating increases thirst. Best foods to eat are those with high carbohydrate content, such as hard candy and fruit bars, if available.

Every bit of work requires additional food and water; remember that the less you work, the less food and water you need.

You can live many days without food if you have water. When water is no problem, drink more than your normal amount to keep fit.

Always be on the lookout for wild foods. Live off the land whenever possible. *Save your rations for emergencies.*

Eat regularly, if possible; don't nibble! On limited rations, plan for one good meal daily; then sit down and make a feast of it. Two meals a day are preferable, especially if one of them is hot. If you are collecting wild foods, plan a hot meal. Cooking usually makes the food safer, more digestible, and more palatable. On the other hand, some foods such as sapodilla, star apple, soursop, and memdrillos are not palatable unless eaten raw. The time you spend cooking will give you a good rest period.

Native foods may be more appetizing if they are eaten by themselves. Mixing rations and native foods usually does not pay. In many countries, vegetables are often contaminated by the human dung which the natives use as fertilizer. Such diseases as dysentery are carried in this way. If possible, you should select and prepare your meals when you find yourself in such a situation. If necessary to avoid offending the natives, indicate that your peculiar taboos require you to prepare your own food.

Learn to overcome your prejudices. Foods that may not look good to eat are often part of the natives' regular diet. Wild foods are good foods, with high vitamin and mineral content. Fleshy-leafed plants make good salad greens and fresh fruits provide fluid when water supplies are low. Eat enough to be satisfied.

With a few exceptions, all animals are edible when freshly killed. Don't eat toads. Avoid fish with sunken eyes, flabby flesh or skin, or an unpleasant odor. If the flesh remains dented when you press your thumb against it, the fish is probably stale and should not be eaten.

Food Preparation

Boiling, roasting, baking, and *frying*—in that order—are the most efficient ways of preparing foods. Pit cooking or clambake style (oven) is slower but requires less attention, protects food from flies and other pests, and reveals no flame at night (an advantage if you are in enemy territory, no advantage if you are signaling for help).

COOKING. Cooking makes for a more enjoyable meal. All wild game, fresh water fish, clams, mussels, snails, and crawfish should be thoroughly cooked for safety. Mince tough mussels or large snails. Avoid eating raw or smoked fresh water fish, as they may be contaminated with parasites. Parrots, hawks, and crows can be tough, but they soften up when stewed thoroughly. Most plant foods are made more digestible and palatable and yield more food value after heating.

Salt water shellfish may be eaten raw out are safest when cooked. Shark meat is edible, except in the arctic, but it must first be cut into small pieces and soaked overnight or boiled in several changes of water to destroy the ammonia flavor which accumulates in the flesh. Shark meat is not poisonous, just unpalatable.

Turtle eggs can be boiled or roasted, but the whites do not harden.

Leaves can be used to wrap certain foods for consignment to the cooking oven. In the southwest Pacific the leaves of the breadfruit, for instance, and those of the banana are commonly used to wrap food before cooking. This keeps the food from getting covered with sand and soil and prevents it from being burnt to a parched ember while cooking. In other parts of the world where breadfruit and banana leaves are not obtainable, any type of thick foliage plant may be used for food wrapping. But avoid using a type that will give an unpleasant flavor. Also, in the southwest Pacific and other areas where the screw pine (*Pandanus,* see illustration in attachment 1) grows, the leaves of this plant are very often used for wrapping fish. Palm leaves or the limber parts of a vine or branch may be used for tying the leaves securely around the wrapped food.

Both green and mature coconut shells form natural casseroles for cooking, as do hollow gourds. Marine shells can be used for scraping, peeling, and grating. Along inland rivers and lakes, fresh water bivalve and clam shells may also be used. Whenever shells are used for scraping or cutting, crack off part of the curved edge to form a straight, sharp edge. Hold the shell with the fingers on the inner surface and the thumb on the outer surface, and make backhand strokes away from your body.

Roasting (in the coals of a fire). You can coat fish, potatoes, fresh water mussels, and many other foods large in size with a layer of mud or clay and roast them directly in the flames or coals of a fire. Loss of food by burning is thus reduced. You need not scale fish prepared in this way; peel off the skin with the baked clay when cooked. You may also wrap food in wet leaves or foil from rations.

Steaming Under the Fire. Foods small in size, such as small bird eggs, fresh water snails, or

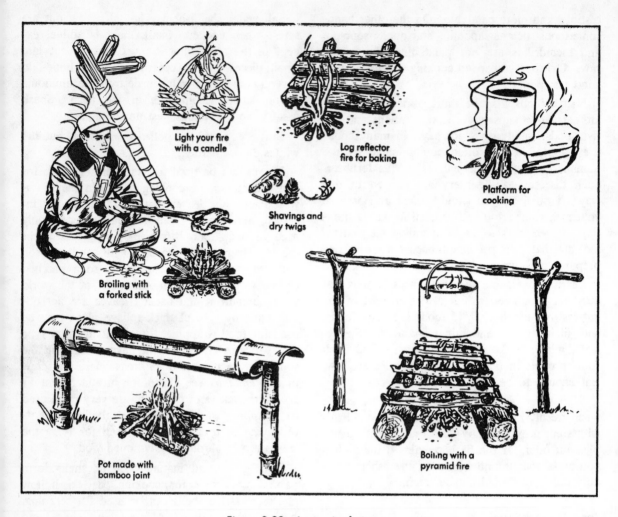

Figure 2-22. Improvised stoves

any other shellfish, may be cooked in quantity in a pit beneath your fire. Fill a small, shallow pit with food, after lining it or wrapping the food in plant leaves, seaweed, cloth, or foil from rations. If nylon is used, do not allow it to scorch or melt. Cover the pit with a ¼- to ½-inch layer of sand or soil, and build your fire directly over it. After cooking for about 1 hour, rake the fire away and uncover the food.

Steaming With Heated Stones (clambake style). Heat a number of stones in a fire, then allow the fire to burn down to coals. Make sure the rocks do not come from a stream bed since they may explode when heated. Place such foods as fresh water mussels (in their shells) directly on and between the stones, and cover the whole with plant leaves, grass, or seaweed, and also with a layer of sand or soil. When thoroughly steamed in their own juices, clams, oysters, and mussels show a gaping shell when uncovered and you may eat the food without further preparation.

Stone Boiling. Fill a big container or hollowed-out log with water and food. Add red-hot stones until the water boils. Cover for about an hour with big leaves, or until food is well done. Containers for stone boiling can also be made out of tree bark or by digging a hole and lining it with signal paneling or watertight materials.

Bamboo Joints. Bamboo joints make good pots. Heat them until they char. When hollow sections of bamboo are used as containers for food or water, remove the powdery substance that coats the inside lining. The powder is somewhat irritating. To remove the powder, rub by hand or rub or shake with a water and sand mixture. Rinse well to remove the sand and powder particles. The cleansing may have to be repeated to remove all the powder.

Rock Oven. Any type of food may be cooked in the ground. First dig a hole approximately 2 feet deep and 2 or 3 feet square, depending on the amount of food to be cooked. Then select rocks, but not from a stream bed, as these rocks explode when heated; green limbs approximately 3 inches in diameter; plenty of firewood; and grass or leaves for insulation.

Lay a fire in the hole. Place the green limbs across the hole. Pile the rocks on the green limbs. Light the fire and keep it stoked. When the green limbs burn through and the rocks fall into the hole, the oven is ready to use.

Remove the rocks and ashes. Clean any live fire from the hole. Line the bottom of the hole with hot rocks. Place a thin layer of dirt over the rocks. Place grass, moss or other insulating material on the dirt. Put in the food to be cooked, more insulating material, a thin layer of dirt, hot rocks, and cover over with remaining earth.

Small pieces of meat (steak, chops, etc.) cook in 1½ to 2 hours. Large roasts take 5 to 6 hours.

Planking. Meat may be cooked by leaving it on a plank close to the fire. This method is wasteful as the meat loses most of its liquid content and *thorough* cooking is difficult.

Broiling is the quickest way of preparing fish. A *rock broiler* may be made by placing a layer of small stones on top of hot hardwood coals, and laying the fish on the top. Scaling the fish before cooking by this method is not necessary, and small fish need not be cleaned. Cooked in this manner, fish have a moist and delicious flavor. Crabs and lobsters may also be placed on the stones and broiled. Breadfruit is frequently cooked in this manner.

The *earth oven* is used by some South Pacific islanders, and it is particularly well suited to their foods. Make a shallow excavation about 2½ feet wide by 8 or 12 inches deep in soft soil or sand. Build a fire of hardwood and let it burn until a heavy bed of coals has accumulated. Lay over this a grate of hardwood sticks and pile on a large number of small rocks. By the time the grate has burned through, the rocks should be quite hot. Remove the larger coals and burning brands and spread the stones smoothly over the bottom and along the sides of the pit. Spread a thin layer of breadfruit leaves on the hot stones. Wrap the fish, or other food, in more leaves and place it in the oven. Sprouted coconuts, lobsters, large clams, and crabs may be put in without wrapping. Cover with a final layer of leaves and loose sand so that the oven is covered. The size of the oven and cooking time vary with the type of food.

Food Preparation in Hostile Areas

Civilized man has become accustomed to cooking all, or nearly all, of his foods. This has come about for two reasons, palatability and health.

Palatability. Cooking unquestionably improves the flavor of most foods. Some green vegetables and fruits are notable exceptions.

Health. Cooking is recognized as one of the primary methods of removing harmful parasites from food, particularly animal foods.

The problem of preparing food in a hostile area becomes acute when a fire, even a small cooking fire, can bring about capture. When you have secured food in a hostile area, you will be faced with the preparation of your food in a manner which will not compromise your presence. Of course it would be simple to state that the best solution would be to eat the food without cooking.

In some respects, this would be a more reasonable solution than it might initially seem to be. From the standpoint of palatability, it is mostly a matter of adjusting your frame of mind. Animal foods are recognized as being palatable when cooked to a very minor degree. The need for food cannot be ignored and the situation may demand that it be eaten partially cooked or even uncooked.

In regard to the health considerations involved, many of the reasons for cooking are long-range in nature. Thorough cooking is recognized as a means of destroying organisms that may be present in the food, and which will cause sickness or ill effects if they gain entry. Under survival conditions in a hostile area, you may be forced to forego thorough cooking and accept the risk involved until you can return to friendly hands where professional treatment is available.

Assuming that some means of preparing food under hostile conditions must be employed, you should be aware of some of the means to which you may resort to achieve some degree of safety and at the same time improve palatability.

Parasites and other organisms living in the flesh of an animal depend upon the body temperature of the animal, the moisture within the flesh of the animal, and other factors to support their life. Any action that modifies these conditions improves the food. For example, freezing or thorough drying of the meat may bring about an untenable situation for some parasites.

If cooking is deemed mandatory, exercise extreme care in selecting the site for your fire and insure that security considerations are in your favor. Prepare the food in very small quantities in order to keep the size of the fire as low as possible.

ANIMAL FOOD

Animal food gives you the most food value per pound. *Anything that creeps, crawls, swims, or flies is a possible source of food.* People eat grasshoppers, hairless caterpillars, wood-boring beetle larvae and pupae, ant eggs, spider bodies, and termites. Such insects are high in fat and should be cooked until dried. You have probably eaten insects as contaminants in flour, corn meal, rice, beans, fruits, and greens of your daily food.

Hunting and Stalking

• Carry your weapon so that, if you fall, it will not be damaged.

• Get as close as possible to the game before shooting.

• Don't shoot rapid fire. One shot does the job if aimed properly.

• Fire from as steady a position as possible. Remember—survival rifles are light and any unsteadiness on your part due to exertion or excitement will set the barrel to trembling. The prone position is best for a steady shot, but sitting or kneeling positions may have to be used. Use a rest such as a log or stone for the barrel whenever you can, but put your hand between the rest and

the gun barrel or the gun will shoot wild. Never fire offhand unless time prevents your taking another position.

• Aim at a vital spot. The shoulder or chest is probably the best spot for medium and large game. Do not shoot unless a vital spot is open.

• Do not trust your first shot, even if game appears to have fallen dead. Reload immediately but keep your eye on the game.

• Look for blood if game runs away after first shot. If you find blood, wait at least 30 minutes before following. Wounded game will lie down and stiffen if given time.

• An indiscriminate shot fired in hostile territory can compromise your position and alert enemy forces. The practice of hunting in hostile territory must be generally discouraged except in very remote areas when extreme need exists. After the kill is made, either take a small amount of meat and move out, or better yet, move to a safe vantage point and watch your kill to see whether or not the shot has attracted attention.

• Hunting with a hand gun is difficult at best. Careful stalking must precede the actual attempt to kill. A well aimed shot at a vital spot must be made. Use both hands on the gun if necessary to get a good shot.

Most warm-blooded, hairy animals are wary and hard to catch. To hunt them requires skill and patience. The best method for a beginner is "still hunting." Find a place where animals pass —a trail, watering place, or feeding ground. Hide nearby, always downwind so the animal can't smell

Figure 2-23. Stalk Animals Upwind

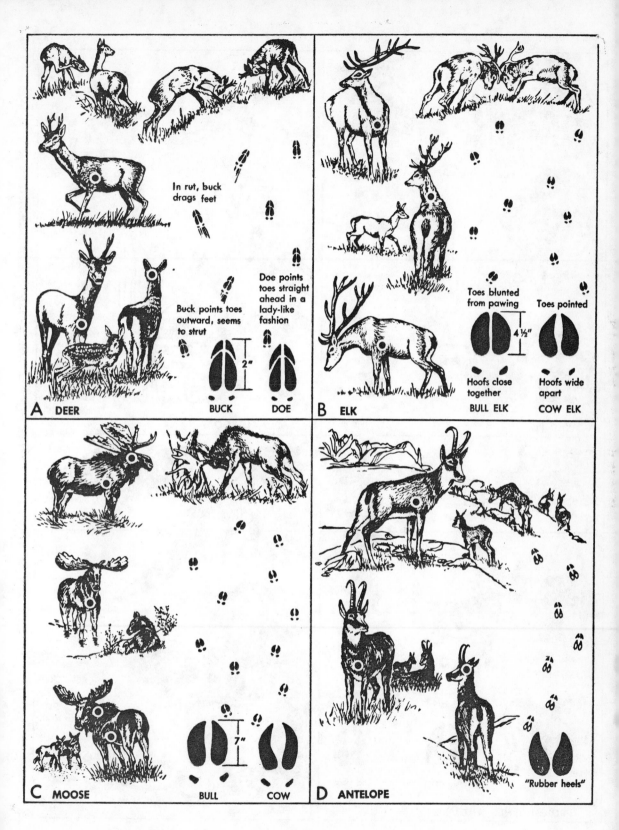

A DEER

In rut, buck drags feet

Buck points toes outward, seems to strut

Doe points toes straight ahead in a lady-like fashion

2"

BUCK   DOE

B ELK

Toes blunted from pawing

Toes pointed

4 ½"

Hoofs close together

Hoofs wide apart

BULL ELK   COW ELK

C MOOSE

7"

BULL   COW

D ANTELOPE

"Rubber heels"

Figure 2-24. Vital Spot

A WILD PIG

2½″

Dew claws

B MOUNTAIN GOAT

"Rubber heels"

C PRONGHORNED ANTELOPE

Only two toes register—
dew claws absent

Fore Hoofs wider than Hind Hoofs

D FOX

Tail mark

2¼″

Fore

Hind

Figure 2-25. Vital Spot

you, and wait for game to come within range. Remain absolutely motionless. You can stalk an animal upwind by moving very slowly and noiselessly, keeping under cover as much as possible. Move only when the animal is feeding or looking the other way. Freeze when he looks your way.

The best time to hunt is in the very early morning or dusk. When traveling, keep alert for animal signs such as tracks, trampled underbrush, or droppings. On narrow trails, be ready for game using the same pathways.

Game is most plentiful and most easily found near water, in forest clearings, or along the edge of thickets. Many animals live in holes in the ground or in hollow trees. Poke a flexible stick into the hole to determine if it is inhabited. If you use a forked stick, twist it quickly when you come in contact with the body of a small animal, and you may entangle enough fur in the small fork to pull the animal out of the hole. Use a stick to tease the animal into running out, but first close off other exits. Animals in hollow trees can be smoked out by a fire built at the base of the tree; be ready to club the animal as it comes out.

Night hunting or fishing is usually best, since most animals move at night. Use a flashlight or make a torch to shine in the animal's eyes. They will be partly blinded by the light and you can get much closer than in the daytime. If you have no gun, try to kill the animals with a club or a

Figure 2-27. Look for Turtles

Figure 2-26. Animals can be Smoked from Hollow Trees

sharpened stick used as a spear. Eyes of spiders and insects are good reflectors, so don't be surprised if you "shine up" eyes and can't find the rest of the creature. Eyes of spiny lobsters on reefs shine red. Remember that large animals, when wounded or with their young, can be dangerous. Be sure that the animal is dead, not just wounded and playing possum.

Along river and lake shores, small freshwater turtles often can be found sunning themselves (figure 2-27) If they dash into shallow water, you can still get them. Watch out for mouth and claws. Frogs and snakes also sun and feed along streams. Use both hands to catch a frog—one to attract it and keep it busy while you grab it with the other. All snakes, except sea snakes, are good to eat; catch them behind the head with a long forked stick.

Both marine and dry-land lizards are edible. Use a noose or small fishhook baited with a bright cloth lure, or use a slingshot or club.

You can make a slingshot with the elastic from your parachute pack and a forked stick or the metal rods in your tie-down kit. With practice, you can kill any small animal.

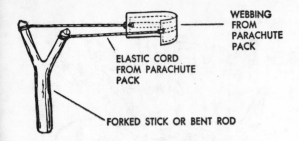

WEBBING FROM PARACHUTE PACK

ELASTIC CORD FROM PARACHUTE PACK

FORKED STICK OR BENT ROD

Figure 2-28. Improvised Slingshot

Never overlook small birds and their nests. All bird eggs are edible when fresh, even with embryos. Large wading birds such as cranes and herons often nest in mangrove swamps or in high trees near water. Ducks, geese, and swans are to be expected in tundra areas. During the moulting season, these birds can be clubbed or netted. Sea birds along low coastlines frequently nest on sand bars or low sand islands. Steep rocky coasts are favorite nesting places for gulls, auks, murres, and cormorants. Try catching birds at night when they are roosting.

Snares, Traps, Deadfalls, and Nets

Snaring of *small game* is useful during periods of food shortages, especially in the absence of firearms or during periods of imposed silence. Set your snares in game trails or frequently used runways, which you can recognize by fresh tracks and droppings.

All snares and traps should be simple in construction and should be set out as soon as possible and before darkness. Any spot used as a butchering place attracts other animals. This is a good place to watch for game during the next 24 hours. Use entrails for bait.

Place your traps where the trail is narrow. Arrange pickets, brush, or obstacles in such a manner as to force the animal to pass through the snare. Be sure that the loop is large enough for the head to pass through but not so large that the body will go through. Disturb natural surroundings as little as possible.

Small rodents may be snared in any area with a string noose laid around a hole or burrow. Conceal yourself or lie flat on the ground a short distance away. Jerk the noose tight when the animal pops his head out or steps into the noose.

The twitch-up snare—a noose attached to a sapling—jerks the animal up into the air and keeps his carcass out of reach of other animals. This type of snare is not recommended for very cold climates, since the bent sapling may freeze in position and not spring up when released.

Medium to large animals can be captured in deadfalls, but this type trap is recommended only where big game exists in such quantities as to justify the time and effort spent in construction. Build your deadfall close to or across a game trail, beside a stream, or on a ridge. Be sure that the fall log slides smoothly between upright guide posts and that the bait is placed at a sufficient distance from the bottom log to insure time for the fall log to fall before the animal can withdraw its head.

In a trip-string deadfall, no bait is used. The log is tripped by the animal's touching a trip string set across the trail.

An untended noose or deadfall is preferred, since it leaves you free for other duties. Check traps early in the morning.

Birds can be caught with the gill net from your survival kit. At night, set up the net vertically to the ground in some natural flyway, such as an opening in dense foliage. During the day, anchor one end of the net to the ground and attach the other end to a tree limb so that you can release it from a distance. Bait the area under the net, wait for the birds to gather, and then pull down the net.

A gill net can be made using suspension line and the core liners pulled from the inside. See figure 2-31.

Fishing

To catch fish use the hook and line in your emergency kit, trying the smaller hooks first. Use insects, shellfish, worms, or meat for bait. Try to see what the fish are eating. Artificial lures can be made from pieces of brightly colored cloth, feathers, or bits of bright metal or foil. A length of wire between the line and the hook prevents a fish from biting the line in two. If you have no hooks, improvise them from wire or insignia pins, or carve them out of bone or hard wood. You can make a line by unraveling a parachute

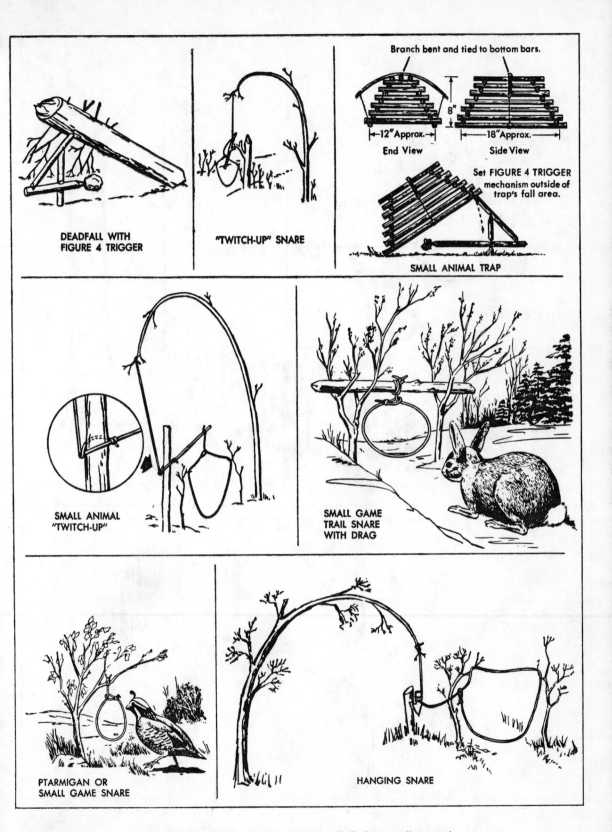

DEADFALL WITH FIGURE 4 TRIGGER

"TWITCH-UP" SNARE

Branch bent and tied to bottom bars.

8"

←12" Approx.→
End View

←18" Approx.→
Side View

Set FIGURE 4 TRIGGER mechanism outside of trap's fall area.

SMALL ANIMAL TRAP

SMALL ANIMAL "TWITCH-UP"

SMALL GAME TRAIL SNARE WITH DRAG

PTARMIGAN OR SMALL GAME SNARE

HANGING SNARE

Figure 2-29. Traps, Snares, and Deadfalls for Small Animals

35

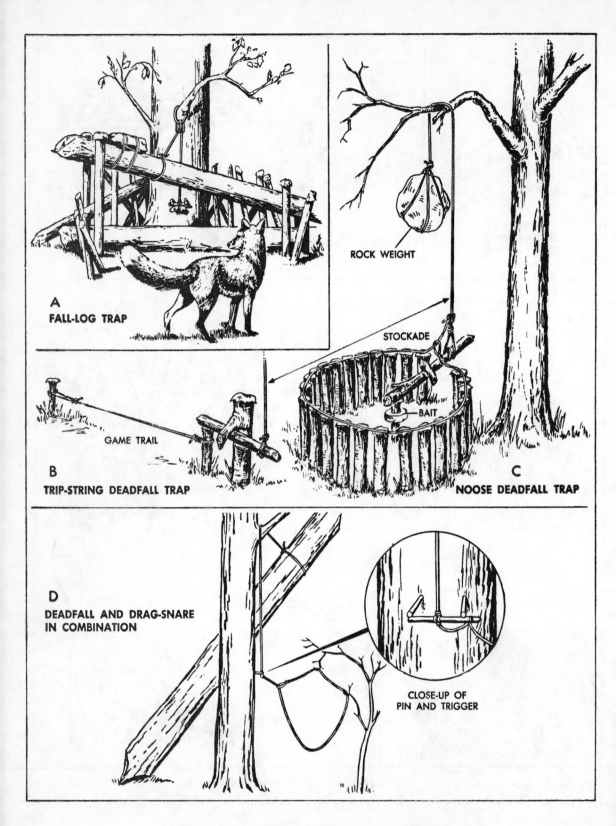

A
FALL-LOG TRAP

ROCK WEIGHT

STOCKADE

BAIT

B
TRIP-STRING DEADFALL TRAP

GAME TRAIL

C
NOOSE DEADFALL TRAP

D
**DEADFALL AND DRAG-SNARE
IN COMBINATION**

CLOSE-UP OF
PIN AND TRIGGER

Figure 2-30. Deadfalls for Medium to Large Animals

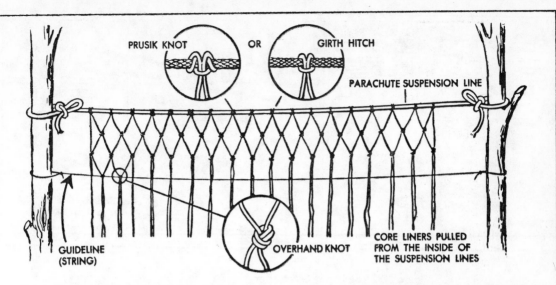

PRUSIK KNOT OR GIRTH HITCH

PARACHUTE SUSPENSION LINE

GUIDELINE (STRING)

OVERHAND KNOT

CORE LINERS PULLED FROM THE INSIDE OF THE SUSPENSION LINES

1. Suspend a suspension line casing (from which the core liners have been pulled) between 2 uprights, approximately at eye level.

2. Hang core liners (an even number) from the line suspended as in 1, above. These lines should be attached with a Prusik knot or girth hitch and spaced in accordance with the mesh you desire. One-inch spacing will result in a 1-inch mesh, etc. The number of lines used will be in accord with the width of the net desired. If more than one man is going to work on the net, the length of the net should be stretched between the uprights, thus providing room for more than one man to work. If only one man is to make up the net, the depth of the net should be stretched between the uprights and step 8, below, followed.

3. Start at left or right. Skip the first line and tie the second and third lines together with an overhand knot. Space

according to mesh desired. Then tie fourth and fifth, sixth and seventh, etc. One line will remain at the end.

4. On the second row, tie the first and second, third and fourth, fifth and sixth, etc., to the end.

5. Third row, skip the first line and repeat step 3 above.

6. Repeat step 4, and so on.

7. You may want to use a guide line which can be moved down for each row of knots to insure equal mesh. Guide line should run across the net on the side opposite the one you are working from so that it will be out of your way.

8. When you have stretched the depth between the uprights and get close to ground level, move the net up by rolling it on a stick and continue until the net is the desired length.

9. String suspension line casing along the sides when net is completed to strengthen it and make the net easier to set.

Figure 2-31. Making a Gill Net

suspension line or by twisting threads from cloth or plant fibers. If the fish won't take bait, try to hook them in the stomach as they swim by.

Better and more efficient than a line is a net (figure 2-32). If you have a seine, attach poles at each end and work it up or downstream as rapidly as possible, moving stones and threshing the bottom or edges of the stream banks. Gather up the net quickly every few moments so the fish can not escape. If you have a gill net, avoid damaging it in rough water. Use stones as anchors and wood for floats. A gill net set at a slight angle to the current tends to drain clear any floating refuse that comes down the stream, making the net less visible. Absolutely quiet stream water is hard to find. The net will occasionally catch diving birds which try to rob your gill net.

In fresh water, usually the deepest water is the best place to fish. In shallow streams the best places are pools below falls, at the foot of rapids, or behind rocks. The best time to fish is usually early morning or late evening. Sometimes fishing is best at night, especially in moonlight or if you have a light to attract the fish. Fish can sometimes be killed with the back side of a machete; or they can be speared with a sharpened stick. Before you give up, try fishing in all kinds of water and depths, at all times, and with all types of bait. But watch out for slippery rocks; and keep out of the surf, particularly when the tide is changing.

Shrimp and prawns live on or near the sea bottom and may be scraped up. They may also be lured to the surface by light at night. Catch them with a hand net made from parachute cloth.

Figure 2-32. Setting a Gill Net or Fish Trap in a Stream

Lobsters and crawfish are creeping crustaceans found on the bottom in water 10-30 feet deep. Use lobster traps, a jig, or a baited hook, or lift your catch out of the water with a dip net. Crabs creep, climb, and burrow; they are easily caught in shallow water with a dip net or in traps baited with fish heads or animal guts.

Fish traps or weirs are very useful for catching both fresh and salt water fish, especially those that move in schools. In lakes or large streams, fish tend to approach the banks and shallows in the morning and evening. Sea fish, traveling in large schools, regularly approach the shore with the incoming tide, often moving parallel to the shore and guided by obstructions in the water.

A fish trap is basically an inclosure with a

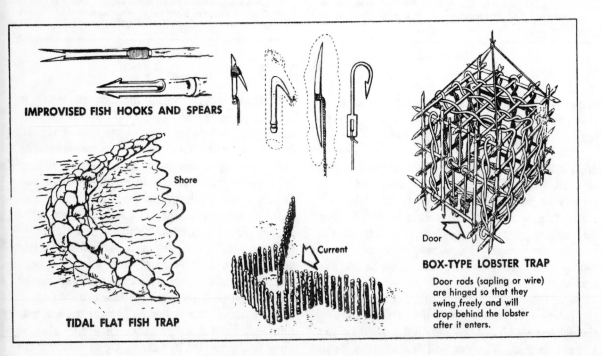

Figure 2-33. Maze-Type Fish Traps

38

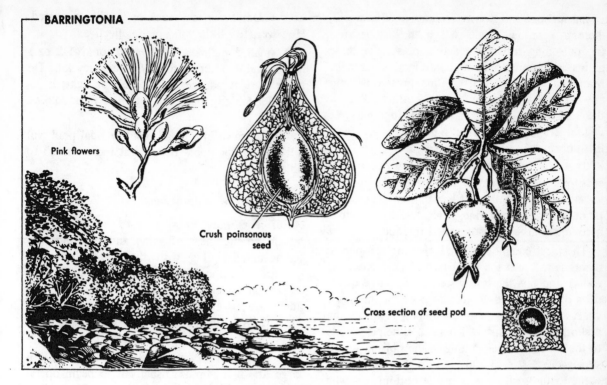

Pink flowers

Crush poinsonous seed

Cross section of seed pod

Figure 2-34. Plants Used to Stupefy Fish

blind opening where two fencelike walls extend out, like a funnel, from the entrance. The time and effort you put into building a fish trap should depend on your need for food and the length of time you plan to stay in one spot.

Pick your trap location at high tide; build at low tide. One to two hours of work should do the job. Consider your location, and try to adapt natural features to reduce your labors.

On rock shores, use natural rock pools. On coral islands, use natural pools on the surface of reefs, by blocking openings as the tide recedes. On sandy shores, use sand bars and the ditches they inclose. The best fishing off sandy beaches is in the lee of offshore sand bars.

Note the swimming habits of fish. Build your simple weir as a low stone wall extending out into the water and forming an angle with the shore. If you plan a more complex brush weir, choose protected bays or inlets, using the narrowest area and extending one arm almost to the shore. Place nets across mouths of streams.

In small, shallow streams, make your fish traps with stakes or brush set into the stream bottom or weighted down with stones so that the stream is almost blocked except for a small narrow opening into a stone or brush pen or shallow water. Wade into the stream, herding the fish into your trap. Catch or club them when they get into shallow water. Mud-bottom streams can be trampled until roiled, then seined. The fish are blinded and cannot avoid the nets.

Look for fresh water crawfish, snails, and clams under rocks, logs, overhanging bushes, or in mud bottoms.

Fish may be confined in properly built inclosures and kept for days, since the incoming water keeps them fed. In many cases, it may be advantageous to keep them alive until needed and thus assure a fresh supply without danger of spoilage.

Mangrove swamps are often good fishing grounds. At low tide, clusters of oysters and mussels are exposed on the mangrove "knees," or lower branches. Clams can be found in the mud at the base of trees. Crabs are very active among branches or roots and over mud. Fish can be caught at high tide. Snails are found on mud or clinging to roots. *Do not eat shellfish that are not covered at high tide or those from a colony containing diseased members.*

Throughout the warm regions of the world, there are various plants which the natives use for poisoning fish. The active poison in these plants is harmful only to cold-blooded animals. Man can eat fish filled by this poison without any ill effects whatsoever. In the southwest Pacific, the seeds and bark from the barringtonia tree (figure 2-34), are commonly used as a source of fish poison.

The barringtonia tree usually grows along the seashore. In southeast Asia, the derris plant is widely used as a source of fish poison. The derris plant, a large woody vine, is also used to produce a commercial fish poison called rotenone.

The most common method of using fish-poison plants is to crush the plant parts (most often the roots) and mix them in water. Drop large quantities of the crushed plants into pools or the head-waters of small streams containing fish. Within a short time, the fish will rise in a helpless state to the surface. After putting in the poison, follow slowly down stream and pick up the fish as they come to the surface, sink to the bottom, or swim crazily to the bank. A stick dam or obstruction will aid you in collecting fish as they float down-stream.

The husk of "green" black walnuts can be crushed and sprinkled into small, sluggish streams and pools to act as a fish stupefying agent.

Commercial rotenone can be used in much the same manner as crushed derris roots. However, rotenone has no effect if dusted over the surface of a pond. Mix it to a malted-milk consistency with a little water, and then distribute it in the water. If the concentration is strong, it takes effect within 2 minutes in warm water, or it may take an hour in colder water. Fish sick enough to turn over on their backs will eventually die. An ounce of 12% rotenone kills every fish for a half mile down a stream that is about 25 feet wide.

A few facts to remember about the use of rotenone are:

• It is very swift-acting in warm water at 70°F. and above.

• It works more slowly in cold water and is not practical in water below 50° or 55°F.

• It can best be applied in small ponds, streams, or tidal pools.

• Don't use too much or it will be wasted. However, too little will not be effective.

A small container of 12% rotenone (1-2 oz.) is a valuable addition to any emergency kit. Do not expose it unnecessarily to air or light; it retains its toxicity best if kept in a dark-colored vial.

Lime thrown in a small pond or tidal pool will kill a fish in the pool. Burn coral and sea shells to obtain lime.

Preparation of Animal Food

Survivors must know how to exploit to their advantage the meat of game and fish and how to accomplish this with the least effort and physical exertion. Many men have died from starvation because they had failed to take full advantage of a game carcass. They abandoned the carcass on the mistaken theory that they could secure more game whenever needed.

TRANSPORTATION OF MEAT. If the animal is large, the first impulse usually is to begin operations by packing the meat to camp. If possible, pack your camp to the animal so more of the meat can be used.

A procedure often advocated for transporting the kill is to use the skin as a sled for dragging the meat to camp. When the entire animal is dragged, this procedure may prove satisfactory only on frozen lakes or rivers, over very smooth snow-covered terrain, or, in the case of seals, on polar ice. In rough or brush-covered country, however, it is generally most difficult, if not impossible, to use this method. Mountain sheep or other large mountain animals frequently can be dragged down a snow-filled gully to the base of the mountain. If meat is the only consideration, and you do not care about the condition of the skin, mountain game can sometimes be rolled for long distances. First, gut the animal and sew up the incision. Once the bottom of the hill is reached, almost invariably the method is either to back-pack your meat to camp, making several trips if no other survivors are present, or to pack your camp to the animal. Under survival conditions, your home is on your back. Obviously, there is no reason to pack 100 pounds of meat to camp when you can pack your outfit to the animal.

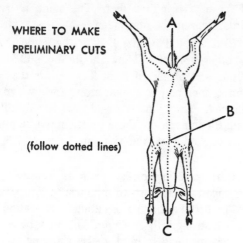

WHERE TO MAKE
PRELIMINARY CUTS

(follow dotted lines)

The first step in skinning is to turn the animal on its back and with a sharp knife cut through the skin on a straight line, from the end of the tail bone to a point under its neck, A-C on the diagram. In making this cut, pass around the anus and, with great care, press the skin open until you can insert the first two fingers between the skin and the thin membrane inclosing the guts. When the fingers can be forced forward, place the blade of the knife between the fingers, blade up, with the knife held firmly. As you force the fingers forward, palm upward, follow with the knife blade, cutting the skin but not cutting the membrane.

If the animal is a male, cut the skin parallel to, but not touching, the penis. If the tube leading from the bladder is accidentally cut, a messy job and unclean meat will result. If the gall or urine bladders are broken, washing will help clean the meat. Otherwise, it is best not to wash meat but to allow it to form a protective glaze.

On reaching the ribs, it is no longer possible to force the fingers forward, because the skin adheres more strongly to flesh and bone. Furthermore, care is no longer necessary. The cut to point C can be quickly completed by alternately forcing the knife under the skin and lifting it. With the central cut completed, make side cuts consisting of incisions through the skin, running from central cut A-C up the inside of each leg to the knee and hock joints. Then make cuts around the front legs just above the knee and around the hind legs above the hocks. Make the final cross cut at point C, and then cut completely around the neck and the back of the ears. Now is the time to begin skinning.

On a small or medium-sized animal, one man can skin on each side. The easiest method is to begin at the corners where the cuts meet. When the animal is large, three men can skin at the same time. However you should remember that when it is getting dark and hands are clumsy because of the cold, a sharp skinning knife can make a deep wound. So, keep well away from the man next to you.

When you have skinned down on the animal's side as far as you can, roll the carcass on its side to continue on the back. Before doing so, spread out the loose skin to prevent the meat from touching the ground and picking up sand and dirt. Follow the same procedure on the opposite side until the skin is free.

In opening the membrane which incloses the guts, follow the same procedure you followed in cutting the skin by using the fingers of one hand as a guard for the knife and to separate the intestines from the membrane. You can cut away this thin membrane along the ribs and sides in order to see better. Be careful to avoid cutting the intestines or bladder. The large intestine passes through an aperture in the pelvis. This tube must be separated with a knife from the bone surrounding it. Tie a knot in the bladder tube to prevent the escape of urine. With these steps accomplished, the insides can be easily disengaged from the back and removed from the carcass.

The intestines of a well-conditioned animal are covered with a lace-like layer of fat, which can be lifted off and placed on nearby bushes to dry for later use. The kidneys are embedded in the back, forward of the pelvis, and are covered with fat. Running forward from the kidneys on each side of the backbone are two long strips of chop-meat or muscle called tenderloin or backstrap. Eat this after the liver, heart, and kidneys as it is usually very tender (tenderloin). Edible meat can also be removed from the head, brisket, ribs, backbone, and pelvis.

Large animals should be quartered. To do this, cut down between the first and second rib and then sever the backbone with your axe or machete. Cut through the brisket of the front half and then chop lengthwise through the backbone so that you have two front quarters. On the rear half, cut through the pelvic bone and lengthwise through the backbone. When speed is advisable, the front legs and shoulders can be quickly separated from the body with a knife.

Figure 2-35. Skinning and Butchering

When the weight of the meat proves excessive and moving of the base camp is not practicable, eat some of the animal at the scene of the kill. To avoid spoilage, eat the heart, liver, and kidneys as soon as possible. All of the meaty parts of the skull such as the brain, tongue, eyes, and flesh should also be eaten.

In a severe hunger emergency, the intestines are palatable if thoroughly cleaned in water, then wrapped around a stick and roasted over coals. The large intestine, cooked in this manner, is considered a delicacy by some natives.

Remove the bones from the meat. Leg bones laid on a bed of coals roast quickly and can be easily cracked with light taps of a knife or stone to expose the marrow, which is highly prized as food by hunters.

SKINNING AND BUTCHERING. Under survival conditions, skinning and butchering must be done carefully so that every edible pound of meat can be saved.

If you decide before skinning that you do not want the skin, a rough job can be done. However, think well before throwing the skin away. A square of skin, long enough to reach from your head to your knees, will not weigh much when green dried, and is one of the best ground cloths to use under your sleeping bag on frozen ground or snow. Snow will not stick to the skin if you lay it hair side up.

Immediately after a kill is the best time to skin and butcher. However, if you kill an animal late in the day, you can make the preliminary cut. A-C, gut the animal, and return early next morning to do the skinning. Be sure to place the carcass so that predators cannot get to it. Then, if the site is visited, the marauder will usually eat only the guts.

When preparing meat under survival conditions, take care not to discard edible fat. This is especially important when, as is often the case in the arctic, diet must consist almost entirely of meat. Fat must be eaten in order to provide a complete diet. Many men think that they are unable to eat fat. This is because with a plentiful, civilized diet, meat fat is not a necessity. Under emergency conditions, however, when sugar or vegetable oils are lacking, fat *must* be eaten. Rabbits lack fat,

and the fact that a man will die on a diet consisting of rabbit *meat alone* indicates the importance of fat in a primitive diet. The same is true of birds, such as the ptarmigan.

Birds should be handled in the same manner as other animals. They should be gutted after killing and protected from flies. Birds that carry no fat, such as ptarmigan, crow, and owl, may be skinned. The skins of waterfowl are usually fat and, for this reason, these birds should be plucked and cooked with the skin on. The giblets may also be eaten.

Carrion-eating birds, such as vultures, must be boiled for at least 20 minutes, to kill parasites, before further cooking or eating. Fish-eating birds have a strong, fish-oil flavor. This may be lessened by baking them in mud, or by skinning them before cooking.

The best meat on a lizard is the hind quarters and tails. Eat the legs of a frog. Turtles have edible flesh on legs, neck, and tail, and on their bodies.

Skin all frogs and snakes. Remove and discard skin, head, and internal organs.

CARE OF MEAT. The greatest danger to meat comes during weather warm enough to allow flies to deposit their eggs, or "blow" the meat. Even while you are skinning an animal, flies can enter bullet holes or any small cavity and lay eggs, which turn into maggots in a few days. The *only* way to prevent fly-blow is to make it impossible for a fly to touch the meat. Do this by wrapping the meat loosely in parachute material or other fabric. Wrap it loosely, so that an airspace of an inch or two is formed between the meat and the sack.

When meat is to be backpacked during the day, it should be rolled in fabric or clothing and placed inside the pack to be carried. This soft material acts as a nonconductor in keeping the meat cool.

In sparsely settled regions, native dogs will smell meat at incredible distances and raid the meat cache at night. Be careful to guard meat from dogs and other predatory animals.

Smoking or Drying Meat. Cutting meat across the grain in thin strips and either drying it in the wind or smoking it will produce "jerky." In warm or damp weather when meat deteriorates rapidly, smoking over a smoldering fire can prevent its spoiling for some time. Take care to keep the meat from getting too hot.

Willow, alders, cottonwood, birch, and dwarf birch make the best smoking woods. Do not use pitch woods, such as fir and pine, as they make the meat unpalatable.

A paratepee (figure 2-15) would work well for the smoking process. By tying meat to the upper ends of the poles and closing the smoke flaps, a good concentration of smoke is obtained. Efficient smoking also can be done by laying fabric over a drying rack and building the fire underneath.

Hang all drying meat high to keep it away from animals. Cover to prevent blowfly infestation. If mold forms on the outside, brush or wash off before eating. In damp weather, smoked or air-dried meat must be redried to prevent molding.

Reptile meat may be dried by placing on hot rocks or hanging in the sun.

Preserving Cooked Meat. To preserve cooked animal food, recook it once each day, especially in warm weather.

Care of Fish and Shell Food

Cleaning and Scaling Fish. Immediately after you land a fish, bleed it by cutting out the gills and large blood vessels that lie next to the backbone. Scale and wash the fish in clean water.

Some fish, such as members of the trout family, do not need to be scaled. Others such as catfish and sturgeon have no scales, but you can skin them.

Some small salt water fish can be eaten with a minimum of cleaning. Their scales are loose and drop off or can be washed off immediately after the fish are caught. The stomach and intestines can be flipped out with the thumb. These fish are oily, highly nutritious, and good—even raw.

Preservation of Fish. The method used to preserve fish through several days of warm weather is similar to that used in preserving meat.

When there is no danger of predatory animals disturbing the fish, lay the fish on available fabric. Allow fish to cool all night. Early the next morning, before the air gets warm, roll the fish in the fabric (figure 2-36). This bundle can be placed inside your pack. During rest periods, or whenever the pack is removed, place it in the shade, if

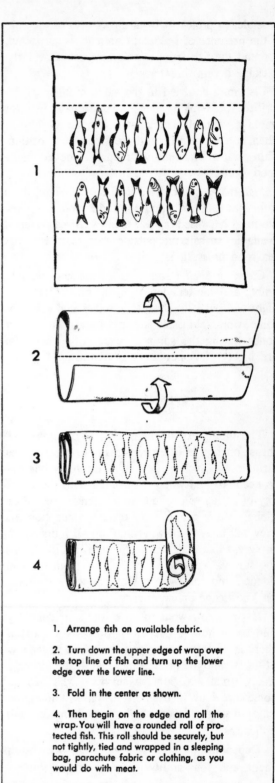

1. Arrange fish on available fabric.

2. Turn down the upper edge of wrap over the top line of fish and turn up the lower edge over the lower line.

3. Fold in the center as shown.

4. Then begin on the edge and roll the wrap. You will have a rounded roll of protected fish. This roll should be securely, but not tightly, tied and wrapped in a sleeping bag, parachute fabric or clothing, as you would do with meat.

Figure 2-36. Fish Preservation

possible, to protect it from direct rays of the sun. If the presence of predatory animals is suspected, suspend the fish from a pole or tree. Cover the package if rain threatens.

Fish may be dried in the same manner as described for smoking meat. To prepare fish for smoking, cut off heads and remove backbone. Then, spread them fat and skewer in that position. Thin willow branches with bark removed make good skewers.

Fish may also be dried in the sun. Hang them from branches or spread on hot rocks. When the meat has dried, splash them with sea water, if available, to salt the outside. Do not keep any sea food unless it is well dried or salted.

Cleaning Shell Food. Clams, oysters, mussels, crabs, and lobsters left in clean sea water overnight will partially clean themselves and save you some work. Mussels are poisonous in tropical zones during the summer, especially when seas are highly phosphorescent or reddish.

PLANT FOOD

The thought of having a diet of "rabbit food" thrust on him is often repugnant to the stranded airman, and such an idea is likely to be the first to occur to him when confronted with the necessity of eating wild plants in a strange area of the globe. Many people have the misconception that they will have to crawl around on all fours, chewing grass like a sick dog. Such is not the case if the survival episode is entered into with the confidence and intelligence that can only be based on knowledge or experience.

If you know what to look for, can identify it, and know how to prepare it properly for eating, there is no reason why you can't find sustenance, at least, and perhaps some real tasty food. In many isolated regions, a survivor who has had some previous instruction in plant finding can enjoy dishes which the folks back home consider delicacies.

Depending on your survival area, your equipment, and your ability to forage for all kinds of food, your diet possibly will be unbalanced—too much meat and fat in some cases, too much fruit and vegetables in others. But remember, if your diet tips in favor of plant foods, you'll be much better off in most cases than if you were existing mainly on a menu of meat. Of course, in the arctic regions, the heat-producing ingredients of meat and fats are essential to the diet, but elsewhere a strictly vegetarian diet will sustain you quite well. Meat supplies the body with proteins, which build muscle, but many plant foods (especially seeds and nuts) supply enough for normal efficiency. Plants provide carbohydrates, which give the body energy and supply calories. Carbohydrates keep your weight and energy up, and include such important food products as starches and sugars.

Plant food can be dried by wind, air, sun, or fire, with or without the aid of smoke. A combination of these can be used. The main object is to get rid of the water. Plantains, bananas, breadfruit, leaves, berries and other wild fruits can be dried. Cut them into thin slices and place in the sun or dry over a fire.

As a documented and authoritative example of the value of a strictly plant diet in survival, the case of a Chinese botanist who had been drafted into the Japanese Army during World War II can be cited. Isolated with his company in a remote section of the Philippines, this Chinese botanist kept 60 of his fellow soldiers alive for 16 months by finding wild plants and preparing them properly. He selected 6 men to assist him, and then found 25 examples of edible plants in the vicinity of their camp. He acquainted the men with these samples, showing them what parts of the plants could be used as food. Then he sent the men out to look for similar plants and had them separate the new plants according to the original examples, to avoid any poisonous plant mingling with the edible ones.

The results of this effort were impressive. Though all the men had a natural desire for ordinary food, none suffered physically from the plant food diet. The report was especially valuable because the botanist kept a careful record of all the food used, the results, and the comments of the men. This case history reflects the same opinions as those found in questionnaires directed to American survivors during World War II.

Another advantage of a plant diet is availability. In many cases, you may be in a situation in which

1

Never eat large quantities of a strange plant food without first testing it.

2

When cooking facilities are available:

a. Get rid of any disagreeable taste by boiling the plant in water for 5 to 15 minutes.

b. Take a teaspoonful of the plant food, prepared in the way it will be used, hold it in your mouth for 5 minutes.

3

If, by this time, no burning sensation occurs, swallow it. Wait 8 hours. If no ill effects such as nausea, cramps, or diarrhea result, eat a handful and wait 8 hours. If no ill effects show up at the end of this time, the plant food may be considered edible. Remember that olives are bitter and grapefruit is sour, and that you are trying a new food, so that an unpleasant taste does not always mean the plant is poisonous or even unpalatable.

4

When cooking facilities are not available; follow instructions in rule 2b.

In general, it is considered safe to try foods that you observe being eaten by birds and mammals. Food eaten by rodents (mice, rats, rabbits, beavers, squirrels, muskrats), or by monkeys, baboons, bears, raccoons, and various other omnivorous animals (meat and plant eaters) is usually safe for eating.

CAUTION

1. Cook all plant foods when in doubt about the edibility (see illustration of poisonous plants, attachment 1.)

2. Small quantities of a poisonous plant are not necessarily dangerous. A noteworthy exception is the death angel mushroom (Amanita phalloides), which may prove fatal after eating a few spoonfuls. Avoid mushrooms and other fungi.

3. Cooking will not dissipate the poisonous properties of mushrooms.

4. Avoid eating untested plants that have a milky juice. Also avoid letting the juice contact your skin. Exceptions to this include wild figs, breadfruit, and ripe papayas, all of which contain milky juice but which are quite harmless and nonpoisonous, cooked or uncooked.

5. To avoid ergot poisoning from eating infected heads of cereal grains or other food grasses, discard all grain heads having black spurs in place of normal seed grains.

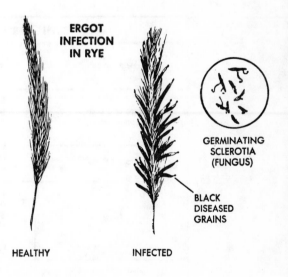

ERGOT INFECTION IN RYE

GERMINATING SCLEROTIA (FUNGUS)

BLACK DISEASED GRAINS

HEALTHY   INFECTED

Figure 2-37. Edibility Rules

you can't forage for animal food. You may be injured, unarmed, in enemy territory, exhausted, or in an area which lacks wild life.

If you're convinced that you can depend on plants for your daily food needs, the next question in your mind is "where to get what, and how."

Kinds of Plants and Where to Find Them

Experts estimate that there are about 300,000 classified plants growing on the surface of the earth, including many which thrive on mountain tops and on the floors of the oceans. However, you won't need to know about all these plants. For the purpose of your study, and perhaps your later use, the brief discussions and the illustrations in attachment 1 touch only on plant foods which fill certain requirements.

The first consideration, of course, is that the plant be edible, and preferably palatable. Next, it must be fairly abundant in the area or areas in which it is found, and if it includes an inedible or poisonous variety in its family, the edible plant must be distinguishable to the average eye from the inedible or poisonous one. Usually a plant has been selected because one special part is edible, such as the stalk, the fruit, or the nut.

Most of the plants, especially those illustrated in this manual, are good general examples of food courses which are similar to many other plants of the same variety. *Familiarity with these "pilot plants" should enable you to evaluate the food possibilities of other plants with which you are not directly acquainted.* For example, the color of the juice in the stalk of one plant might lead you to try another one in which the juice seems to be of the same color and consistency. Since there are an estimated 120,000 varieties of edible plants, you will have to rely on a bit of training and a lot of sound judgment in selecting plants.

Before you learn what to look for and where to look for it, you will find it valuable to know just a bit about the edible parts of plants.

Edible Parts of Food Plants

You will find new plants of which every component is edible, but many plants which you may encounter will have one or more identifiable parts that have considerable food or thirst-quenching value. The great variety of plant component-parts which might contain substance of food value is shown in figure 2-38. Each of these parts is described and illustrated, and the accompanying discussion defines the climatic or geographic zone in which plants bearing each part can be found.

EDIBLE PARTS OF PLANTS	
Underground Parts	Tubers Roots and Rootstalks Bulbs
Stems and Leaves (potherbs)	Shoots and Stems Leaves Pith Bark
Flower Parts	Flowers Pollen
Fruits	Fleshy Fruits (dessert and vegetable) Seeds and Grains Nuts Seed Pods Pulps
Gums and Resins	
Saps	

Figure 2-38. Edible Parts of Plants

Tubers. The potato is an example of an edible tuber. Many other kinds of plants produce tubers including the tropical yam, the Eskimo potato, and tropical water lilies. Tubers are usually found below ground and must be dug out. Tubers are rich in starch and should be cooked by roasting in an earth oven or by boiling.

The following plants with edible tubers are illustrated in attachment 1.

Arrowroot, East Indian
Bean, Yam
Chufa (Nut Grass)

Taro
Water Lily (Tropical)
Yam, Tropical

Roots and Rootstalks. Edible roots are often several feet in length and usually are not swollen. Many plants produce roots which may be eaten for food.

Edible rootstalks are underground stems which have become much thickened. Some kinds are several inches thick, and in comparison to true roots, are usually relatively short and jointed.

Both true roots and rootstalks are storage organs rich in stored starch.

The following plants with edible roots or rootstalks (rhizomes) are illustrated in attachment 1.

Baobab
Bean, Goa
Bracken
Calla, Wild (Water Arum)
Canna Lily
Cattail
Chicory
Horse-Radish
Lotus Lily
Manioc

Pine, Screw
Plantain, Water
Polypody
Reindeer Moss
Rock Tripe
Rush, Flowering
Spinach, Ceylon
Ti Plant
Tree Fern
Water Lily (Temperate Zone)

Bulbs. The most common edible bulb is the wild onion, which easily can be detected by its characteristic odor. In Turkey and central Asia, the bulb of the wild tulip may be eaten. Wild onions may be eaten uncooked, but other kinds of bulbs are more palatable if cooked. All bulbs contain a high percentage of starch. *(Some bulbs are poisonous; see death camas, attachment 1.)*

The following plants with edible bulbs are illustrated in attachment 1.

Lily, Wild
Onion, Wild

Tulip, Wild

Shoots and Stems. All edible shoots grow in much the same fashion as asparagus. The young shoots of ferns (fiddleheads) and especially those of bamboo and numerous kinds of palms are desirable for food. Some kinds of shoots may be eaten uncooked, but most are better if first parboiled for 5 to 10 minutes, the water drained off, and the shoots reboiled until they are sufficiently cooked for eating.

The following plants with edible shoots and stems are illustrated in attachment 1.

Agave (Century Plant)	Palm, Coconut	Purslane
Bamboo	Palm, Fishtail	Reindeer Moss
Bean, Goa	Palm, Nipa	Rhubarb, Wild
Bracken	Palm, Rattan	Rock Tripe
Cattail	Palm, Sago	Spinach, Ceylon
Colocynth	Palm, Sugar	Spreading Wood Fern
Lotus Lily	Papaya	Sugar Cane
Luffa Sponge	Pokeweed	Tree Fern
Palm, Buri	Polypody	Water Lily (Tropical)
		Willow, Arctic

Leaves. The leaves of spinach-type plants (pot-herbs), such as wild mustard, wild lettuce, lambs quarter, and many others may be eaten either raw or cooked. Prolonged cooking, however, destroys most of the vitamins. Plants which produce edible leaves are perhaps the most numerous of all edible plants.

The young tender leaves of nearly all nonpoisonous plants are edible. Testing the different kinds is one of the joys of the survival experience.

The following plants with edible leaves are illustrated in attachment 1.

Amaranth	Luffa Sponge	Rock Tripe
Baobab	Orach, Sea	Sorrel, Wild
Bean, Goa	Papaya	Spinach, Ceylon
Chickory	Pine, Screw	Spreading Wood Fern
Dock	Plantain	Tamarind
Luffa	Pokeweed	Taro
Horse-Radish	Prickly Pear	Ti Plant
Lettuce, Water	Purslane	Willow, Arctic
Lotus Lily	Reindeer Moss	

Pith. Some plants have an edible pith in the center of the stem. The pith of some kinds of tropical plants is quite large. Pith of the sago palm is particularly valuable because of its high food value.

The following palms with edible pith (starch) are illustrated in attachment 1.

Buri	Fishtail	Sago
Coconut	Rattan	Sugar

Barks. The inner bark of a tree—the layer next to the wood—may be eaten raw or cooked. Under famine conditions, it is possible in northern areas to make flour from the inner bark of such trees as the cottonwood, aspen, birch, willow, and pine. The outer bark should be avoided in all cases, because this part contains large amounts of bitter tannin. Pine bark is high in vitamin C. The outer bark of pines can be scraped away and the inner bark stripped from the trunk and eaten fresh, dried, or cooked, or it may be pulverized into flour. Bark is most palatable when newly formed in spring. As food, bark is most useful in the arctic regions, where plant food is often scarce.

Flowers and Buds. Fresh flowers may be eaten as part of a salad or to supplement a stew. The hibiscus flower is commonly eaten throughout the southwest Pacific area. In South America, the people of the Andes eat nasturtium flowers. In India, it is common to eat the flowers of many kinds of plants as part of a vegetable curry. Flowers of desert plants may also be eaten.

Plants with edible flowers are illustrated in attachment 1.

Abal	Colocynth	Papaya
Banana	Horse-Radish	
Caper, Wild	Luffa Sponge	

Pollen. Pollen looks like yellow dust. All pollen is high in food value, and in some plants, especially the cattail, quantities of pollen may easily be collected and eaten as a kind of gruel (see illustration of cattail in attachment 1).

FRUITS

Edible fruits can be divided into *dessert,* or sweet kinds, and *vegetable,* or non-sweet kinds. Both are the seedbearing part of the plant.

Dessert fruits are often plentiful, in all areas of the world where plants grow. For instance, in the far North there are blueberries and crowberries; in the temperate zones, cherries, plums, and apples; and in the American deserts, fleshy cactus fruits. Tropical areas have more kinds of edible fruit than other areas, and a list would be endless. Dessert fruits may be cooked or, for maximum vitamin content, left uncooked.

Common vegetable fruits include the tomato, cucumber, pepper, eggplant, and okra.

Fleshy Fruits (Dessert). Plants with edible fruits (dessert) are illustrated in attachment 1.

Apple, Wild	Cranberry	Plum, Batako
Bael Fruit	Fig, Wild	Pokeberry
Banana	Grape, Wild	Prickly Pear
Bignay	Huckleberry	Rose-Apple
Blueberry, Wild	Jujube, Common	Soursop
Bullocks Heart	Mango	Sweetsop
Cloudberry	Mulberry	Whortleberry
Crabapple	Papaya	

Fleshy Fruits (Vegetable). Plants with edible fruits (vegetables) are in attachment 1.

Breadfruit	Horse-Radish	Plantain
Caper, Wild	Luffa Sponge	

Seeds and Grains. Seeds of many plants, such as buckwheat, ragweed, amaranth, goosefoot (chenopodium), and the beans and peas from beanlike plants, contain oils and are rich in protein. The grains of all cereals and many other grasses, including millet, are also an extremely valuable source of plant protein. They may either be ground between stones, mixed with water and cooked to make porridge, or parched or roasted over hot stones. In this state, they are still wholesome and may be kept for long periods without further preparation.

The following plants with edible seeds and grains are illustrated in attachment 1.

Amaranth	Millet, Italian	Rice
Bamboo	Millet, Pearl	Sterculia
Baobab	Orach, Sea	St. Johns Bread
Bean, Goa	Palm, Nipa	Tamarind
Colocynth	Pine, Screw	Water Lily (Tropical)
Lotus Lily	Purslane	Water Lily (Temperate Zone)
Luffa Sponge		

Nuts. Nuts are among the most nutritious of all raw plant foods and contain an abundance of valuable protein. Plants bearing edible nuts occur in all the climatic zones of the world and in all continents except the arctic regions. Inhabitants of the temperate zones are familiar with walnuts, filberts, almonds, hickory nuts, acorns, hazelnuts, beechnuts, and pine nuts, to mention just a few. In the tropical zones are found coconuts and other palm nuts, brazil nuts, cashew nuts, and macadamia nuts.

Most nuts can be eaten raw, but some kinds, such as acorns, are better cooked.

The following plants with edible nuts are illustrated in attachment 1.

Almond	Filbert (Hazelnut)	Palm, Sago
Almond, Indian or Tropical	Oak, English (Acorn)	Palm, Sugar
Beechnut	Palm, Buri	Pine
Cashew	Palm, Coconut	Pistachio, Wild
Chestnut, Water (Trapa Nut)	Palm, Fishtail	Walnut
Chestnut		

Seed Pods. Seed pods are really fruits (vegetable), but it is better to list them as a separate food source, because of the large number of edible seed pods in the bean and pea family.

Young bean pods may be boiled until tender.

Plants with edible seed pods are illustrated in attachment 1.

Bean, Goa	Lotus Lily	Tamarind
Horse-Radish		

Pulps. The pulp around the seeds of many fruits is the only part eaten, as, for example, the pomegranate. Some fruits produce sweet pulp; others have a tasteless or even bitter pulp. Plants that produce edible pulp include the custard apple, inga pod, breadfruit, and tamarind. In the case of breadfruit, the pulp must be cooked, whereas in other plants the pulp may be eaten uncooked. Use the edibility rules in all cases of doubt.

Plants with edible pulp are illustrated in attachment 1.

Baobab	Pine, Screw	St. Johns Bread
Juniper	Rose, Wild	Tamarind
Palm, Rattan		

--- GUMS AND RESINS ---

When plant sap collects on the outside of the plant and hardens as a deposit, it is called *gum*, if soft and soluble in water, and *resin*, if hard and not soluble in water. You are perhaps familiar with the gum which exudes from cherry trees and the resin which seeps from pine trees. These plant byproducts are edible and are a good source of nutritious food which should not be overlooked.

In desert and tropical forests areas, drinking water is often scarce. Vines or other plant parts may be tapped as a potential source of drinking water or water substitute. The sap of palms, for instance, is a thirst-quencher. The liquid is obtained by decapitating the flower stalk and letting the fluid drain into some sort of vessel (such as a bamboo joint). Furthermore, palm sap, with its high sugar content, is highly nutritious. Drinking water can be obtained from the ti plant, grape vine, rattan palm, coconut palm, cactus, and the malee plant.

The best method of procuring drinking water from vines is as follows: Make a slanting cut high on the stem, and then cut the vine off about 6 feet below this cut. Water will begin to flow at the lower end. Either drink directly from the freshly cut end or let the liquid drain into a container.

Plants with edible sap and drinking water are illustrated in attachment 1.

Acacia, Sweet (water)	Palm, Fishtail (sap)	Palm, Fishtail
Agave (water)	Palm, Nipa (sap)	Palm, Sago
Banana (water)	Palm, Rattan (water)	Palm, Sugar
Cactus (water)	Palm, Sago (sap)	Sugar Cane
Colocynth (water)	Palm, Sugar (sap)	Coffee substitutes:
Cuipo Tree (water)	Saxaul (water)	Beechnut
Grape (water)	Sugar Cane (sap)	Chicory
Palm, Buri (sap)	Sugar producing plants:	Chufa (Nut Grass)
Palm, Coconut (sap)	Palm, Buri	

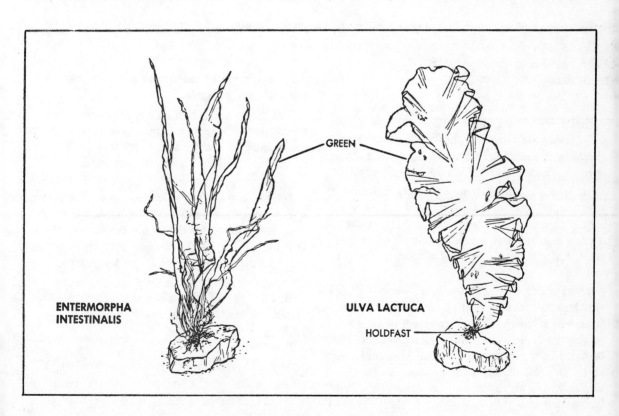

GREEN

ENTERMORPHA INTESTINALIS

ULVA LACTUCA

HOLDFAST

Figure 2-39a. Edible Green Seaweeds

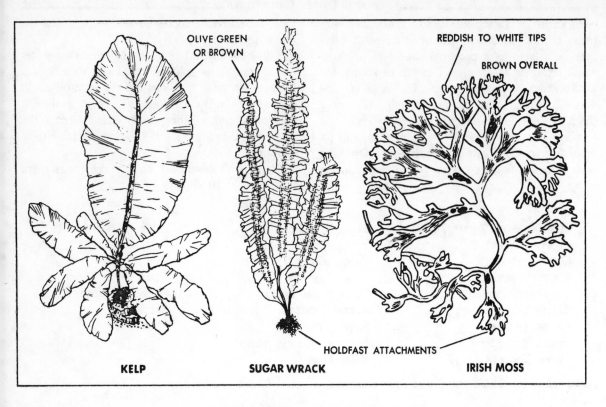

OLIVE GREEN OR BROWN

REDDISH TO WHITE TIPS

BROWN OVERALL

HOLDFAST ATTACHMENTS

KELP   SUGAR WRACK   IRISH MOSS

Figure 2-39b. Edible Brown Seaweeds

Seaweeds

Seaweed is a form of marine algae, and many varieties which are quite edible may be found on or near the shores of the larger ocean areas. Properly prepared seaweed can be an important part of the diet, and is for millions of people.

In large quantities, and especially before the stomach is conditioned to it, seaweed may be a violent cathartic. Eaten in moderation, however, it is a valuable source of iodine, other minerals, and vitamin C, which is a good scurvy preventive.

In selecting seaweeds for food, choose plants attached to rocks or floating free, because those stranded on the beach for any length of time may be spoiled or decayed. Thin, tender varieties can be dried over a fire or dried in the sun until crisp and then crushed and used in a soup or broth to add flavor. The thick, leathery seaweeds should be washed and then boiled for a short time to soften them, after which they may be eaten together with other foods, such as fish or vegetables.

Some kinds can be eaten raw, after you have first tested them for edibility.

The following list of edible seaweeds gives a description of the plant, tells where it may be found, and in many cases suggests a method of preparation. Each variety is illustrated.

GREEN SEAWEEDS. Common green seaweed, often called sea lettuce *(Ulva lactuca),* occurs abundantly on both sides of the Pacific and North Atlantic oceans. After washing it in clean water, use it in the same manner as garden lettuce.

BROWN SEAWEEDS. The most common edible brown seaweeds are the sugar wrack, kelp, and Irish moss.

SUGAR WRACK (Laminaria saccharina). The young stalks of the sugar wrack are sweet to the taste. This seaweed is found on both sides of the Atlantic, and on the coasts of China and Japan.

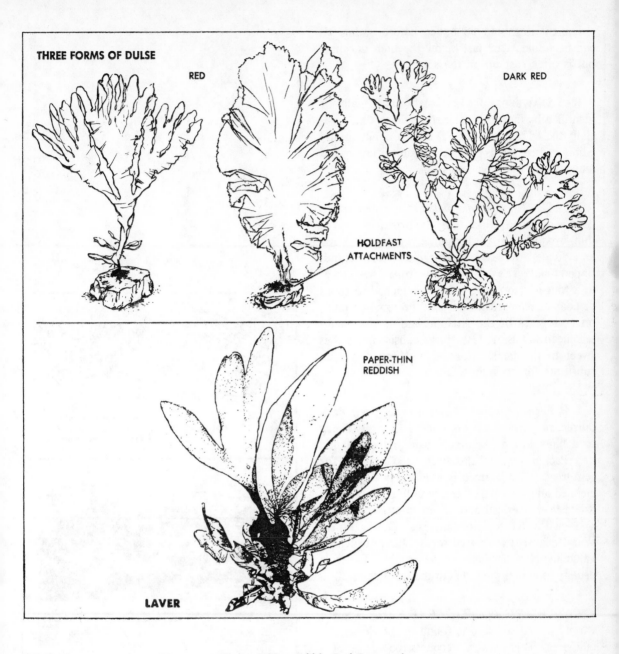

Figure 2-39c. Edible Red Seaweed

EDIBLE KELP (Alaria esculenta). Edible kelp has a short cylindrical stem and thin, wavy olive-green or brown fronds from 1 to several feet in length. It is found in both the Atlantic and Pacific Oceans, usually below the high tide line on submerged ledges and rocky bottoms. Kelp should be boiled before eating to soften it, after which it can be mixed with vegetables or soup.

IRISH MOSS (Chondrus crispus). Irish moss, a variety of brown seaweed, is quite edible, and is often sold in market places. It is found on both sides of the Atlantic Ocean and can be identified by its tough, elastic, and leathery texture. However, when dried it becomes crisp and

53

shrunken; it should be boiled before eating. It can be found at or just below the high tide line, but is often cast up on the shore.

RED SEAWEEDS. Red seaweeds can usually be identified by their characteristic reddish tint, especially the edible varieties. The most common and edible red seaweeds include the dulse, laver, and many warm-water varieties.

DULSE (Rhodymenia palmata). Dulse has a very short stem which quickly broadens into a thin, broad, fan-shaped expanse which is dark red and divided by several clefts into short, round-tipped lobes. The entire plant is from a few inches to a foot in length. It is found attached to rocks or coarser seaweeds, usually at the low-tide level, on both sides of the Atlantic and in the Mediterranean. Dulse is leathery in consistency but is sweet to the taste. If dried and rolled, it can substitute for chewing tobacco.

LAVER (Porphyra). Laver is usually red, dark purple, or purplish-brown, and has a satiny sheen or a filmy luster. Common to both the Atlantic and Pacific areas, it has been used as food for centuries. This seaweed is used as a relish, or is cleaned and then boiled gently until tender. Also, it can be pulverized and added to crushed grains and fried in the form of flatcakes. During World War II, laver was chewed for its thirst-quenching value by New Zealand native troops. Laver is usually found on the beach at the low tide level.

RED WARM-WATER SEAWEED. A great variety of red seaweed is found in the South Pacific area. This seaweed accounts for a large portion of the native diet.

FRESHWATER ALGAE. A freshwater variety of seaweed which is common in China (and also in America and Europe) is the marine alga known as common Nostoc (nostoc commune), and its variety, flagellated nostoc. The latter is peculiar to northwestern China, but common Nostoc may be found in pools in the spring. It forms green, round jellylike lobules about the size of marbles. It is usually dried and used in soups.

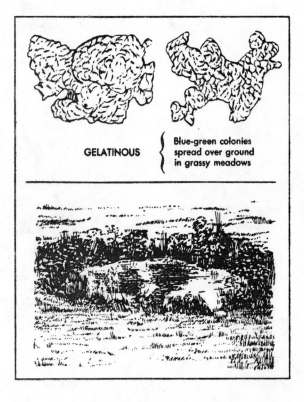

GELATINOUS

Blue-green colonies spread over ground in grassy meadows

Figure 2-39d. Fresh Water Algae

Whether you plan to stay in one place or to .ravel, you will want to know where you are. If you are traveling, you need to know what direction to take. If you are staying, you want to know your location so that you can radio the information to your rescuers. Your position report doesn't have to be accurate to the mile to be helpful; any data you can give reduces the area to be searched.

MAP READING

A map is, in its primary conception, a conventionalized picture of the earth's surface as seen from above, simplified to bring out important details and lettered for added identification. A map represents what is known about the earth rather than what can be seen by an observer. However, a map is selective, in that only that information which is necessary for the map's intended use is included on any one map. Maps also commonly include features which are not visible on the earth, such as parallels, meridians, and political boundaries.

Since it is impossible to portray accurately a round object, such as the earth, on a flat surface, all maps have some elements of distortion. Depending on the intended use, some maps sacrifice constant scale for accuracy in measurement of angles, while others sacrifice accurate measurement of angles for a constant scale. However, most maps used for ground navigation use a compromise projection in which a slight amount of distortion is introduced into the elements which a map portrays, but in which a fairly true picture is given.

Map Symbols

By means of standard symbols, maps show important roads, side roads, trails, towns, villages, woods, streams, lakes, and the features that help you recognize the terrain as you look at it or travel over it. Conventional signs and symbols are standardized. Those which require special explanation are usually contained in the legend included at the bottom of most maps. A great deal of information which is necessary for the proper interpretation of a map is usually printed on the borders of the map. To avoid making serious mistakes, *always read the marginal information before using a map.*

Contour Lines

Contour lines are wavy brown lines on a map and are drawn linking all points at a given height above sea level. These lines are broken in intervals and a figure inserted in the break, such as 6,500, 7,000, 7,500, or 8,000. These figures indicate the height in feet of the contour line above mean sea level. (Some foreign maps have the height indicated in meters, so be careful when using a map for the first time.) Always check the marginal information to find the contour interval. Some of the lines carry no identifying numbers, but since the contour interval is known, the height of any unnumbered line can be determined by its relation to the numbered lines. For example: the contour interval is 100 feet and an unnumbered line is two lines away from the 9,000-foot line and three lines from the 9,500-foot line, the elevation at any point on the unnumbered line is obviously 9,200 feet. The height of any point on a map can be determined by reference to adjacent contour lines. Elevations are further indicated on maps and charts by measured elevations for the peak or highest point of a mountain. The arrangement of the contour lines indicates the form of the land. The contour lines around a ridge point downhill, and those in a valley point upstream. The spacing of contours indicates the steepness of a slope. Contour lines close together indicate a steep slope, and contour lines which are far apart indicate a gentle slope. These are points for people who are traveling on foot to consider when planning a route.

Distance Scales

How far is it fom where you are to where you want to go? Maps give this information by providing the user with a scale to measure distance on the map. These scales can be used to find the distances between any two points on the map. Lay any available straight edge, a folded piece of paper, a string, or the edge of a pencil on the map so that it joins the two points. Mark on the straight edge the position of the two points. Lay the marked straight edge on the graphic scale and read off the distance directly. The same technique can be used to measure distance along a crooked course such as a road or river by breaking the course up into short straight segments.

Proceeding as above discloses the distance in miles on the map only. When traveling across country on the ground, vertical distance as you climb or descend adds to the total distance traveled. For this reason, the transition from air travel to ground travel is difficult for most fliers, and ample allowance must be made for vertical movement when planning travel.

Longitude and Latitude Lines

To describe a location in a city, the intersection of two streets is commonly used. Knowing the name of only one street establishes the general area of the location, but the intersection of two streets constitutes an exact location. In the same fashion, in order to locate a point on a map or chart you must indicate the coordinates of this particular point, in degrees of longitude and latitude.

Latitude can be described as a division of the surface of the earth into north and south. An imaginary circle known as the Equator, drawn around the earth midway between the North and South Poles, serves as the starting point. The surface of the earth north of the Equator is divided into 90 equal divisions by circles drawn parallel to the Equator. Each circle is called a parallel of latitude and is numbered starting from 0° at the Equator to 90° at the North Pole. Any parallel of latitude north of the equator is known as north latitude. The earth's surface south of the Equator is divided in the same manner and is known as south latitude. Each degree is further subdivided into 60 divisions, called minutes. Using this sys-

tem, you will find Offutt AFB, Nebraska, is about 41° and 15′ north of the equator.

Longitude can be described as an east and west division of the earth's surface. Longitude is measured in degrees east and west of a base line which passes through Greenwich, England. This line is a circle which passes through both the North and South Poles and is called the prime meridian. Longitude is divided into 360 equal parts, or degrees. If you stand on the circle passing through Greenwich and face the North Pole, the lines on your left are numbered 1° W, 2° W, to 180° W, and the ones on your right are numbered 1° E, 2° E, to 180° E. Longitudes 180° E and 180° W coincide. Again by using this system, you will find Offutt AFB, Nebraska, to be about 95° and 56′ west of Greenwich.

All navigational maps and charts are laid out in latitude and longitude. The position of any point on the earth is described as so many degrees and minutes east or west of the prime meridian and so many degrees and minutes north or south of the Equator. The approximate location of Offutt AFB, Nebraska, would thus be 41° and 15′ north latitude and 95° and 56′ west longitude.

How to Use a Map

The information printed on a map can be used in any number of ways. In cases where extended travel must be accomplished, a map for planning the route and maintaining travel is extremely valuable.

If you can position yourself on a map, which is a graphic portrayal of the earth's surface, you will provide the basic criteria for planning your travel. Three of the most important steps in movement across country will be:

1. To establish position before movement,

2. To determine an accurate destination, and

3. To be able periodically to pinpoint your progress and position.

To give an accurate picture of the country, a map must be oriented to agree with terrain features. The map can be roughly oriented by holding it so that you can see landmarks in their proper perspective on the printed map. This tech-

Figure 2-47. Map Reading

nique is known as inspection and is particularly useful to you while moving across country. Ideally, the map should be oriented with the help of a compass.

Carefully study the map to determine the best route for your specific needs. The map also provides information on the availability of water, and, to a degree, food, shelter and safety. Learn in advance to use a map well—to predict what you will find when you arrive at some point you cannot now see—then when you have to rely on the map, it will be of maximum value.

To be able to select the route which will offer the fewest obstacles to travel, or which will provide security from observation is of extreme importance.

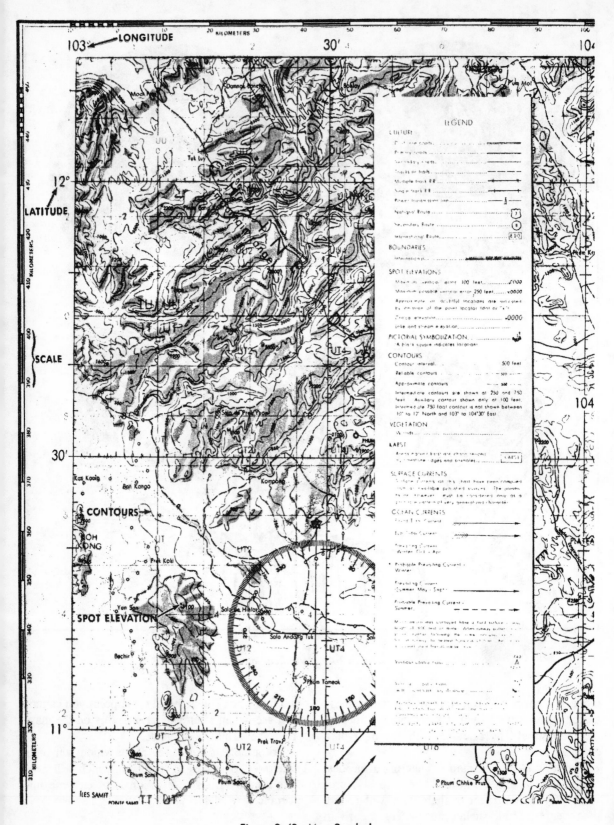

Figure 2-48. Map Symbols

58

DIRECTION FINDING

Use of the Magnetic Compass

Direction is measured in degrees clockwise from north (360° or 0°) through 360 degrees. The most common instrument for measuring direction is the *magnetic compass*. Since most survival kits contain some type of magnetic compass, it is imperative that you know something of its use. Compasses are generally marked in degrees from 0° to 360°; east is 90°, south 180°, and west 270 degrees. The easiest way to understand direction is to consider yourself to be at the center of a large compass. The 360 degrees of your compass dial are now 360 different paths or streets that you may use in following a map. The direction to a given point on the map is determined by measuring the angular distance clockwise from north to that point. This angular distance, expressed in degrees, is the direction of that point from you.

The term "north" is usually considered to mean the direction of the North Geographic Pole. The compass needle points directly to the North Geographic Pole in only a few places on the surface of the earth. The reason for this is that the North and South *Magnetic Poles* do not coincide with the North and South *Geographic Poles*. In ad-dition, deposits of magnetic materials in various regions of the earth keep the compass from pointing to the North Magnetic Pole. A magnetic compass, therefore, points not toward the North Geographic Pole, nor exactly toward the North Magnetic Pole, but to the *magnetic north* for that particular area. The difference between true north and magnetic north is called "variation." Variation is represented on a map by lines joining points of equal variation and is expressed in degrees east and west of a base line where the variation is zero. If you are east of this line, your compass points west of true north, and if you are west of this line, your compass points east of true north.

The right and left borders of any map may be viewed as meridians of longitude. From the bottom to the top, these borders are arrows pointing true north, with only a minor distortion resulting from the portrayal of a spherical surface on a flat plane. The map is a "truc" directional navigational aid which is to be used in conjunction with a "magnetic" device.

The information from the two devices must be merged to allow for practical application. The procedure that accomplishes this merger is referred to as map orientation and is done as shown in figure 2-49.

1. Place the map on a level surface and stabilize it.

2. Place the compass on the map in a manner that brings the true north-south line of the compass (lubber line, sighting wire, compass straight edge, etc.) into line with a north-south line of the map, north-to-north.

3. Now turn map and compass until the magnetic indicator (arrow or needle) of the compass is as many degrees east or west of the true north-south line of the compass as the variation which the area calls for. Variation may be stated or indicated on the map, or may be determined by using celestial aids.

Figure 2-49. Use Compass to Orient Map

Once the map has been oriented, you can pinpoint your position by plotting azimuths on recognizable land features, either natural or manmade, as they appear on the map. To use three such features is best, although two will give good results. This technique is known as triangulation and is performed as follows:

1. Identify the land features to be used and shoot an azimuth to it from your location.

2. Set your compass on the oriented map so that it points to the landmark (on the map) with the same reading.

3. From the landmark, direct your attention back through the center of the compass.

4. Draw a line from the landmark on this heading.

If you repeat this operation using two or three known landmarks, your position on the ground (and on the map) will be where the lines intersect when using two points, or within the triangle formed by the lines when three points are used.

In hostile territory, remember that *the map must not be marked.* You can perform triangulation by using strings and stretching them across the map and then removing them when you have completed your computation.

If you are captured and have in your possession a marked map, the markings would disclose your planned travel and possibly the travel plans of other survivors.

Finding Your Way by Natural Landmarks

Rain or fog may hide the sun, and at times you may have to orient a course by observing landmarks—such as vegetation, sand contours, or snowdrifts—that are affected by prevailing winds. Travel under such conditions is difficult until streams, hills, or a seacoast running in a definite direction comes to your aid.

VEGETATION. Near a seacoast where prevailing winds blow inland from the ocean, thicket growth is dead or stunted on the windward side and slowly increases in height toward the lee side. Individual trees lean away from the prevailing wind and their branches are thicker and longer on the lee side.

SAND. Sand contours are affected by wind but less so than those of snow. Old sand drifts formed by strong winds are more firmly packed than recently formed drifts, and sand lies deeper on the leeward side.

SNOW. Learn the characteristics of drifts by studying snow surfaces after storms. You can tell the direction of the wind by the fact that a snowdrift is, generally, lower and narrower to windward and higher and wider to leeward before dropping off abruptly to a general level. When you travel at night and there is only diffused light which makes no shadows, or if it is so dark that you cannot see the drifts, stop and carefully feel the drifts with your feet or drop on all fours, and examine them with your hands.

Certain desert and arctic regions have characteristic dune and drift patterns. Some of these patterns tend to be seasonal and have been known to change with every storm according to the quadrant from which the storm has developed. If you fly regularly in arctic or desert areas, you should study the patterns in the areas where you fly and understand their value as aids to ground travel.

Daytime Direction and Position Finding

DETERMINING DIRECTION BY STICK AND SHADOW. If the sun is casting a shadow, a simple way to determine direction is the stick and shadow method. Figure 2-50 shows the position of earth from both the summer sun and the winter sun. Between 66.6°N and 66.6°S shadows progress to the east, regardless of the season.

Whether the sun is north or south of you at midday depends on your latitude. North of 23.4° N., the sun is always due south of local noon; and the shadow points north. South of 23.4°S., the sun is always due north at local noon; and the shadow points south. In the tropics, the sun can be either north or south at noon, depending on the date (season) and your position but the shadow progresses to the east regardless of the season.

DIRECTION FROM THE SUN AT SUNRISE AND SUNSET. Figure 2-51 shows the true azimuth of the rising sun and the relative bearing of the setting sun for all the months in the year in the Northern and Southern Hemispheres (the table assumes a level horizon and is inaccurate in

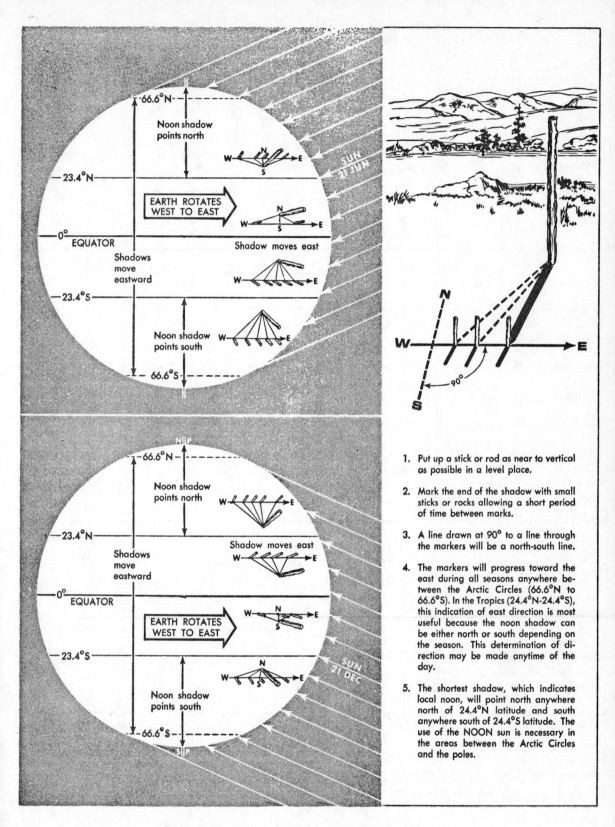

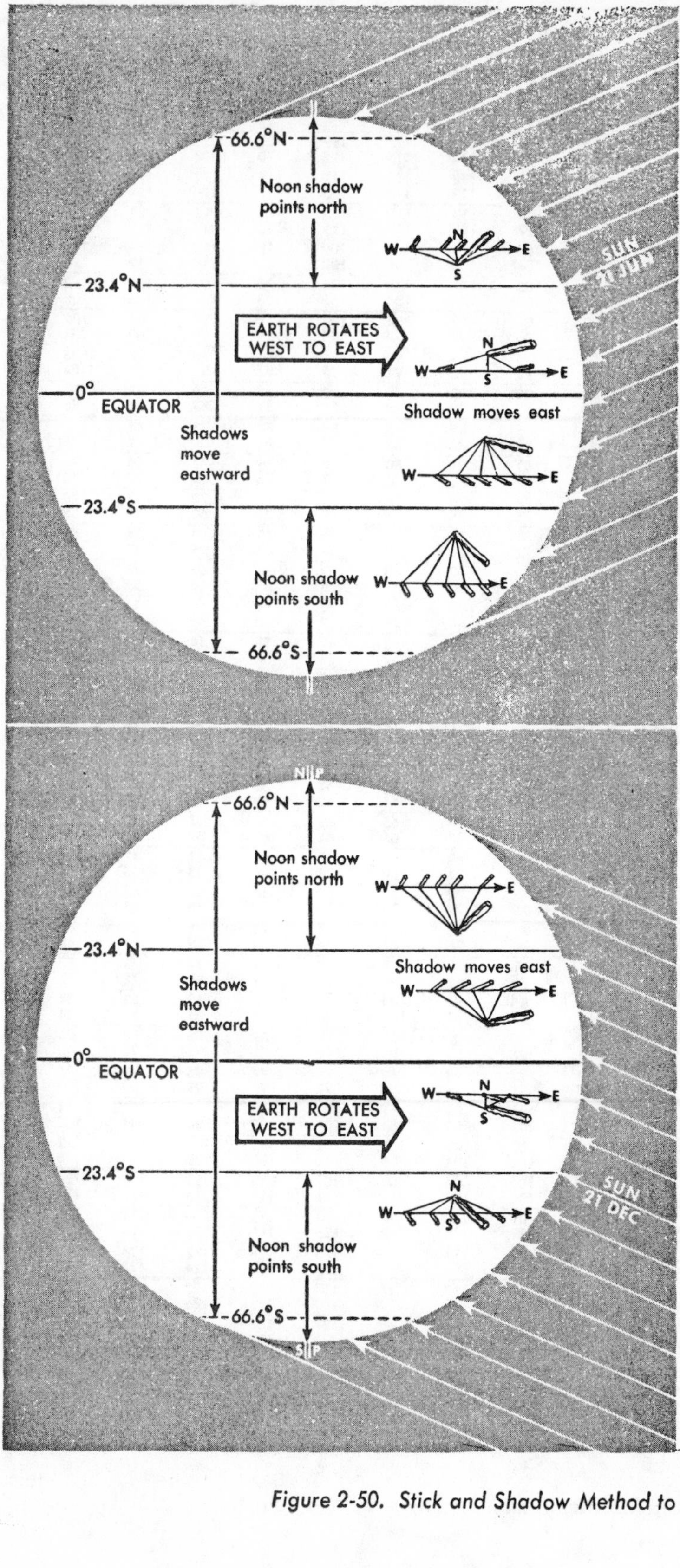
SUN
21 JUN
66.6°N
Noon shadow points north
W
N
S
E
23.4°N
EARTH ROTATES WEST TO EAST
0°
EQUATOR
Shadow moves east
Shadows move eastward
23.4°S
Noon shadow points south
66.6°S
N P
66.6°N
Noon shadow points north
23.4°N
Shadow moves east
Shadows move eastward
0°
EQUATOR
EARTH ROTATES WEST TO EAST
23.4°S
SUN
21 DEC
Noon shadow points south
66.6°S
S P

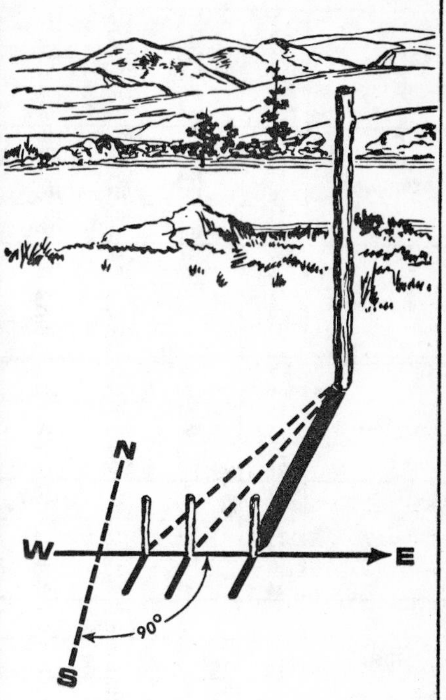
N
W
E
90°
S

1. Put up a stick or rod as near to vertical as possible in a level place.
2. Mark the end of the shadow with small sticks or rocks allowing a short period of time between marks.
3. A line drawn at 90° to a line through the markers will be a north-south line.
4. The markers will progress toward the east during all seasons anywhere between the Arctic Circles (66.6°N to 66.6°S). In the Tropics (24.4°N-24.4°S), this indication of east direction is most useful because the noon shadow can be either north or south depending on the season. This determination of direction may be made anytime of the day.
5. The shortest shadow, which indicates local noon, will point north anywhere north of 24.4°N latitude and south anywhere south of 24.4°S latitude. The use of the NOON sun is necessary in the areas between the Arctic Circles and the poles.

Figure 2-50. Stick and Shadow Method to Find Direction

DATE		Angle to North from the rising or setting sun (level terrain) LATITUDE												
		0°	5°	10°	15°	20°	25°	30°	35°	40°	45°	50°	55°	60°
JANUARY	1	113	113	113	114	115	116	117	118	121	124	127	133	141
	6	112	113	113	113	114	115	116	118	120	123	127	132	140
	11	112	112	112	113	113	114	115	117	119	122	125	130	138
	16	111	111	111	112	112	113	114	116	118	120	124	129	136
	21	110	110	110	111	111	112	113	115	117	119	122	127	133
	26	109	109	109	109	110	111	112	113	115	117	120	124	130
FEBRUARY	1	107	107	108	108	108	109	110	111	113	115	117	121	126
	6	106	106	106	106	107	107	108	109	111	113	115	118	123
	11	104	104	105	105	105	106	107	108	109	110	112	116	120
	16	103	103	103	103	103	104	105	106	107	108	110	112	116
	21	101	101	101	101	101	102	102	103	104	105	107	109	112
	26	99	99	99	99	100	100	100	101	102	103	104	106	108
MARCH	1	98	98	98	98	99	99	99	100	100	101	102	104	106
	6	96	96	96	96	96	97	97	97	98	98	99	100	102
	11	94	94	94	94	94	94	95	95	95	96	96	97	98
	16	92	92	92	92	92	92	92	92	93	93	93	93	94
	21	90	90	90	90	90	90	90	90	90	90	90	90	90
	26	88	88	88	88	88	88	88	88	87	87	87	87	86
APRIL	1	86	86	86	86	85	85	85	85	84	84	83	82	81
	6	84	84	84	83	83	83	83	82	82	81	80	79	77
	11	82	82	82	82	81	81	81	80	80	79	77	76	74
	16	80	80	80	80	79	79	78	78	77	76	74	72	70
	21	78	78	78	78	78	77	76	76	75	73	72	69	66
	26	77	77	76	76	76	75	75	74	72	71	69	66	63
MAY	1	75	75	75	74	74	73	73	72	70	69	66	63	59
	6	74	74	73	73	73	72	71	70	68	67	64	61	56
	11	72	72	72	72	71	70	69	68	67	64	62	58	52
	16	71	71	71	70	70	69	68	67	65	63	60	55	49
	21	70	70	70	69	69	68	67	65	63	61	58	53	47
	26	69	69	69	68	68	67	66	64	62	60	56	51	44
JUNE	1	68	68	68	67	66	66	64	63	61	58	54	49	41
	6	67	67	67	67	66	65	64	62	60	57	53	48	40
	11	67	67	67	66	65	64	63	62	59	56	53	47	39
	16	67	67	67	66	65	64	63	62	59	56	53	47	39
	21	67	67	67	66	65	64	63	62	59	56	53	47	39
	26	67	67	67	66	65	64	63	62	59	56	53	47	39
JULY	1	67	67	67	66	65	64	63	62	59	56	53	47	39
	6	67	67	67	66	66	65	64	62	60	57	53	48	40
	11	68	68	68	67	66	65	64	63	61	58	54	49	41
	16	69	68	68	67	67	66	65	64	62	59	55	50	43
	21	69	69	69	69	68	67	66	65	63	60	57	52	45
	26	70	70	70	70	69	68	67	66	64	62	59	54	48
AUGUST	1	72	72	72	71	71	70	69	68	66	64	61	57	51
	6	73	73	73	73	72	71	71	69	68	66	63	60	55
	11	75	75	74	74	74	73	72	71	70	68	66	63	58
	16	76	76	76	76	75	75	74	73	72	70	68	65	61
	21	78	78	77	77	77	76	76	75	74	72	71	68	65
	26	79	79	79	79	79	78	78	77	76	75	73	71	68
SEPTEMBER	1	82	82	82	81	81	81	80	80	79	78	77	75	73
	6	83	83	83	83	83	83	83	82	82	81	80	78	77
	11	85	85	85	85	85	85	85	84	84	83	83	82	81
	16	87	87	87	87	87	87	87	86	86	86	85	85	84
	21	89	89	89	89	89	89	89	89	89	89	88	88	88
	26	91	91	91	91	91	91	91	91	91	91	92	92	92
OCTOBER	1	93	93	93	93	93	93	93	94	94	94	95	95	96
	6	95	95	95	95	95	96	96	96	97	97	98	99	100
	11	97	97	97	97	97	98	98	99	99	100	101	102	104
	16	99	99	99	99	99	100	100	101	101	102	104	105	108
	21	101	101	101	101	101	102	102	103	104	105	107	109	112
	26	102	102	103	103	103	104	104	105	106	108	109	112	115
NOVEMBER	1	104	104	105	105	105	106	107	108	109	110	113	116	120
	6	106	106	106	107	107	108	109	110	111	113	115	119	123
	11	107	107	108	108	108	109	110	111	113	115	117	121	126
	16	109	109	109	109	110	111	112	113	115	117	120	124	130
	21	110	110	110	111	111	112	113	114	116	118	122	126	133
	26	111	111	111	112	112	113	114	116	118	120	124	128	135
DECEMBER	1	112	112	112	113	113	114	115	117	119	122	125	130	138
	6	112	112	113	113	114	115	116	118	120	123	126	132	140
	11	113	113	113	114	115	116	117	118	121	124	127	133	141
	16	113	113	113	114	114	115	116	117	118	121	124	127	141
	21	113	113	113	114	115	116	117	118	121	124	127	133	141
	26	113	113	113	114	115	116	117	118	121	124	127	133	141

NOTE: When the sun is rising, the angle is reckoned from East to North.
When the sun is setting, the angle is reckoned from West to North.

Figure 2-51. *Finding Direction from the Rising or Setting Sun*

mountainous terrain). On January 26, your position is 50°00′ N and 165°06′ W. In figure 2-51, at that date and under 50°N latitude, you find the azimuth of the rising sun to be 120 degrees. Therefore, north will be 120° to your left when you are facing the rising sun.

To find north from the setting sun, consider the same problem as above. Since the sun sets in the west, north must be to the right of the sun. Therefore, north will be 120° to your right when you face the sun.

The table does not list every day of the year, nor does it list every degree of longitude. If you want accuracy within 1° of azimuth, you may have to interpolate (split the difference) between the values given in the table. However, for all practical purposes, using the closest day and the closest degree of latitude listed in the table will give you an azimuth which will enable you to hold your course. For example: If you are at 32° N latitude on 13 April, the azimuth of the rising sun is actually 79°22′; however, by entering the table with the closest day listed, 11 April, and the closest latitude, 30°, you get 81° as the azimuth of the rising sun. The value is accurate enough for field purposes.

LATITUDE BY NOON ALTITUDE OF SUN. On any given day, there is only one latitude on the earth where the sun passes directly overhead or through the zenith at noon. In all latitudes north of this, the sun passes to the south of the zenith; and in those south of it, the sun passes to the north. For each 1° change of latitude, the zenith distance also changes by 1 degree.

Figure 2-52c gives for each day of the year the latitude where the sun is in the zenith at noon.

If you have a Weems plotter or other protractor, you can use the maximum altitude of the sun to find latitude by measuring the angular distance of the sun from the zenith at noon. Find the time of local noon with the methods described earlier in this section. Stretch a string from the top of a stick to the point where the end of the noon shadow rested; place your plotter along the string and drop a plumb line from the center of the plotter. The intersection of the plumb line with the outer scale of the plotter shows the angular distance of the sun from your zenith.

LATITUDE BY LENGTH OF DAY. When you are in any latitude between 60° N and 60° S, you can determine your exact latitude within 30 nautical miles (½°), if you know the length of the day within 1 minute. This is true throughout the year except for about 10 days before and 10 days after the equinoxes—approximately 11-31 March and 13 September-2 October. During these two periods, the day is approximately the same length at all latitudes. To time sunrise and sunset accurately, you must have a level horizon.

Observations for Latitude. Find the length of the day from the instant the top of the sun first appears above the ocean horizon to the instant it disappears below the horizon. This instant is often marked by a green flash. Write down the times of sunrise and sunset. Don't count on remembering them. Note that only the length of day counts in the determination of latitude; your watch may have an unknown error and yet serve to determine this factor. If you have only one water horizon, as on a seacoast, find local noon by the stick and shadow method. The length of day is twice the interval from sunrise to noon or from noon to sunset.

Knowing the length of day, you can find the latitude by using the nomogram shown in figure 2-53.

LONGITUDE FROM LOCAL APPARENT NOON. To find longitude, you must know the correct time. You should know the rate at which your watch gains or loses time. If you know this rate and the time you last set the watch, you can compute the correct time. Correct the zone time on your watch to Greenwich time; for example, if your watch is on Eastern Standard Time, add 5 hours to get Greenwich time.

You can find longitude by timing the moment when a celestial body passes your meridian. The easiest body to use is the sun. Use one of the following methods.

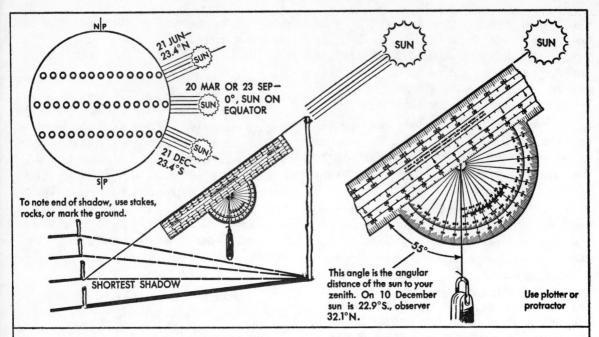

N|P

21 JUN — 23.4°N

20 MAR OR 23 SEP — 0°, SUN ON EQUATOR

21 DEC — 23.4°S

S|P

SUN

SUN

To note end of shadow, use stakes, rocks, or mark the ground.

SHORTEST SHADOW

This angle is the angular distance of the sun to your zenith. On 10 December sun is 22.9°S., observer 32.1°N.

55°

Use plotter or protractor

DECLINATION OF SUN

(IN DEGREES AND TENTHS OF A DEGREE)

Declination is tabulated to the nearest tenth of a degree rather than to the nearest minute of arc. To convert 1/10° (0.1°) to minutes, multiply by 6. (ie. 27.9°=27° 54')

DAY	JAN	FEB	MAR	APR	MAY	JUN	JUL	AUG	SEP	OCT	NOV	DEC
1	S 23.1	S 17.5	S 7.7	N 4.4	N 15.0	N 22.0	N 23.1	N 18.1	N 8.4	S 3.1	S 14.3	S 21.8
2	23.0	17.2	7.3	4.8	15.3	22.1	23.1	17.9	8.1	3.4	14.6	21.9
3	22.9	16.9	6.9	5.2	15.6	22.3	23.0	17.6	7.7	3.8	15.0	22.1
4	22.9	16.6	6.6	5.6	15.9	22.4	22.9	17.3	7.3	4.2	15.3	22.2
5	22.8	16.3	6.2	5.9	16.2	22.5	22.8	17.1	7.0	4.6	15.6	22.3
6	S 22.7	S 16.0	S 5.8	N, 6.3	N 16.4	N 22.6	N 22.7	N 16.8	N 6.6	S 5.0	S 15.9	S 22.5
7	22.5	15.7	5.4	6.7	16.7	22.7	22.6	16.5	6.2	5.4	16.2	22.6
8	22.4	15.4	5.0	7.1	17.0	22.8	22.5	16.3	5.8	5.7	16.5	22.7
9	22.3	15.1	4.6	7.4	17.3	22.9	22.4	16.0	5.5	6.1	16.8	22.8
10	22.2	14.8	4.2	7.8	17.5	23.0	22.3	15.7	5.1	6.5	17.1	22.9
11	S 22.0	S 14.5	S 3.8	N 8.2	N 17.8	N 23.1	N 22.2	N 15.4	N 4.7	S 6.9	S 17.3	S 23.0
12	21.9	14.1	3.5	8.6	18.0	23.1	22.0	15.1	4.3	7.3	17.6	23.1
13	21.7	13.8	3.1	8.9	18.3	23.2	21.9	14.8	3.9	7.6	17.9	23.1
14	21.5	13.5	2.7	9.3	18.5	23.2	21.7	14.5	3.6	8.0	18.1	23.2
15	21.4	13.1	2.3	9.6	18.8	23.3	21.6	14.2	3.2	8.4	18.4	23.3
16	S 21.2	S 12.8	S 1.9	N 10.0	N 19.0	N 23.3	N 21.4	N 13.9	N 2.8	S 8.8	S 18.7	S 23.3
17	21.0	12.4	1.5	10.4	19.2	23.4	21.3	13.5	2.4	9.1	18.9	23.3
18	20.8	12.1	1.1	10.7	19.5	23.4	21.1	13.2	2.0	9.5	19.1	23.4
19	20.6	11.7	0.7	11.1	19.7	23.4	20.9	12.9	1.6	9.9	19.4	23.4
20	20.4	11.4	0.3	11.4	19.9	23.4	20.7	12.6	1.2	10.2	19.6	23.4
21	S 20.2	S 11.0	N 0.1	N 11.7	N 20.1	N 23.4	N 20.5	N 12.2	N 0.8	S 10.6	S 19.8	S 23.4
22	20.0	10.7	0.5	12.1	20.3	23.4	20.4	11.9	0.5	10.9	20.1	23.4
23	19.8	10.3	0.9	12.4	20.5	23.4	20.2	11.6	N 0.1	11.3	20.3	23.4
24	19.5	9.9	1.3	12.7	20.7	23.4	20.0	11.2	S 0.3	11.6	20.5	23.4
25	19.3	9.6	1.7	13.1	20.9	23.4	19.7	10.9	0.7	12.0	20.7	23.4
26	S 19.0	S 9.2	N 2.1	N 13.4	N 21.1	N 23.4	N 19.5	N 10.5	S 1.1	S 12.3	S 20.9	S 23.4
27	18.8	8.8	2.5	13.7	21.2	23.3	19.3	10.2	1.5	12.7	21.1	23.3
28	18.5	8.5	2.9	14.0	21.4	23.3	19.1	9.8	1.9	13.0	21.3	23.3
29	18.3	8.1	3.2	14.4	21.6	23.3	18.8	9.5	2.3	13.3	21.4	23.3
30	18.0	...	3.6	14.7	21.7	23.2	18.6	9.1	2.7	13.7	21.6	23.2
31	S 17.7	...	N 4.0	...	N 21.9	...	N 18.4	N 8.8	...	S 14.0	...	S 23.1

EXAMPLE: On 10 December the declination of the sun is 22.9°S., so an observer who measures the zenith distance as 0° would know that he is at latitude 22.9°S. If he measures a zenith distance of 5° with the sun south of this zenith, he is 5° north of 22.9°S, or at a latitude 17.9°S; and if the sun is north, he is 5° south of 22.9°S, or in latitude 27.9°S.

Figure 2-52. Determining Latitude by Noon Sun

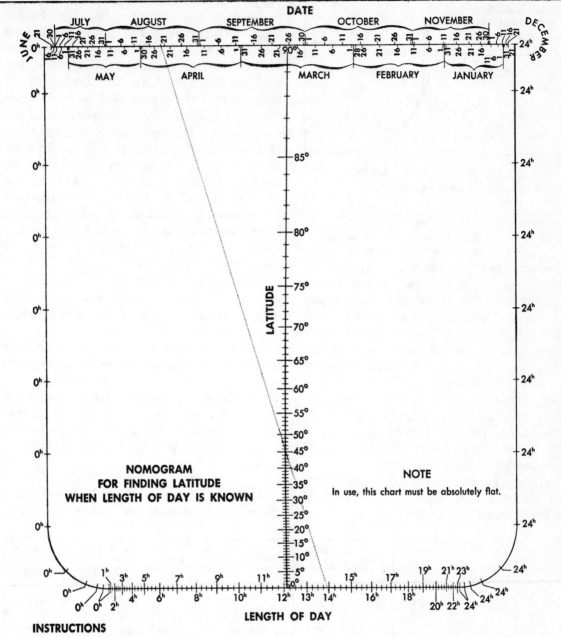

DATE

JULY AUGUST SEPTEMBER OCTOBER NOVEMBER

JUNE DECEMBER

MAY APRIL MARCH FEBRUARY JANUARY

LATITUDE

NOMOGRAM
FOR FINDING LATITUDE
WHEN LENGTH OF DAY IS KNOWN

NOTE

In use, this chart must be absolutely flat.

LENGTH OF DAY

INSTRUCTIONS

To find your latitude:

In Northern Latitudes:

1. Find length of the day from the instant the top of the sun appears above the ocean horizon to the instant it disappears below the horizon. This instant is often marked by a green flash.

2. Lay a straight edge or stretch across the Nomogram, connecting the observed length of the day on the Length of Day Scale with the date on the Date Scale.

3. Read your latitude on the Latitude Scale.

EXAMPLE: On August 20, observed length of the day is 13 hours and 54 minutes. Latitude is 45°30'N.

In Southern Latitudes:

Add six months to the date and proceed as in northern latitudes.

EXAMPLE: On 11 May observed length of day is 10 hours and 4 minutes. Adding 6 months gives 11 November. Latitude is 41°30'S.

Figure 2-53. Nomogram

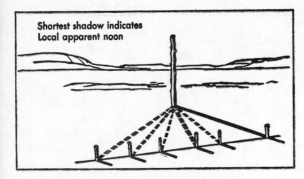

Figure 2-54. Stick-and-shadow method
of determining local apparent noon

• Put up a stick or rod (figure 2-54) as nearly vertical as possible, in a level place. Check the alignment of the stick by sighting along the line of a makeshift plumb bob. (To make a plumb bob, tie any heavy object to a string and let it hang free. The line of the string indicates the vertical.) Sometime before midday begin marking the position of the end of the stick's shadow. Note the time for each mark. Continue marking until the shadow definitely lengthens. The time of the shortest shadow is the time when the sun passed the local meridian or local apparent noon. You will probably have to estimate the position of the shortest shadow by finding a line midway between two shadows of equal length, one before noon and one after.

• If you get the times of sunrise and sunset accurately on a water horizon, local noon will be midway between these times.

• Erect two plumb bobs approximately one foot apart so that both strings line up on Polaris, much the same as a gun sight. Plumb bobs should be set up when Polaris is on the meridian and has no east-west correction. The next day, when the shadows of the two plumb bobs coincide, they will indicate local apparent noon.

Mark down the Greenwich time of local apparent noon. The next step is to correct this observed time of meridian passage for the equation of time—that is, the number of minutes the real sun is ahead of or behind the mean sun. (The mean sun was invented by astronomers to simplify the problems of measuring time. Mean sun rolls along the equator at a constant rate of 15° per hour. The real sun is not so considerate; it changes its angular rate of travel around the earth with the seasons.)

Figure 2-55 gives the values in minutes of time to be added to or subtracted from mean (watch) time to get apparent (sun) time.

Now that you have the Greenwich time of local noon, you can find the difference of longitude between your position and Greenwich by converting the interval between 1200 Greenwich and your local noon from time to arc. Remember that 1 hour equals 15° of longitude, 4 minutes equal 1° of longitude, and 4 seconds equal 1' of longitude.

Example: Your watch is on Eastern Standard Time, and it normally loses 30 seconds a day.

Date	Eq. of Time*	Date	Eq. of Time*	Date	Eq. of Time*	Date	Eq. of Time*	Date	Eq. of Time*	Date	Eq. of Time*
Jan. 1	−3.5 min.	Mar. 4	−12.0	May 2	+3.0 min.	Aug. 4	−6.0	Oct. 1	+10.0 min.	Dec. 1	+11.0
2	−4.0	8	−11.0	14	+3.8	12	−5.0	4	+11.0	4	+10.0
4	−5.0	12	−10.0	May 28	+3.0	17	−4.0	7	+12.0	6	+9.0
7	−6.0	16	−9.0			22	−3.0	11	+13.0	9	+8.0
9	−7.0	19	−8.0	June 4	+2.0	26	−2.0	15	+14.0	11	+7.0
12	−8.0	22	−7.0	9	+1.0	Aug. 29	−1.0	20	+15.0	13	+6.0
14	−9.0	26	−6.0	14	0.0			Oct. 27	+16.0	15	+5.0
17	−10.0	Mar. 29	−5.0	19	−1.0	Sept. 1	0.0			17	+4.0
20	−11.0			23	−2.0	5	+1.0			19	+3.0
24	−12.0	Apr. 1	−4.0	June 28	−3.0	8	+2.0	Nov. 4	+16.4	21	+2.0
Jan. 28	−13.0	5	−3.0			10	+3.0	11	+16.0	23	+1.0
		8	−2.0	July 3	−4.0	13	+4.0	17	+15.0	25	0.0
Feb. 4	−14.0	12	−1.0	9	−5.0	16	+5.0	22	+14.0	27	−1.0
13	−14.3	16	0.0	18	−6.0	19	+6.0	25	+13.0	29	−2.0
19	−14.0	20	+1.0	July 27	−6.6	22	+7.0	Nov. 28	+12.0	Dec. 31	−3.0
Feb. 28	−13.0	Apr. 25	+2.0			25	+8.0				
						Sep. 28	+9.0				

* Add plus values to mean time and subtract minus values from mean time to get apparent time.

Figure 2-55. Equation of Time

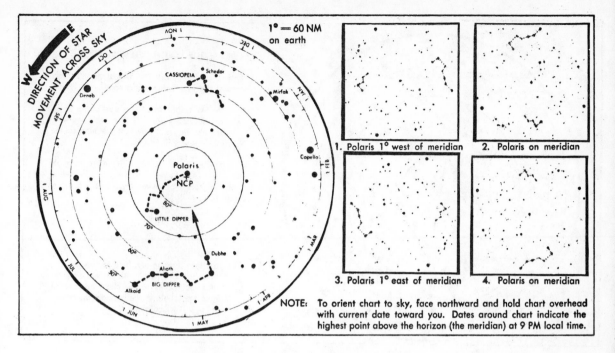

Figure 2-56. Finding Direction from Polaris

You haven't set it for 4 days. You time local noon at 15:08 on your watch on 4 February.

Watch correction is 4 × 30 seconds, or plus 2 minutes. Zone time correction is plus 5 hours. Greenwich time is 15:08 plus 2 minutes plus 5 hours or 20:10. The equation of time for 4 February is minus 14 minutes. Local noon is 20:10 minus 14 minutes or 19:56 Greenwich. Difference in time between Greenwich and your position is 19:56 minus 12:00 or 7:56. A time of 7:56 equals 119° of longitude.

Since your local noon is later than Greenwich noon, you are west of Greenwich. Your longitude then is 119° W.

Nighttime Direction and Position Finding

DIRECTION FROM POLARIS. In the Northern Hemisphere one star, Polaris (the Pole Star), is never more than approximately 1° from the North Celestial Pole. In other words, the line from any observer in the Northern Hemisphere to the Pole Star is never more than one degree away from true north. You find the Pole Star by locating the Big Dipper or Cassiopeia, two groups of stars which are very close to the North Celestial Pole. The two stars on the outer edge of the Big Dipper are called pointers, as they

point almost directly to Polaris. If the pointers are obscured by clouds, Polaris can be identified by its relationship to the constellation Cassiopeia. Figure 2-56 indicates the relation between the Big Dipper, Polaris, and Cassiopeia.

DIRECTION FROM THE SOUTHERN CROSS. In the Southern Hemisphere, Polaris is not visible. There the Southern Cross is the most distinctive constellation. As you fly south, the Southern Cross appears shortly before Polaris drops from sight astern. An imaginary line through the long axis of the Southern Cross, or True Cross, points toward the South Pole. The True Cross should not be confused with a larger cross nearby known as the False Cross, which is less bright and more widely spaced. Two of the four stars in the True Cross are among the brightest stars in the heavens; they are the stars on the southern and eastern arms. Those of the northern and western arms are not as conspicuous but are bright.

There is no conspicuous star above the South Pole to correspond to Polaris above the North Pole. In fact, the point where such a star would be, if one existed, lies in a region devoid of stars. This point is so dark in comparison with the rest of the sky that it is known as the *Coal Sack.*

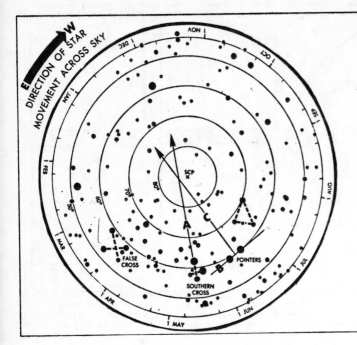

TO LOCATE THE SOUTH CELESTIAL POLE:

1. Extend an imaginary line (A) along the long axis of the True Cross to the south.

2. Join the two bright stars to the east of the Cross with an imaginary line (B). Bisect this line with one at right angles (C) and let it extend southward to intersect line (A).

3. The intersection of line (C) with the line through the Cross (A) is a few degrees from the South Celestial Pole (approximately 5 or 6 full moon widths).

NOTE: To orient chart to sky, face southward and hold chart overhead with current date toward you. Dates around chart indicate the highest point above the horizon (the meridian) at 9 PM local time.

Figure 2-57. Finding Direction from Southern Cross

Figure 2-57 shows the True Cross and—to the west of it—the False Cross. Hold the page above your head (E toward east) for realism and note two very bright stars just to the east of the True Cross. With them and the True Cross as guides, you can locate the spot within the *Coal Sack* which is exactly above the South Pole.

FINDING DUE EAST AND WEST BY EQUATORIAL STARS. Due to the altitude of Polaris above the horizon, it may be sometimes difficult to use it as a bearing. To use a point directly on the horizon may be more convenient. In the Southern Hemisphere, of course, Polaris is not visible, and an accurate bearing is difficult to obtain.

The celestial equator, which is merely a projection of the earth's equator onto the imaginary celestial sphere, always intersects the horizon line at the due east and west points of the compass. Therefore, any star on the celestial equator rises due east and sets due west (disallowing a small error because of atmospheric refraction). This holds true for all latitudes except those of the North and South Poles, where the celestial equator and the horizon have a common plane. However, if you are at the North or South Pole you will probably know about it beforehand, so this technique can be assumed to be of universal applicability.

Certain difficulties arise in the practical use of this technique. Unless you are quite familiar with the constellations, you may have difficulty spotting a specific rising star as it first appears above the eastern horizon. Thus, it will probably be simpler to depend upon the identification of an equatorial star before it sets in the west.

Another problem is that caused by atmospheric extinction. As stars near the horizon they grow fainter in brightness, since the line of sight between the observer's eyes and the star passes through a constantly thickening slice of atmosphere. Therefore, faint stars disappear from view before they actually set. However, a fairly accurate estimate of the setting point of a star can be made some time before it actually sets. Also, the atmospheric conditions of the locality have a great effect on the obstruction of a star's light as it sets. Atmospheric haze, for example, is much less a problem on an arid desert than along a temperate zone coastal strip.

Figure 2-58 shows the brighter stars and some prominent star groups which lie along the celestial equator. There are few bright stars which are actually *on* the celestial equator. However, there

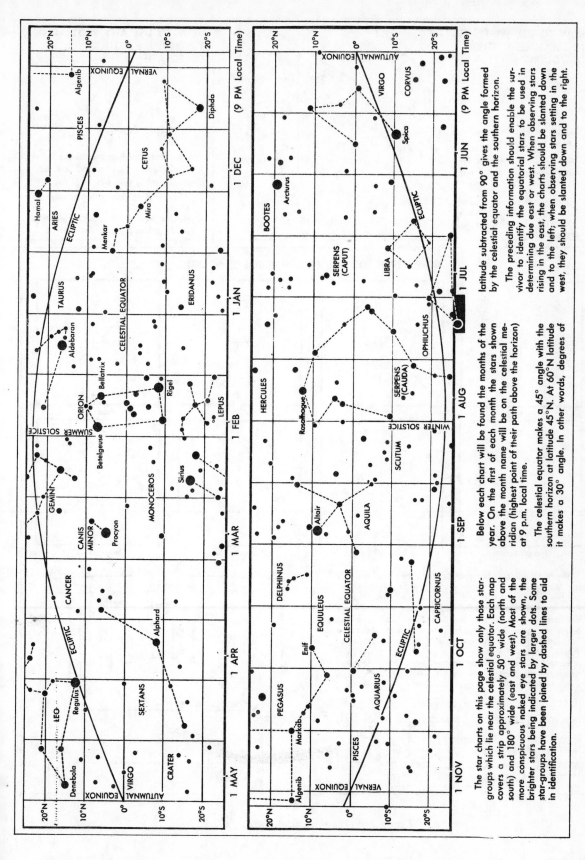

The star charts on this page show only those star-groups which lie near the celestial equator. Each map covers a strip approximately 50° wide (north and south) and 180° wide (east and west). Most of the more conspicuous naked eye stars are shown, the brighter stars being indicated by larger dots. Some star-groups have been joined by dashed lines to aid in identification.

Below each chart will be found the months of the year. On the first of each month the stars shown above the month name will be on the celestial meridian (highest point of their path above the horizon) at 9 p.m. local time.

The celestial equator makes a 45° angle with the southern horizon at latitude 45°N. At 60°N latitude it makes a 30° angle. In other words, degrees of latitude subtracted from 90° gives the angle formed by the celestial equator and the southern horizon.

The preceding information should enable the survivor to identify the equatorial stars to be used in determining due east or west. When observing stars rising in the east, the charts should be slanted down and to the left; when observing stars setting in the west, they should be slanted down and to the right.

Figure 2-58. Charts of Equatorial Stars

69

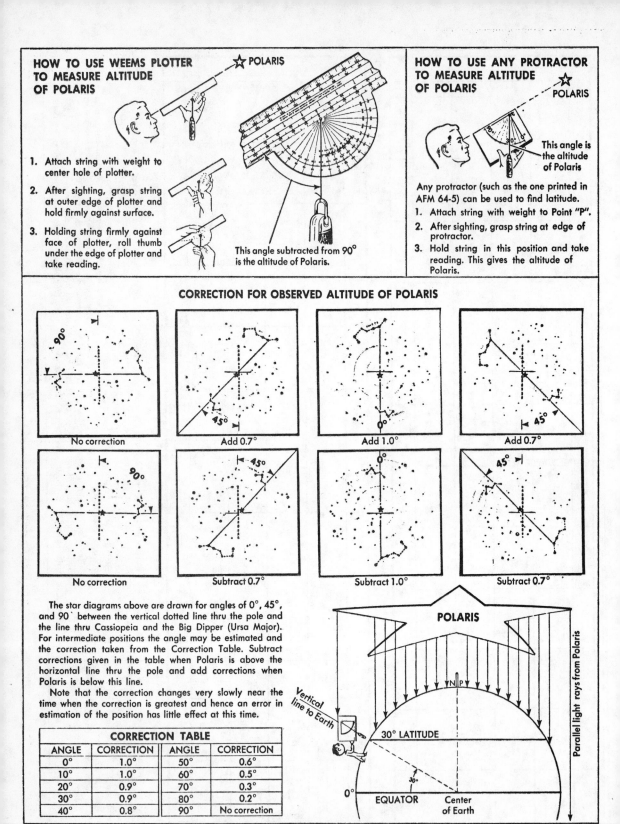

HOW TO USE WEEMS PLOTTER TO MEASURE ALTITUDE OF POLARIS

1. Attach string with weight to center hole of plotter.
2. After sighting, grasp string at outer edge of plotter and hold firmly against surface.
3. Holding string firmly against face of plotter, roll thumb under the edge of plotter and take reading.

This angle subtracted from 90° is the altitude of Polaris.

HOW TO USE ANY PROTRACTOR TO MEASURE ALTITUDE OF POLARIS

This angle is the altitude of Polaris

Any protractor (such as the one printed in AFM 64-5) can be used to find latitude.
1. Attach string with weight to Point "P".
2. After sighting, grasp string at edge of protractor.
3. Hold string in this position and take reading. This gives the altitude of Polaris.

CORRECTION FOR OBSERVED ALTITUDE OF POLARIS

No correction	Add 0.7°	Add 1.0°	Add 0.7°
No correction	Subtract 0.7°	Subtract 1.0°	Subtract 0.7°

The star diagrams above are drawn for angles of 0°, 45°, and 90° between the vertical dotted line thru the pole and the line thru Cassiopeia and the Big Dipper (Ursa Major). For intermediate positions the angle may be estimated and the correction taken from the Correction Table. Subtract corrections given in the table when Polaris is above the horizontal line thru the pole and add corrections when Polaris is below this line.

Note that the correction changes very slowly near the time when the correction is greatest and hence an error in estimation of the position has little effect at this time.

CORRECTION TABLE

ANGLE	CORRECTION	ANGLE	CORRECTION
0°	1.0°	50°	0.6°
10°	1.0°	60°	0.5°
20°	0.9°	70°	0.3°
30°	0.9°	80°	0.2°
40°	0.8°	90°	No correction

POLARIS

Parallel light rays from Polaris

Vertical line to Earth

30° LATITUDE

0°

EQUATOR   Center of Earth

Figure 2-59. Finding Latitude by Polaris

are a number of stars which lie quite near it, so an approximation within a degree or so can be made. Also, a rough knowledge of the more conspicuous equatorial constellations will give the survivor a continuing checkpoint in maintaining his orientation.

FINDING LATITUDE FROM POLARIS. You can find your latitude in the Northern Hemisphere north of 10° N. by *measuring the angular altitude of Polaris above the horizon, as shown in figure 2-59.*

Position Finding Using the Fishline Sextant

One of the oldest known means of establishing position is to determine the instant that an infinitely distant celestial body passes directly overhead. The celestial body is then at the instant of Meridian Transit. The time that various celestial bodies will be over any point on the earth's surface has been established, and almanacs containing this calculated position of stars at any given time have been printed for centuries.

A simple system for determining Meridian Transit is shown in figure 2-60 and can be set up under survival conditions. The only requirements are:

- A watch that is running and which is set on a time zone that you can convert to GMT by adding or subtracting the correct number of hours. (A watch already showing GMT is ideal.)
- Approximately 20 feet of string.
- The proper forms for computation.

Two 3-way swivels are very handy to assist in setting up the sextant. Nylon leader is ideal for use as the triangle itself since it tends to gather prevailing light which will assist in making sightings under minimum light conditions.

The computation itself may be completed at any time, once the observations that were made have been recorded. (Check and recheck your arithmetic.) The position fix resulting from this procedure will be accurate within approximately ten miles if your sightings were made carefully and your GMT is accurate.

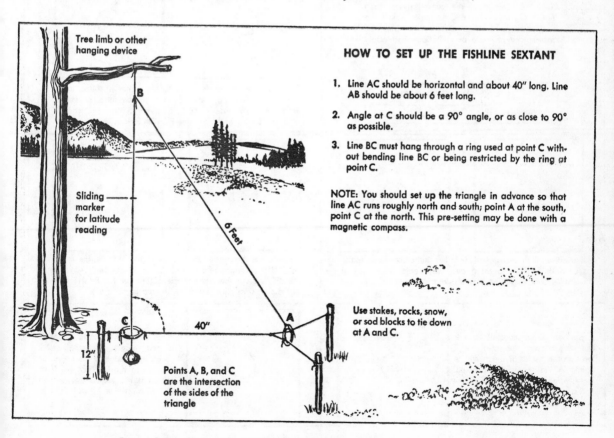

HOW TO SET UP THE FISHLINE SEXTANT

1. Line AC should be horizontal and about 40" long. Line AB should be about 6 feet long.

2. Angle at C should be a 90° angle, or as close to 90° as possible.

3. Line BC must hang through a ring used at point C without bending line BC or being restricted by the ring at point C.

NOTE: You should set up the triangle in advance so that line AC runs roughly north and south; point A at the south, point C at the north. This pre-setting may be done with a magnetic compass.

Use stakes, rocks, snow, or sod blocks to tie down at A and C.

Tree limb or other hanging device

Sliding marker for latitude reading

6 Feet

B

40"

12"

C

A

Points A, B, and C are the intersection of the sides of the triangle

Figure 2-60. *Using the Fishline Sextant to Find Longitude and Latitude*

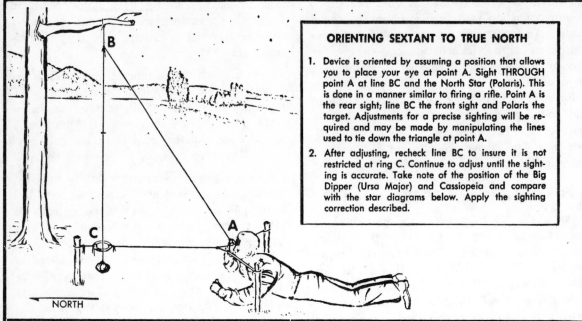

ORIENTING SEXTANT TO TRUE NORTH

1. Device is oriented by assuming a position that allows you to place your eye at point A. Sight THROUGH point A at line BC and the North Star (Polaris). This is done in a manner similar to firing a rifle. Point A is the rear sight; line BC the front sight and Polaris the target. Adjustments for a precise sighting will be required and may be made by manipulating the lines used to tie down the triangle at point A.

2. After adjusting, recheck line BC to insure it is not restricted at ring C. Continue to adjust until the sighting is accurate. Take note of the position of the Big Dipper (Ursa Major) and Cassiopeia and compare with the star diagrams below. Apply the sighting correction described.

POLARIS SIGHTING CORRECTION

Note the position of the constellations, Ursa Major (Big Dipper) and Cassiopeia. Select the illustration which most closely resembles the appearance of these constellations and apply the sighting correction (if any) required.

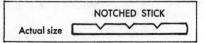

NOTCHED STICK

Actual size

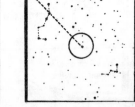

If position of the constellations is like either of these, insert the small stick through the center of the swivel at point "A" from the RIGHT side to the FIRST notch. Sight from the LEFT end of the stick and align line BC with Polaris.

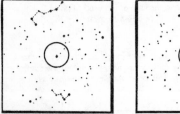

If position of the constellations is like either of these, make NO CORRECTION. Sight through the center of swivel at point "A" and align line BC with Polaris.

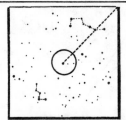
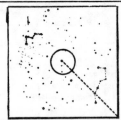

If position of the constellations is like either of these, insert the small stick through the center of the swivel at point "A" from the LEFT side to the FIRST notch. Sight from the RIGHT end of the stick and align line BC with Polaris.

If position of the constellations is like this, insert the small stick through the center of the swivel at point "A" to the CENTER notch. Sight from the LEFT end of the stick and align line BC with Polaris.

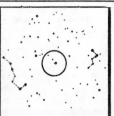
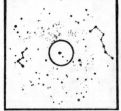

If position of the constellations is like this, insert the small stick through the center of the swivel at point "A" to the CENTER NOTCH. Sight from the RIGHT end of the stick and align line BC with Polaris.

Figure 2-60. Continued

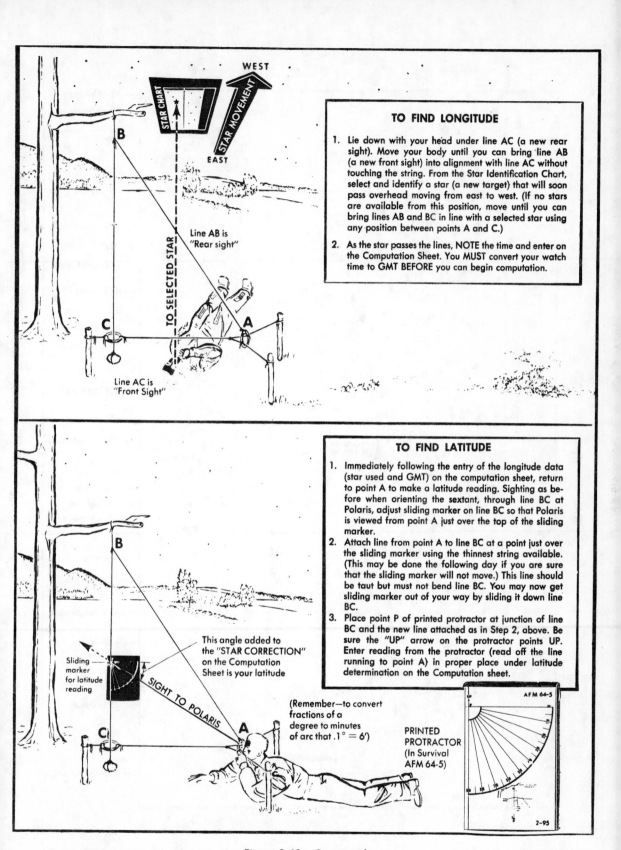

TO FIND LONGITUDE

1. Lie down with your head under line AC (a new rear sight). Move your body until you can bring line AB (a new front sight) into alignment with line AC without touching the string. From the Star Identification Chart, select and identify a star (a new target) that will soon pass overhead moving from east to west. (If no stars are available from this position, move until you can bring lines AB and BC in line with a selected star using any position between points A and C.)

2. As the star passes the lines, NOTE the time and enter on the Computation Sheet. You MUST convert your watch time to GMT BEFORE you can begin computation.

WEST

STAR CHART

STAR MOVEMENT

EAST

B

Line AB is "Rear sight"

TO SELECTED STAR

C

A

Line AC is "Front Sight"

TO FIND LATITUDE

1. Immediately following the entry of the longitude data (star used and GMT) on the computation sheet, return to point A to make a latitude reading. Sighting as before when orienting the sextant, through line BC at Polaris, adjust sliding marker on line BC so that Polaris is viewed from point A just over the top of the sliding marker.

2. Attach line from point A to line BC at a point just over the sliding marker using the thinnest string available. (This may be done the following day if you are sure that the sliding marker will not move.) This line should be taut but must not bend line BC. You may now get sliding marker out of your way by sliding it down line BC.

3. Place point P of printed protractor at junction of line BC and the new line attached as in Step 2, above. Be sure the "UP" arrow on the protractor points UP. Enter reading from the protractor (read off the line running to point A) in proper place under latitude determination on the Computation sheet.

B

This angle added to the "STAR CORRECTION" on the Computation Sheet is your latitude

Sliding marker for latitude reading

SIGHT TO POLARIS

C

A

(Remember—to convert fractions of a degree to minutes of arc that .1° = 6')

PRINTED PROTRACTOR (In Survival AFM 64-5)

AFM 64-5

2-95

Figure 2-60. Continued

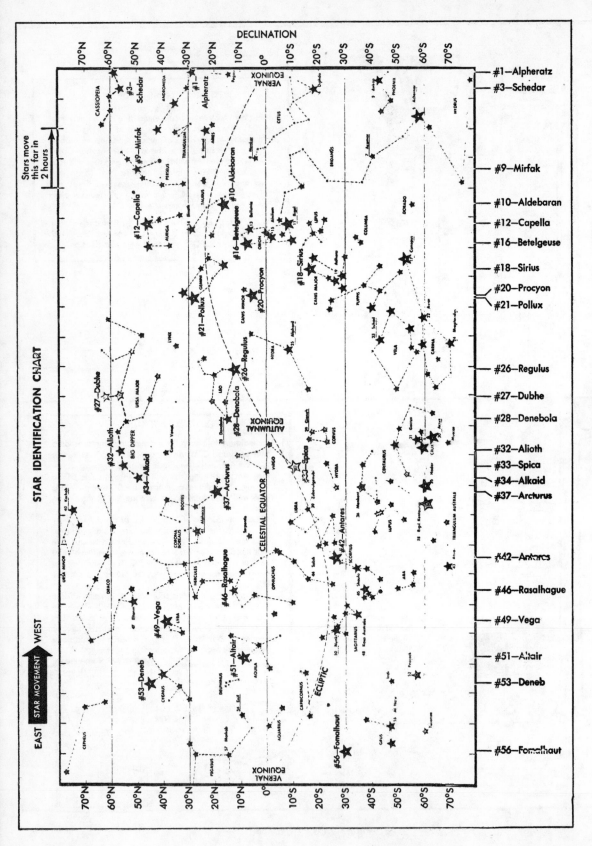

Figure 2-60. Continued

74

COMPUTATION SHEET

LONGITUDE DETERMINATION

(A) Enter proper information in space provided:

Time of star transit in Greenwich mean time, 24 hour clock.

DAY_____   MONTH_____   YEAR 19_____   HOURS_____   MINUTES_____

DAY	
1st--00059	16th--00946
2nd--00118	17th--01005
3rd--00177	18th--01065
4th--00237	19th--01124
5th--00296	20th--01183
6th--00355	21st--01242
7th--00414	22nd--01301
8th--00473	23rd--01360
9th--00532	24th--01420
10th--00591	25th--01479
11th--00650	26th--01538
12th--00709	27th--01597
13th--00769	28th--01656
14th--00828	29th--01715
15th--00887	30th--01774
	31st--01834

MONTH
Jan-- 05918
Feb--07751
Mar--09407
Apr--11241
May--13015
Jun--14848
Jul--16622
Aug--18456
Sep--20289
Oct--00463
Nov--02296
Dec--04070

YEAR 19
1969 00053
1970 00039
1971 00025
1972 (Jan-Feb) 00011
1972 (Mar-Dec) 00070
1973 00056
1974 00042
1975 00028
1976 (Jan-Feb) 00014
1976 (Mar-Dec) 00073
1977 00059
1978 00035
1979 00021

HOURS
1hr --00902
2hr --01805
3hr --02707
4hr --03610
5hr --04512
6hr --05415
7hr --06317
8hr --07220
9hr --08122
10hr --09025
11hr --09927
12hr --10830
13hr --11732
14hr --12635
15hr --13537
16hr --14439
17hr --15342
18hr --16244
19hr --17147
20hr --18049
21hr --18952
22hr --19854
23hr --20757

MINUTES	
1min--00015	31min--00466
2min--00030	32min--00481
3min--00045	33min--00496
4min--00060	34min--00511
5min--00075	35min--00526
6min--00090	36min--00541
7min--00105	37min--00557
8min--00120	38min--00572
9min--00135	39min--00587
10min--00150	40min--00602
11min--00165	41min--00617
12min--00180	42min--00632
13min--00196	43min--00647
14min--00211	44min--00662
15min--00226	45min--00677
16min--00241	46min--00692
17min--00256	47min--00707
18min--00271	48min--00722
19min--00286	49min--00737
20min--00301	50min--00752
21min--00316	51min--00767
22min--00331	52min--00782
23min--00346	53min--00797
24min--00361	54min--00812
25min--00376	55min--00827
26min--00391	56min--00842
27min--00406	57min--00857
28min--00421	58min--00872
29min--00436	59min--00887
30min--00451	

TRANSIT STAR USED

# 1--21508	#21---14660	#37--08795
# 3--21029	#26--12509	#42--06798
# 9--18582	#27--11684	#46--05806
#10--17499	#28--10997	#49--04867
#12--16898	#32--10018	#51--03770
#16--16308	#33--09556	#53--03000
#18--15552	#34--09212	#56--00971
#20--14745		

(E) To obtain value (Z) which will be your longitude, you must do one of the following:

1. If (Y) is less than 10800, divide by 60. Carry the division to two (2) decimal places. The whole number will be degrees of West longitude. Round off the decimal remainder to one (1) number. (If second figure is five or over, add 1 to the first figure following the decimal; if less than 5, drop it.) Multiply the remaining figure by 6; the result will be minutes of West longitude.

2. If (Y) is between 10800 and 21600, subtract the figure from 21600. Divide the result by 60. The whole number will be degrees of East longitude. Round off as above. When figure following decimal has been multiplied by 6, the result will be minutes of East longitude.

LONGITUDE: ....° ......' (Z)

(B) Enter below, proper value from each table as indicated:

Month ....

Date ....

Year ....

Star ....

Hours ....

Mins ....

(C) ADD: .... (W)

SUBTRACT .... (X)
(W-X)
.... (Y)

(D) At (X) above, enter 00000, 21600, 43200 or 64800 whichever is next smaller than (W).

LATITUDE DETERMINATION

STAR CORRECTION

# 1-- 10'		
# 3-- 8'	#21-- 58'	#37--1° 56'
# 9-- 9'	#26--1° 31'	#42--1° 44'
#10-- 17'	#27--1° 41'	#46--1° 33'
#12-- 24'	#28--1° 48'	#49--1° 19'
#16-- 32'	#32--1° 54'	#51--1° 2'
#18-- 43'	#33--1° 56'	#53-- 49'
#20-- 57'	#34--1° 56'	#56-- 20'

Enter reading from protractor:

.... ° .... '

.... ° .... ' (J)

ADD _____

LATITUDE: .... ° .... ' (K)

Enter at (J) the correction for the star used in the longitude computation. When added to the protractor reading, (K) is your latitude.

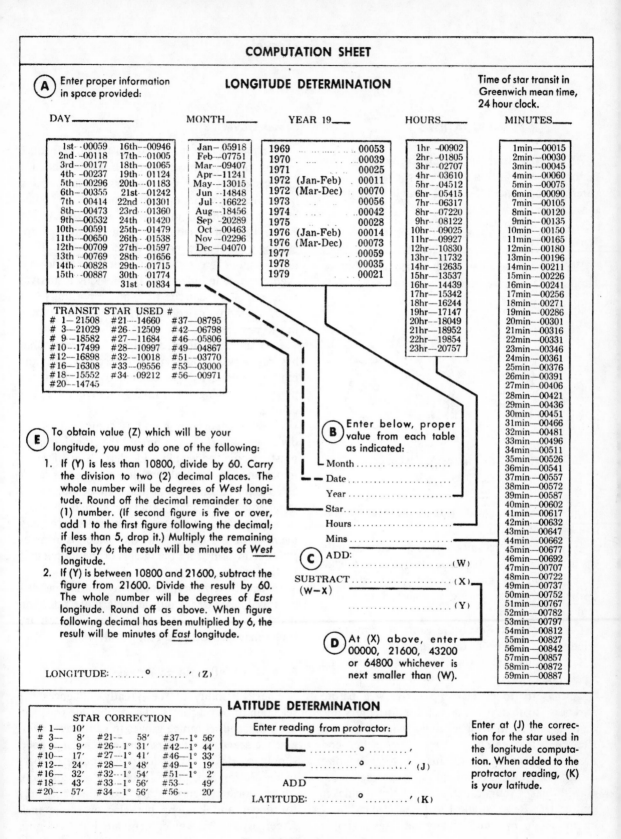

Figure 2-60. Continued

PREPARATIONS

Before you start to travel, consider all the factors at the beginning of this chapter. Lay careful plans, and make a thorough estimate of the situation.

Travel Hints

Wear shoes you can walk in comfortably or improvise footgear adequate for walking. Re-

Figure 2-61. Improvised Shoes

member that you must depend on your feet to bring you out.

If you are in friendly territory, leave a note at the aircraft for rescuers, as well as a sign visible from the air. Describe your estimated destination and the route you intend to travel, and mark your trail.

Carry your anti-exposure suit; it is a good windbreak and protection from the elements. Also, it is invaluable when crossing streams and small bodies of water.

Always try to make camp early, well before darkness, so that you can get comfortable while there is still light. Unpack only what you need. Repack before going to sleep. For shelter and fire making, see section C, this chapter. Organize campwork crews. Assign set tasks for each man; it will make your camping operations quicker and easier. Be methodical and neat around your camp. A sloppy camp usually indicates a sloppy plan and weak leadership.

Group Travel

In almost every group, at least one individual refuses to follow travel rules or lacks the patience and wisdom of a trained outdoorsman in selecting trails, locating game, or solving some of the countless other problems that arise during travel. He is the type of person who can, if allowed to, endanger an entire party. Some survival situations require great skill in order to avoid the slightest error in judgment. By breaking a survival rule, one man can destroy an opportunity for securing food or jeopardize the lives of others in the party.

In a survival episode involving an aircrew that has regrouped following the emergency, the aircraft commander is in command. If he is not present, the highest ranking individual takes charge.

When the survival group is composed of individuals other than aircrew, the ranking man must assume leadership. Leadership is of great importance in survival, and the party must work as a team to insure that all tasks are accomplished in an equitable manner. Full use should be made of any survival experience or knowledge of any member of the group, and the leader is responsible for insuring that the talents of the individuals in the group are used.

In enemy territory, group travel must be discouraged. A large group attracts more attention than a small group of two or three, and solitary travel may prove to be best of all.

Fuel As An Influence on Travel

The availability of fuel greatly influences the selection of travel routes. The timberline travelers must descend to spruce groves to camp overnight, and the seacoast travelers must watch for a good supply of driftwood. Along the southern coast of the Bering Sea, outcrops of coal are common. Many northern grasses are excellent not only for tinder and kindling but also as staple fuel. Green willow and alder generate hot fires and, when laid in the shape of a grill, help to start a coal fire. Green willow branches thrown on a fire at night form coals that last until morning.

A generous supply of wood makes a comfortable camp, but a fire that can be a survivor's best friend can also be his most dangerous enemy if it burns important equipment or irreplaceable clothing. *Never leave a fire without first taking precautions to put it out.*

Route-Finding

The novice is prone to follow a compass line. The experienced man follows lines of least resistance, recognizing at a glance that a curved route may be shorter and easier, that an apparently innocuous stretch of forest may be filled with windfalls, or that a smooth, green meadow may contain a series of beaver ponds, which hamper travel or make it almost impossible.

Use game trails when they follow your projected course. Trails made by migrating caribou are frequently extensive and useful. On scree or rock slides, mountain sheep trails are helpful. Moose and bear trails are almost always unreliable, frequently leading into almost impenetrable thickets or swamps. Other routes offer varying prospects, such as the chance of securing game or of locating waterholes.

Route-finding through wild country requires great concentration, knowledge of wilderness "road signs," common sense, and judgment. Fortunately, trailwalking techniques develop progressively with experience, and a clear mind registers observations and forms deductions almost subconsciously.

Calmness, self-confidence, constant watchfulness, courage, caution, and unlimited patience— all characteristics of the best types of outdoorsmen —develop with time.

Backpacking

When you must carry heavy loads for comparatively long distances, backpacking is essential.

Although a heavy load is a burden, using a suitable harness and following certain approved loading and carrying techniques can eliminate unnecessary hardships and assist you in carrying the load with greater safety and comfort.

Carrying a burden initially develops mental irritation and fatigue, either of which can lower morale or cause hysteria. Experienced men know that when packing a heavy load it is advisable to keep the mind occupied with other thoughts. A survivor can divert his attention from a heavy load by surveying the landscape for the best travel routes and the safest means of passing undetected through hostile territory, or by searching for game or other sources of food.

Make slight adjustments during each rest stop to improve the fit and comfort of your pack. Also, constantly regulate your pace to the weight of your pack and the nature of the terrain being crossed.

Packing Means

Packing is not a pleasant task but, under most survival conditions, a task to which you must resort. Often, you must quickly gather your equipment and move out, perhaps before you can construct a good pack.

Sometimes you may have time only to gather your gear under your arm and rapidly leave the scene. In such an instance, it would be better to fashion a roll of your gear and wear it around your neck, or quickly lash it into a bundle and carry it on your shoulder.

When you have plenty of time, it may be desirable to make a more rigid pack such as a well-padded pack board and some type of sack. The convenience of being able to keep track of your equipment, particularly small items, is of great importance.

PACK BOARD. A pack board can be made by bending branches which are about ¾ to 1 inch in diameter and placing parachute webbing across starting at the ends, so that the webbing is stretched tight where it rests against your back. Make the frame in the shape of a rectangle or a triangle.

PACK SACK. The pack sack can be fashioned from the canvas or fabric from the parachute canopy. The sack can be sewed with cores from suspension line and needle.

Backpacking is one of the skills of survival that must be learned and practiced with the aim of making the best of a trying situation. The better you perfect the technique, the better you can perform necessary survival travel

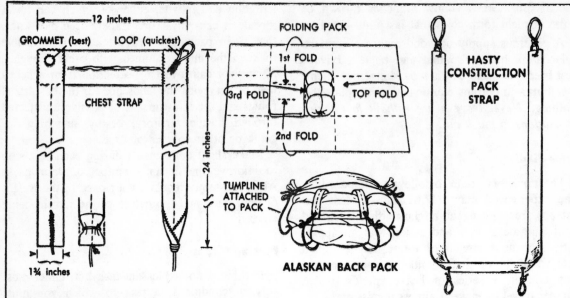

You can make this type of pack strap out of any soft, pliable, and strong material. Suitable materials usually available to a survivor include animal skins, canvas, and parachute-harness webbing. It can be made in the following manner:

1. Cut a strip approximately 12 inches long (outside measurement) and 3 inches wide for a cheststrap.

2. Use any soft material, such as an old sock or parachute cloth, for padding; however, take care to maintain an even surface in order to reduce or eliminate unnecessary body friction.

3. Sew loops or grommets into the lower outside corners of the cheststrap.

4. On the outer edges of the cheststrap, sew two shoulder straps about 2 inches wide and long enough to extend from the cheststrap over and beyond the shoulders. The shoulder straps need no padding if they are flat and smooth, but pad them if they irritate or cut into your shoulder.

5. At the end of the shoulder straps attach strings about 6 feet long. These strings may be made from rawhide or thin rope. You can also make excellent straps by braiding or twisting parachute shroud lines.

6. Encircle the pack with these strings and pass them under each arm before attaching them with a half hitch to the loops or grommets in the cheststrap. Tie the half hitch with a slip-loop so that you can quickly release the pack with a single pull.

Figure 2-62. Alaskan Back Pack

ALASKAN PACKSTRAP. The Alaskan packing method, which combines a fabric pack strap and a tumpline, is used with minor variations by primitive peoples throughout the world (figure 2-62).

The pack should be worn so that it can be released with a single pull in the event of emergency. Such an emergency can happen when crossing streams or when the going is hazardous and the pack can be the cause of a serious fall. You should make the knot with an end readily available which can be pulled to drop the pack quickly.

Advantages of the Alaskan Packstrap. Because it is so small in bulk and so light in weight, you can carry it over one shoulder, tie it around your waist, or carry it in a pocket while hunting.

In an emergency, you can quickly release it.

The broad top of the pack bundle provides a firm, steady platform on which you can carry bulky items.

You can adjust this packstrap to pack efficiently items of a variety of shapes and sizes.

When properly assembled, the pack is soft and lies flat against your back.

When you use the packstrap with a tumpline, the two together distribute a pack's weight over your shoulders, neck, and chest, thereby eliminating sore muscles and chafed areas.

Disadvantages of the Alaskan Packstrap. Experience and ingenuity are necessary to use it with maximum efficiency.

The packstrap is not immediately available after an emergency landing but must be constructed.

The pack must be assembled and lashed before you can adjust the packstrap to it.

You must anticipate your needs for an entire day and keep outside the pack those articles you will need.

A novice canot quickly remove or put on the pack when stopping to rest; however, it need not be taken off during the course of an entire day's travel.

TUMPLINE. A tumpline is the greatest single aid to backpacking, since it transfers part of the weight of a pack from your shoulders to your head and neck (figure 2-63).

How To Use A Tumpline. Have the tumpline just tight enough to transfer about half of the weight of the pack from your shoulders to your head.

Occasionally, a heavy pack can cut off the blood circulation of the shoulders and arms. In such cases, a tumpline is of great value. By slight adjustments, you can transfer most of the weight to your head and neck, thereby instantly loosening the shoulder straps and permitting circulation to return to numb arms.

For the first few days, a tumpline may cause neck muscles to be slightly sore from the unusual strain placed on them; however, this discomfort soon disappears. With practice, you can support heavy weights with only your neck and head.

A tumpline can be used very handily to pack an animal carcass, firewood, or camp equipment. Since it can be rolled up and carried in a pocket, it can be a real aid to survival.

LAND TRAVEL

Land travel techniques are based largely on experience, which in turn is acquired only through actual physical performance. However, experience can be replaced somewhat by the intelligent application of certain specialized practices that can be learned through instruction and observation. For example, travel routes may be established by observing the direction of a bird's flight, the actions of wild animals, the way a tree grows, or even the shape of a snowdrift. Bearings read from a compass or the sun or stars can improve on these observations and confirm original headings. All observations are influenced by the location and physical characteristics of the area where they are made and by the season of the year.

Successful primitive travel presupposes the ability of the individual to survive; however, never forget that you must depend on *regional* food supplies when traveling. *You must forage as you travel.*

Land travel requires knowledge beyond mere travel techniques. You should have at least a

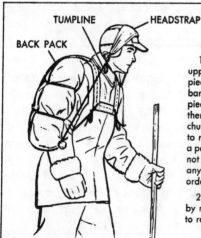

TUMPLINE   HEADSTRAP
BACK PACK

TUMPLINE CONSTRUCTION

1. Attach a soft band, which rests on the upper forehead, to the pack by means of pieces of light line. You can make the band of any strong, soft material, such as pieces of animal skin with the hair still on them, tanned skin, an old sock, or parachute cloth. Make the band long enough to reach over your forehead and down to a point opposite each ear. A tumpline does not require sewing since the end knots keep any loose material along the edges in order.

2. Adjust the tumpline to fit your head by making loops at the ends. It is difficult to reach down and behind to make neces-sary adjustments at the bottom of your pack, but you can easily reach up to adjust the pack by means of loops on either side of your forehead.

3. Make mainstrings from rawhide or parachute suspension lines. Tie them to the lower corners of the pack, bring them up to the loops at the ends of the tumpline, and tie them there with a slipknot.

You will learn from experience how to estimate proper adjustments before putting on your pack, but you can always make closer adjustments after the packstraps are adjusted.

Figure 2-63. Tumpline Construction

general idea of the location of your starting place and of your ultimate destination. You should know something about the country through which you will travel and the people in it. If the population is hostile, you must adapt your entire method of travel and mode of living to this one condition.

WILDERNESS travel requires continuous sightings. A novice views a landscape from the top of a hill with what he considers care and interest, and then says, "Let's go." The experienced man settles down comfortably and starts carefully surveying the surrounding countryside. A distant blur may be mist or smoke; a faint, winding line on a far-off hill may be a manmade or an animal trail; a blur in the lowlands may be a herd of caribou or cattle. Plan your travel route for each day only after carefully reconnoitering the terrain. Carefully study distant landmarks for characteristics that insure their recognition from other locations or angles. Careful and intelligent observation will train you to interpret correctly the things you see, whether they are distant landmarks or a broken twig at your feet.

Before leaving a place, study your back trail carefully. After you have passed by, game may move out from cover to watch your movements. Know your route both forward and backward. An error in route planning may make it necessary to backtrack in order to take a new course.

MOUNTAIN RANGES frequently affect the climate of a region, and the climate in turn influences the vegetation, wild life, and the character and number of people living in the region. For example, the ocean side of mountains has more fog, more rain, and more snow than the inland side of a range. Forests may grow on the ocean side while the inland side is semiarid. Therefore, a complete change in route-finding procedures and survival techniques may be necessary when crossing a mountain range.

Travel in mountainous country is simplified by conspicuous drainage landmarks, but it is complicated by the roughness of the terrain. A mountain traveler can readily determine the direction in which rivers or streams flow; however, he must reconnoiter to determine whether a river is safe for rafting, or if a snowfield or mountainside can be traversed safely. Mountain travel differs from travel through rolling or level country, and certain cardinal rules govern climbing methods. A group descending into a valley, where descent becomes increasingly steep and walls progressively more perpendicular, may be obliged to climb up again in order to follow a ridge until an easier descent is possible. In such a situation, rappeling with a suspension line rope may save many weary miles of travel. In mountains, a traveler must avoid possible avalanches of earth, rock, and snow, as well as crevasses (deep cracks in the ice) in ice fields.

In mountainous country, it is sometimes best to travel on ridges—the snow surface is probably firmer and you have a better view of your route from above. Watch out for snow and ice overhanging steep slopes. Avalanches are a hazard on steep snow-covered slopes, especially on warm days and after heavy snowfalls.

GLACIERS. Many glaciers offer possible travel routes. Their main contribution to emergency travel is that they serve as routes across mountain ranges. Glacier crossing demands special knowledge and techniques, such as the use of a lifeline and poles for locating crevasses. There are, however, numerous places in the north where mountain ranges can be negotiated on foot in a single day by following glaciers.

Be especially careful on glaciers. Watch out for crevasses that may be covered by snow. Travel in groups of not fewer than 3 men, roped together at intervals of 30 to 40 feet. Probe before every step. Always cross a snow-bridged crevasse at right angles to its course.

Find the strongest part of the bridge by poking with a pole or ice axe. When crossing a bridged crevasse, distribute your weight by crawling or by wearing snowshoes or skis.

FORESTS grow in humid areas. When forested areas are dense, river trails and ridges usually afford the easiest travel. In open forests, land travel is easy and offers a greater choice of direction of movement, but such forests may not offer sufficient cover or concealment. Isolated homes, villages, and towns may be found along rivers, and these may require changes in travel methods. Where populations are unfriendly, it is often necessary to travel at night.

In certain parts of *northern prairies*, the direction in which streams flow can be determined only with difficulty. Countless lakes with poor drainage also can add to travel difficulties.

WATERWAYS. Rivers offer easy and fast avenues of communication through wilderness. In summer, the use of rafts or boats insures speedy travel; frozen, level river surfaces afford easy walking in winter. Large lakes or connecting systems of smaller waterways also provide good travel avenues.

The greatest population densities are found along waterways. In enemy territory, the chances of being seen or apprehended are much greater along waterways.

"Overflows," caused by *river* water flowing over ice, are extremely dangerous at low temperatures. Thin ice on lakes or streams is always dangerous. However, if you guard against these dangers, the level surfaces of water routes permit rapid traveling.

Avoid swamps and wet mud flats. If you come down in one, step on roots or bunches of grass. Avoid "slick spots." In soft mud, lie flat and travel on your belly. Anti-exposure suits are invaluable in this type of terrain. If you have a life raft, you may be able to make your way out through meandering water channels.

Don't cross quicksand without testing it to see if it will bear your weight. Quicksand may have a firm crust and yet be almost fluid underneath, so try to puncture the crust when testing. Use a pole for a probe if you can find one. Wear a life preserver if you have one. If you do get caught in quicksand, fall on your back and stretch out your arms, so that your weight will be spread over the largest area possible. If you have companions, lie still until they throw a line or reach you with a pole. If you are alone, inflate your life preserver, try to get a pole, or other support under your hips and then pull your legs out of the sand; rest, then roll to firm ground. If you have to rest while getting to shore, lie on your back and spread out your arms.

MOUNTAIN TRAVEL

Mountain Walking

Mountain walking involves four different techniques, depending on the general formation of the ground to be crossed. The different types of ground are hard ground, grassy slopes, scree slopes, and talus slopes. Two fundamental procedures apply to all four techniques, and you must master both of these procedures in order to expend minimum energy and time. (1) You must keep the weight of your body *directly* over your feet. (2) You must place the soles of your shoes *flat* on the ground. You can accomplish both of these most easily by taking small steps and moving at a slow, steady pace.

Hard ground generally is firmly packed dirt that will not give way under the weight of a man's step.

When ascending hard ground, apply the two fundamental procedures and the following in addition:

• Lock your knees briefly at the end of each step in order to rest your leg muscles.

• Traverse steep slopes and, if necessary, climb in a zigzag direction and not straight up.

• Turn at the end of each traverse by stepping off in the new direction with the uphill foot. This prevents crossing your feet and possibly losing your balance.

When traversing hard ground, you can place the full sole of your shoe down flat most easily by rolling your ankle away from the hill with each step.

For narrow stretches, you may use the herringbone step. Ascend straight up a slope with your toes pointed out and use all of the other principles already outlined.

Descending over hard ground is best accomplished by the following procedures:

• Come straight down without traversing.

• Keep your back straight and your knees bent so that they take up the shock of each step.

• Keep your weight directly over your feet and place the full sole on the ground at each step.

• Walk with a slight forward lean and with your feet slightly pigeon-toed.

In mountainous terrain, *grassy slopes* are usually made up of small hummocks of growth rather than a continuous field of grass. To ascend, step on the *upper side* of each hummock where the ground is more level than on the

A. CIRQUE
B. RIDGE
C. PEAK
D. ICEFALL
E. BUTTRESS
F. CATCHMENT BASIN
G. TERMINAL MORAINE
H. CREVASSE
I. MEDIAL MORAINE
J. LATERAL MORAINE
K. GLACIER
L. GULLIES
M. CORNICE
N. TALUS SLOPE

Figure 2-64. Typical Mountain Terrain

lower side. Traverse with a slow, rhythmic, walking motion. Never run, because running on hard or uneven terrain can result in a sprained ankle. To *descend,* use the techniques mentioned for hard ground.

Scree slopes consist of small rocks and rock particles which have collected under cliffs. Scree varies in size from sand particles to pieces the size of your fist. Occasionally it is a mixture of various sizes, but normally each scree slope is made up of the same size particles.

To *ascend* scree is extremely difficult—avoid it when possible. All principles of ascending hard ground apply, but you must pack each step carefully so that your foot does not slide down when weight is placed on it. You can do this best by kicking in with the toe of the upper foot and the heel of the lower foot.

To *descend* scree, come down in a straight line. It is important to keep your feet in a slightly pigeon-toed position as well as to keep your back straight and your knees bent. Since there is a tendency to run down scree, take care not to attain too great a speed and thereby lose control. By leaning slightly forward, you can obtain greater control.

When a scree slope must be *traversed* and no gain or loss of altitude is desired, use the hop-skip method. This is a hopping motion in which the lower foot takes all the weight and the upper foot is used only for balance.

Talus slopes are similar in makeup to scree slopes, but the rocks are larger. To walk on talus, step on top of and on the uphill side of the rocks to keep them from tilting and rolling downhill. All other previously mentioned procedures apply.

Some general precautions in mountain travel are:

• It is of the utmost importance that you do *not* kick loose rocks so that they roll down hill. Falling rocks are extremely dangerous to men below, and they also make a great deal of noise. Carelessness by anyone in this respect can cause a well-planned mission to fail, since one rock no larger than a man's head can kill or severely injure several men, as well as ruin all security measures.

• Step over rather than on top of obstacles such as rocks and fallen logs to help avoid fatigue.

• Talus usually is easy to ascend and traverse while scree is a better avenue of descent.

Balance Climbing

Balance climbing is the type of movement used to travel on steep slopes. It combines the balanced movement of a tightrope walker and the unbalanced climbing of a man ascending a ladder. Body position is very important.

Climb with the body in balance—that is, with your weight poised over your feet or just ahead of them as you move. Your feet, not your hands, carry the weight except on the steepest cliffs—your hands are for balance. Your feet do not hold well when you lean in toward the rock.

With your body in balance, move with a slow, rhythmic motion. Use three points of support,

Figure 2-65. Body Position

such as two feet and one hand, whenever possible. Handholds that are waist- to shoulder-high are preferable. Use small intermediate holds rather than stretching and changing to widely separated big holds. Avoid a spread-eagle position in which you stretch so far that you cannot let go.

In descending, face out when the going is easy, face sideways when it is hard, and face in when it is extremely difficult. Use the lowest possible handholds.

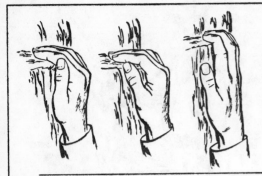

PULL HOLDS

PULL HOLDS are those with which you pull down; they are the easiest to use but also the most likely to break out.

PUSH HOLD

PUSH HOLDS are ones with which you push down; they help you to keep your arms low. They rarely break out, but are more difficult to maintain in case of a slip. A push hold is often used to advantage in combination with a pull hold.

JAM HOLDS

JAM HOLDS involve jamming any part of your body or an extremity into a crack. Put one hand into a crack and clench it into a fist or put one arm into a crack and twist the elbow against one side of the crack and the hand against the offset side.

PINCH HOLDS

PINCH HOLDS involve a protruding piece of rock being firmly held between your fingers and thumb, or clasped between your hands.

FRICTION HOLDS depend solely on the friction of your hands or feet against a smooth surface. They are difficult to use because they give you a feeling of insecurity, which most climbers try to correct by leaning close to the rock, thereby increasing their insecurity. Friction holds often serve well as intermediate holds, some of which give needed support while you move over them but which would not support you were you to stop on them.

FRICTION HOLDS

Figure 2-66. Basic Holds

You must relax, because tensed muscles tire quickly. When resting, keep your arms low so that circulation is not impaired.

BASIC HOLDS. Refer to figure 2-66.

COMBINATION HOLDS. You can combine and vary basic holds. The number of variations depends only upon the limit of your imagination. A few common combination holds are illustrated in figure 2-67.

USE OF HOLDS. A hold need not be large to be good nor must it be solid as long as the pressure you apply keeps it in place. Experienced climbers use small holds that are scarcely visible. You must roll your feet and hands over your holds and *not* try to skip or jump from one hold to another.

When traversing, however, it is often desirable to use either the hop step, in which you change feet, or a small hold with which you may move sideways more easily. This useful step involves a slight upward hop followed by precise footwork.

MARGIN OF SAFETY. Carefully test each and every hold before applying full pressure to it. Keep a margin of safety by never attempting to climb to the full limit of your ability. Carefully assess the climbing ability of yourself and all other members of your climbing party. Then, with equal care, study the terrain to be covered. Make every effort to plan climbs so that the *least* able climber in a group is never pushed to the fullest extent of his ability.

Roped Climbing

In group climbing, two or three men are tied into a 60- to 120-foot length of rope. *Belaying* provides the necessary safety factor that enables each man to climb. When any one man is climbing, he is belayed from above or below by another man to whom he is tied with a belay rope (figure 2-68). Without belaying skill, using a rope is a hazard and not a help to group climbing. Figure 2-68 also explains roped climbing for a 2-man party and a 3-man party.

RAPPELING. A climber with a rope can descend quickly by means of a rappel—sliding down a rope which has been looped around such rappel (or holding) points as a tree or projecting rock (figure 2-68).

GLACIERS AND GLACIAL TRAVEL

To cope with the problems that can arise in using glaciers as avenues of travel, it is important that you understand something of the nature and composition of glaciers.

A *valley glacier* is essentially a river of ice. The valley glacier flows at a rate of speed that depends largely on its mass and the slope of its bed.

A glacier consists of two parts:

(1) The lower glacier, which has an ice surface that is devoid of snow during the summer.

(2) The upper glacier, where the ice is covered, even in summer, with layers of accumulated snow that grade down into glacier ice.

To these two integral parts of a glacier may be added two others which, although not a part of the glacier proper, generally are adjacent to it and are of similar composition.

These adjacent features, the *ice* and *snow slopes*, are immobile, since they are anchored to underlying rock slopes. A large crevasse separates such slopes from the glacier proper and defines the boundary between moving and anchored ice.

Ice is plastic near the surface, but not sufficiently so to prevent cracking as the ice moves forward over irregularities in its bed. Fractures in a glacier surface, called crevasses, vary in width and depth from only a few inches to many feet.

Crevasses form at right angles to the direction of greatest tension and, since within a limited area tension usually is in the same direction, crevasses in any given area tend to be roughly parallel to each other.

Generally, crevasses develop across a slope. Therefore, when traveling up the middle of a glacier, you usually encounter only transverse crevasses (crossing at right angles to the main direction of the glacier).

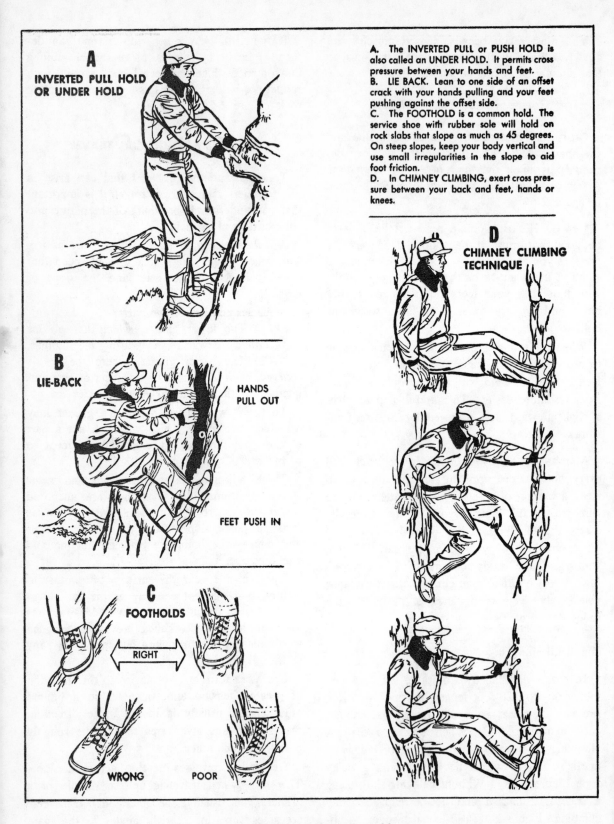

A. The INVERTED PULL or PUSH HOLD is also called an UNDER HOLD. It permits cross pressure between your hands and feet.

B. LIE BACK. Lean to one side of an offset crack with your hands pulling and your feet pushing against the offset side.

C. The FOOTHOLD is a common hold. The service shoe with rubber sole will hold on rock slabs that slope as much as 45 degrees. On steep slopes, keep your body vertical and use small irregularities in the slope to aid foot friction.

D. In CHIMNEY CLIMBING, exert cross pressure between your back and feet, hands or knees.

A
INVERTED PULL HOLD
OR UNDER HOLD

B
LIE-BACK

HANDS
PULL OUT

FEET PUSH IN

C
FOOTHOLDS

RIGHT

WRONG   POOR

D
CHIMNEY CLIMBING
TECHNIQUE

Figure 2-67. Combination Holds

BELAYING

1. Run the rope through your guiding hand (the hand on the rope running to the climber) and around your body to your braking hand, making certain that the rope will slide readily.
2. Make sure that the remainder of the rope is so laid out that it will run freely through your braking hand.
3. See that the rope does not run over the sharp edge of a rock.
4. Use the guiding hand to avoid letting too much slack develop in the rope as the climber moves.
5. Gently tug the line running to the climber to sense his movements.
6. Avoid taking up slack suddenly, since this may throw the climber off balance.
7. Brace well for the expected direction of a fall, so that the force of a fall, whenever possible, will pull you more firmly into position. Neither trust nor assume a belay position that has not been tested.

IN CASE OF A FALL, be able to perform the following movements automatically:
1. Relax your guiding hand.
2. Let the rope slide enough so that braking action is applied gradually by bringing your braking hand slowly across the chest.
3. Hold the belay position, even if this means letting the rope slide several feet.

THE SITTING BELAY

1. The belayer sits or leans against the rocks and attempts to get good triangular bracing between his two legs and his buttocks. Whenever possible, his legs should be straight. The rope should run around his hips in such a manner that a fall will maintain the belayer more firmly in position. This is facilitated by making certain that the rope always runs along the belayer's *best braced leg* to the climber.
2. After the belayer has found a belay position and has settled himself there, he calls "On belay," which is answered by the climber with "Up rope" (in order to have the belayer take up the slack).
3. When the slack has been taken up, the belayer calls "Test." The climber then calls "Testing" and puts his weight gradually on the rope. The climber must be careful not to jerk the rope suddenly, as this might pull the belayer out of position.
4. If the position is satisfactory, the belayer calls "Climb," and the climber calls "Climbing."
5. If the belayer finds his position unsatisfactory, he must call "Off belay," and the climber must release all tension at once. The belayer must then find another position and repeat the test procedure.

SITTING HIP BELAY

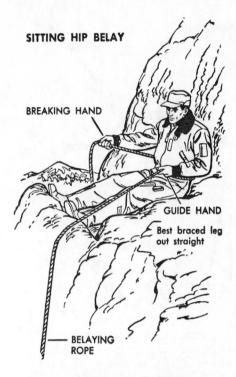

BREAKING HAND

GUIDE HAND

Best braced leg out straight

— BELAYING ROPE

ROPED CLIMB (2-MAN PARTY)

1. One man, chosen as leader because of his ability and experience, always climbs first.
2. Both men tie in with a bowline or a bowline on a coil.
3. The second man takes a belay and starts the test procedure.
4. After finding that his position is satisfactory, he gives the order "Climb."
5. The leader then climbs to a suitable belay position. He should not take long leads, particularly where climbing is difficult. If there is no suitable belay position and he must take a long lead or if climbing is precarious, the leader should, whenever possible, lay the rope over rock nubbins. The belay man adapts his position to an upward pull of the rope.
6. The belayer should watch the slack and inform the climber, "20 feet," "15 feet," "10 feet," and "5 feet," by estimating the length of rope left at the belayer's position.
7. When the climber has reached a belay point, he establishes a firm belay position and follows test procedures. The No. 2 man climbs to his position, then the No. 1 man climbs again. Only when it is determined that both climbers are of equal ability is leapfrogging permissible.
8. The procedure is repeated until the objective is reached.

Figure 2-68. Roped Climbing Techniques

RAPPELING

FRONT VIEW

REAR VIEW

SIMULTANEOUS MOVEMENT. When a slope becomes gentler for a stretch, all men can move at once. The No. 2 and No. 3 men carry the slack rope in neat coils which can be payed out or rolled up as the distance between the men varies. The rope must be kept off the ground but not taut.

ROPED CLIMB (3-MAN PARTY)

1. In a 3-man party each man has a number: the leader is No. 1, the middle man No. 2, and the end man No. 3.
2. The signals are the same as for a 2-man party, except that the number of the man involved must be called out along with the signal. For example, the middle man may give the order "No. 1 climb," or "No. 3 climb."
3. The leader climbs from the starting point to the first belay position, brings up No. 2, and climbs to the second belay position. He provides what security he can while No. 2 brings up No. 3. No. 2 then follows No. 1 who climbs to the third belay position. When not climbing, No. 3 provides security as anchor man for No. 2 when he is belaying.
4. NO MAN CLIMBS UNTIL ORDERED TO DO SO, AND ONLY ONE MAN CLIMBS AT A TIME.

Certain other *general rope signals*, in addition to the belay signals, are often useful. These signals are given orally.

a. "Up rope," is used when a climber discovers excess slack in his belay rope.

b. "Slack," is used when the belay rope is too tight to permit maneuvering.

c. "Tension," means the climber is in trouble and wants a tight rope.

d. "Falling," is used to warn the belay man if the climber believes he is about to fall.

e. When silence is necessary or when a high wind distorts oral signals, you can convey information by a prearranged system of jerks or gentle tugs on the rope.

RAPPELING

A climber with a rope can descend quickly by means of a rappel—sliding down a rope which has been doubled around such rappel (or holding) points as a tree or projecting rock.

In selecting a route, be sure that the rope reaches the bottom or an intermediate point from which additional rappels will reach the bottom. Test the rappel point carefully. Check to see that the rope will run freely around it when one end is pulled from below to retrieve the rope after the rappel has been completed.

To assume the body rappel position, face the anchor point and straddle the rope. Then pull the rope from behind and run it around either hip, diagonally across the chest, then back over the opposite shoulder. From there the rope runs to the braking hand, which is the hand on the same side as the hip that the rope crosses. (For example, from the right hip to the left shoulder to the right or braking hand.)

The climber should lead with the braking hand down and should face slightly sideways. He should keep the other hand on the rope above him as a guide and not as a brake.

He must lean out at a sharp angle to the rock. He should keep his legs well spread and relatively straight for lateral stability and his back straight to reduce unnecessary friction.

Turning up the collar prevents rope burns on the neck. Wear gloves and other articles of clothing as padding for the hands, shoulders, and buttocks.

Figure 2-68. Continued

Near the margins or edges of a glacier, the ice moves more slowly than it does in midstream. This speed differential causes the formation of crevasses which trend diagonally upstream away from the margins or sides.

While crevasses are almost certain to be encountered along the margins of a glacier and in areas where a steepening in gradient occurs, the gentlest slopes may also contain crevasses.

An *icefall* forms where an abrupt steepening of slope occurs in the course of a glacier. Here stresses are set up in many directions. As a result, the icefall consists of a varied mass of ice blocks and troughs with no well-defined trend to the many crevasses.

Moraines

As a glacier moves forward, debris from the valley slopes on either side is deposited on its surface. Shrinkage of the glacier from subsequent melting causes this debris to be deposited along the receding margins of the glacier. Such ridges are called *lateral (side) moraines*.

Where two glaciers join and flow as a single river of ice, the debris on the adjoining lateral margins of the glaciers also unites and, flowing with the major ice-stream, forms a *medial (middle) moraine*. (By examining the lower part of a glacier, it often is possible to tell how many tributaries have joined to form the lower trunk of the glacier.)

Where the snout of the glacier has pushed forward as far as it can go—that is, to the point at which the rate of melting equals the speed of advance of the ice mass—a *terminal (end) moraine* is usually found. This moraine may be formed of debris pushed forward by the advancing snout or it may be formed by a combination of this and other processes.

Lateral and medial moraines may provide excellent avenues of travel. When the glacier is heavily crevassed, moraines may be the only practicable routes.

Ease of progress along moraines depends upon the stability of the debris that composes them. If the material consists of small rocks, pebbles, and earth, the moraine usually is loose and unstable and the crest may break away at each footstep. If larger blocks compose the moraine, they have probably settled into a compact mass and progress may be easy.

In moraine travel, it is best either to proceed along their crest or, in the case of lateral moraines, to follow the trough which separates it from the mountainside. Since the slopes of moraines are usually unstable, there is great risk of spraining an ankle on them.

Medial moraines usually are less pronounced than lateral moraines, because a large part of their material is transported within the ice. Travel on them usually is easy but do not rely upon them as routes for long distances since they may disappear beneath the glacier's surface.

Only rarely is it necessary for a party traveling along or across moraines to be roped together.

Glacial Surface Streams

On those portions of a glacier where melting occurs, runoff water cuts deep channels in the ice surface and forms surface streams. Many such channels exceed 10 feet in depth and width. They usually have smooth sides and their banks are usually undercut. Many of these streams terminate at the margins of the glacier where in summer they contribute to the torrent that constantly flows between the ice and the lateral moraine. You must exercise the greatest caution in crossing a glacial surface stream, since the bed and undercut banks are usually of hard, smooth ice which offers no secure footing.

Glacial Mills

Other streams, however, disappear abruptly into crevasses or into round holes, called glacial mills, and then flow as subglacial streams. Glacial mills are cut into the ice by the churning action of water. They vary in diameter. Glacial mills differ from crevasses not only in shape but also in origin, since they do not develop as a result of moving ice. In places, the depth of a glacial mill may equal the thickness of the glacier.

Glacial Rivers

Northern rivers are varied in type and present numerous problems to those who must cross or navigate them.

A MOUNTAIN AREA
SEEN VISUALLY

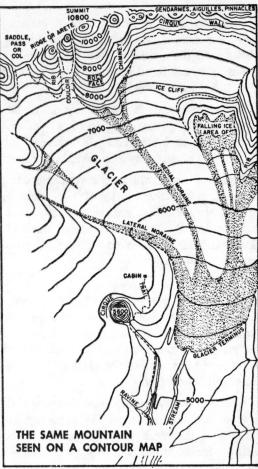

THE SAME MOUNTAIN
SEEN ON A CONTOUR MAP

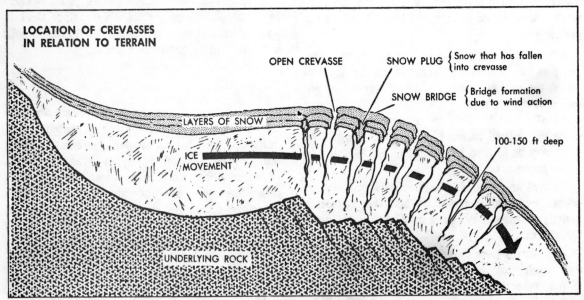

**LOCATION OF CREVASSES
IN RELATION TO TERRAIN**

OPEN CREVASSE

SNOW PLUG { Snow that has fallen into crevasse

SNOW BRIDGE { Bridge formation due to wind action

LAYERS OF SNOW

ICE MOVEMENT

100-150 ft deep

UNDERLYING ROCK

Figure 2-69. Typical Glacier Construction

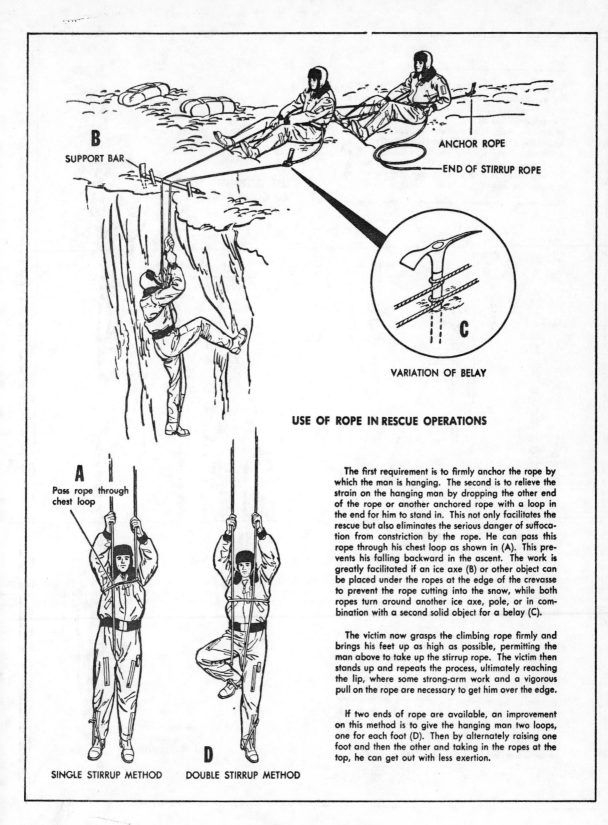

B

SUPPORT BAR

ANCHOR ROPE

END OF STIRRUP ROPE

C

VARIATION OF BELAY

USE OF ROPE IN RESCUE OPERATIONS

A

Pass rope through chest loop

D

SINGLE STIRRUP METHOD   DOUBLE STIRRUP METHOD

The first requirement is to firmly anchor the rope by which the man is hanging. The second is to relieve the strain on the hanging man by dropping the other end of the rope or another anchored rope with a loop in the end for him to stand in. This not only facilitates the rescue but also eliminates the serious danger of suffocation from constriction by the rope. He can pass this rope through his chest loop as shown in (A). This prevents his falling backward in the ascent. The work is greatly facilitated if an ice axe (B) or other object can be placed under the ropes at the edge of the crevasse to prevent the rope cutting into the snow, while both ropes turn around another ice axe, pole, or in combination with a second solid object for a belay (C).

The victim now grasps the climbing rope firmly and brings his feet up as high as possible, permitting the man above to take up the stirrup rope. The victim then stands up and repeats the process, ultimately reaching the lip, where some strong-arm work and a vigorous pull on the rope are necessary to get him over the edge.

If two ends of rope are available, an improvement on this method is to give the hanging man two loops, one for each foot (D). Then by alternately raising one foot and then the other and taking in the ropes at the top, he can get out with less exertion.

Figure 2-70. Crevasse Rescue

CERTAIN PRECAUTIONS SHOULD BE OBSERVED. The exact edge of the crevasse should be ascertained; it may overhang and drop the rescuer into the void if approached too closely. An overhanging lip should be cut away if possible, otherwise the rope will cut into it, and the man cannot easily be brought over the lip. If the edge is sharp ice, it should be rounded off so that the rope will not be cut. The handle of an ice-imbedded axe can be laid at the edge of the overhang to protect the rope.

USE OF PRUSIC KNOT TO CLIMB A ROPE

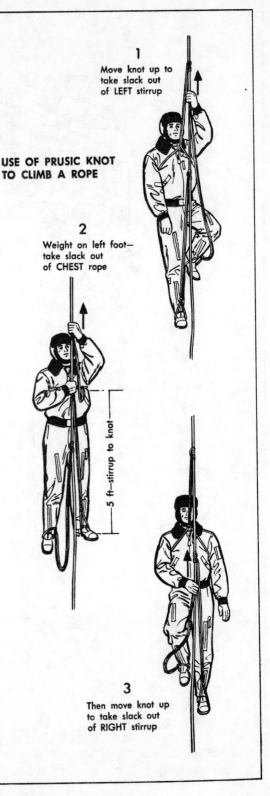

1
Move knot up to take slack out of LEFT stirrup

2
Weight on left foot—take slack out of CHEST rope

5 ft—stirrup to knot

3
Then move knot up to take slack out of RIGHT stirrup

THE PRUSIK KNOT

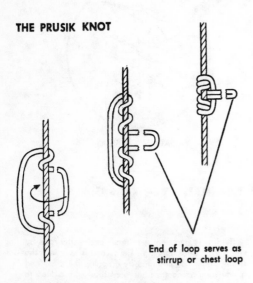

End of loop serves as stirrup or chest loop

The Prusik knot is a valuable means of climbing a rope and saving yourself if you fall into a crevasse, and it is useful if you need to bring a man up a rock face. The knot holds tightly when weight is applied, but it slides easily when unweighted. The method of tying is shown in (E). Take a bight loop or double part of line and turn it twice around the rope, then pull the loose ends of the line through the loop.

For climbing a rope, use three slings fashioned from lengths of line. Make two stirrups and a chest loop fastened by Prusik knots to the climbing rope, as shown in (F). There should be about 5 feet between the stirrup and the knot in order to have the knot in front of the chest in an easy handling position. Then, by moving first one stirrup and then the other, you can climb the rope. At the same time, by pushing up the chest loop, you are secured against loss of balance and can take a rest by leaning back at any time. This is a valuable means of extrication from a crevasse or of rescuing someone from a difficult rock face when strength fails or bad weather intervenes.

Figure 2-70. Continued

Wherever mountains and highlands exist in the arctic regions, melting snows produce concentrations of water that pour downward in series of cataracts, falls, and swift chutes. Their current is churned to foam and the roar drowns out the human voice. Such rivers cannot be successfully rafted in canoes, but *at times they must be crossed.*

Rivers flowing from icecaps and hanging, piedmont (lakelike), or serpentine (winding or valley) glaciers are all notoriously treacherous.

Northern glaciers may be vast in size, and the heat of the summer sun can release vast quantities of water from them.

Glacial ice is extremely unpredictable. An icefield may look innocent enough from above, but countless subglacial streams and water reservoirs may be under its smooth surface. These reservoirs are either draining or are temporarily blocked or damned. Mile-long lakes may lie under the upper snowfield, waiting only for a slight movement in the glacier to liberate them and to send their millions of gallons of water flooding into the valleys below.

Because of variations in the amounts of water released by the sun's heat, all glacial rivers fluctuate in water level. The peak of the flood water usually occurs in the afternoon as a result of the noonday heat of the sun on the ice. For some time after the peak has passed, rivers which drain glaciers may be unfordable or even unnavigable; however, by midnight or the following morning, the water may recede so that fording is both safe and easy.

When following a glacial river that is broken up into many shifting channels, choose routes next to the bank rather than taking a chance on getting caught betwen two dangerous channels.

Flooding Glaciers

Glaciers from which torrents of water descend are called flooding glaciers. Two basic causes of such glaciers are: (1) The violent release of water which the glacier carried on its surface as lakes, or (2) The violent release of large lakes which have been dammed up in tributary glaciers because of the blocking of the tributary valley by the main glacier. This release is caused by a crevasse or a break in the moving glacial dam

coming opposite the lake, the water of which then roars down in an all-enveloping flood.

Flooding glaciers can be recognized from above by the floodswept character of the lower valleys—the influence of such glaciers is sometimes felt for many miles below. Prospectors have lost their lives while rafting otherwise safe rivers because a sudden flood entered by a side tributary and descended as a wall of white, rushing water.

Crevasse Rescue

See figure 2-70.

WATER TRAVEL

Fording Streams

Every man traveling on foot through wilderness must ford some streams. These may range from small, ankle-deep brooks that rush down from side valleys, to large, snow- or ice-fed rivers. The latter are so swift that you can hear waterborne boulders on the bottom being crashed together by the current. If these streams are of glacial origin, wait for them to decrease in strength during the night hours before attempting to ford them.

You must find a ford that is basically safe; this requires careful study. If there is a commanding hill beside the river, leave your pack in a safe spot, and climb the rise. Carefully examine the valley for:

• Level stretches where the river breaks into a number of channels. Like an army, a river can best be defeated when it is separated into a number of parts.

• Obstacles on the opposite bank which might hinder travel. Make certain that you end up on the side where travel is easier and safer.

• A ledge of rocks which crosses the river and which often indicates the presence of rapids or canyons.

• Any heavy timber growths, since they indicate where the channel is deepest.

When selecting a site for fording, remember the following: ·

• Whenever possible, choose a course that leads across the current at about a 45° angle downstream.

THE PACK

1. Remove your pants and underdrawers and lash them to the top of your pack. The water will then have less grip on your bare legs.

2. Keep your shoes and socks on to protect your feet and ankles from boulders and to give you firmer footing.

3. Tie important articles securely to the top of your pack. If you are forced to release your pack, you probably can eventually locate it; but, if single pieces of valuable equipment fall separately, you probably can never recover them.

4. Shift your pack well up on your shoulders; have the slipnooses in good operating condition in case it is necessary to drop your pack. Regardless of the type of pack you are carrying, make certain that you can quickly extricate yourself from it. PREPARE YOURSELF AND YOUR GEAR SO THAT, IF SWEPT OFF YOUR FEET, YOU CAN QUICKLY RELEASE YOUR PACK; then, unencumbered, you can hold onto one end of the pack-strap and, half-swimming and half-wading, fight your way to the far bank. Many competent swimmers have drowned because they could not get out of a heavy pack quickly enough.

USE OF POLE IN CROSSING A SWIFT STREAM

A strong pole can greatly aid a man fording a swift stream. The pole should be about 5 inches in diameter and about 7 or 8 feet long.

Use the pole on your UPSTREAM side to break the current. Do not use it on your downstream side where the current tends to push you down on the pole and to lift your feet from under you.

Keep the pole grasped firmly on your upstream side and firmly plant your feet with each step. Lift the pole a little ahead and downstream from its original position but still upstream from you.

Step below the pole. Keep the pole well slanted so that the force of the current keeps the pole against your shoulder.

SEVERAL MEN entering a swift ford should follow the procedures already mentioned.

The pole is used differently when there is more than one man. The HEAVIEST man forms the DOWNSTREAM anchor with the pole held PARALLEL to the current. The LIGHTEST man is placed at the UPSTREAM end of the pole where he breaks the current; those below move in the eddy formed by his body.

If the current comes from the right, grasp the pole under the left armpit with the right hand extended for balance. If the current comes from the left, grasp the pole under the right armpit and extend the left hand for balance.

At times the upstream man may be temporarily swept from his feet, but the eddy formed by his body enables the man or men below him to move with comparative ease.

As in all fording, the route should quarter downstream. Currents too strong for one man to stand against usually can be crossed safely in this manner.

Experience can' enable you to judge water and the swiftness of its flow with great accuracy, but there is always danger in fording. Take all possible precautions for your personal safety and that of your equipment.

Do not worry about having a heavy pack on your back, since nothing helps more in swift water than weight—IF you can release it quickly. Indians used to shoulder heavy stones to help them to keep their footing in swift streams. The weight of your pack makes it inadvisable to complicate matters further with heavy stones, but REMEMBER THAT THE WEIGHT OF A PACK IS A HELP AND NOT A HINDRANCE.

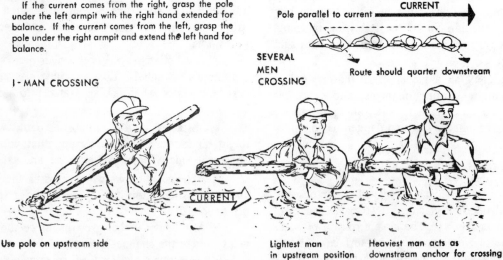

Figure 2-71. Fording a Treacherous Stream

• Never attempt to ford a stream directly above, or even close to, a deep or rapid waterfall or a deep channel.

• Always ford where you would be carried to a shallow bank or sandbar if you should lose your footing.

• Avoid rocky places, since a fall can cause serious injury; however, an occasional rock that breaks the current may be of some assistance to you.

Depth is not necessarily a deterrent if you can keep your footing. Deep water may run more slowly and be safer than shallow water; you can always dry out your clothing later.

In some places, it is easier to swim. Before entering the water, plan exactly what you are going to do and how you are going to do it. Take all possible precautions, and if the stream appears to be treacherous take the steps shown in figure 2-71.

Rafts and Rafting

Rafting rivers is one of the oldest known forms of travel and, under survival conditions, often the best and quickest mode of travel. You can make rafts of dry, dead, standing trees. Spruce, which is found near polar and subpolar rivers, makes the best rafts.

BUILDING A RAFT. The greatest problem in raft construction (figure 2-72a, b, and c) is to make the craft strong enough to withstand the buffeting it may have to take from rocks and swift water. Even if 6- to 8-inch spikes are available, they are not satisfactory since they pull or twist out easily. Rope quickly wears out from frequent, rough contact with rocks and gravel.

Northern woodsmen have evolved a construction method (figure 2-72b) that requires neither spikes nor rope, yet produces a raft that is superior in strength. The only materials you need are logs, although rope is sometimes useful, and the only tools you need are an axe and a sheath knife.

PROTECTING YOUR GEAR AND RIFLE WHEN RAFTING. One of the most important items of equipment you have is your rifle, and few things sink faster. A raft is not foolproof and can turn over when it hits a rock. As a result, the beds of some northern streams are liberally spotted with rifles lost from rafts and canoes. Even when attached to rafts, rifles have gone to the bottom when the raft logs broke apart upon hitting obstructions. Tie your rifle to the raft, but lash it firmly to only one log. Thus, if the raft should be broken, you have a chance of recovering your rifle by going downstream and finding the one log to which your rifle is tied. You may have to swim to reach the log, but at least you have a chance to recover intact a valuable piece of equipment.

Protect packs and other gear by wrapping them in waterproof covering.

RAFTING. You can steer a raft by using sweeps and poles; a pole is more efficient in fairly shallow water, but a sweep is preferable in deep water. Use poles and sweeps from both ends of the raft. The bow (front) man can see any obstructions ahead and the stern (rear) man can follow his directions in steering. Poles are also useful for pushing a raft in quiet water.

The most important rule in navigating an unknown stream is to study cautiously stretches that may be dangerous. Scout swift-water rapids or sharp bends, where the current is strong and the view ahead is obstructed, by beaching the raft and carefully studying the questionable stretch in order to plan the safest route.

Sweepers are among the most dangerous obstructions in northern rivers. A sweeper is a large tree growing on a river bank that is being undermined by a swift current. As the bank washes away, the tree leans farther and farther out until it may actually bounce up and down with the current. While rounding a bend in a river, you may be suddenly confronted with a sweeper that blocks the channel. A rafting party is relatively helpless when it encounters such an obstacle in swift water—hundreds of men have met disaster by hitting sweepers in dangerous rapids. The only precautionary measure is to land above a bend in order to study the river ahead.

Snags and sunken boulders make characteristic disturbances on the surface of a current which you soon learn to recognize.

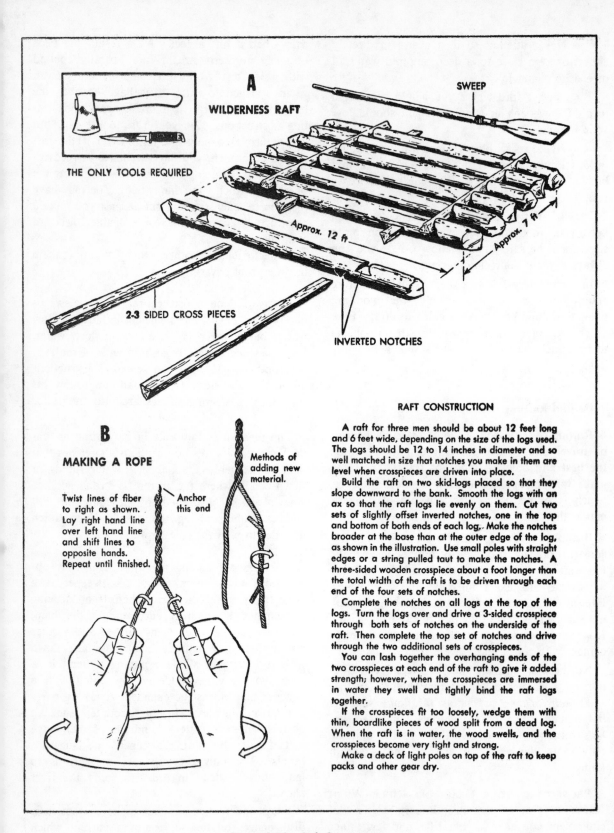

A

WILDERNESS RAFT

SWEEP

THE ONLY TOOLS REQUIRED

Approx. 12 ft

Approx. 7 ft

2-3 SIDED CROSS PIECES

INVERTED NOTCHES

B

MAKING A ROPE

Twist lines of fiber to right as shown. Lay right hand line over left hand line and shift lines to opposite hands. Repeat until finished.

Anchor this end

Methods of adding new material.

RAFT CONSTRUCTION

A raft for three men should be about 12 feet long and 6 feet wide, depending on the size of the logs used. The logs should be 12 to 14 inches in diameter and so well matched in size that notches you make in them are level when crosspieces are driven into place.

Build the raft on two skid-logs placed so that they slope downward to the bank. Smooth the logs with an ax so that the raft logs lie evenly on them. Cut two sets of slightly offset inverted notches, one in the top and bottom of both ends of each log. Make the notches broader at the base than at the outer edge of the log, as shown in the illustration. Use small poles with straight edges or a string pulled taut to make the notches. A three-sided wooden crosspiece about a foot longer than the total width of the raft is to be driven through each end of the four sets of notches.

Complete the notches on all logs at the top of the logs. Turn the logs over and drive a 3-sided crosspiece through both sets of notches on the underside of the raft. Then complete the top set of notches and drive through the two additional sets of crosspieces.

You can lash together the overhanging ends of the two crosspieces at each end of the raft to give it added strength; however, when the crosspieces are immersed in water they swell and tightly bind the raft logs together.

If the crosspieces fit too loosely, wedge them with thin, boardlike pieces of wood split from a dead log. When the raft is in water, the wood swells, and the crosspieces become very tight and strong.

Make a deck of light poles on top of the raft to keep packs and other gear dry.

Figure 2-72. Raft Construction

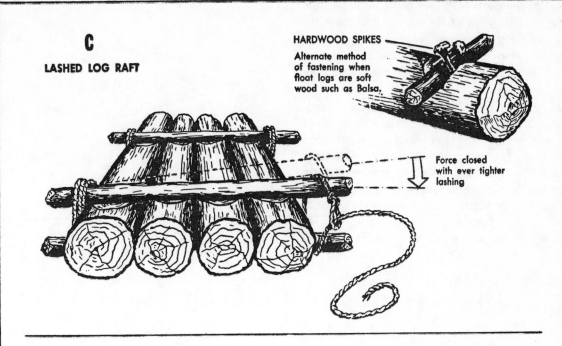

C
LASHED LOG RAFT

HARDWOOD SPIKES

Alternate method of fastening when float logs are soft wood such as Balsa.

Force closed with ever tighter lashing

D CONSTRUCTION OF A BULL BOAT

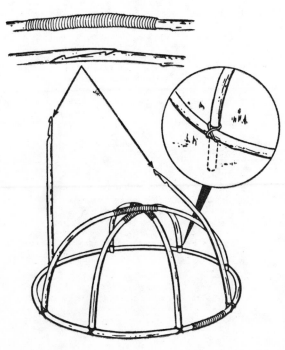

An emergency boat can be made by stretching a tarpaulin or light canvas cover over a skillfully shaped framework of willows and adding a well-formed keel of green wood, such as slender pieces of spruce.

Attach gunwales (sides) of slender saplings to both ends and equalize the spreaders or thwarts as in a canoe. Tie ribs of strong willows to the keel, bend the ends of the ribs upward and tie them to the gunwales. Closely cover the inside of the frame with willows to form a deck upon which to stand.

Such a boat is easy to handle, buoyant, and lacks only strength to be suitable for long journeys. This boat is entirely satisfactory for ferrying a group across a broad, quiet stretch of river.

When such a boat has served its purpose, remove the canvas cover and take it along for constructing shelters or making other boats.

Figure 2-72. Continued

Navigating rivers in hostile territory is possible but difficult because of the necessity of traveling at night. Night navigation requires extremely close adherence to all normal precautionary measures. The raft should be camouflaged during daylight hours.

While hard and fast rules are usually inadvisable, it is always wise to stay close to the *point* of a river bend. If the river bends to the left, keep close to the left bank; if it bends to the right, stay close to the right bank. Water is shallower along these points, and you frequently can jump out to ease your raft gently around the point. Attach a coil of rope of parachute suspension lines to the stern of the raft to help you to control it.

LAND SURVIVAL
-MOIST TROPICS

Some people think of the tropics as an enormous and forbidding tropical rain forest through which every step taken must be hacked out, and where every inch of the way is crawling with danger. Actually, much of the tropics is not rain forest. What rain forest there is must be traveled with some labor and difficulty, it is true, but with little danger from anything bigger or more terrifying than malaria-carrying mosquitoes. Your tropical area may be rain forest, mangrove or other swamps, open grassy plains, or semi-arid brushland. The tropics may contain deserts or cold mountainous districts. So, you may find useful information for survival in all parts of this manual.

EARLY CONSIDERATIONS

Take shelter from tropical rain, sun, and insects. Malaria-carrying mosquitoes and other insect pests are the immediate dangers, so protect yourself against bites. Don't leave the crash area without carefully blazing or marking your route. Use your compass. Know what direction you are taking.

In the tropics, even the smallest scratch can quickly become dangerously infected, so promptly disinfect any wound.

SIGNALING

Sending up smoke signals from a jungle is difficult—the trees disperse the smoke so much that it cannot be recognized as a signal. Set up your fires and other signals in natural clearings and along edges of streams.

Small radio transmitters do not operate effectively under wet jungle foliage; find a clearing.

DECISION TO STAY OR TRAVEL

If you come down in dense jungle where your aircraft and signals can't possibly be seen from the air, you will probably do wisely to travel out. You can find shelter, food, and water along the way. Streams are plentiful in most places; they are often good routes to habitation.

With the proper equipment, care, and common sense, you should be able to travel successfully.

SPECIAL MEDICAL ASPECTS

Most stories about the animals, snakes, spiders, and nameless terrors of the jungle are not based on fact. You are safer from sudden death in the jungle than in most big cities. You might never see a poisonous snake or a large animal. What may bother you most are the howls, screams, and crashing sounds made by noisy monkeys, birds, night insects, and falling trees. The real dangers of the tropics are the insects, many of which pass on diseases or parasites.

Insects

MOSQUITOES. Malaria may be your worst enemy. It is transmitted by mosquitoes, which are normally encountered from late afternoon until early morning. They may also bite in the shade during the day. Guard against bites by camping away from swamps, on high land. Sleep under mosquito netting if you have it; otherwise, smear mud on your face as a protection against insects, especially when sleeping. Wear full clothing, especially at night; tuck your pants into the tops of your socks or shoes. Wear mosquito headnet and gloves if available. Rub mosquito repellent on your hands and all exposed skin. Take antimalaria tablets, if available, according to directions as long as the supply lasts.

TICKS. Ticks may be numerous, especially in grassy places; you may get dozens of them on your body. Strip to the skin once a day or oftener and inspect *all* parts of your body for ticks, leeches, bed bugs, and other pests. If there are several men in your group, examine each other. Brush ticks off clothing; flick them off the skin. If they get attached, cover them with a drop of iodine—they will let go. Heating them will also make them let go, but don't burn your skin. Touch up the bite with antiseptic. Be careful when removing a tick—the head may stay in and start infection.

FLEAS. Fleas are common in dry, dusty buildings. The females will burrow under your toenails or into your skin to lay their eggs. Remove them with a sterilized knife; keep the cut clean. In India and southern China, bubonic plague is a constant threat. Rat fleas carry this disease, and discovery of dead rats usually means a plague epidemic in the rat population, which may be a prelude to an outbreak among human beings. Fleas may also transmit typhus fever and in many parts of the tropics—especially Malaya and Indonesia—rats also carry parasites which cause

jaundice and other fevers. Keep your food in ratproof containers or in rodent proof caches.

MITES. In many tropical and temperate parts of the Far East, a type of typhus fever is carried by tiny red mites. These mites resemble the chiggers of southern and southwestern United States. They live in the soil and burrowed a few inches into the ground, are common in tall grass, cutover jungle, or stream banks. When you lie or sit on the ground, the mites emerge from the soil, crawl through your clothes, and bite. Usually you don't know that you have been bitten, for the bite is painless and does not itch. Mite typhus is a serious disease; prevent it by not getting bitten. Clear your camping ground and burn it off, sleep above the ground, and treat your clothing with insect repellent.

OTHER INSECTS. Leeches are most common in wet underbrush and during the wet season. You may pick them up from plants, the ground, or water. They will get through your shoe eyelets or over your shoe tops. If the leech is embedded, try smothering it with mud, applying heat, or, as a last resort, pull it off.

Spiders, scorpions, and centipedes are often abundant, and some are large. Shake out your shoes, socks, and clothing; and inspect your bed morning and evening—especially for scorpions. A few spiders have poisonous bites, which may be as painful as a wasp sting. Black widow spiders are dangerous. The large spiders called tarantulas rarely bite, but if you touch them, the short hard hairs which cover them may come off and irritate the skin. This is also true of some moth wings.

Centipedes sting if you touch them, and their sting is like that of a wasp. Avoid all types of many-legged insects.

Scorpions are real pests, for they like to hide in clothing, bedding, or shoes, and they strike without being touched. They have poison glands in the large claws and tail; their sting can make you sick.

Stings of all these insects cause swelling and pain. Use cold compresses, mud, or coconut meat applied locally.

Chiggers, wasps, and wild bees are pests and may be harmful. Chiggers, mites, and fleas bore under the skin and cause painful sores; but a drop of oil, resin, or pitch kills them.

Treat ant, wasp, and bee stings with cold compresses. Don't camp near an ant hill or an ant trail. Use caution in climbing trees, for many types of biting ants live in branches and foliage of tropical trees. Mangrove swamps have hanging plants attached to the branches of the mangroves which are almost always inhabited by biting ants.

Never walk barefoot—your shoes guard against crawling mites, ticks, cuts, and subsequent bacterial infection. When you are accidentally dunked or forced to wade in fresh waters suspected of being infested with fluke parasites, observe the following precautions: wring out your clothes, drain and dry your shoes, and rub your body dry of all droplets. Apply insect repellent over exposed areas.

Poisonous Snakes

See attachment 2 for descriptions and illustrations of poisonous snakes.

Crocodiles

The marine crocodile of the Indo-Australian region is very dangerous. They are abundant along the seashores, in coral reef areas as well as in salt water estuaries and in bays. Either crocodiles or alligators may be expected in any tropical waters. They prefer to lie on banks or float like logs with just their eyes above the water. Exercise the greatest caution in fording deep streams, in bathing, and whenever you have occasion to be in or near the water, especially where crocodiles or alligators are evident. Do not attract them to you by thrashing in the water. Avoid them at all times.

Contaminated Fish

Food poisoning will result from eating contaminated or decomposed fish. All freshly caught fish are very susceptible to spoilage, and fresh water fish often contain parasites that also infect humans.

Dangerous Fish

Watch out for poisonous, venomous, and ferocious fish.

POISONOUS FISH. Many species of reef fish have flesh containing toxic substances. These substances are found in some species of fish at all times, and in other species during certain periods of the year. Fish poisoning may occur during any season. The toxins are found in all parts of the fish, especially in the liver, intestines, and eggs. An ounce of liver or flesh of the puffer fish will kill a man in 20 minutes.

The toxins produce a numbness of the lips, tongue, tips of fingers and toes. They also produce severe itching, and a reversal of temperature sensations, which makes hot objects feel cold, and cold feel hot. These sensations are accompanied by nausea, vomiting, dizziness, loss of speech, and a paralysis which may result in death.

Fish toxins are water-soluble, so that even broth from a chowder containing parts of a poisonous fish is harmful. Fish toxins cannot be destroyed by heat, and no amount of cooking will destroy the poison. Nor is freshness any guarantee of safety, since fish toxins are not the result of food spoilage. You cannot distinguish a poisonous fish from a nonpoisonous one by appearance, even if you know it by sight. The best example of this is the red snapper, a well-known table delicacy in many parts of the world, but which in the tropics accounts for many fatal cases of fish poisoning. The red snapper (red pargo) of the Gulf of Mexico and the Caribbean is not poisonous.

No reliable rules exist for testing the edibility of questionable fish. Various methods, such as the discoloration of a silver coin in contact with cooking fish, black discoloration at the base of fish teeth, unusually dull appearance of fish eyes, variation in color, or the tests that are normally used to detect spoiled fish, are valueless. standard edibility rules are useless, since the toxins are tasteless and the flesh usually appears palatable. Birds are least susceptible to the poison, so fish should not be accepted just because birds are seen eating questionable fish. The cat and pig are least affected, while dogs and rats are most susceptible to fish poisons. Even in these animals, reactions to the poison may not be noted for 24 hours. In general, the severity of illness from eating the poisonous flesh of fish is dependent upon the amount eaten. The illness will be more severe if the liver, intestines, or eggs are eaten. An attack of fish poisoning does not give the victim any immunity. Antidotes are not known. Induced vomiting and bowel movements should be attempted. Aside from this, only the symptoms can be alleviated, and these only to a degree.

Poisonous fish are widely distributed in the warm waters of the tropics and are especially numerous in the shallow waters of the Caribbean, and Central and South Pacific. In the Central Pacific around the Phoenix, Canton, Sidney, Midway, Fanning, Line, and Johnston islands, it has been estimated that there are some 300 species of poisonous reef fishes. Fish poisoning may occur at any time of the year and is more dangerous during the breeding period. The information in the paragraphs which follow will help you to avoid poisonous fish.

Characteristics of poisonous fish. There are no simple rules to tell desirable fish from undesirable ones. The worst offenders are illustrated in figures 3-1 and 3-2. These have the following characteristics:

• Almost all live in the shallow waters of lagoons or reefs.

• Many have round or boxlike bodies with hard shell-like skins which are covered with bony plates or spines. They have small parrot-like mouths, small gill openings, and the belly fins are small or absent. Their names suggest their shape: puffer fish, file fish, globe fish, trigger fish, trunk fish, trumpet fish, moon fish, butterfly fish.

Some fish which are usually considered edible, such as red snapper and barracuda, are poisonous when taken from atolls and reefs.

Survivors stranded on inhabited islands may follow the advice of the local natives. But, natives are not infallible guides to the edibility of fish in their home waters. In many cases the development of poison in a previously edible species has been so sudden and unpredictable that local inhabitants eat them and fall ill. However, natives are aware of the most common offenders and should provide some information of the safer fishing grounds.

General Precautions. Survivors without benefit of local information should observe the following precautions:

• Lagoons are normally shallow with sandy or broken coral bottoms. Reef-feeding species predominate. Some are undesirable as food.

• Be especially careful to avoid dangerous or poisonous fish on the leeward or protected side of an island. This area of shallow water consists of patches of living corals interspersed with open spaces and may extend seaward for some distance. Numbers and varieties of fish are usually very abundant; some are undesirable as food.

• Don't eat fish caught in any area where the water is unnaturally discolored. Popular belief is that most fish become poisonous after feeding on microscopic marine algae or small animals whose presence can be noted by eye only when they occur in sufficient mass to change the color of the water. This condition best exists in warm, shallow, protected sides of an island.

• Try fishing on the seaward or windward side, or in deep passages leading from the open sea to the lagoon but be careful of currents and waves. The reefs of live coral drop off sharply into deep water and form a dividing line between the *suspected fish of shallows* and the *desirable deep water species*. Strong swells and wind tend to keep the waters free of toxic foods that may affect fish, and the deep water permits ocean fish to approach close to the island. Even in this area, morays, snappers, barracuda, parrot fish, rockfish, sea bass, and other reef fish may be caught; all *suspected reef fish* should be discarded, whether caught on the ocean or reef side. Survivors on life rafts on the open ocean have less to worry about from fish poisoning.

FISH AND SHELLFISH WITH SPINES. Venomous fish produce their injurious effects only by means of spines, stingers, or "teeth" which inject irritating toxins into the hands or feet of the unwary. Some fish, such as the surgeon, may be armed with venomous spines and have poisonous flesh as well. Typical members of the venomous group are shown in figure 3-2.

Coral reefs are no place for bare feet. Coral, dead or alive, can cut them to ribbons. Seemingly harmless sponges and sea urchins can slip fine needles of lime or silica into your skin, and they will break off and fester. Don't dig them out; use citrus fruit juice, if available, to dissolve

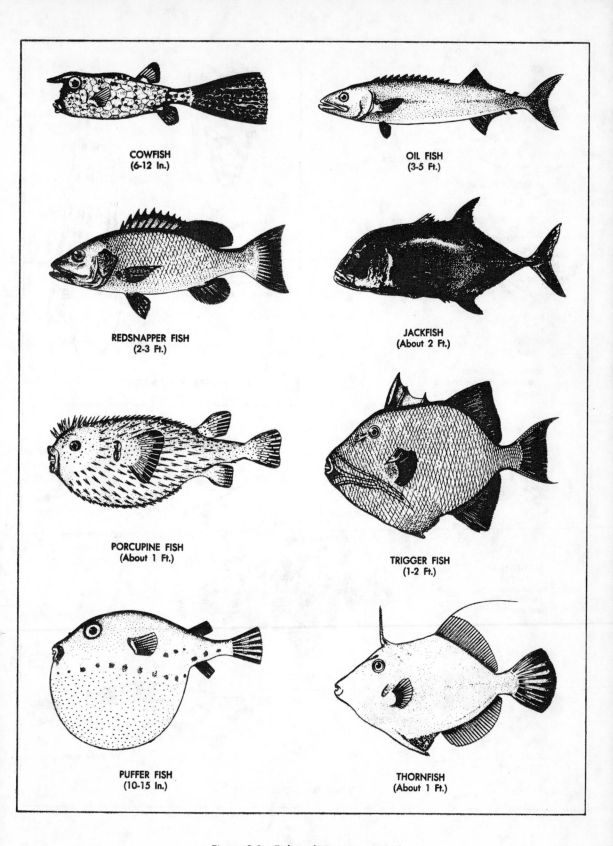

COWFISH
(6-12 In.)

OIL FISH
(3-5 Ft.)

REDSNAPPER FISH
(2-3 Ft.)

JACKFISH
(About 2 Ft.)

PORCUPINE FISH
(About 1 Ft.)

TRIGGER FISH
(1-2 Ft.)

PUFFER FISH
(10-15 In.)

THORNFISH
(About 1 Ft.)

Figure 3-1. Fish with Poisonous Flesh

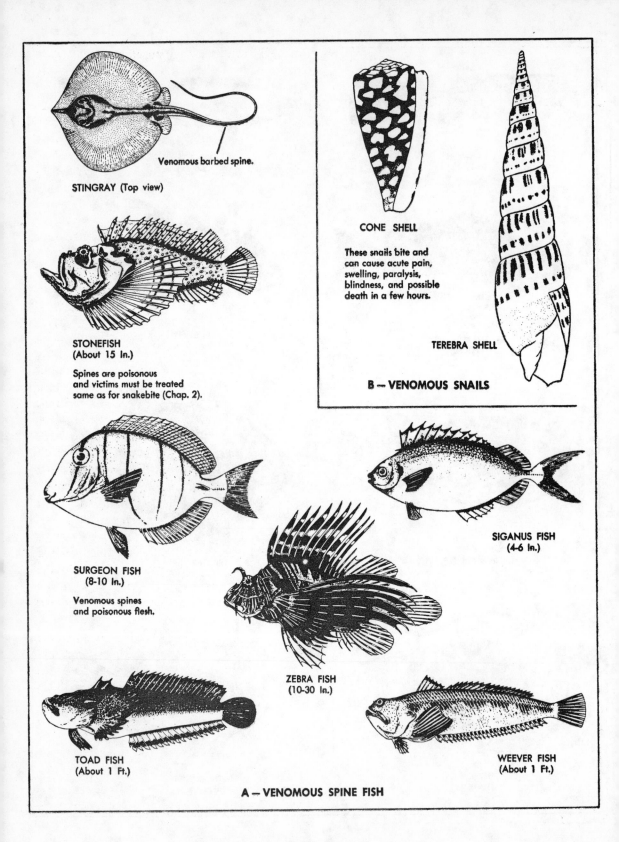

STINGRAY (Top view)

Venomous barbed spine.

STONEFISH
(About 15 In.)

Spines are poisonous
and victims must be treated
same as for snakebite (Chap. 2).

CONE SHELL

These snails bite and
can cause acute pain,
swelling, paralysis,
blindness, and possible
death in a few hours.

TEREBRA SHELL

B — VENOMOUS SNAILS

SURGEON FISH
(8-10 In.)

Venomous spines
and poisonous flesh.

SIGANUS FISH
(4-6 In.)

ZEBRA FISH
(10-30 In.)

TOAD FISH
(About 1 Ft.)

WEEVER FISH
(About 1 Ft.)

A — VENOMOUS SPINE FISH

Figure 3-2. Venomous Spine Fish and Snails

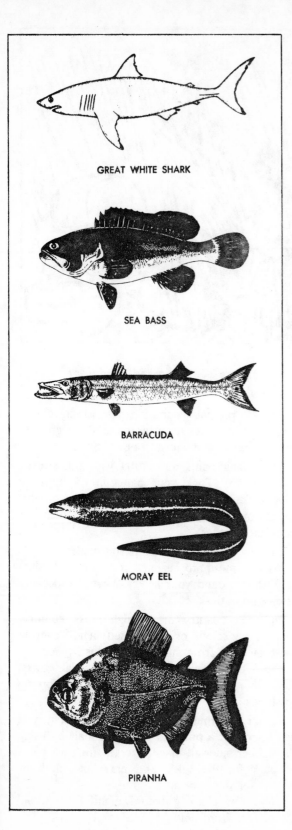

GREAT WHITE SHARK

SEA BASS

BARRACUDA

MORAY EEL

PIRANHA

Figure 3-3. Ferocious Fish

them. The almost invisible stonefish will not move from your path. This fish has poisonous spines that will cause you agony or death. *Treat as for snakebite* (chapter 2).

Don't probe with your hands into dark holes; use a stick. Don't step freely over muddy or sandy bottoms of rivers and seashores; slide your feet along the bottom. In this way you will avoid stepping on stingrays or other sharp-spined animals. If you step on a stingray, you push its body down, giving it leverage to throw its tail up and stab you with its stinging spine. A stingray's broken-off spine can be removed only by cutting it out.

Cone snails and long, slender, pointed terebra snails have poison teeth and can bite. Cone snails have smooth, colorful mottled shells with elongate, narrow openings. They live under rocks, in crevices of coral reefs, and along rocky shores of protected bays. They are shy and are most active at night. They have a long mouth and a snout or proboscis which is used to jab or inject their teeth. These teeth are similar to tiny hypodermic needles, with a tiny poison gland on the back end of each. This action is swift, producing acute pain, swelling, paralysis, blindness, and possible death within a few hours. Avoid handling all cone snails.

Handle the big conches with caution. These snails have razor-sharp trapdoors, which they may suddenly jab out, puncturing your skin in their effort to get away. Don't use your hands to gather large abalones and clams. Pry or wedge them loose with a stick or some such device. They will hold you if they clamp down on your fingers.

FEROCIOUS FISH. In crossing deeper portions of a reef, check the reef edge shadows for sharks, barracudas, and moray eels (figure 3-3). Morays are vicious and aggressive when disturbed. They hide in dark holes among the reefs.

In northeastern South America, the rivers are infested with piranha fish, which, though small, attack in schools and can devour a 300-lb. hog in a few minutes.

In salt water estuaries, bays, or lagoons, man-eating sharks may come in very close to shore. Many sharks have attacked in shallow water on bathing beaches in the tropic seas. Barracudas have also made such attacks. Usually sharks 4 feet long and shorter are timid. Beware, however, of all larger ones, including hammerheads. They are potentially dangerous. Not all sharks show fins above the water.

Portuguese Man-of-War

In warm salt water, watch out for the Portuguese man-of-war. These jellyfish-like creatures have stinging tentacles which may be as much as 50 feet long. The sting is extremely painful and may even disable a swimmer who tangles with a man-of-war in the water.

Figure 3-5. Improvised Head Gear

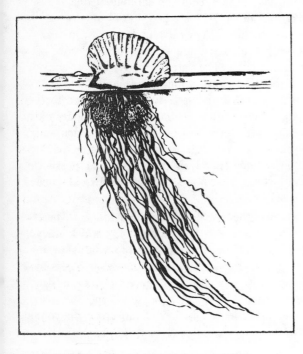

Figure 3-4. Portuguese Man-of-War

Floating on the surface of the sea, the man-of-war appears like a blue bladder 4-5 inches long. Figure 3-4 shows the wrinkled topsail and a mass of long stinging streamers underneath. They are especially common in the Gulf Stream.

CLOTHING

Keep your body covered to (1) prevent malaria-carrying mosquitoes and other pests from biting

you, (2) protect your skin against infections caused by scratches from thorns or sharp grasses, and (3) prevent sunburn in open country.

Wear long pants and shirts with the sleeves rolled down. Tuck your pants in the tops of your socks and tie them securely, or improvise puttees of canvas or parachute cloth to keep out ticks and leeches.

Loosely worn clothes keep you cooler.

Wear a mosquito headnet or tie an undershirt or T-shirt around your head. Wear it especially at dawn and dusk.

In open country or in high grass country, wear a neckcloth or improvised head covering for protection from sunburn and dust. (See figure 3-5.) Move carefully through high grass; some sharp-edged grasses can cut your clothing to shreds.

If you lose your shoes or if they wear out, you can improvise a practical pair of sandals by using the rubber sidewall of an aircraft tire or a piece of bark for the soles, and parachute cloth or canvas for the uppers.

Dry your clothing before nightfall to avoid discomfort from cold.

If you have an extra change of clothes, especially socks, keep it dry to replace wet clothing.

Wash clothing, especially socks, daily. Dirty clothes not only rot but may lead to skin diseases.

SHELTER

Try to pick a campsite on a knoll or high spot, in an open place well back from swamps; you'll be bothered less by mosquitoes, the ground will be drier, and there will be more chance of a breeze.

Cutting away a great deal of the underbrush around your permanent campsite is a good idea; you will let out more of your firelight, which will keep prowling animals away.

You can make a fair bed by covering a pile of brush with layers of palm fronds or other broad leaves. A better bed can be made by building a frame of poles and covering the top with long, spineless palm leaves to a depth of 4 or 5 layers; cut the corner poles long enough to support a mosquito net or parachute fabric cover.

A thick bamboo clump or matted canopy of vines for cover reflects the smoke from a campfire and discourages insects. This cover will also keep the extremely heavy dew of early morning off your bed.

A few don'ts are:

• Don't sleep on the ground. Contact with the ground is chilling. Leaves or grass on the ground make a camp more comfortable.

• Don't sleep or build a shelter under a coconut tree—a falling coconut can disable you.

• Don't camp too near a stream or pond, especially during the rainy season.

• Don't camp on game trails or near waterholes.

• Don't build a shelter under dead trees or trees with dead limbs. They may fall and wreck your camp or hurt someone.

The easiest improvised shelter is made by draping a parachute, tarpaulin, or poncho over a rope or vine stretched between two trees (figure 3-6a). Keep one end of the canopy higher than the other. Discourage insects by having few openings and by burning a smudge. A hammock made from your parachute will keep you off the ground and discourage ants, spiders, leeches, scorpions, and other pests.

In the wet jungle forest you need shelter from dampness. If you stay with the aircraft, use it for shelter. Try to make it mosquito-proof by covering openings with nettings or parachute cloth.

A good rain shelter can be made by constructing an A-type framework and then covering it with a good thickness of palm or other broad leaves, pieces of bark, or mats of grass as shown in figure 3-6b.

Nights are cold in the mountain areas. Get out of the wind. Make your fire a few feet from a cliff or against a rock pile. Build your shelter so that you get reflected heat. Arrange the reflector so that the fire doesn't blow back at you.

FIRE-MAKING

Fuel is usually plentiful in the tropics. During the rainy season, the fire problem may be more complicated by the difficulty of finding dry wood, but many of the larger trees—whether dead or alive—have hollow trunks. Cut strips of the dry inner lining for kindling. When the fire is burning good and high, you can add wet deadwood; even if the outside is wet, you can burn the heart of deadwood. You may also find dry wood hanging in the network of vines or lying on bushes.

A few pieces of green wood mixed in are good for cooking. Dried green wood gives more heat than seasoned wood.

A partly decayed log is the best bank for your campfire; it smoulders all through the night.

Don't use green bamboo for fuel; it emits dangerous fumes. If you use dry bamboo, cut into each section before burning. The sealed sections will explode when they get hot. Shavings of seasoned bamboo are excellent for tinder purposes even when everything seems to be wet.

In palm country you can get good *tinder* by using the fibers at the bases of palm leaves. The insides of dry termite nests make good tinder.

Green leaves thrown on a fire makes a smudge that discourages mosquitoes. If you can recognize plants that are skin irritants, don't burn them; their smoke is also toxic.

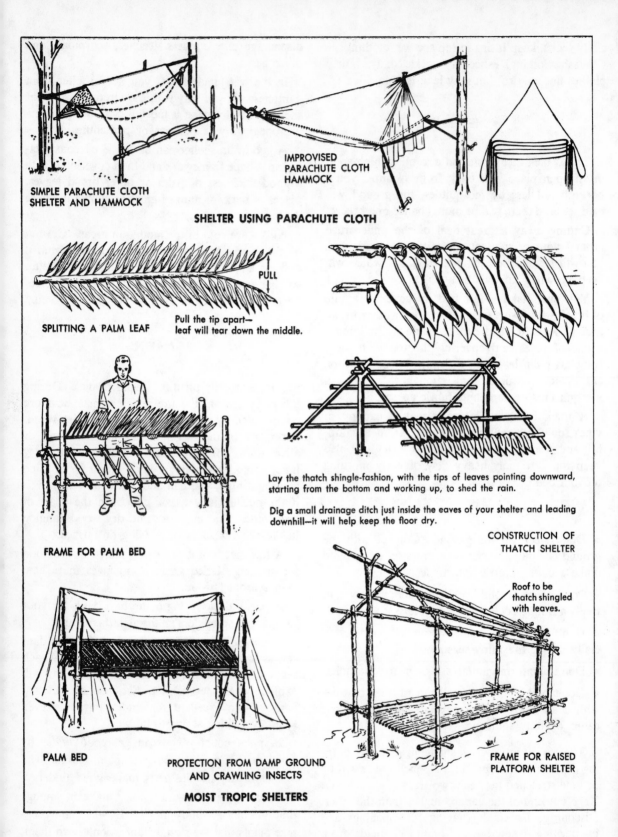

SIMPLE PARACHUTE CLOTH
SHELTER AND HAMMOCK

IMPROVISED
PARACHUTE CLOTH
HAMMOCK

SHELTER USING PARACHUTE CLOTH

SPLITTING A PALM LEAF

PULL

Pull the tip apart—
leaf will tear down the middle.

FRAME FOR PALM BED

Lay the thatch shingle-fashion, with the tips of leaves pointing downward,
starting from the bottom and working up, to shed the rain.

Dig a small drainage ditch just inside the eaves of your shelter and leading
downhill—it will help keep the floor dry.

CONSTRUCTION OF
THATCH SHELTER

Roof to be
thatch shingled
with leaves.

PALM BED

PROTECTION FROM DAMP GROUND
AND CRAWLING INSECTS

MOIST TROPIC SHELTERS

FRAME FOR RAISED
PLATFORM SHELTER

Figure 3-6. Tropic Shelters

By having several logs handy, you can keep your fire going for days. Keep spare wood dry by stowing it under your shelter or beneath broad green leaves. Continuously dry out wet kindling and fuel near your fire for future use.

If your camp is moved, carry some dry tinder and kindling with you to your destination. Use common sense if you must use fires in enemy territory. Fires can be hidden in the jungle but should only be started as an absolute necessity. If the necessity exists, start your fire after dark in a heavy thicket well off trails, and keep the fire burning hot but small to eliminate as much smoke as possible. Remember that jungle people can smell smoke from a great distance, day or night.

WATER

You can get nearly clear water from muddy streams or lakes by digging a hole in sandy soil 1 to 6 feet from the bank. Allow water to seep in, and then wait for the mud to settle.

Water from tropical streams, pools, springs, and swamps is safe to drink only *after it has been purified*. Some discolored or turbid water may be partially cleared by filtering through an improvised filter such as parachute cloth.

You can get water from some plants, and it can be used without further treatment. Coconuts contain refreshing water—the green, unripe coconuts about the size of a grapefruit are best. (See attachment 1.) Do not drink the fluid in mature coconuts as it contains oil which acts as a purgative and causes griping. Vines are often good sources. Choose a good-sized vine and cut off a 3- to 6-foot length. Make first cut at the top. Sharpen one end and hold a container or your mouth to the sharpened end. The water will be fresh and pure. Never drink from a vine that has milky, sticky, or bitter tasting sap. Bamboo stems sometimes have water in the hollow joints. Shake the stems of old, yellowish bamboo—if you hear a gurgling, cut a notch at the base of each joint and catch the water in a container.

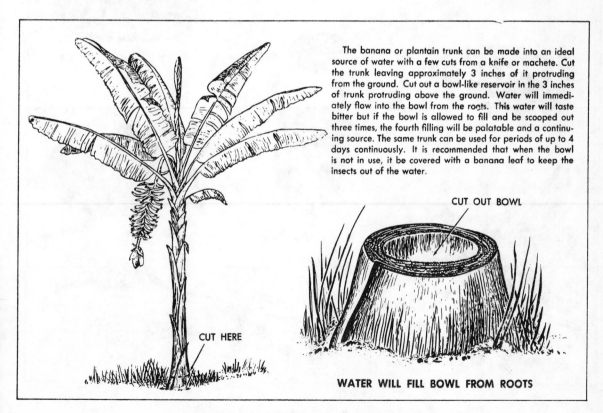

The banana or plantain trunk can be made into an ideal source of water with a few cuts from a knife or machete. Cut the trunk leaving approximately 3 inches of it protruding from the ground. Cut out a bowl-like reservoir in the 3 inches of trunk protruding above the ground. Water will immediately flow into the bowl from the roots. This water will taste bitter but if the bowl is allowed to fill and be scooped out three times, the fourth filling will be palatable and a continuing source. The same trunk can be used for periods of up to 4 days continuously. It is recommended that when the bowl is not in use, it be covered with a banana leaf to keep the insects out of the water.

CUT OUT BOWL

CUT HERE

WATER WILL FILL BOWL FROM ROOTS

Figure 3-7. Water from the Banana Tree Stump

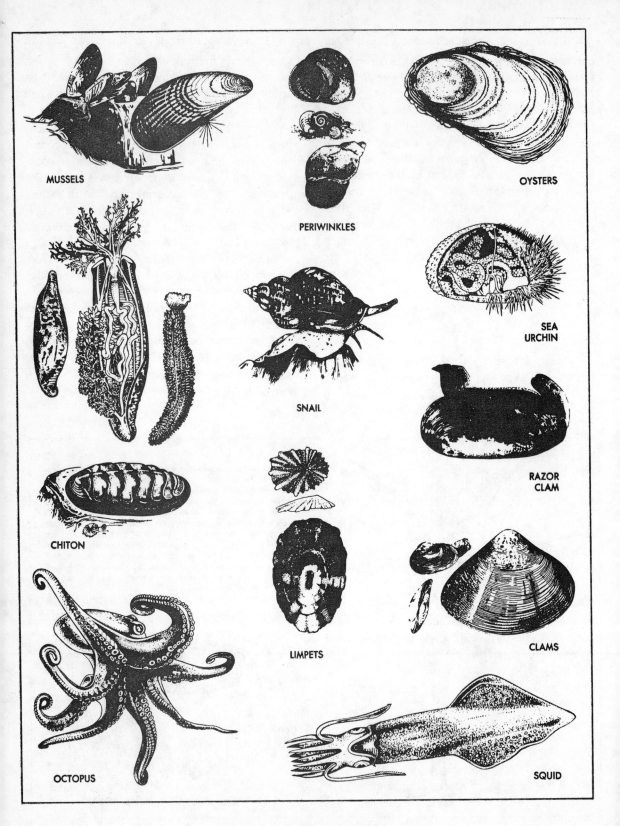

MUSSELS

PERIWINKLES

OYSTERS

SEA
URCHIN

SNAIL

RAZOR
CLAM

CHITON

LIMPETS

CLAMS

OCTOPUS

SQUID

Figure 3-8. Edible Invertebrates

In the American Tropics, the branches of large trees often support air plants (relatives of the pineapple) whose overlapping, thickly growing leaves may hold a considerable amount of rainwater. Strain the water through cloth to eliminate most of the dirt and the water insects. In climbing one of these trees, you may also find small frogs or snakes.

Collect rainwater by digging a hole and lining it with a tarpaulin or a piece of canvas. Catch water from dripping trees by wrapping a clean cloth around a sloping tree, and arrange one end of the cloth to drip into a container.

Animal trails often lead to water. Follow them, but take care not to get lost.

FOOD

Animal Food

LAND ANIMALS. Paths and roads are the normal passageways along which animals travel through tropical forests. Look on the ground for hedgehogs, porcupines, anteaters, mice, wild pigs, deer, and wild cattle. Look in the trees for bats, squirrels, rats, and monkeys. Dangerous beasts— tiger, rhinoceros, elephant—are rarely seen and best left alone. In the Old World Tropics, fruit bats or flying foxes are good sources of meat.

SEA FOOD. Review the discussion of dangerous fish earlier in this chapter.

Rocks, along beaches or extending out into deeper water as reefs, provide a fruitful source of survival food.

Rocks often bear clinging shellfish. Be sure that all shellfish you take are healthy. Do not select them from colonies where some are dead or dying, or where shellfish are not covered with water at least 5 percent of the time.

Fish, crabs, lobsters, crayfish, sea urchins, and small octopi can be poked out of holes, crevices, or rock pools. Be ready to spear them before they move off into deep water. If they are in deeper water, tease them shoreward with a baited hook, piece of string, or stick. You will find flower-like anemones in pools and crevices. They shrink closed when you touch them. Detach them with a knife. Wash well to remove slime and dirt in and outside of animal; boil or simmer.

A small heap of empty oyster shells near a hole may indicate an octopus. Drop a baited hook into the hole and wait until the octopus has entirely surrounded the hook and line; then lift it quickly. To kill, pierce it with your fish spear. Octopi are not scavengers like sharks, but hunters, fond of spiny lobster and other crablike fish. At night, they come into shallow water and can be easily seen and speared.

Snails and limpets cling to rocks and seaweed from the low-water mark up. Large snails called chitons adhere tightly to rocks just above the surf line.

Mussels usually form dense colonies in rock pools, on logs, or at the base of boulders. *Mussels are poisonous in tropical zones during the summer,* especially when seas are highly phosphorescent or reddish.

Sluggish sea cucumbers and conchs (large snails) live in deep water. The sea cucumber can and does shoot out his stomach when excited. Don't eat the stomach, boil the animal and eat the skin and the five strips of muscle inside the body.

The safest fish to eat are those from the open sea or deep water beyond the reef. Silvery fishes, river eels, butterfly fishes, and flounders from bays and rivers are good to eat. Remember that fish caught in the tropics spoil quickly.

Land crabs are common on tropical islands and are often found in coconut groves. Use an open coconut for bait.

HUNTING AND FISHING. If you want to shoot game in the jungle, you'll have a better chance of getting it if you make it come to you. Stalking animals without making any noise is difficult and you will probably frighten them away. Animals will often come if you just sit on a log and don't make any noise. Find a comfortable place and stay there quietly for 5 to 10 minutes. Animals and birds can be "called" by experts, but this is a form of woodsmanship not easily taught in a manual.

Hook and Line Fishing. Hook and line fishing on a rocky coast requires a lot of care to keep the line from becoming entangled or cut on sharp edges. Most shallow water fish are nibblers. Unless your bait is well placed and hooked and the

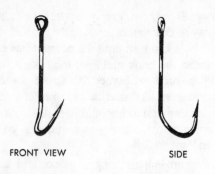

FRONT VIEW   SIDE

Figure 3-9. Snell Hook with Offset Barb

barb of the hook offset by bending (see figure 3-9), you will lose the bait without gaining a fish. Use hermit crabs, snails, or the tough muscle of a shellfish. Take the cracked shells and any other animal remains and drop it into the area you wish to fish. This brings the fish to your area and gives you a somewhat better selection.

If hook-and-line fishing doesn't work out, try chop fishing.

Chop Fishing. Chop fishing is effective at night during low tide. This method requires a torch and a machete. The fish are attracted by the light of the torch and then may be stunned by slashing at them with the back of the machete blade. You should get enough fish for several days by this method. Be careful while swinging the machete. In a situation such as this, fish may also be speared.

Spear Fishing. Underwater spear fishing will produce good catches, provided you have goggles, spears, and lung attachments. But it takes a good swimmer to go after fish with a minimum of home-made equipment, and the danger of cuts from coral, venomous fish, and ferocious fish is hardly justified under survival conditions. You will also find that fish can be wary and hard to corner. Fish swimming in shallow areas or close to the surfaces can be speared from shore or from a raft.

Fishing in Tides, Rips, Currents, and Surf. The survivor should take careful note of tides in his locality, for his schedule of living and traveling

Figure 3-10. Use Torch and Machete for Chop Fishing

will be affected by the daily change of tides. Normal low tide is the best time for lobster fishing and hunting shellfish on the reefs.

The islands of the Pacific have fairly regular diurnal tides with an approximate range of 2½ feet. Normal ebb and flow may be interrupted by periods of prolonged high and low tides caused by the presence of storms in the general vicinity. Low tide is best for gathering shellfish and other forms of reef life. Small fish, and at night, lobsters and sharks, are particularly active during the first few hours of the incoming tide. Dangerous rip tides are not noticeable where tidal inlets are wide. During any change of tide, a great volume of water passes through atoll inlets, and a swimmer should not atempt to swim or raft across the deeper channels until the tide reaches a lull at peak or ebb. Don't get caught far out on a reef by incoming tides, since these may sweep over a reef with a current that makes walking difficult and swimming dangerous.

Surf is not dangerous unless the survivor is in a weakened condition or unless storms have built the wave action above the normal 8-foot height. Waves do not break until they are almost on the reef, and they move shoreward in a definite cycle. The swimmer should take advantage of the lull between series of large waves to get through the surf. It is important to head *into* the waves. If a large wave is ready to break in front of you in shallow water, dive, grab hold of a rock and hang on until the crest of the wave is passed. Let the declining force of the wave carry you shoreward.

Practically all shorelines of atoll islands are rimmed by coral reefs, backed by sandy beaches in sheltered spots and outcrops of coral limestone in exposed areas. Reefs of windward shores are usually reduced to flat, waveswept shelves. The leeward side of islands has more of a tendency for barrier formation to take place, creating shallow lagoons which are very productive to sea life, but some of this sea life is frequently poisonous or dangerous. Deep inlets cut the reefs at the mouths of island streams. Many of these streams appear insignificant, but they discharge enough fresh water, especially in rainy seasons, to stop the formation of coral growth in reef inlets. As a consequence, many of these inlets are abrupt

canyons, and dangerous rip tides may form at change of tide. Surf may be dangerous on the windward side. Steady northeast trades or storm winds pile up breakers 7 to 15 feet high. Surf is usually highest near the peak of the incoming tide. Surf is less dangerous in coves and there is a good chance that inlets through the reef will be found in such places.

Poisoning Fish. The extreme lows of moon tides (those with the lowest ebb occurring at daybreak) are best for poisoning fish. Fish are most active on the incoming tide.

To prepare fish poison, crush the ripe, fallen seeds of barringtonia and allow them to stand overnight. Seashells burned in a fire can also be used. Place these in coarse sacks or nets and drag through the water of the tide pools. The poison stupefies the fish, and they can be caught as they rise to the surface. However, many hide out in crevices and must be pulled out by hand.

Edible Plants of Tropical Areas

Plant foods of the tropics are found in four general vegetation areas—the tropical rain forests, the tropical semievergreen seasonal forests, the scrub and thorn forests, and the savanna. These areas are discussed in the paragraphs which follow.

TROPICAL RAIN FOREST. The jungle in America, Asia, and Africa is more correctly called tropical rain forest. The tropical rain forest forms a belt around the entire globe, bisected somewhat equally by the equator, so that more rain forest lies in the Northern Hemisphere than the Southern Hemisphere. Actually, the tropical rain forest belt, as shown in figure 3-11, is not a continuous one, even in any of the various regions in which it occurs. Usually it is broken by mountain ranges, plateaus, and even by small semi-desert areas, according to the irregular pattern of climate which regulates the actual distribution of rain forest.

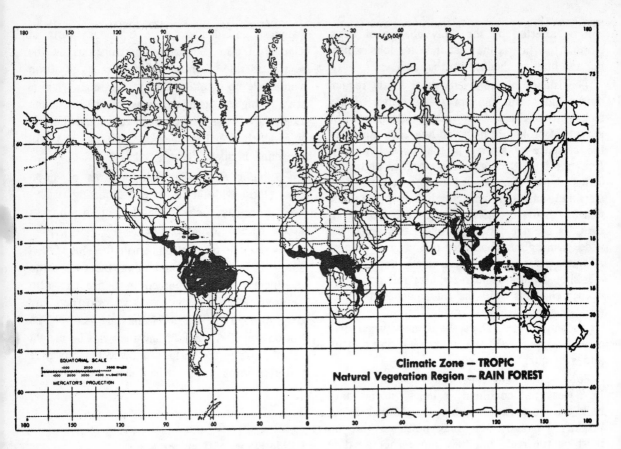

Figure 3-11. Tropic Zone—Rain Forest

Some of the leading characteristics of the tropical rain forest common to these areas in America, Asia, and in Africa, are as follows:

- Vegetation consists of five stories.

- High rainfall (100 inches or more) distributed more or less equally throughout the year.

- Areas of occurrence lie betwen 20° N, and 20° S. latitude.

- Evergreen trees predominate, many of large girth (10 feet in diameter) with thick leathery leaves.

- Vines (lianas) and air plants (epiphytes) are abundant.

- Herbs, grasses, and bushes rare in understory.

- Uniformity in aspect wherever rain forest is well developed.

- Tree bark thin, green, smooth and usually lacking fissures.

The overwhelming majority of plants that grow in the forest of the rainy tropics are woody and of the dimensions of trees. The vines and air plants that grow on the trunks and branches of trees are woody. Grasses and herbs, which are common in the temperate woods of the United States, are rare in the tropical rain forest. Trees form the principal elements of the vegetation in the rain forest. The undergrowth consists of woody plants—seedling and sapling trees, shrubs, and young woody climbers. All of the plants grow very large. The bamboos, which are really giant grasses, (see attachment 1), grow to giant proportions, 20-80 feet high in some cases. Bamboo thickets in parts of some rain forests are impenetrable.

The variety of trees and other plants in the rain forest is great. There are wide variations in size. It is rare, indeed, to find in the rain forest stands of trees which consist of but one of a few kinds, such as exist in the coniferous

114

forest belt of America and Europe. The plants that produce edible parts in the jungle are often scattered, and searching to find several of the same kind will be a part of the survivor's activities.

Jungle trees are never as large, however, as the giant redwoods of California nor as tall as the eucalyptus of Australia. The average height of the taller trees in the rain forest is rarely more than 150-180 feet. Occasionally, venerable giants of the tropical rain forest attain 300 feet in height, but this is extremely rare. Trees more than 10 feet in diameter are also rare in the jungle, but scattered ones of this size may occur. The trunks are, as a rule, straight and slender and do not branch until near the top. The base of many trees is provided with plank buttresses, flangelike outgrowths which are common in all tropical forests. The bark of tropical trees generally is thin and smooth and rarely has deep fissures.

The greatest majority of mature tropical trees have large, leathery, dark-green leaves which resemble laurel leaves in size, shape, and texture. The foliage is so uniform that the casual observer might easily be excused for supposing that the forest was predominantly composed of species of laurel. The general aspect is monotonous, and large and strikingly colored flowers are uncommon. Most of the trees and shrubs have inconspicuous, often greenish or whitish, flowers.

The undergrowth of the rain forest consists of shrubs, herbaceous plants, and vast numbers of saplings and seedling trees. Travel books often give a misleading impression of the density of tropical forests. On river banks or in clearings, where much light reaches the ground, there is a dense growth which is often quite impenetrable. But in the interior of old undisturbed forest, it is not difficult to walk in any direction. Photographs give an exaggerated notion of the density of the undergrowth; it is usually possible to see another person at least 60 feet away.

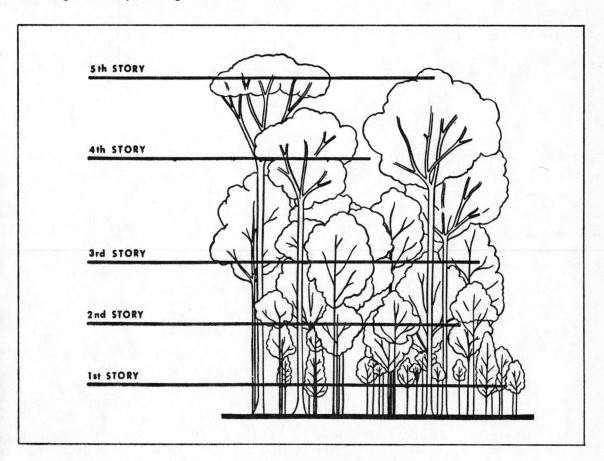

Figure 3-11a. Five Stories of Tropical Rain Forest Vegetation

LAND SURVIVAL
-DESERT

CHARACTERISTICS OF DESERTS

Desert areas are characterized by scanty rainfall and the absence of trees. Usually there is no open water in deserts, but some deserts do have true lakes. Permanent desert lakes with no outlets are salt lakes. Fresh water pools may last days or weeks in any desert after unusual rainstorms. However, don't count on them, for there may be many years between those rainstorms.

Extremes of temperature are as characteristic of deserts as lack of rain and great distances. Hot days and cool nights are usual. A daily minimum-maximum range of 45° F. in the Sahara and a 25° to 35° difference between night and day in the Gobi is the rule. The difference between summer and winter temperatures is also extreme in deserts. Because from these extremes, it is often difficult to keep from freezing in some desert areas. However, summer daytime heat in any desert of the world will make your sweat glands work at capacity. You'll need drinking water to maintain that production.

There are more than 50 important named deserts in the world. They occupy nearly one-fifth of the earth's land surface, but only about 4% of the world's population lives there.

The term "desert" is applied to a variety of areas. There are salt deserts, rock deserts, and sand deserts. Some are barren gravel plains without a spear of grass, a bush, or cactus spine for a hundred miles. In other deserts, there are grasses and thorny bushes where camels, goats, or even sheep can munch and nibble a subsistent diet.

In this study, references are most often cited from two deserts of climatic extremes, a north temperate desert and a near tropic desert. Other deserts fall in between these extremes. Check the latitude before you apply this information to a particular desert.

Anywhere you find them, deserts are places of extremes. They can be extremely dry, hot, cold, and often devoid of plants or trees or lakes or rivers. But most important in any desert, it is an extremely long time between drinks unless you carry your water with you

117

Sahara

The Sahara is the largest desert in the world, as well as the best known. It stretches across North Africa from the Atlantic Ocean to the Red Sea and from the Mediterranean and the Sahara Atlas Mountains in the north to the Niger River in tropical Africa. It consists of three million square miles of level plains and jagged mountains, rocky plateaus, and graceful sand dunes. There are thousands of square miles where there is not a spear of grass, not a bush or tree, not a sign of vegetation. But Sahara oases—low spots in the desert where water can be reached for irrigation—are among the most densely populated areas in the world. Date groves and garden patches supporting 1,000 people per square mile are surrounded by barren plains devoid of life.

Only 10% of the Sahara is sandy. By far the greater part of the desert is flat gravel plain from which the sand has been blown away and piled up in the low places where the dunes are located. There are rocky mountains rising 11,000 feet above sea level, and there are a few depressions 50 to 100 feet below sea level.

The change from plain to mountain is abrupt in the Sahara. Mountains generally go straight up from the plain like jagged skyscrapers from a city street. Sharp-rising mountains on a level plain are especially noticeable in many desert landscapes, because there is no vegetation to modify that abruptness. The lack of trees or bushes makes even occasional foothills appear more abrupt than in temperate climates.

Arabian

Some geographers consider the Arabian Desert as a continuation of the Sahara. Half a million square miles in area, the Arabian Desert covers most of the Arabian Peninsula except for fertile fringes along the Mediterranean, the Red Sea, the Arabian Sea, and the valleys of the Tigris-Euphrates Rivers. Along much of the Arabian coastline the desert meets the sea.

There is more sand in the Arabian Desert than in the Sahara, and there are fewer date grove oases. These are on the east side of the desert at Gatif, Hofuf, and Medina. Also there is some rain in Arabia each year, in contrast to the decades in the Sahara that pass without a drop. Accordingly, Arabia has more widespread vegetation, but nomads find scanty pasture for their flocks of sheep and goats over large sections. They depend on wells for water.

The Arabian Desert differs in one great respect from the Sahara—Arabia has oil. Oil companies have established modern communities on the edge of the desert. They have drilled many water wells over the area for use of the nomads and their flocks.

Oil is carried across the desert in great pipelines which are regularly patrolled by aircraft. Pumping stations are located at intervals. All these evidences of modern civilization have increased the well-being of the desert people and, as a result, your chances for a safe journey afoot. However, the desert of Arabia is rugged, and native Arabs still get lost and die from dehydration.

Gobi

As used here, "Gobi" means only that basin or saucer-like plateau north of China, and covering 125,000 square miles. The plateau includes Inner and Outer Mongolia.

On all sides of the Gobi, mountains form the rim of the basin. Many of them slope gently on the desert side but are abrupt and steep on the other side. The basin itself slopes so gently that much of it appears to be a level plain. The Gobi has rocks and buttes and numerous badlands, or deeply gullied areas.

For a hundred miles or so around the rim of the Gobi, there is a band of grassland. In average years, the Chinese find this to be productive farm land. Year by year they push the Mongol herdsman farther and farther toward the true Gobi. In drought years, agriculture retreats.

As you move toward the center of the Gobi, there is less and less rainfall; soil becomes thinner, and grass grows in scattered bunches. This is the home of the Mongol herdsman. His wealth is chiefly horses, but he also raises sheep, goats, camels, and a few cattle.

Beyond the rich grassland the Gobi floor is a mosaic of tiny pebbles, which often glisten in the sunlight. These pebbles were once mixed with the sand and soil of the area, but in the course of centuries the soil has been washed or blown away and the pebbles have been left behind as a loose pavement.

What rain there is in the Gobi drains toward the basin; almost none of it cuts through the mountain rim to the ocean. There are some distinct and well-channeled watercourses, but these are usually dry. Many of them are remnants of prehistoric drainage systems. In the east, numerous shallow salt lakes are scattered over the plain. They vary in size and number with the changes of rainfall in the area.

Sand dunes are found in the eastern and western Gobi, but these are not as pronounced a feature as they are in certain sections in the Sahara. The Gobi is not a starkly barren waste like the great African desert. Some grass is everywhere, although it is often scanty. Mongols live in scattered camps all over the plains instead of being concentrated in oases.

Southwest United States

The flat plains with scanty vegetation and abruptly rising buttes of our Southwest are reminders of both the Gobi and the Sahara. But the spectacular rock-walled canyons found in the Southwest have few counterparts in the deserts of Africa or Asia. The gullied badlands of the Gobi resemble similar formation in both the Southwest and the Dakotas, but our desert rivers—the lower Colorado, lower Rio Grande and tributaries, such as the Gila and Pecos—have a more regular supply of water than is found in Old World deserts. The Nile and Niger are, in part, desert rivers but get their water from tropical Africa. They are desert immigrant rivers (like the Colorado, which collects the melting snows of the eastern Rockies) and gain sufficient volume to carry them through the desert country.

The scattered population of Navajo, Apache, and Papago Indians, who live in our southwestern desert regions, parallel the scattered population of Mongolia.

In general, our southwest deserts have more varied vegetation, greater variety of scenery, and more rugged landscape than either the Gobi or the Sahara. In all three areas it is often a long time between drinking water stops, and that spells "desert" in any man's language.

Death Valley, a part of the Mohave lying in southern California, probably has more water holes and more vegetation than exist in vast stretches of the Sahara. The evil reputation of the Valley appears to have been started by unwise travelers who were too terrified to make intelligent search for water and food. The dryness of Death Valley atmosphere is unquestioned, but it lacks the vast barren plains stretching from horizon to horizon in the Sahara.

Compared to the Sahara, the desert country of southwestern United States sometimes looks like a luxuriant garden. There are many kinds of cactus plants in the American desert, but these are not found in either the Sahara or Gobi (unless imported from America).

After a good spring rain—not every year, by any means, but sometimes—there are more than 140 different kinds of plants which blossom in the American desert. Many of these are "quickies," whose seeds can withstand long months and even years of drought. White primroses, lavender verbenas, orange poppies, and yellow desert sunflowers are just a few of the colorful flowers which carpet the desert floor after a hard spring rain.

In contrast to the "quickies," which blossom only after desert rains, are the cactus plants. These store up moisture in their stems or trunks, and their blossomtime is not so dependent on uncertain rains.

Although the cactus plants are not found in either the Gobi or the Sahara, both of these larger deserts do show a few of the quick-flowering plants after a hard rain. The displays of flower colors in these Old World deserts, however, are very poor shows compared to the variety and brilliance of the American desert.

South America

Generally there are two regions of deserts in South America. The first and by far the largest is along the west coast, beginning in the southern part of Ecuador, extending the entire coastline of Peru, and reaching nearly as far south as Valparaiso in Chile. This region of about 2,000 miles in length and averaging approximately 100 miles in width is classified as true desert. Even so, along the shoreline of Peru as far south as Arica and inland a few miles there is often a low cloud layer or misty fog layer called "garuas." The layer is approximately 1,000 feet thick and produces a fine drizzle that often turns the streets muddy and clings to clothes, making them quite damp. From Arica, Peru, south to Coquimbo, Chile, or about 30 degrees south, the cloud cover does not exist and this region may truly be called rainless. The rare and uncertain showers are valueless for cultivated vegetation. Because of this frequent cloud cover and other phenomena, the temperature along the coastal desert is remarkably cool, averaging about 72° in the summer daytime and about 55° in the winter daytime.

Behind the coastal ranges in the higher elevations, the aridity is at a maximum. In the nitrate fields of the Great Atacama Desert, shut off from the sea mists, the air is very dry and the slightest shower is very rare. Here the summer daytime temperatures rise to 85 or 90 degrees.

The second desert region is entirely in Argentina east of the Andes, extending in a finger-like strip from about 30 degrees south, southeast to about 50 degrees south. This region is approximately 1200 miles long and 100 miles wide. In this highly dissected plateau region the temperature ranges from a yearly average of 63°F in the north to 47°F in the south. The average annual rainfall pattern is from about 4 inches in the north to about 6 inches in the south.

EARLY CONSIDERATIONS

Water is your biggest problem if you are down in the desert. Get into the shade as soon as possible. Wait until nightfall to travel. If you have crashed or bailed out, reserve any decisions or activity until possible effects of shock have passed. In hot deserts, reserve all strenuous activities for the cooler portions of the day or for nighttime. Keep your head, the back of your neck and other unprotected areas such as arms, covered.

SIGNALING

You can make a good improvised flare from a tin can filled with sand soaked with gasoline. Light it with care. Add oil and pieces of rubber to make dense smoke for daytime signal. Burn gasoline or use other bright flame at night.

Dig trenches to form signals, or line up rocks to throw shadow.

If you can find brush in the area, gather it into piles and have it ready to light when a search aircraft is heard or sighted.

Smoke fires and smoke grenades are best for use in daytime. Flares and bright flames are hard to see.

The mirror is a very good desert signal. Practice using it. Use metal, brightly polished on both sides, as a substitute.

DECISION TO STAY OR TRAVEL

The best advice generally is to stay with the aircraft. You'll last much longer without water if you stay near the aircraft, in the shade rather than exhausting yourself by trying to walk out.

Travel only if you are sure that you can walk easily to assistance, and if you are absolutely certain that you have enough water (see desert water supply table, figure 4-4), or if there is reasonable doubt that rescue is possible.

SPECIAL MEDICAL ASPECTS

Exposure to desert sun can be dangerous. It can cause three types of heat collapse: heat cramps, heat exhaustion, and heat stroke.

Heat Cramps

The first warning of heat exhaustion usually is cramps in leg or belly muscles. Keep the patient resting; give him salt dissolved in water, but only if there is plenty of water to drink. (Two salt tablets per canteen of water [1-quart] or equivalent proportion.)

Heat Exhaustion

Patient is first flushed, then pale; sweats heavily. His skin is moist and cool; he may become delirious or unconscious. Treat him by placing him in the shade, flat on his back. Give him salt dissolved in water—two tablets to a canteen.

Heat Stroke

Heat stroke may come on suddenly. The face is red, skin hot and dry. All sweating stops. The head aches severely; pulse is fast and strong. Unconsciousness may result. Treat the patient by cooling him off. Loosen his clothing; lay him down flat, but off the ground, in the shade. Cool him by saturating clothes with water and by fanning. Do not give stimulants.

Note: People whose bodies have become acclimatized to working in high temperatures will find their normal salt needs are satisfied at mealtime by food salted to their taste. During acclimatization a man's heart action, circulation, sweat glands, and all body functions become adjusted to function in the heat. This is the period of natural adjustment to the conservation of body salt.

Sunglare

The color of the ground varies a great deal in different deserts. In areas where there is light sand, as much as 80% of the light which falls on it is reflected back. That is getting near the amount of reflection from snow.

Snow blindness (photophthalmia) is due to the reflection of short wavelength ultraviolet light. Since there is a higher percentage of ultraviolet light in equatorial regions, there is probably a damaging concentration of these light rays at eye level from the reflected light in some desert regions.

Solar retinitis produced by the short infrared and visible light rays can also occur in deserts. You won't be bothered by this, however, unless you look at the sun or are scanning the sky in the area immediately adjacent to the sun.

In other words, sunglasses of some sort are good for you. Even though the glare does not seem painful to you, the very high light intensities of the desert will cause a decrease in your night vision.

Regular flying sunglasses in large frames are the easy and satisfactory solution to the problem of sunglare. They should be large enough to prevent side light from striking the eye. Such glasses will be some protection against dust, but by no means complete protection.

Figure 4-1. Improvised Glasses

If you do not have flying sunglasses, the next best help is to make slit goggles as shown in figure 4-1. Another method is to shade the eyes from above with a hat or a turban which has cloth down the sides of your face. Smear charcoal or dirt on the bridge of your nose and below your eyes, to cut down glare.

Sunblindness

Symptoms of sunblindness are burning, watering, or inflamed eyes, poor vision, the halo seen when looking at lights, and headaches.

Treat sunblindness by protecting the eyes from light and relieving the pain. The patient should either stay in a dark shelter or wear a lightproof bandage. Relieve the patient by putting cold compresses on the eyes. Give the patient aspirin. Use no eye drops or ointment. If patient has complete rest, he will probably recover within 18 hours. When travel is necessary before 18 hours, patient will have to be led. Remember: the first attack of sunblindness makes the victim more susceptible to future attacks.

Hazards

Deserts are quite healthful places, since dry air is not favorable to bacteria. Wounds usually heal rapidly in the desert, even without treatment. Except in some oases of the Sahara, malaria does not exist. The venereal diseases, however, are prevalent in both Gobi and Sahara. They are much more common in Mongolia than in Africa. Unless you lose your senses of sight and smell, you probably will not become infected.

Summertime dysentery can be avoided by watching your diet and not eating or drinking uncooked native food. In the fall and early winter, typhoid and paratyphoid are present, but your inoculations or shots give normal protection from these.

MOSQUITOES. Ordinarily mosquitoes do not travel far from their breeding place. They breed in quiet or stagnant water such as rain pools, swamps, water pockets in plants, old tin cans, or similar places. Since their usual life span is 15 to 20 days, under some conditions even a couple of months, their presence does not mean that you are near a supply of water.

All mosquitoes are unwelcome company, but only some species of the anopheles carry malaria. You can usually distinguish the anopheles from other mosquitoes by the way they settle on your skin or other surface. The anopheles settles with the proboscis and long axis of the body in one straight line at an angle of 45° with its "landing field." The culicine mosquitoes, which in general do not carry disease, land with the abdomen parallel to or inclined toward the surface upon which it rests. Cold weather slows them down.

Singing mosquitoes are not anopheles. The singers do not generally carry disease.

Malaria, yellow fever, dengue, filariasis (elephantiasis) and other ills are mosquito-borne.

Unless the female anopheles has bitten a patient with malaria or other mosquito-carried disease before she bites you, no harm is done. She is only a vector, not an originator. If a strong silent mosquito drills you at a 45° angle, play safe and reach for the antimalaria pill.

FLIES. Flies are sometimes found so far out in the desert that you wonder how they got there. In Egypt and Libya they are *bad*. They buzz and pry about any exposed part of your body without letup. They settle on your lips, the corners of your eyes, your ears. There is no rest from flies unless you cover your face and every part of your body when you are in a fly-infested desert.

OTHER INSECTS. Other insects are less numerous. In some regions you might shake a scorpion out of your shoes in the morning. On the other hand, you can spend months in the desert without seeing one.

SNAKES. Snakes are not numerous in desert areas. Cold weather keeps them sluggish, and you probably will not see one in wintertime even in southern deserts.

CLOTHING

In hot deserts you need your clothing for protection against sunburn, heat, sand, and insects, so don't discard any of it. Keep your head and body covered during the day—you'll last longer on less water. Wear long pants and blouse them over the tops of your boots. Roll down your shirtsleeves, but keep them loose and flapping to stay cooler.

Wear a cloth neckpiece to cover the back of your neck from the sun. Your T-shirt makes an excellent neck drape, with the extra material used as padding under your cap. If you have no hat, make a headpiece like that worn by the Arabs, as shown in figure 4-2. You can adapt your pilot chute for use as a parasol; don't be too proud to use one. During duststorms, wear a covering for your mouth and nose; parachute cloth will do.

Deserts are not always hot. Heat is a desert characteristic in summer daytime—from May to October in the Sahara; during July and August in the Gobi. During the rest of the year, you'll need winter clothing in the Sahara, arctic winter clothing in the Gobi.

If you have lost your shoes, or if they wear out, make sandals as shown in figure 4-2. Those hardy desert soldiers, the French Foreign Legionnaires, follow the practice of wearing "Russian socks" on their long desert hikes. These are prepared as follows: Wash your feet in lukewarm water; then dry them and rub grease on them. Cut parachute cloth into strips 2 feet long and 4 inches wide, and wrap these strips, bandage fashion, around your feet and ankles. They will feel and look like ordinary white socks. They will enable you to walk in comfort, even with blishered heels.

SHELTER

The summer months bring hot days, and shelter from the midday sun is advisable.

You will need shelter mostly from sun and heat.

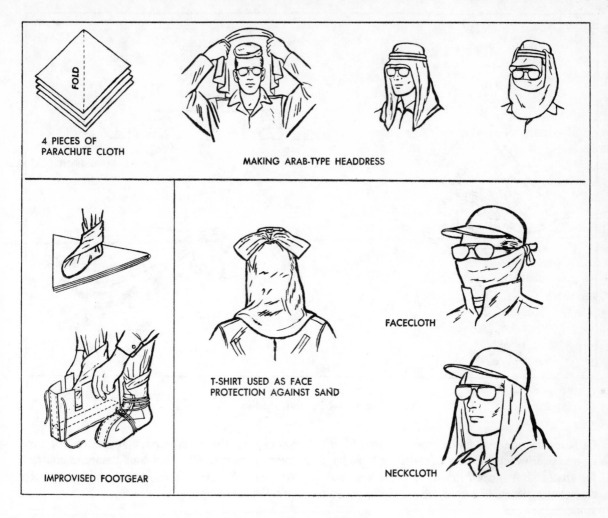

FOLD

4 PIECES OF
PARACHUTE CLOTH

MAKING ARAB-TYPE HEADDRESS

IMPROVISED FOOTGEAR

T-SHIRT USED AS FACE
PROTECTION AGAINST SAND

FACECLOTH

NECKCLOTH

Figure 4-2. Desert Clothing

During Sahara winter (October to May) the absence of shelter is not serious. Nights are cold, but not much below freezing, while daytime temperatures reach the 80's and low 90's. You will not suffer from exposure if properly dressed. If it should rain, use the inside of the aircraft then for protection against cold and rain, but do your cooking outside to prevent carbon monoxide poisioning.

Aircraft

If you stay with the aircraft, don't use the inside of it for shelter in the daytime—it will be too hot. Get under the shade of a wing, if you have no other shelter. You can make a good shade shelter easily by tying a spreadout parachute as an awning to the wing, leaving the lower edge at least 2 feet clear of the ground for air circulation. Use sections of aircraft tubing (if available) for tent poles and pegs.

Parachute

If the aircraft is not available, make a shelter of your parachute, as shown in figure 4-3. The layers of cloth separated by an airspace of several inches make a cooler shelter than a single thickness. The parachute can also be placed across a trench dug in the sand.

Natural Shelter

Natural shelter is limited to the shade of cliffs or the lee side of hills. In some desert mountains you can find good cavelike protection under the tumbled blocks of rocks broken from cliff sides.

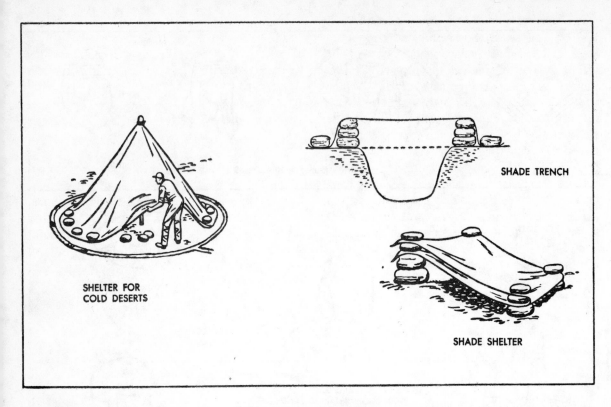

SHELTER FOR COLD DESERTS

SHADE TRENCH

SHADE SHELTER

Figure 4-3. Desert Shelters

Occasionally you may find a twisted, stunted bush or tree over which you can spread your parachute for shade. But out on the open plain you must carry your shelter, like your food and water, with you.

Note: If you camp or travel in a desert canyon or dry river bed, be prepared for a quick exit. Cloudbursts, although rare, do cause sudden and violent floods which sweep along a dry valley in a wall of roaring water.

FIRE-MAKING

In some deserts, fuel is extremely rare. Wherever you find plant growth, use all twigs, leaves, stems, and underground roots for burning.

Stems of palm leaves and similar wood serve as fuel in the near oases. Dried camel dung is the standard fuel where woody fibers are lacking.

In the Gobi, dried heifer dung is the preferred fuel. Heifer dung has a symmetrical shape, in contrast to the broad irregular pattern of cow dung. It burns with a hot blue flame, in contrast to the smokey yellow flame of cow dung, sheep droppings, etc.

WATER

Water Requirements

In the desert, your life depends on your water supply. Figure 4-4 shows how long you can survive on specific amounts of water at various temperatures.

The normal temperature of your body is 98.6°F. Any variation reduces your efficiency. An increase of 6° to 8° for any extended period is fatal. Your body gets rid of excess heat by evaporating water on the skin surface. You can see how effective the system is if you fill a desert water bag and a canteen with water and hang both in the sun. When the water in the canteen is 110°F., the water in the sweating desert bag will be only 70 degrees. Evaporation of sweat on the desert bag keeps it 40° cooler.

When you sweat, however, your body loses water, and you must replace the loss by drinking water. Otherwise you will pay for the loss in reduced efficiency and perhaps death. A man who has lost 2½% of his body weight by sweating (about 1½ quarts) loses 25% of his efficiency. Also, if he is working in temperatures of 110°F., his normal ability will be cut another 25 percent. These data mean that if your body is short 1½ quarts of water and the air around you is 110°F., you can do only about half as much work as you normally do; you can walk only half as far as you could in cooler temperatures with plenty of water.

In hot deserts, you need a minimum of a gallon of water a day. If you walk in the cool desert night, you can get about 20 miles for that daily gallon. If you do your walking in daytime heat, you'll be lucky to get 10 miles to the gallon. Whether you sit out your desert survival or walk home, you'll need water—at least 3 to 4 quarts a day.

The only way to conserve your water is to ration your sweat. Drink water as you need it, but keep heat out of your body by keeping your clothes on. Clothing helps ration sweat by absorbing it and, through its evaporation, cooling your environment within the clothes. You may feel more comfortable in the desert without a shirt or pants, because your sweat evaporates fast. But then you need more sweat—and sunburn is a painful trouble. Desert sun will burn you even if you have a good coat of tan, so wear a hat, use a neckcloth, and keep your clothes on. Light-colored clothing turns away the heat of the sun better than dark clothes. Clothing also keeps out the hot desert air.

NO WALKING AT ALL	MAXIMUM DAILY TEMPERATURE (°F) IN SHADE ▼	AVAILABLE WATER PER MAN, U.S. QUARTS					
		0	1 Qt	2 Qts	4 Qts	10 Qts	20 Qts
		DAYS OF EXPECTED SURVIVAL					
	120°	2	2	2	2.5	3	4.5
	110	3	3	3.5	4	5	7
	100	5	5.5	6	7	9.5	13.5
	90	7	8	9	10.5	15	23
	80	9	10	11	13	19	29
	70	10	11	12	14	20.5	32
	60	10	11	12	14	21	32
	50	10	11	12	14.5	21	32

WALKING AT NIGHT UNTIL EXHAUSTED AND RESTING THEREAFTER	MAXIMUM DAILY TEMPERATURE (°F) IN SHADE ▼	AVAILABLE WATER PER MAN, U. S. QUARTS					
		0	1 Qt	2 Qts	4 Qts	10 Qts	20 Qts
		DAYS OF EXPECTED SURVIVAL					
	120°	1	2	2	2.5	3	
	110	2	2	2.5	3	3.5	
	100	3	3.5	3.5	4.5	5.5	
	90	5	5.5	5.5	6.5	8	
	80	7	7.5	8	9.5	11.5	
	70	7.5	8	9	10.5	13.5	
	60	8	8.5	9	11	14	
	50	8	8.5	9	11	14	

©Reprinted from "Physiology of Man in the Desert," by E. F. Adolph and Associates, Interscience Publishers, New York; 1947

Figure 4-4. Water Requirements

1%-5% OF BODY WEIGHT	6%-10% OF BODY WEIGHT	11%-20% OF BODY WEIGHT
Thirst	Dizziness	Delirium
Vague discomfort	Headache	Spasticity
Economy of movement	Dyspnea (labored breathing)	Swollen tongue
Anorexia (no appetite)	Tingling in limbs	Inability to swallow
Flushed skin	Decreased blood volume	Deafness
Impatience	Increased blood concentration	Dim vision
Sleepiness	Absence of salivation	Shriveled skin
Increased pulse rate	Cyanosis (blue skin)	Painful urination
Increased rectal temp.	Indistinct speech	Numbness of the skin
Nausea	Inability to walk	Anuria (decreased or deficient urination)

Figure 4-5. Signs and Symptoms of Dehydration

Keep in the shade as much as possible during the day. Desert natives have tents open on all sides to allow free circulation of air during the daytime. Sit up a few inches off the ground, if possible do not lie right on it. The temperature can be 30° cooler a foot above the ground, and that dffierence can save you a lot of sweat.

Slow motion is better than speed in hot deserts. Slow and steady does it. If you must move about in the heat, you'll last longer on less water if you take it easy. Remember the Arab—he is not surviving in the desert; he lives there and likes it. He isn't lazy—he's just living in slow motion, the way the desert *makes* him live. Don't fight the desert—you won't win.

Figure 4-5 lists the signs and symptoms of dehydration.

Sources of Desert Water

Although it is not wise to depend on finding natural water in an unfamiliar area, there are a number of sources from which water may be obtained.

WELLS. In all deserts, wells are the sources of most water. Hand-dug wells have furnished water to irrigate Sahara oases for many centuries, and there are almost as many ways of hauling the water to the surface as there are wells. Hand-dug wells, like the oases themselves, are located in low

places of the desert. Basins, dry river valleys, and hollows in the dunes are typical locations. The best of these, of course, are ancient river beds.

In the western Sahara, the natives have dug elaborate tunnels for irrigation. Starting at the edge of a basin or in the bed of an old river, they dig a ditch toward the desert, keeping the bottom of the ditch on a gentle slope down from the basin. As the ditch extends out into the desert, it soon becomes too deep to be maintained as an open trench. The workmen extend it as a tunnel as far as they can see without artificial light. Leap-frogging ahead along the same line, they set down a well and tunnel back and forward. Then another jump is made to another well. These chains of wells, connected by a tunnel in the moist sand, extend for miles into the desert. Water collects in the underground channel and flows to the basin, where it irrigates the gardens. A similar system has been discovered in the central Asian desert nearly ten thousand miles from the tunnels in Sahara. Although they are still being used and are being extended in modern times, the origins of these tunnels are still hidden to historians.

In some areas, governments have provided for keeping wells open or digging new wells, but most desert travelers are public-spirited enough to fix a well that needs repairs. Their generosity doesn't extend to leaving a rope for the next traveler. Unless you are agile enough to go down and up

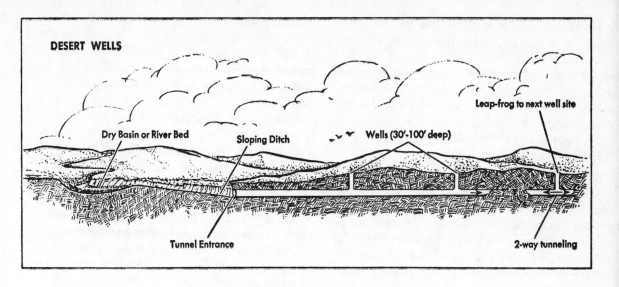

DESERT WELLS

Dry Basin or River Bed

Sloping Ditch

Wells (30'-100' deep)

Leap-frog to next well site

Tunnel Entrance

2-way tunneling

Figure 4-6. Hand-dug Irrigation Systems

a chimney like Santa Claus, you had better carry a 100-foot rope in the Sahara. A 30-foot rope will reach water in most Gobi wells.

The Gobi is itself a great basin with only internal drainage, so that water falling on its mountain edges, if not evaporated, replenishes the ground water supply. Wells dug in valley bottoms or other low places of the Gobi tap that water supply at a depth of 10 to 15 feet. Natives dip the water with a skin bag on the end of a stick to which a rope is attached, or use a bucket on a hand rope. Elaborate pulleys, well sweeps, or pumps so common in the Sahara are not necessary at shallow Gobi wells.

In northern Mongolia, wells are less numerous than in the south, because there are more springs. All roads lead to water, however. You'll know you are going in the right direction when your trail joins another. The "arrow" formed by two connecting trails points toward the water.

Desert wells are generally located along trails. In rocky deserts and on some gravel plains, however, the well is not always easy to find. This is particularly true if it does not have any super structure or is in a protected valley.

In desert and near-desert regions, wells are gathering places for native peoples as well as stopping places for caravans. Permanent camps or habitations may be as much as 2 or 3 miles away from the well. Passing caravans may camp within a few yards or a few hundred yards from a well. Camp fire ashes, animal droppings, and generally disturbed surface show that others have camped there. Such indications will also tell you that a well is not far off. Paths leading from the camping area should lead you to the well.

On some flat plains, wells which are not often used are covered against sandstorms. Even though there is no sand in the immediate area, sandstorms would in time fill up such wells. In sand dune areas, this is even more likely. Desert people have learned to cover such wells a little below the top. Sand drifts in, but the well is protected. You can dig out the cover and reach water easily in such wells but be careful not to dump the sand into the cavity. There may be only a shallow pool of water in the well bottom.

You sometimes hear stories about poisoned wells. Many of these are based on bad-tasting water which is not necessarily poisonous. Actually the danger of poison from water in the Sahara can only be cited as a curiosity, for there are just two wells in this class. One, at Tini-Hara in Esh-Shish-Erg, is so strong of chlorine that it will burn clothing. In the same Erg, General Laperine found another well so strong of saltpeter that it caused vomiting. Occasionally in the Gobi, a traveler will encounter a well so strongly alkali that he will prefer to go the 6 or 8 miles to a fresher water supply.

RIVERS. Great desert rivers like the Nile, the Tigris, and the Euphrates have been used to irrigate the desert for centuries. Shorter streams on the desert edges are also diverted into irrigation ditches to water the feet of palm trees. At other points, where mountain streams lose themselves in desert sands, the natives plant their trees and crops right over the lost rivers so that roots can reach the water without difficulty.

LAKES. There are shallow lakes in most deserts, and many of them are undrained. These have been without outlets for many thousands of years so that evaporation has concentrated the amount of salt in the water and has made them distinctly salt water lakes. Some of the salt water tastes like table salt. In other areas it may contain magnesium or alkali.

NATURAL POOLS AND CISTERNS. In the Sahara, deep hollows on rocky plains (figure 4-7a) act as cisterns and collect surface water from the rare torrential rains. These tanks may be dry for 10 or 15 years, then suddenly be deep enough for a good swimming hole. The water in them is fresh and drinkable and may take several weeks or months to dry up. Unfortunately there is no way for the casual traveler or stranger to the area to know of the existence of such water holes, and there is no rule to guide one to them. They are natural drainage basins like any depression on a plain or plateau. If you know there has been a rain recently in your area, then keep an eye out for hollows or any protected cavity which would naturally collect surface drainage.

Many desert water holes are not true wells but are natural tanks or cisterns. These may be located behind rocks, in gullies or side canyons and under cliff edges (figure 4-7b). Often the ground surface near them is solid rock or hard-packed soil on which paths do not show up. In such cases, you may have to search for the water point.

In the Libyan Sahara, doughnut-shaped mounds of camel dung often surround the wells. Unless you recognize the small mound ring you could easily miss the well.

PLANTS. The thirsty traveler in tropical jungles will find many plants containing suitable drinking water. In the Gobi and Sahara, plants are not a source of water supply. American deserts are slightly better favored. The large barrel cactus does contain considerable moisture which can be squeezed out of the pulp if you have the energy to cut through the tough, outer spine-studded rind. Botanists argue both that the juice *can* and *cannot* be used to quench thirst.

Three men did drink it and found the taste bitter. "Reminded me of the taste when I take an aspirin tablet without a drink of water to wash it down," said one. The taste disappeared in about half an hour. A barrel cactus 3½ feet high contained moisture from top to bottom and "about a quart of liquid could be obtained by crude methods of crushing the pulp and squeezing out the milky juice." (This is an exception, like dandelions, to the rule that milky or colored sap-bearing plants should not be eaten. Working with a scout knife, one of the men took 40 minutes to get to the moisture-bearing pulp of this kind of plant. Less time was required when a machete was available. So far the evidence for getting your water supply out of desert plants indicates that you had better find a well or other source.

WATER CREEPS ALONG CRACKS IN THE ROCKS

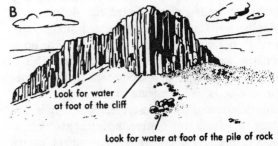

Look for water at foot of the pile of rock

Figure 4-7. Where to Look for Springs

Cut off top, mash pulp, suck water through grass straw or mash the pulp in a cloth and squeeze directly into the mouth.

INTERIOR OF BARREL CACTUS —WATERY PULP

Figure 4-8. Water from the Cactus Plant

CONDENSED MOISTURE. In the Arabian Desert near the Persian Gulf and the Red Sea and in the Libyan Sahara near the Mediaterranean Sea, the air is quite moist. This moisture condenses on cool objects. Often condensed moisture or dew will be heavy enough to drip from metal awnings or roofs on cool mornings. In Arabia, this morning dew and even fog extends inland several miles. Occasionally fog occurs as much as 200 miles from the Persian Gulf.

If you find dew on the metal wings of your crashed aircraft, you may collect the drip in a container or you might get more water by wiping it off the cool metal with a handkerchief or soft cloth and wringing it out into a container.

Cool stones, collected from below the hot surface of the desert, if placed on a waterproof tarp may cause enough dew to collect for a refreshing drink. Exposed metal surfaces like aircraft wings or tin cans are best dew condensers. They should be clean of dust or grease to get the best flavored water.

Soon after sunrise in the desert, the dew evaporates. If you expect a good drink, you must collect the dewdrops very soon after sunup.

SOLAR STILL. A solar still can be made from a sheet of clear plastic stretched over a hole in the ground. Whatever moisture is in the soil plus that from plant parts (fleshy stems and leaves) when they are used as a supplementary source, will be extracted and collected by this emergency device. Obviously, where the soil is extremely dry and no fleshy plants are available, little, if any, water can be obtained from the still. However, in such situations, the still can be used to purify polluted water such as body wastes. The parts for the still are a piece of plastic film about six feet square, a water collector-container or any waterproof material from which a collector-container can be fashioned, and a piece of plastic tubing about ¼ inch in diameter and 4 to 6 feet long. The tubing is not essential, but makes the still easier to use.

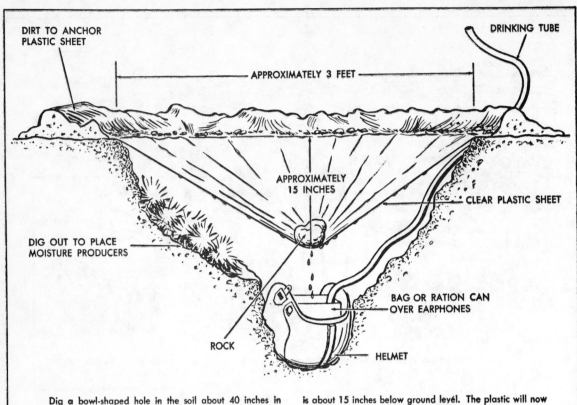

Dig a bowl-shaped hole in the soil about 40 inches in diameter and 20 inches deep. Add a smaller, deeper sump in the center bottom of the hole to accommodate the container. If polluted waters, such as body waste, are to be purified, a small trough can be dug around the side of the hole about half way down from the top. The trough insures that the soil wetted by the polluted water will be exposed to the sunlight and at the same time that the polluted water is prevented from running down around or into the container. If plant material is to be used, line the sides of the hole with pieces of the plant or its fleshy stems and leaves. Place the plastic film over the hole and put a little soil on its edges to hold it in place. Place a rock no larger than your fist in the center of the plastic and lower the plastic until it is about 15 inches below ground level. The plastic will now have the shape of a cone.

CAUTION

Make sure the plastic cone does not touch the earth anywhere causing loss of water.

Put more soil on the plastic around the rim of the hole to hold the cone securely in place and to prevent water vapor losses. Straighten the plastic to form a neat cone with an angle of about 30 degrees so that the water drops will run down and fall into the container in the bottom of the hole. It takes about one hour for the air to become saturated and start condensing on the underside of the plastic cone.

Figure 4-9. Solar Still

A container can be made from such material as plastic, aluminum foil, poncho, emergency ration tins, or a flight helmet. The tubing, when it is available, is to be fastened to the bottom of the inside of the container and used to remove drinking water from the container without disturbing the plastic film.

Some plastics work better than others. Almost any clear plastic film should work, if it is clear, strong, and "wettable." That is, it should be the kind which, when water drops form on the under side, causes the drops to cling to the plastic and run down to drip into the container instead of dropping off where they form.

If fleshy plants are available, or if polluted water is to be purified, the still can be constructed in any convenient spot where it will receive direct sunlight throughout the day. Ease of digging will be the main consideration. If soil moisture is to be the only source of water, some sites will be better than others. Seek a place where there is reason to believe the soil will contain more moisture. A stream bed, even though dry, or a depression where rain water has collected will stay moist longer than other areas. Generally clay soil is better than sand because it holds more water longer. (In any case, after prolonged dry periods the yield from any soil alone may be small.) Although sand generally does not retain as much moisture as clay, a wet sand will work very well. Along the sea coast or in any inland area where brackish or polluted water is available, any wet soil, even sand, produces usable amounts of water. On cloudy days, the yield will be reduced because direct sunlight is necessary if the still is to operate at full efficiency.

Certain precautions must be kept in mind. If you use polluted water, make sure that none is spilled near the rim of the hole where the plastic touches the soil and that none comes in contact with the container, otherwise there is a chance that your freshly distilled water will be contaminated.

Do not disturb the plastic sheet during daylight "working hours" unless it is absolutely necessary. If a plastic drinking tube is not available, raise the plastic sheet and remove the container as few times as possible during daylight hours. It takes from ½ to 1 hour for the air in the still to become resaturated and the collection of water to begin again after the plastic has been disturbed.

Tips on Locating Sources of Water

Desert natives often know of lingering surface pools in dry stream beds or other low places. They cover them in various ways to protect them from excessive evaporation. If you look under brush heaps or in sheltered nooks you may locate such pools in semi-arid brush country.

Birds need water. Some of them fly long distances at sunset and dawn to reach waterholes. If you hear their chirping in the early morning or evening, you may locate their private drinking fountain. In true desert areas, flocks of birds circle over waterholes.

The presence of vegetation does not always mean that surface water is available. Many plants have an extensive shallow root system. This enables them to make maximum use of water from rare desert rains. Other plants have long taproots which go down several feet to reach a permanent supply of ground water. In the American desert, mesquite is an outstanding example. Where it grows, you can reach water if you dig—but you may have to dig down 20 to 60 feet. The roots of this plant are known to grow to those depths to reach ground water.

Places which are visibly damp, where animals have scratched or where flies hover are more reliable places to dig for water, because they indicate that surface water was there recently.

Digging for Water

When you are away from trails or far from wells, you may still find water. Along the seashore or on sandy beaches or desert lakes your best chance is to dig a hole in the first depression behind the first sand dune. Rainwater from local showers collects here. Stop digging when you hit wet sand. Water will seep out of the sand into the hole. This first water is fresh or nearly fresh; it is drinkable. If however, you dig deeper, you may strike salt water.

Damp surface sand anywhere marks a good place to scoop out such a shallow well, from which you can collect water into your canteen or other receptacle. Among sand dunes away from surface water, the lowest point between the dunes, as shown in figure 4-10, is where rain water collects. Dig down 3 to 6 feet. If sand gets damp, keep digging until you hit water. If you dig in the dune itself, you may strike a foot or so of damp sand with dry sand below. When that happens, you had better look for a lower spot to dig your well.

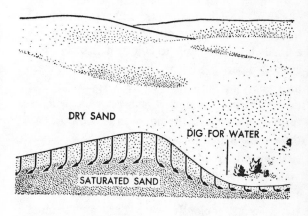

DRY SAND

DIG FOR WATER

SATURATED SAND

Figure 4-10. Sand Dunes

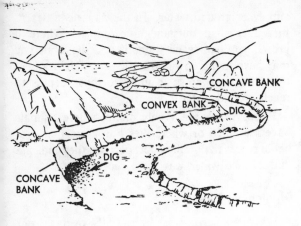

Figure 4-11. *Dry River Bed*

In a sand dune belt, water most likely will be found beneath the original valley floor at the edge of the dunes rather than in the easy digging middle of the belt.

Dry stream beds often have water just below the surface. It accumulates and sinks at the lowest point on the outside of a bend in the stream channel as the stream dries up. You may catch a drink if you dig on such outside bends.

In mud flats during winter you may find wet mud at the lowest point. Wring mud out in a piece of cloth to get water—but don't drink if the water is too salty or soapy tasting.

FOOD

Animal Food

In most deserts, animals are scarce. Their presence depends upon water and vegetation, and true deserts offer little of either. However, a few animals have been able to adjust their body processes to desert conditions, the best known of these are the camel and the gazelle. Apparently the desert antelope, or gazelle, can get enough moisture from its food, for no records indicate that these creatures drink water at any time.

Camels have adapted to an irregular supply of water rather than to its absence. They make up for periods of enforced drought—8 to 10 days—by drinking copiously when they are watered. Camel men say that their charges drink about as much water in the course of a year as other beasts of equal size (about 6 gallons a day). Their advantage is that they carry storage tanks.

Some small rodents (rabbits, prairie dogs, rats), snakes, and lizards have learned to live in deserts. They keep in the shade or burrow into the ground, protecting themselves from the direct sun and heated air as well as from the hot desert surface.

Hunting

Look for animals at waterholes, in grassy canyons, low-lying areas, dry riverbeds—where there is a greater chance of moisture—or under rocks and in bushes. Animals are most commonly seen at dusk or early morning. The smaller animals are your best and most reliable sources of food. You may catch rodents by finding their burrows and snaring them with a loop snare, trap, or deadfall when they come out at dusk or dawn. Look for land snails on rocks and bushes.

Try kissing the back of your hand to make squalling sounds; you may attract birds. Sand grouse, ducks, bustards, pelicans, and even gulls have been seen over some desert lakes. Trap them in baited deadfalls or use a hook or gorge.

When hunting an animal on the desert, remember that distances are deceptive. Make certain the animal is actually within range before you fire. You'll probably get just one shot.

Plant Food

DESERT SCRUB AND WASTE. The plants that grow in deserts are fairly well restricted to particular desert areas. For example, American desert plants are almost wholly different from African desert plants. Possibly one reason for this is that unbroken stretches of desert scrub and waste are usually not so widespread as the other vegetation regions, such as the tropical rain forest, prairie, steppe, or tundra. The northern coniferous forests of America, Europe and Asia are similar, not only in aspect, but also as to the kinds of plants. The general aspects of all hot deserts are much alike, but the similarity ends there. For instance, native cacti occur only in American deserts, and not in Asia and Africa.

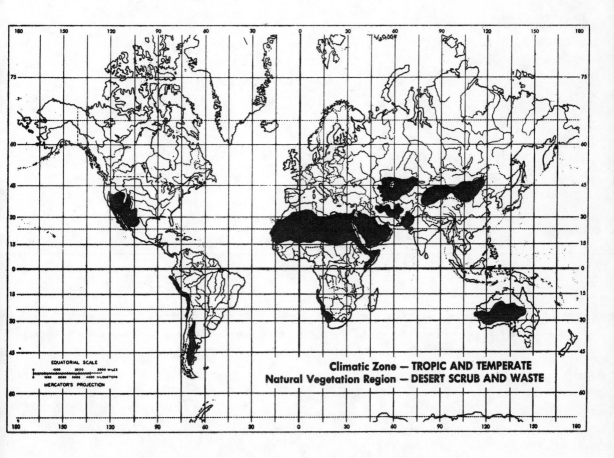

Figure 4-12. Temperate Zone—Desert Scrub and Waste Areas

133

ATTACHMENT ONE
PLANTS

Section A—Poisonous Plants

POISONOUS PLANTS IN THE TROPICS AND TEMPERATE ZONES

There are two types of poisonous plants. One type poisons on contact. An example of this type is poison ivy, which affects the external portions of the body. The other type poisons internally. Poison hemlock is an example. The poisoning occurs from having eaten a portion of the plant—fruit, stem, leaf, root.

Poisonous on Contact

If you are familiar with poison ivy or poison oak in the United States and are aware of the abundance of these plants, you have already seen poisonous plants of this type in as plentiful a state as they occur anywhere in the world.

In tropical regions, many kinds of plants poison by contact. The family to which the American poison oak and poison ivy belong has tropical types which are dangerous. The plants of this family are mostly trees and shrubs. The poison is usually exuded by the bark, which is often identified by streaks of black ooze along the trunk. If you come into contact with a poisonous plant of this sort, the treatment is the same as for poison ivy and poison oak. Wash the poisonous oil away with soap and water and apply a bandage to prevent spreading.

In the moist tropics of southeast Asia, for instance, the poisonous members of the cashew family are called rengas. The leaves of the cashew nut (*Anacarduim occidentale*) are poisonous to some people.

Poisonous Internally

One of the greatest concerns of the survivor is whether or not a strange plant is poisonous to eat. Use the edibility rules explained in figure 2-37 when in doubt. Try to learn what is good, and stick with those kinds. Try a nibble first, not a whole handful. Make sure that you can identify the water hemlock.

Stinging Plants

Nettles are the commonest kind of stinging plants in the North Temperate Zone. In the tropics, the tree nettle and the cowhage have stinging hairs. The tree nettle carries an irritating poison which is formic acid. The action of the cowhage is merely mechanical. Recovery from the effects of these plants occurs in a relatively short time.

POISONOUS PLANTS IN THE ARCTIC (TUNDRA) AND SUBARCTIC

Plants which produce poisoning upon contact do not exist in these cold regions.

The following plants are poisonous only when eaten. They are internal poisons and are the only dangerous ones you are apt to encounter on the tundra and in the subarctic regions adjoining the tundra.

2-3½' Tall

White flowers

RED POISONOUS BERRIES

ROOTSTALK IS A VIOLENT
PURGATIVE AND EMETIC

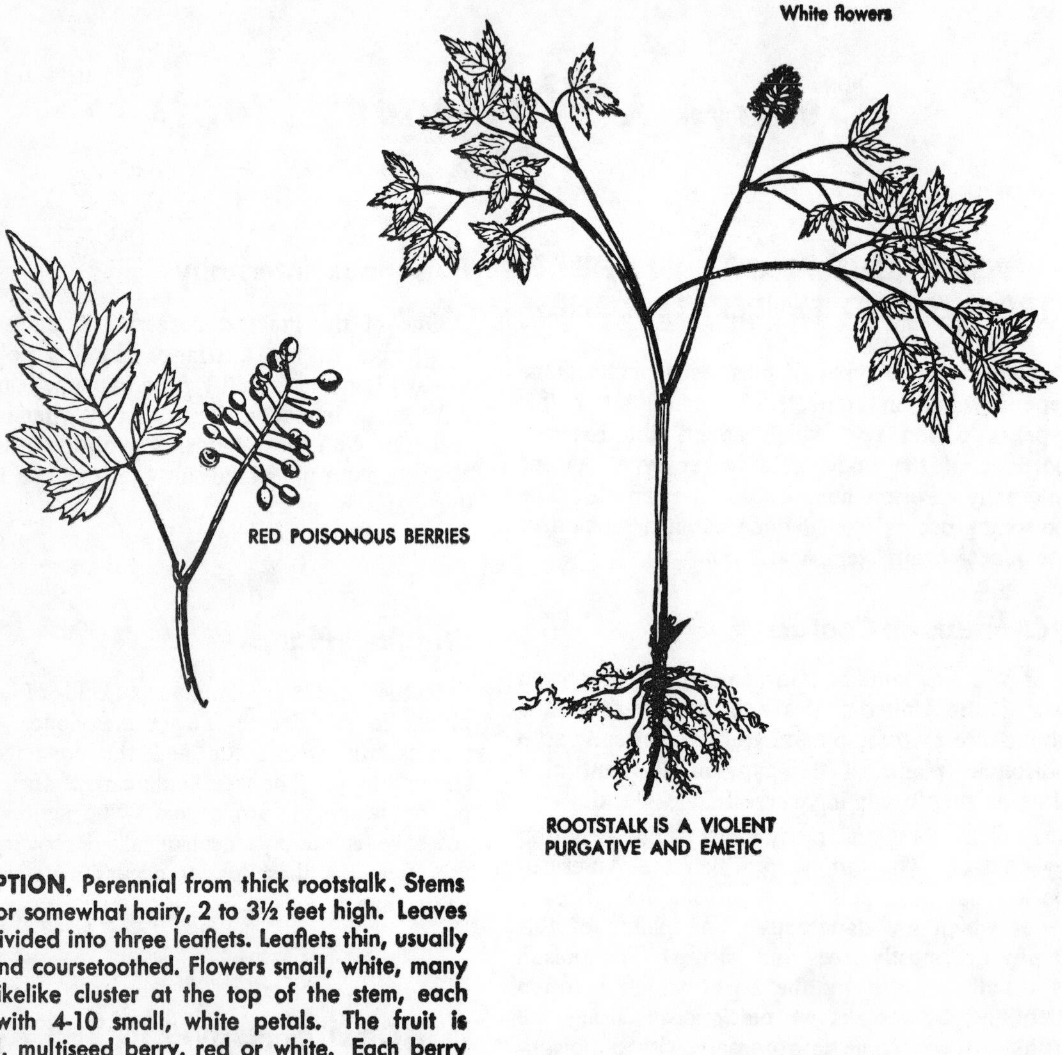

DESCRIPTION. Perennial from thick rootstalk. Stems smooth or somewhat hairy, 2 to 3½ feet high. Leaves large, divided into three leaflets. Leaflets thin, usually lobed and coursetoothed. Flowers small, white, many in a spikelike cluster at the top of the stem, each flower with 4-10 small, white petals. The fruit is a round, multiseed berry, red or white. Each berry is attached to the stem by a short, thick stalk, the white-berried plant having red stalks.

WHERE FOUND. Woods and thickets. This is a typical plant of the North Temperate Zone, especially from about latitude 40° N. to the arctic and sub-arctic areas of Europe, Asia, and North America.

CONDITIONS OF POISONING. The BERRIES of this plant are poisonous. As few as six berries can cause increased pulse, dizziness, burning in the stomach, and colicky pains. The ROOTSTALK is a violent purgative and emetic.

Figure A1-1. Baneberry

POISONOUS

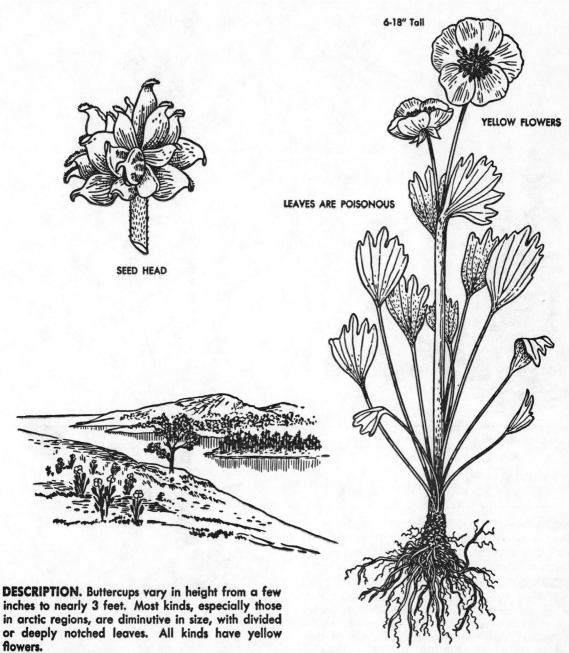

6-18" Tall

YELLOW FLOWERS

LEAVES ARE POISONOUS

SEED HEAD

DESCRIPTION. Buttercups vary in height from a few inches to nearly 3 feet. Most kinds, especially those in arctic regions, are diminutive in size, with divided or deeply notched leaves. All kinds have yellow flowers.

WHERE FOUND. Widely distributed throughout the North Temperate Zone and well into the tundra of Europe, Asia, and America.

CONDITIONS OF POISONING. If the LEAVES are eaten, severe inflammation of the intestinal tract may result.

Figure A1-2. Buttercup

POISONOUS

6-15" Tall

ALL PARTS ARE POISONOUS

(No onion odor)

SEED POD

WHITE FLOWERS

DESCRIPTION. Plant grows from a bulb. Stems 1 to 2 feet high, leafy, with linear leaves clasping the stem at the base. Flower greenish-white in loose terminal clusters—contrasted with wild onion, which has flowers closely aggregated at the top of the stem; also NO ONION ODOR IN DEATH CAMAS.

WHERE FOUND. The death camas occurs in meadows and on edges of forests in parts of western subarctic North American and eastern Siberia; also occurs farther south to western United States.

CONDITIONS OF POISONING. The death camas contains the toxic alkaloid, zygadenine, in ALL PARTS OF THE PLANT FROM THE BULB TO THE SEED. Children have been known to be poisoned by eating the bulbs, probably mistaking them for onions.

Figure A1-3. Death Camas

POISONOUS

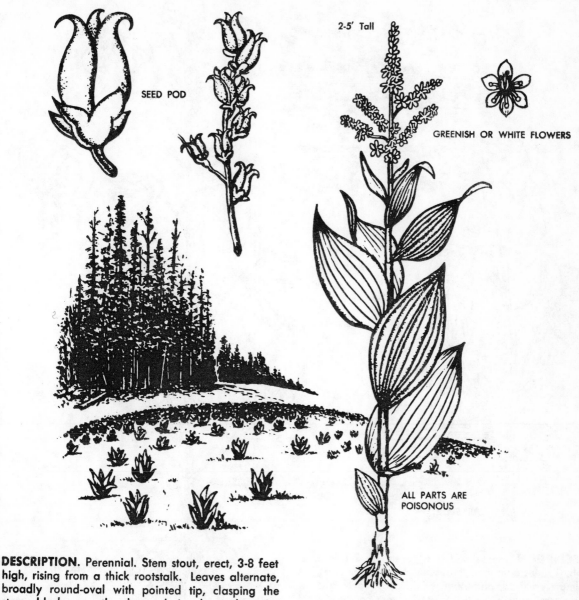

SEED POD

2-5' Tall

GREENISH OR WHITE FLOWERS

ALL PARTS ARE
POISONOUS

DESCRIPTION. Perennial. Stem stout, erect, 3-8 feet high, rising from a thick rootstalk. Leaves alternate, broadly round-oval with pointed tip, clasping the stem; blade smooth above, hairy beneath; veins parallel. Small flowers in large terminal spikelike clusters with drooping branches; three petals, often greenish, but sometimes white.

WHERE FOUND. Swamps and low grounds in Europe, Asia, and America from about 40° N. latitude. Occurs on the edge of the arctic, although probably rare on the tundra.

CONDITIONS OF POISONING. Fatalities among humans from EATING FALSE HELLEBORE are rare but are more common to sheep and other animals. Symptoms are salivation, vomiting, purging, abdominal pain, muscular weakness, general paralysis, tremors, spasms, and occasionally convulsions. Death results from asphyxia.

Figure A1-4. False Hellebore

POISONOUS

Larkspur (Delphinium) and Monkshood (Aconitum)

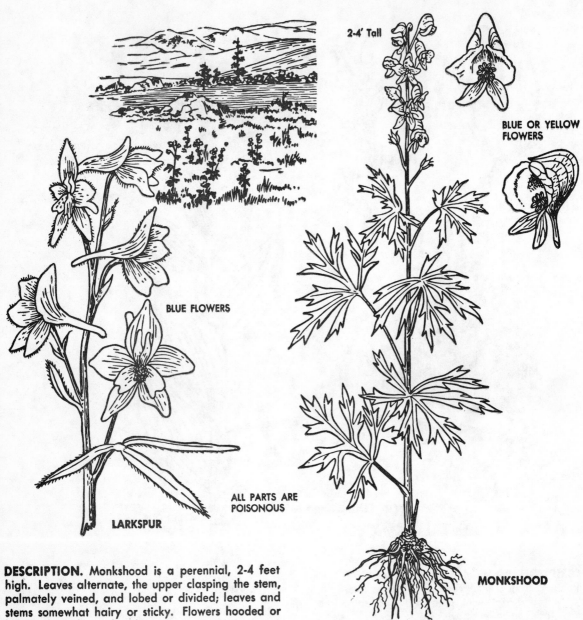

2-4' Tall

BLUE OR YELLOW FLOWERS

BLUE FLOWERS

ALL PARTS ARE POISONOUS

LARKSPUR

MONKSHOOD

DESCRIPTION. Monkshood is a perennial, 2-4 feet high. Leaves alternate, the upper clasping the stem, palmately veined, and lobed or divided; leaves and stems somewhat hairy or sticky. Flowers hooded or helmet-shaped, usually blue.

Larkspur is similar to monkshood, but the flowers are not hooded. Most kinds develop two spurs at the base of the flower.

WHERE FOUND. Monkshood and larkspur are distributed widely over the North Temperate and subarctic zones, especially in mountainous regions.

CONDITIONS OF POISONING. THESE PLANTS while poisonous at all times, seem to be most poisonous just before flowering. Symptoms are muscular weakness, irregular and labored breathing, weak pulse, bloating, belching, constant attempt at swallowing, and pupils contracted or dilated.

Figure A1-5. Larkspur and Monkshood

POISONOUS

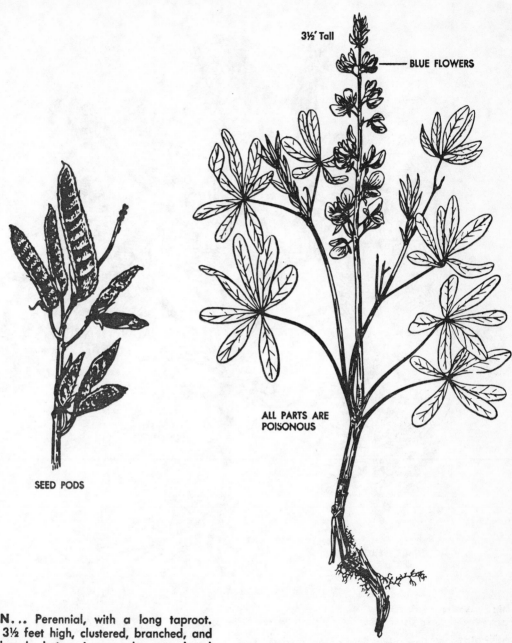

3½' Tall

BLUE FLOWERS

ALL PARTS ARE
POISONOUS

SEED PODS

DESCRIPTION... Perennial, with a long taproot. Stems up to 3½ feet high, clustered, branched, and smooth to densely hairy. Leaves alternate, basal leaves on short stalks, palmately (like a hand) divided with 6-8 leaflets. Flowers blue, often shaded pink or white, rarely pure white.

WHERE FOUND. Found only on the North American Continent. Only one kind occurs in the arctic regions of Alaska.

CONDITIONS OF POISONING. Lupine plants contain alkaloids and are known to cause fatal poisoning in animals. When eaten in excess by humans, it produces serious effects. It is thought that the excess WOODY FIBER produces fatal inflammation of the stomach and intestines.

Figure A1-6. Lupine

POISONOUS

141

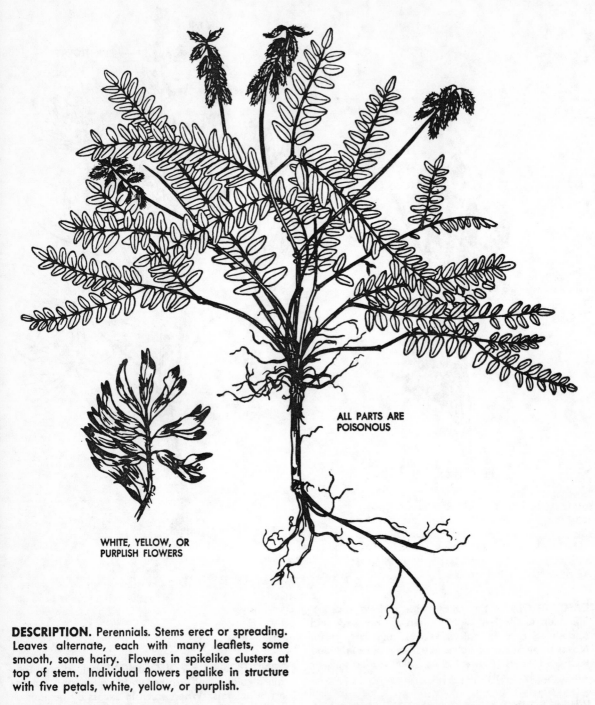

ALL PARTS ARE
POISONOUS

WHITE, YELLOW, OR
PURPLISH FLOWERS

DESCRIPTION. Perennials. Stems erect or spreading. Leaves alternate, each with many leaflets, some smooth, some hairy. Flowers in spikelike clusters at top of stem. Individual flowers pealike in structure with five petals, white, yellow, or purplish.

WHERE FOUND. These plants occur rather abundantly in meadows, on hillsides, and on tundra throughout the North Temperate Zone.

CONDITIONS OF POISONING. Several species of locoweed have been reported as toxic. Avoid ALL KINDS to be on the safe side.

Figure A1-7. Vetch and Locoweed

POISONOUS

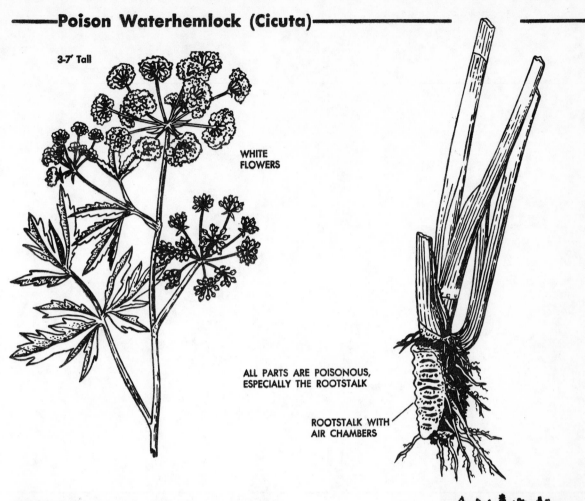

3-7' Tall

WHITE
FLOWERS

ALL PARTS ARE POISONOUS,
ESPECIALLY THE ROOTSTALK

ROOTSTALK WITH
AIR CHAMBERS

DESCRIPTION. Perennial. Stems 3½ to 7 feet high, stout, jointed hollow between the joints, reddish. Leaves alternate, divided into narrow leaflets with toothed edges, and the leaf veins end at or near the tooth notches. Leafstalks sheath the stem. Rootstalk short, ringed on the outer surface and often, especially when young, has many fibrous rootlets; when older, it has many spindle-shaped roots bunched at the base. When root and lower stem are split lengthwise, many cross-partitions or chambers can be easily noticed. Plant exudes drops of a yellow aromatic oil which gives it a characteristic odor. Flowers small and white, in umbrellalike clusters at the top of the stalk.

WHERE FOUND. Wet meadows, ditches, along streams, and around tundra lakes. This plant belongs to the parsley, carrot, and parsnip family, which contains many well-known edible plants, but it is better to avoid all members of this family as food in northern areas, since the related waterhemlock is fairly common in the North Temperate Zone.

CONDITIONS OF POISONING. A piece of waterhemlock root about the size of a walnut is said to be sufficient to kill a cow. This plant contains a sticky, resinlike substance called circutoxin. This substance is most concentrated in the ROOTS but is present in ALL PARTS of the plant. Symptoms of poisoning are stomach pains, nausea, vomiting, weak and rapid pulse, and violent convulsions.

TREATMENT. In cases of hemlock plant poisoning, make the patient vomit, then give a cathartic. If vomiting is produced promptly, the victim is likely to recover.

Figure A1-8. Waterhemlock

POISONOUS

INDEX

Climatic Zone	Natural Vegetation Region	
TEMPERATE	Evergreen Scrub Forest	E
	Hardwood (Seasonal) and Hardwood-Coniferous Forest	H
	Coniferous Forest	C
	Prairie	P
	Steppe	S
TROPIC AND TEMPERATE	Mountainous Areas	M
TROPIC	Rain Forest	RF
	Semievergreen Seasonal Forest	SS
	Scrub and Thorn Forest	ST
	Savanna	SA
ANY ZONE	Desert Scrub and Waste	D
ARCTIC	Tundra	T

145

Section B—Edible Plants
East Indian Arrowroot (Tacca pinnatifida)

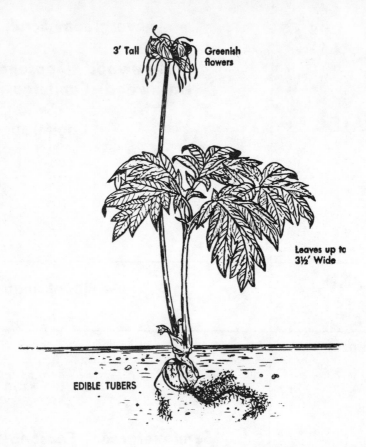

RF

SS

WHERE FOUND:
Tropics—Rain forest.
Tropics—Semievergreen seasonal forest.

The arrowroot is found as a wild plant in parts of tropical Africa, tropical Asia and the islands of the southwestern Pacific. In the wild state, this plant is found in forested areas with a high rainfall and it is a typical rain forest plant. The arrowroot has been cultivated by man, and it is quite possible to find these plants in abandoned fields and gardens and in wet places along roadsides.

APPEARANCE. The arrowroot is a large, coarse herb. The stems are about an inch in diameter and often 3 feet tall. The leaves are from 3 to 3½ feet in diameter and divided into three parts, which are again divided. The flowers are green and purplish. The edible underground tubers are sometimes nearly a foot across.

WHAT TO EAT. The arrowroot has UNDERGROUND TUBERS which sometimes weigh up to 2 pounds. These are very bitter when raw, but when boiled or roasted, they become sweet and quite palatable. The starch content has been found to be as much as 22%, so the survivor should make use of this plant whenever possible.

To prepare flour, first peel the fresh tubers. Then rasp them to a fine pulp directly into a container of water. Use rough stones or pieces of coral for the rasping. The water becomes milky and after the grating process is finished, let the contents stand until the water again becomes clear. Pour off the water and save the white starch on the bottom. Repeat this washing process several times until all trace of bitterness disappears from the starch. After thorough washing, dry the white arrowroot in the sun.

Use the dried arrowroot flour to make bread or pancakes.

Figure A1-9. Arrowroot

Canna Lily (Canna indica)

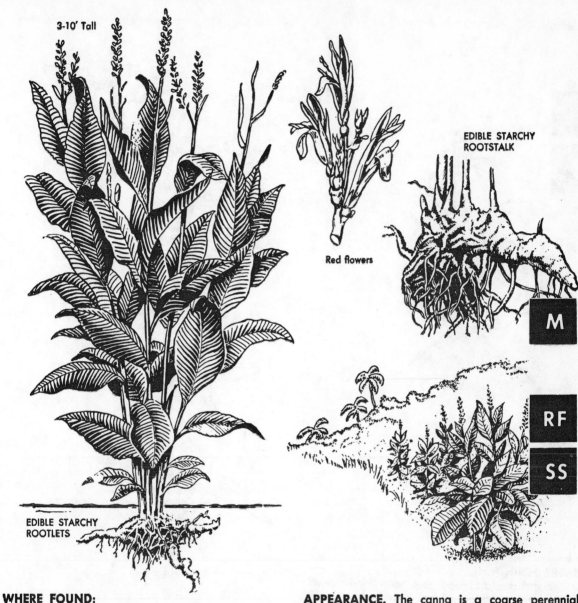

3-10' Tall

Red flowers

EDIBLE STARCHY ROOTSTALK

M

RF

SS

EDIBLE STARCHY ROOTLETS

WHERE FOUND:

    Tropics—Rain forest.
    Tropics—Semievergreen seasonal forest.
    Temperate—Mountainous area (undifferentiated
        highland).

As a wild plant, the canna lily is found in all tropical countries, especially in moist places along streams, springs, ditches, and the margins of woods. The canna is easily recognized, because it is so commonly cultivated in flower gardens in the United States.

APPEARANCE. The canna is a coarse perennial herb, 3-10 feet tall. The plant grows from a large, thick underground rootstalk which is edible. The large leaves resemble the banana but are not so large. The flowers in wild forms of canna are usually small, relatively inconspicuous, and usually red.

WHAT TO EAT. The large and much branched ROOTSTALKS are full of edible starch. The younger parts may be finely chopped and then boiled or pulverized into a sort of meal. Mix in the young shoots of palm cabbage for flavoring.

Figure A1-10. Canna Lily

Lily (Lillium bulbiferum)

H

C

M

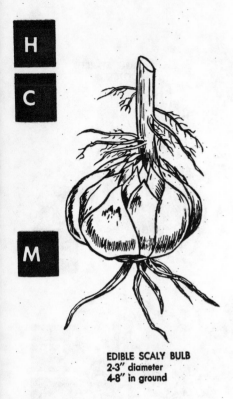

EDIBLE SCALY BULB
2-3" diameter
4-8" in ground

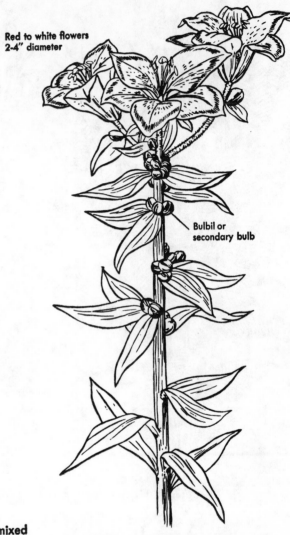

Red to white flowers
2-4" diameter

Bulbil or
secondary bulb

WHERE FOUND:

Temperate—Hardwood (seasonal) and mixed
hardwood-coniferous forest.
Temperate—Coniferous forest.
Temperate—Mountainous area (undifferentiated
highland).

The wild lily occurs over much of the northern hemisphere, particularly in the temperate parts. Lilies are usually found in wooded areas with high to moderate rainfall, from both western and eastern United States, Europe, and across Asia to China and Japan. A large number of lilies are found in Chinese-Himalayan area. The lily illustrated is a native of central Europe.

APPEARANCE. Lilies grow from scaly bulbs. The stems usually rise to several feet in height. The flowers are showy, ranging from white, red, pink to brownish.

WHAT TO EAT. The BULBS are scaly, white, and full of edible starch. They may be eaten cooked or uncooked.

Figure A1-11. Lily

148

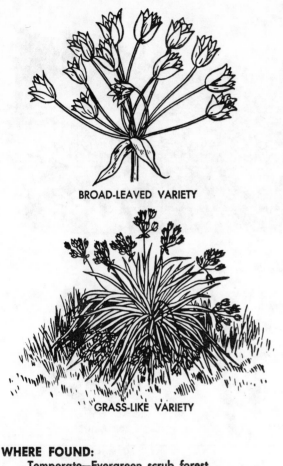

BROAD-LEAVED VARIETY

GRASS-LIKE VARIETY

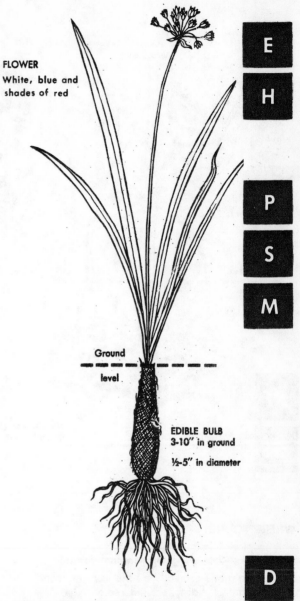

FLOWER
White, blue and
shades of red

Ground
level

EDIBLE BULB
3-10" in ground

½-5" in diameter

WHERE FOUND:

    Temperate—Evergreen scrub forest.

    Temperate—Hardwood (seasonal) and mixed
        hardwood-coniferous forest.

    Temperate—Prairie.

    Temperate—Steppe.

    Any climatic zone—Desert scrub and waste.

    Temperate—Mountainous area (undifferentiated
        highland).

    Wild relatives of the common onion occur widely throughout the North Temperate Zone. Many occur in North America in both moist and arid regions. In Europe and Asia, wild onions are very common over a wide range of habitats: moist areas, deserts, and mountain tops. They are especially common in Central Asia.

APPEARANCE. The onion plant grows from a bulb, which may be buried 3-10 inches below the ground. On most kinds of onions, the leaves are usually somewhat grasslike, although there is a whole group of wild onions with leaves that are several inches wide.

Onion flowers are white, blue, and shades of red. The bulbs of some kinds are very small—½ inch in diameter—whereas some of the larger kinds may be 5 inches in diameter.

WHAT TO EAT. The BULBS of all onions are edible. The foliage and bulbs of all onions emit a characteristic oniony odor and taste. This is a good test to distinguish them from other kinds of bulbous plants.

    Wild onions are never poisonous.

Figure A1-12. Wild Onion

──Taro (Colocasia esculentum)──

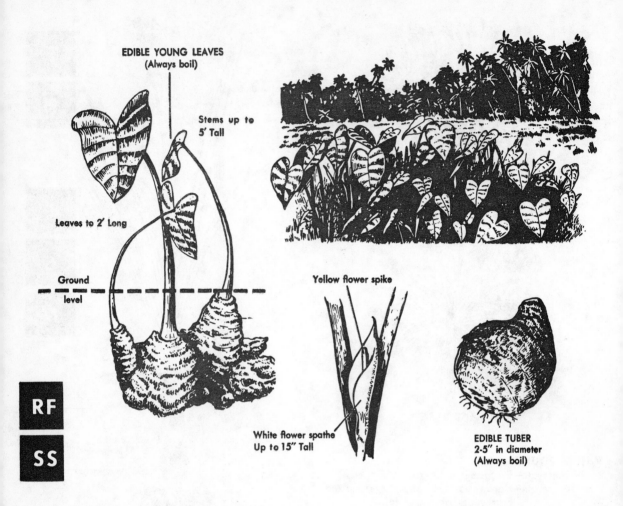

EDIBLE YOUNG LEAVES
(Always boil)

Stems up to
5' Tall

Leaves to 2' Long

Ground
level

RF

SS

Yellow flower spike

White flower spathe
Up to 15" Tall

EDIBLE TUBER
2-5" in diameter
(Always boil)

WHERE FOUND:

Tropics—Rain forest.
Tropics—Semievergreen seasonal forest.

The taro grows in nearly all the tropical countries. It is a plant of moist, forested regions, but it may also be looked for near abandoned villages, along streams, and in ditches.

APPEARANCE: The taro plant has the appearance of a calla lily plant, with leaves to 2 feet long and stems to 5 feet high. The flower is pale yellow and may be up to 15 inches long.

WHAT TO EAT. The TUBERS, only slightly below ground level, can be cooked and eaten like potatoes.

CAUTION

The tubers must be boiled to destroy the minute crystals which are very irritating. The young leaves can be eaten like spinach, but they should always be boiled for the same reason.

NOTE: The taro belongs to a large plant family called the araceae. Many varieties of araceae occur throughout the moist tropics in both America and the Old World, and many of these develop underground tubers. However, all kinds must first be cooked before eating because of the minute irritating crystals contained therein. The foliage of most varieties strikingly resembles the taro.

Figure A1-13. Taro

──Wild Tulip (Tulipa)──

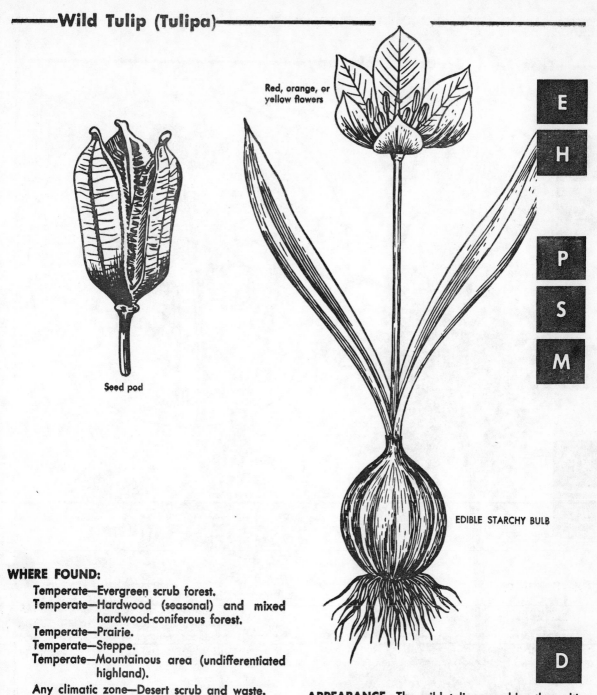

Red, orange, or yellow flowers

E

H

P

S

M

D

Seed pod

EDIBLE STARCHY BULB

WHERE FOUND:

Temperate—Evergreen scrub forest.

Temperate—Hardwood (seasonal) and mixed hardwood-coniferous forest.

Temperate—Prairie.

Temperate—Steppe.

Temperate—Mountainous area (undifferentiated highland).

Any climatic zone—Desert scrub and waste.

The tulip serves to illustrate a kind of plant with relatively large edible bulbs. Wild tulips are common from the Mediterranean region, through Asia Minor to central Asia. Tulips flower for a short time only in the spring, although the plant may be identified by the seed pod which can be found most of the year.

APPEARANCE. The wild tulip resembles the cultivated forms seen in gardens, except the wild ones are smaller. The flowers on the wild sorts are red, yellow, and orange.

WHAT TO EAT. The relatively large fleshy BULBS are full of starch and serve as a good substitute for potatoes. They should be cooked.

Figure A1-14. Wild Tulip

FERNS

Tree Fern, Bracken, Polypody

H

C

M

RF

SS

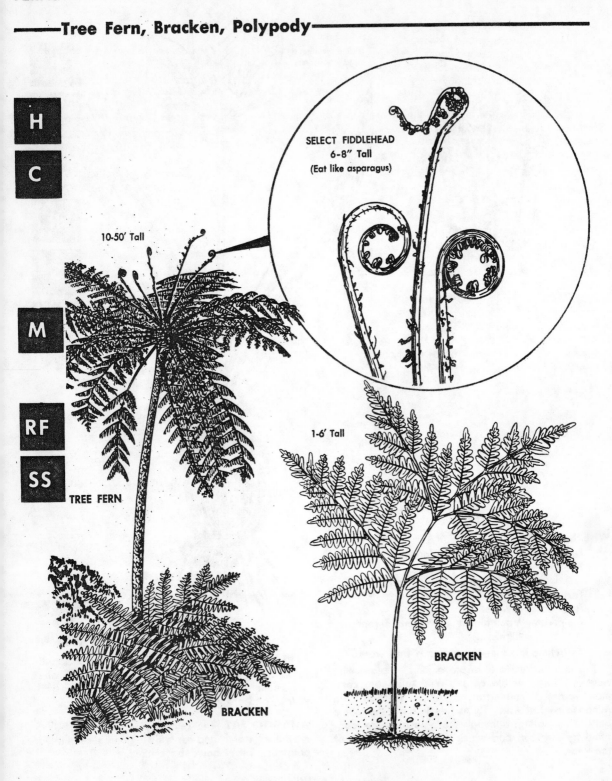

SELECT FIDDLEHEAD
6-8" Tall
(Eat like asparagus)

10-50' Tall

TREE FERN

1-6' Tall

BRACKEN

BRACKEN

Figure A1-15. Bracken, Tree Fern, Polypody

WHERE FOUND:

Tropics—Rain forest.

Tropics—Semievergreen seasonal forest.

Temperate—Hardwood (seasonal) and mixed hardwood-coniferous forest.

Temperate—Coniferous forest.

Temperate—Mountainous area (undifferentiated highland).

In the moist regions of all countries, especially in forested regions, gullies, along streams, and on the edge of woods, ferns are very abundant. Ferns are common throughout the tropical parts of Africa, Asia, Australia, and North and South America.

APPEARANCE.

Fern plants might easily be mistaken for flowering plants, especially with the relatives of the wild parsnip, the water hemlock and the wild carrot. However, with a little care and observation, the survivor can easily distinguish ferns from all other kinds of green plants. In ferns, the underneath surface of the leaves is usually covered with masses of brown dots, which themselves are covered with yellow, brown, or black dust. These dots actually filled with spores (spores are produced in ferns instead of seeds), and the presence of these spore structures easily distinguishes ferns from plants with flowers.

The PASTURE BRAKE, or bracken, is one of the most widely distributed ferns. This fern occurs in every continent in open dry woods, recently burned clearings and pastures, from the subarctic to the tropics. Bracken is a coarse fern with solitary or scattered young stalks often ½-inch thick at the base, nearly cylindrical and covered with rusty felt; the uncoiling frond (fiddlehead) is distinctly 3-forked, usually with a purplish spot at the angles which secretes a sweetish juice; old fronds conspicuously 3-forked; rootstock extensively creeping and branching, blackish and almost woody, about ¼ inch thick.

WHAT TO EAT. This information applies to all ferns. Select young STALKS (fiddleheads) not more than 6-8 inches high. Break them off as low as they remain tender, then draw through the closed hand to remove the wool. Wash and boil in salted water or steam until tender (usually 30 minutes to an hour). Season with salt and pepper and add an edible oil, e.g., coconut oil.

The raw stalks have a very sticky juice. The juice is somewhat altered in cooking, but the boiled vegetable retains some of the sticky quality. Because of this, the pasture brake is not attractive to some tastes, but most people who have tried it properly prepared have found it palatable. As a survival food, it should not be overlooked.

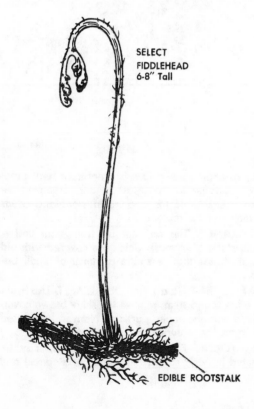

SELECT FIDDLEHEAD 6-8" Tall

EDIBLE ROOTSTALK

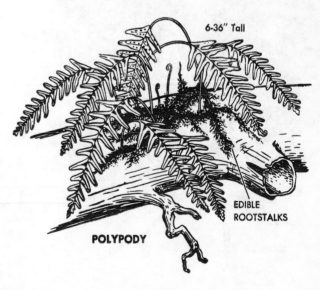

6-36" Tall

EDIBLE ROOTSTALKS

POLYPODY

CAUTION

Unless you are positively able to distinguish a true fern from other plants with delicately cut leaves, do not eat the smaller kinds of ferns. Many plants, such as the notorious poison hemlock (see illustration in this attachment) which is deadly poison, have delicately cut leaves which look something like ferns.

━━Spreading Wood Fern (Dryopteris spinulosa)━━

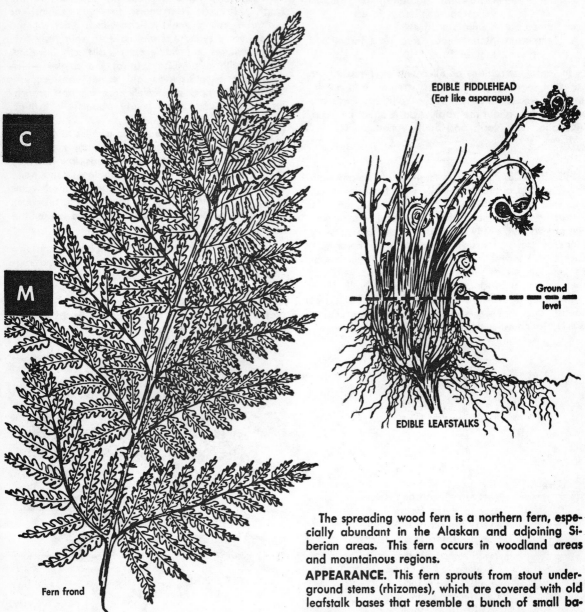

C

M

EDIBLE FIDDLEHEAD
(Eat like asparagus)

Ground
level

EDIBLE LEAFSTALKS

Fern frond

The spreading wood fern is a northern fern, especially abundant in the Alaskan and adjoining Siberian areas. This fern occurs in woodland areas and mountainous regions.

APPEARANCE. This fern sprouts from stout underground stems (rhizomes), which are covered with old leafstalk bases that resemble a bunch of small bananas.

WHAT TO EAT. Roast the OLD LEAFSTALKS from the underground stem, remove the shiny brown covering and eat the inner portion. Natives have used these ferns for centuries as a source of food.

The YOUNG FRONDS, or fiddleheads, may be collected in early spring and boiled or steamed and eaten like asparagus.

WHERE FOUND:
   Temperate—Coniferous forest.
   Temperate—Mountainous area (undifferentiated highland).

Figure A1-16. Wood Fern

154

FORBS AND OTHERS

Agave (Century Plant)

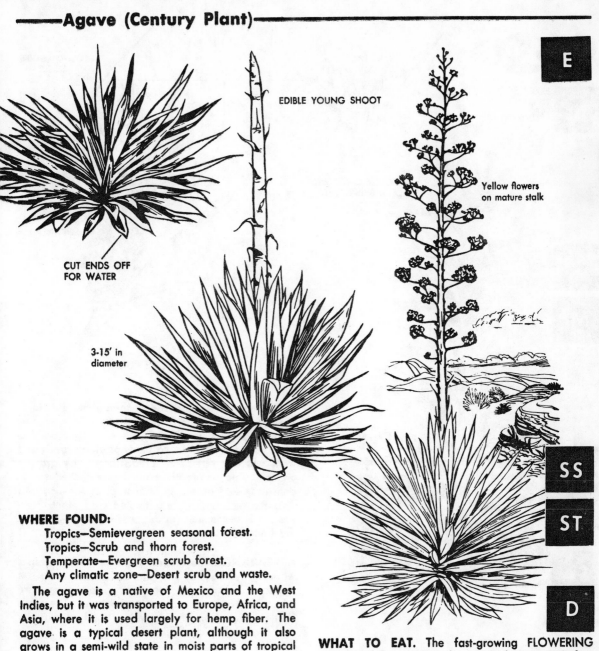

EDIBLE YOUNG SHOOT

E

Yellow flowers
on mature stalk

CUT ENDS OFF
FOR WATER

3-15' in
diameter

SS

ST

D

WHERE FOUND:
   Tropics—Semievergreen seasonal forest.
   Tropics—Scrub and thorn forest.
   Temperate—Evergreen scrub forest.
   Any climatic zone—Desert scrub and waste.

   The agave is a native of Mexico and the West Indies, but it was transported to Europe, Africa, and Asia, where it is used largely for hemp fiber. The agave is a typical desert plant, although it also grows in a semi-wild state in moist parts of tropical areas in Asia.

APPEARANCE: The agave, when fully grown, is an imposing plant because of its size. The thick, tough leaves with stout, sharp tips are borne in an enormous rosette. The flowering stalk in the center of the plant rises very rapidly like a candle to produce the huge flowering head.

WHAT TO EAT. The fast-growing FLOWERING SHOOT of the agave is the part to be eaten. Before the flowers are noticeably developed, these shoots are cut off and roasted in pit ovens (see description in chapter 2). The roasted shoots consist of fibrous, molasses-colored layers, sweet and delicious to the taste and nutritious. Pieces dried in the sun will keep for years. The cut ends of agave leaves can supply drinking water.

Figure A1-17. Agave

Amaranth (Amaranthus)

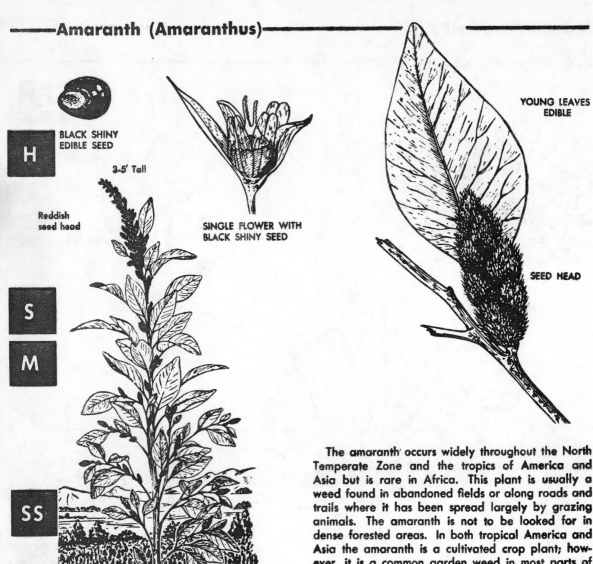

BLACK SHINY EDIBLE SEED

H

3-5' Tall

Reddish seed head

SINGLE FLOWER WITH BLACK SHINY SEED

YOUNG LEAVES EDIBLE

SEED HEAD

S

M

SS

SA

WHERE FOUND:
Tropics—Semievergreen seasonal forest.
Tropics—Savanna.
Temperate—Hardwood (seasonal) and mixed hardwood-coniferous forest.
Temperate—Steppe.
Temperate—Mountanious area (undifferentiated highland).

The amaranth occurs widely throughout the North Temperate Zone and the tropics of America and Asia but is rare in Africa. This plant is usually a weed found in abandoned fields or along roads and trails where it has been spread largely by grazing animals. The amaranth is not to be looked for in dense forested areas. In both tropical America and Asia the amaranth is a cultivated crop plant; however, it is a common garden weed in most parts of the United States.

APPEARANCE. The amaranth grows quickly after a warm rainy seaosn. The plant is usually coarse in appearance and 3-5 feet tall. The flowers are minute and occur in a dense, plumy head. The seeds shatter away from the flowering head at maturity and are easily picked up.

WHAT TO EAT. The black, shiny SEEDS may be beaten out and then pulverized with stones. The flour produced by this method may be used as an additive in soup, or it can be cooked as porridge of high food content.

The YOUNG, TENDER LEAVES of the amaranth may be eaten like spinach.

Figure A1-18. Amaranth

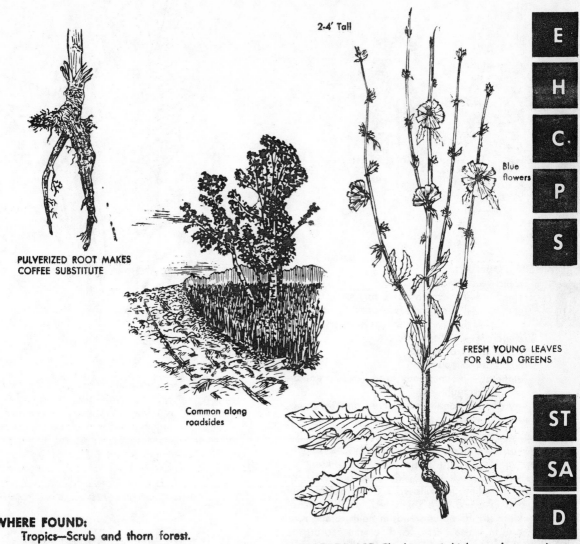

PULVERIZED ROOT MAKES
COFFEE SUBSTITUTE

2-4' Tall

Blue
flowers

FRESH YOUNG LEAVES
FOR SALAD GREENS

Common along
roadsides

E

H

C.

P

S

ST

SA

D

WHERE FOUND:

    Tropics—Scrub and thorn forest.

    Tropics—Savanna.

    Temperate—Evergreen scrub forest.

    Temperate—Hardwood (seasonal) and mixed hardwood-coniferous forest.

    Temperate—Coniferous forest.

    Temperate—Prairie.

    Temperate—Steppe.

    Any climatic zone—Desert scrub and waste.

Wild chicory is a native of Europe and Asia, but it is now very generally distributed throughout the United States as a weed along roadsides and in fields. In Europe and Asia it is also a weed and is abundant in fields and pastures. It also occurs in Africa.

APPEARANCE. The leaves (which may be eaten) are clustered at ground level at the top of a strong underground carrotlike root. The leaves resemble the dandelion in shape but are thicker and rougher. The wiry stems rise 2 to 4 feet and are covered in summer with numerous bright blue heads of flowers.

WHAT TO EAT. The TENDER YOUNG LEAVES are eaten fresh as a salad. The ROOTS have long been the source of chicory, which is the bitter constituent in adulterated coffee. A brew of chicory root makes a somewhat bitter substitute for coffee. The roots may be dug at any time of the year (but preferably in autumn) and pulverized.

Figure A1-19. Wild Chicory

─── Wild Dock and Wild Sorrel (Rumex vesicarius) ───

Flower
(Enlarged)

Flower

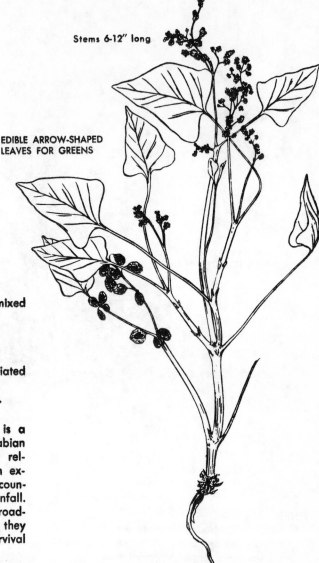

Stems 6-12" long

EDIBLE ARROW-SHAPED
LEAVES FOR GREENS

WHERE FOUND:

> Tropics—Savanna.
> Temperate—Evergreen scrub forest.
> Temperate—Hardwood (seasonal) and mixed
>   hardwood-coniferous forest.
> Temperate—Coniferous forest.
> Temperate—Prairie.
> Temperate—Steppe.
> Temperate—Mountainous area (undifferentiated
>   highland).
> Any climatic zone—Desert scrub and waste.
> Arctic—Tundra.

The wild dock illustrated in this figure is a native of the Middle East, especially the Arabian Desert and adjoining areas. However, many relatives of wild dock and wild sorrel are often extremely abundant in temperate and tropical countries, and in areas of high as well as low rainfall. Many kinds are found as weeds in fields, along roadsides, and in waste places, and for this reason they make a most useful addition to the list of survival plants.

APPEARANCE. WILD DOCK is a stout plant with most of its leaves at the base of its stem, which is commonly 6-12 inches long. The plants usually develop from a strong, fleshy, carrotlike taproot. The flowers are usually very small, growing in green to purplish plumelike clusters.

WILD SORREL is similar to the docks but smaller. Many of the basal leaves are arrow-shaped but smaller than those of the docks and containing a sour juice. The plant shown here is a desert type of sorrel which occurs from the Mediterranean eastward into Arabia.

WHAT TO EAT. Because of the tender nature of the foliage, both the sorrels and docks are useful plants, especially in the desert areas. Their succulent LEAVES may be eaten either fresh or slightly cooked. In order to take away the strong taste, the water should be changed once or twice during cooking. This latter tip is a useful hint in the preparation of many kinds of wild greens

Figure A1-20 Wild Dock and Wild Sorrel

158

Pokeweed (Phytolacca)

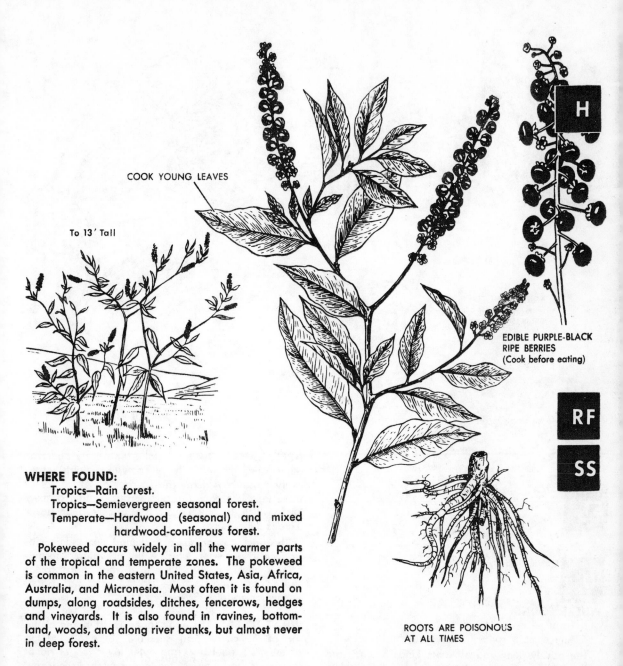

COOK YOUNG LEAVES

To 13' Tall

H

EDIBLE PURPLE-BLACK
RIPE BERRIES
(Cook before eating)

RF

SS

ROOTS ARE POISONOUS
AT ALL TIMES

WHERE FOUND:
　　Tropics—Rain forest.
　　Tropics—Semievergreen seasonal forest.
　　Temperate—Hardwood (seasonal) and mixed
　　　　hardwood-coniferous forest.

Pokeweed occurs widely in all the warmer parts of the tropical and temperate zones. The pokeweed is common in the eastern United States, Asia, Africa, Australia, and Micronesia. Most often it is found on dumps, along roadsides, ditches, fencerows, hedges and vineyards. It is also found in ravines, bottomland, woods, and along river banks, but almost never in deep forest.

APPEARANCE. The pokeweed is a large, coarse, perennial herb up to 13 feet high. The whole plant, especially while young, is tender and quite succulent. The branches are green, magenta, or purple. The leaves are 4-12 inches long. The flowering and fruiting spikes usually droop, and the flowers are followed by deep reddish-purple berries.

WHAT TO EAT. The TENDER YOUNG SHOOTS and LEAVES of poke can be eaten as a cooked vegetable.
　　The juicy BERRIES are bitter and may be toxic when raw, but they are palatable when cooked.

CAUTION
The roots are poisonous at all times.

Figure A1-21. Pokeweed

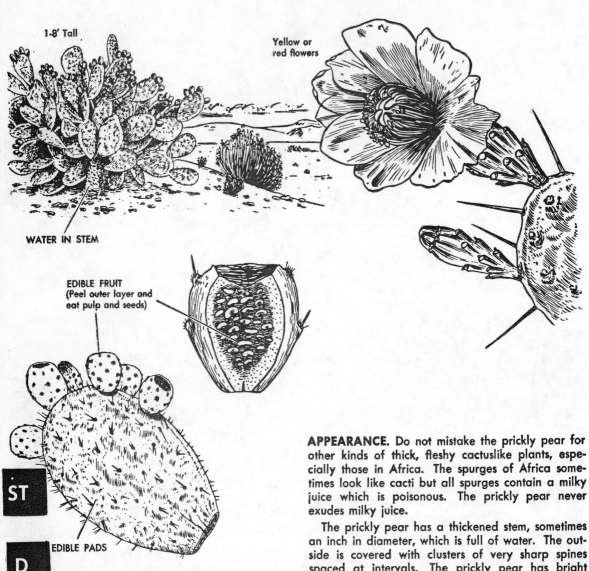

1-8' Tall

Yellow or
red flowers

WATER IN STEM

EDIBLE FRUIT
(Peel outer layer and
eat pulp and seeds)

ST

D

EDIBLE PADS

WHERE FOUND:

Tropics—Scrub and thorn forest.

Any climate zone—Desert scrub and waste.

The prickly pear and all other kinds of cacti are native only to America, but they have been taken to many desert areas in the Old World and also in Australia. The prickly pear is native to the American Southwest, Mexico, and South America. In the Old World, it is now found along the shores of the Mediterranean into Asia Minor and India.

APPEARANCE. Do not mistake the prickly pear for other kinds of thick, fleshy cactuslike plants, especially those in Africa. The spurges of Africa sometimes look like cacti but all spurges contain a milky juice which is poisonous. The prickly pear never exudes milky juice.

The prickly pear has a thickened stem, sometimes an inch in diameter, which is full of water. The outside is covered with clusters of very sharp spines spaced at intervals. The prickly pear has bright yellow or reddish flowers.

WHAT TO EAT. The egg-shaped FRUIT borne at the top of the cactus pad is edible. Slice off the top of the fruit, peel back the outer layer to get rid of the spines, and then eat the inner contents, seeds and all. They are mildly sweet and very juicy. The prickly pear PADS also may be eaten raw or boiled. Cut away the spines and slice the pad lengthwise into strips like string beans.

The prickly pear is not poisonous.

Figure A1-22. Prickly Pear

Purslane (Portulaca oleracea)

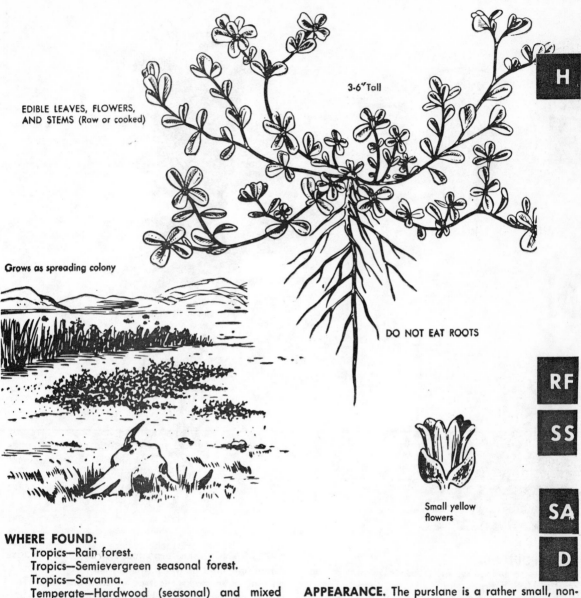

3-6" Tall

EDIBLE LEAVES, FLOWERS, AND STEMS (Raw or cooked)

Grows as spreading colony

DO NOT EAT ROOTS

H

RF

SS

SA

D

Small yellow flowers

WHERE FOUND:
  Tropics—Rain forest.
  Tropics—Semievergreen seasonal forest.
  Tropics—Savanna.
  Temperate—Hardwood (seasonal) and mixed
    hardwood-coniferous forest.
  Any climatic zone—Desert scrub and waste.

The purslane is extremely common as a weed in many parts of the United States and throughout the tropics and temperate zones. It is found in abandoned fields, along roadsides and trails, and on beaches. Wherever it occurs, large quantities may be found.

APPEARANCE. The purslane is a rather small, nondescript-looking plant which might easily be overlooked. The whole plant has a reddish hue, and the stems are quite fleshy. Its flowers are small and yellow. The plant grows no more than 3 to 6 inches high, but it spreads along the ground for a foot or so.

WHAT TO EAT. All parts of the plant, except the roots, may be eaten raw as a salad or cooked like spinach.

Figure A1-23. Purslane

161

Wild Rhubarb (Rheum)

White to pinkish flowering seed pods

H

C

M

EDIBLE SEEDS

3-10' Tall

EDIBLE STEMS

Figure A1-24. Wild Rhubarb

WHERE FOUND:

Temperate—Hardwood (seasonal) and mixed hardwood-coniferous forest.
Temperate—Coniferous forest.
Temperate—Mountainous area (undifferentiated highland)

The cultivated rhubarb of the gardens has about 20 wild relatives which occur from southeastern Europe to Turkey through the mountainous regions of central Asia to China. The wild rhubarbs grow mainly in open places, borders of woods, along streams, and on mountain slope:

APPEARANCE. The large leaves, sometimes nearly 3 feet long and as wide, arise mainly from the base on long stout stalks, most of which are edible. The plants often assume a handsome appearance because of the large leaves. The flowering stems rise above the large leaves, and while in flower the plants seem to be covered by large white plumes.

WHAT TO EAT. Like the common cultivated rhubarb, the STEMS of the wild sorts may be eaten as a vegetable. Some kinds are strong and bitter, but this condition can be alleviated by repeated boilings in water.

162

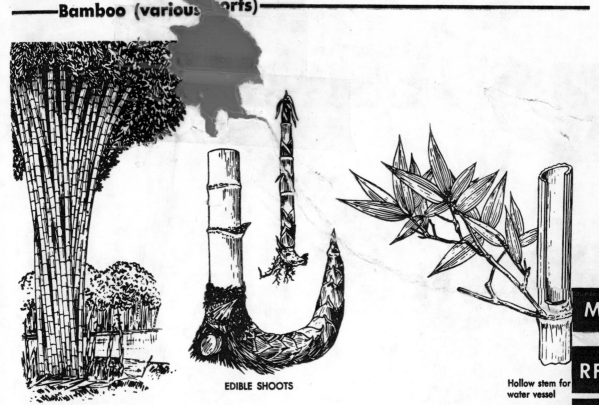

EDIBLE SHOOTS

Hollow stem for water vessel

M

RF

SS

WHERE FOUND:

    Tropics—Rain forest.
    Tropics—Semievergreen seasonal forest.
    Temperate—Mountainous area (undifferentiated
        highland).

These giant members of the grass family occur chiefly in the moist areas of the warm temperate and tropical zones. They are found in clearings, around abandoned gardens, in forests, and along rivers and streams. Bamboo thickets form one of the densest kinds of jungle growth. Bamboos abound in the warm, moist parts of Asia, Indonesia, and Africa. The American tropics support fewer kinds of bamboo than the eastern tropics.

APPEARANCE. Nearly everyone recognizes bamboo in some form or other. Fishing poles are the commonest use for bamboo in the United States. Bamboo canes resemble corn plants and sugar cane. The stems of the bamboo become very hard and woody when they mature. The young shoots, on the other hand, are very tender and succulent. Bamboo varies in size from a few inches to nearly 100 feet, with canes of the largest kinds growing to nearly a foot in diameter.

WHAT TO EAT. The YOUNG SHOOTS of bamboo are edible and appear in quantity during and immediately following rains. They grow very rapidly, some kinds as much as 15 inches a day. Cut these young shoots in the same way as asparagus, and eat the soft tip ends. Freshly cut bamboo shoots are bitter and must be boiled before eating. A second change of water may even be necessary. In fact, some kinds of bamboo shoots may have to be buried in mud for 3 or 4 days to remove the bitterness. Bamboo shoots may be salted, either raw or boiled, and eaten as a pickle; they have as much food value as fresh asparagus.

Bamboo shoots are wrapped in protective sheaths which are tough and coated with tawny or red hairs. If eaten, these hairs cause much irritation to the throat. Remove these outer sheaths carefully before eating bamboo shoots.

The SEED GRAIN of the flowering bamboo may be eaten. Pulverize, add a little water, and press into cakes or boil as you would rice.

Figure A1-25. Bamboo

163

─Cattail, or Elephant Grass (Typha)─

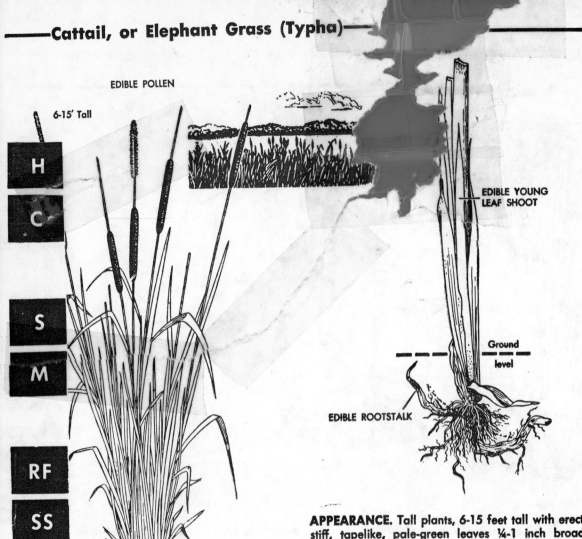

EDIBLE POLLEN

6-15' Tall

H

C

S

M

RF

SS

EDIBLE YOUNG
LEAF SHOOT

Ground
level

EDIBLE ROOTSTALK

APPEARANCE. Tall plants, 6-15 feet tall with erect, stiff, tapelike, pale-green leaves ¼-1 inch broad. Rootstalk creeping and branching, ½ to 1-inch thick. Flowers in dense terminal spikes, the lower part of the spike at first green, finally brown and producing "cotton" (fluffy seeds); the topmost flowering spike is yellow, and sheds edible pollen.

WHAT TO EAT. The YOUNG GROWING SHOOTS are succulent and nutritious when boiled like asparagus. The ROOTSTALKS produce the most nutritious part of the cattail; these contain up to 46% starch and 11% sugar. The best time for collecting these underground parts is late in the fall and through the winter to early spring. At this time, the storage organs have the most food value.

To prepare the rootstalks for food, peel off the outer covering and grate the white inner part. This may be eaten boiled or raw.

The yellow POLLEN from the flowers can be cooked as a gruel or mixed with water into small cakes and steamed as a kind of bread.

WHERE FOUND:

  Tropics—Rain forest.
  Tropics—Semievergreen seasonal forest.
  Temperate—Hardwood (seasonal) and mixed hardwood-coniferous forest.
  Temperate—Coniferous forest.
  Temperate—Steppe.
  Temperate—Mountainous area (undifferentiated highland).

The cattail is worldwide in distribution, with the exception of the tundra and forested regions of the far north. The cattail is a marshland plant which is found over large areas along lakes, ponds, and the backwaters of rivers.

Figure A1-26. Cattail (Elephant Grass)

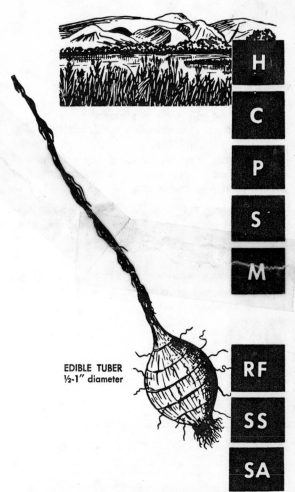

EDIBLE TUBER
½-1" diameter

H
C
P
S
M

RF
SS
SA

Nut grass is widespread in many parts of the world and may be looked for in any moist sandy place, along the margins of streams, ponds, and in ditches. This plant occurs as frequently in tropical as in temperate climates but is not found in arctic regions.

WHERE FOUND:
  Tropics—Rain forest.
  Tropics—Semievergreen seasonal forest.
  Tropics—Savanna.
  Temperate—Hardwood (seasonal) and mixed hardwood-coniferous forest.
  Temperate—Coniferous forest.
  Temperate—Prairie.
  Temperate—Steppe.
  Temperate—Mountainous area (undifferentiated highland).

APPEARANCE. The nut grass has a grasslike appearance but differs from true grasses by having a 3-angled stem and thick underground tubers, which grow to a diameter of ½-1 inch.

WHAT TO EAT. The underground nutlike TUBERS contain starch. They are slightly sweetish and nutty, although the tough, dry rind is not easily chewed. They can be boiled, peeled, and ground into a palatable and wholesome flour, which may be brewed as a coffee substitute.

Figure A1-27. Chufa (Nut Grass)

Pearl Millet (Pennisetum glaucum)

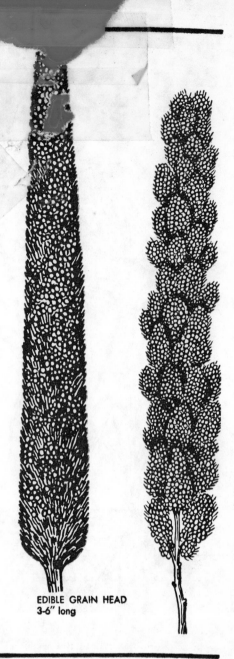

WHERE FOUND:
Tropics—Rain forest.
Tropics—Semievergreen seasonal forest.
Temperate—Mountainous area (undifferentiated
    highland).
Pearl millet may be found around abandoned dwellings and in clearings in the tropical areas of southeastern Asia and Africa.

APPEARANCE. This is a coarse grass several feet tall. The heads are from 3-6 inches long and compact. The edible grains in the head are the size of a mustard seed.

WHAT TO EAT. Pearl millet GRAIN can be pulverized and cooked as porridge, pressed into cakes, or used to thicken soup.

M

RF

SS

EDIBLE GRAIN HEAD
3-6" long

Italian Millet (Setaria italica)

WHERE FOUND:
Tropics—Rain forest.
Tropics—Semievergreen seasonal forest.
Temperate—Mountainous area (undifferentiated
    highland).
Italian millet is widely grown in Asia and Africa, especially where the cultivation of rice is not possible.

APPEARANCE. The Italian millet is a coarse grass, over 2 feet tall. The millet grains are produced in a fairly loose, whiskery head.

WHAT TO EAT. The small yellowish grains are produced in abundance in the head. The GRAINS, if pulverized and eaten as a porridge, are very high in food value.

Figure A1-28. Millet, Pearl and Italian

Rice (Oryza sativa)

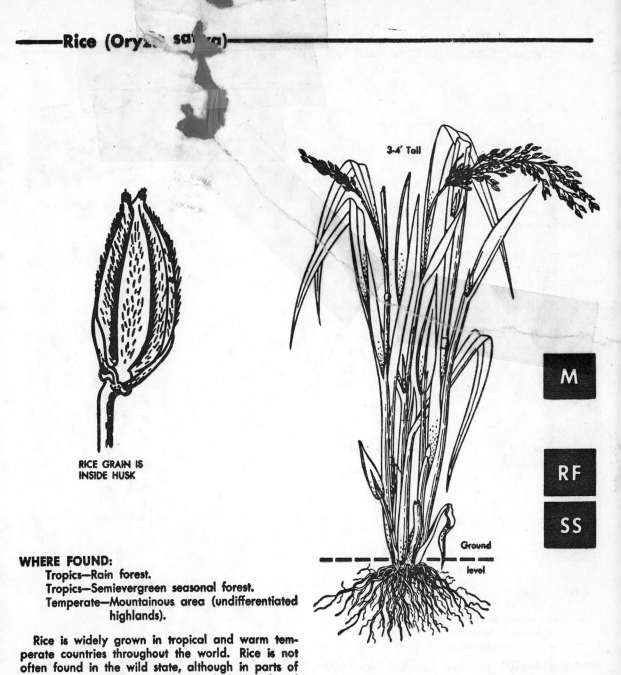

3-4' Tall

M

RF

SS

RICE GRAIN IS
INSIDE HUSK

Ground
level

Figure A1-29. Rice

WHERE FOUND:
Tropics—Rain forest.
Tropics—Semievergreen seasonal forest.
Temperate—Mountainous area (undifferentiated
highlands).

Rice is widely grown in tropical and warm temperate countries throughout the world. Rice is not
often found in the wild state, although in parts of
southeastern Asia it is possible to find abandoned
fields where rice has persisted in a semiwild condition. Truly wild rice does occur, however, in both
Asia and Africa. Rice grows always in wet places.

APPEARANCE. The rice plant is a coarse grass
which grows to a height of 3-4 feet. The leaf blades
are rough and quite hard and from ½-2 inches wide.
The rice grains are inclosed in a hairy, straw-colored
covering out of which the mature rice grains shatter
when ripe.

WHAT TO EAT. Native rice GRAIN can be roasted
and beaten to a fine flour together with native
honey and often a small quantity of palm oil. Then
it can be carried as a powder or as a cake wrapped
in large green leaves to preserve it. Properly dried,
it will keep for a long time.

Rice may also be prepared in the ordinary way
by boiling in water.

167

Sugar Cane (Saccharum officinarum)

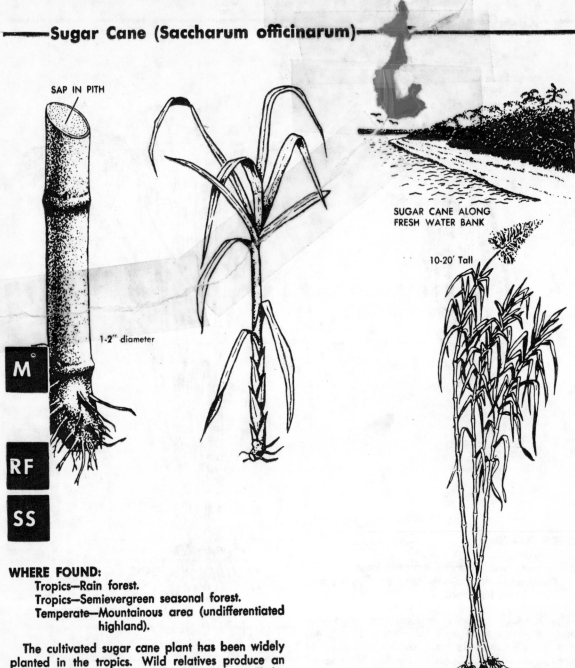

SAP IN PITH

1-2" diameter

SUGAR CANE ALONG
FRESH WATER BANK

10-20' Tall

M°

RF

SS

WHERE FOUND:
   Tropics—Rain forest.
   Tropics—Semievergreen seasonal forest.
   Temperate—Mountainous area (undifferentiated
      highland).

The cultivated sugar cane plant has been widely planted in the tropics. Wild relatives produce an inferior grade of sugar, but both forms will be found. Sugar cane also grows semiwild in many regions, especially in parts of southeastern Asia, on the neighboring islands of the Indies, in Africa, and in America.

APPEARANCE. Both the cultivated and wild relatives of sugar cane are large, coarse grasses, similar to ordinary corn in appearance. Sugar cane produces a large tassel of flowers at the summit of the plant. The stems are yellow, green, or reddish.

WHAT TO EAT. As survival food, the sugarcane and its wild relatives are valuable for the sweet juice which may be chewed out of the ripe cane. The outer layer of the stem may be peeled off and the inside PITH chewed for the refreshing and nourishing SWEET SAP. This sweetness is characteristic of many kinds of grasses, especially the young growing parts.

Figure A1-30. Sugar Cane

168

LICHENS

Iceland Moss (Cetraria islandica)

Lichens are abundant and widespread in the far North and can be used as a source of emergency food. However, some of them contain a bitter acid which causes irritation of the digestive tract.

If lichens are boiled, dried, and powdered, this acid is removed and the powder can then be used as flour or made into a thick soup.

WHERE FOUND:
Arctic—Tundra.
Iceland moss is found on sandy soil.

APPEARANCE. Looks very much like an upright brown seaweed.

Reindeer Moss (Cladonia rangiferina)

WHERE FOUND:
Arctic—Tundra.
Reindeer moss is common in all tundra areas.

APPEARANCE. Gray-green and multibranched.

WHAT TO EAT. Wash the whole plant and boil or roast it.

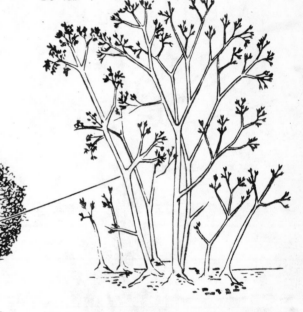

2-6" Tall

REINDEER MOSS
Grows in coral-like clumps

Rock Tripe (Umbilicaria sp.)

WHERE FOUND:
Arctic—Tundra.
Rock tripe is found on certain rocks throughout the northern areas.

APPEARANCE. Grayish-black, leathery and brittle when dry. When it is wet, it takes on a dark green color.

WHAT TO EAT. Eat the whole plant. Unless it is dried before it is cooked, it will cause diarrhea. Boiling is best.

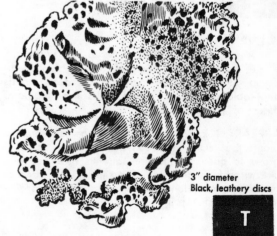

3" diameter
Black, leathery discs

T

Figure A1-31. Iceland Moss, Reindeer Moss, Rock Tripe

SHRUBS

——Abal (Calligonum comosum)——

EDIBLE FLOWERS

About 4' High

ABAL ON ARABIAN DESERT

D

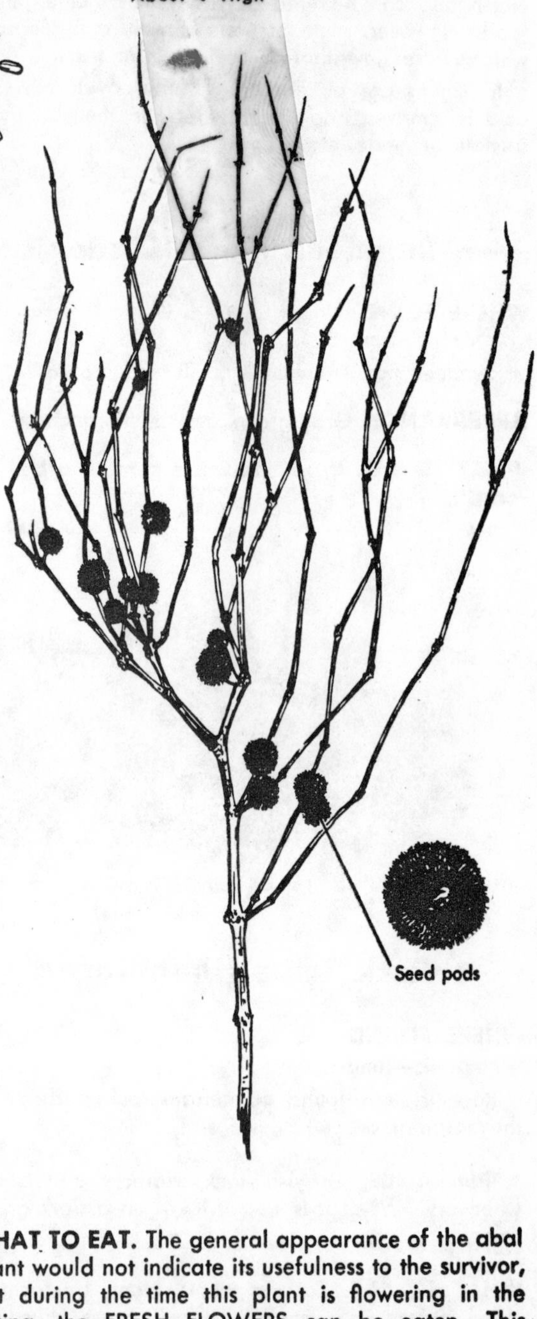

Seed pods

WHERE FOUND:
Any climatic zone—Desert scrub and waste.
The abal inhabits much of the North African desert. It may also be found on the desert sands of Arabia and as far eastward as the Rajputana desert of Western India.

APPEARANCE. The abal is one of the few shrubby plants that exists in the sandy deserts. This plant grows to about 4 feet high, and its branches look like wisps from a broom. The stiff, green branches produce an abundance of flowers in the early spring months (March, April).

WHAT TO EAT. The general appearance of the abal plant would not indicate its usefulness to the survivor, but during the time this plant is flowering in the spring, the FRESH FLOWERS can be eaten. This plant is common in the areas it is found. An analysis of the food value of this plant has shown it to be high in sugar and nitrogenous components.

Figure A1-32. Abal

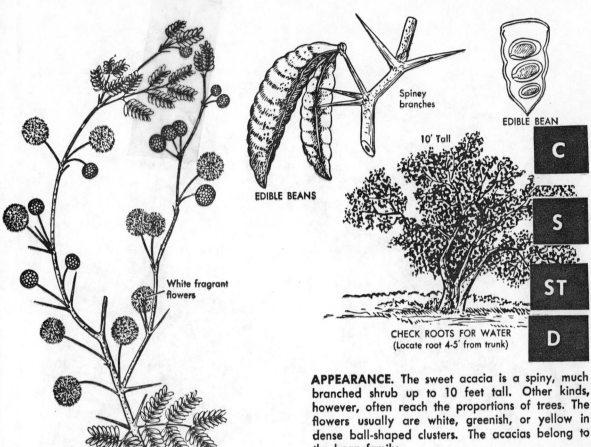

White fragrant flowers

EDIBLE BEANS

Spiney branches

10' Tall

EDIBLE BEAN

C

S

ST

D

CHECK ROOTS FOR WATER
(Locate root 4-5' from trunk)

APPEARANCE. The sweet acacia is a spiny, much branched shrub up to 10 feet tall. Other kinds, however, often reach the proportions of trees. The flowers usually are white, greenish, or yellow in dense ball-shaped clusters. The acacias belong to the bean family.

WHAT TO EAT. Most acacias are desert plants and for this reason are dormant over much of the year, except during rainy seasons. However, acacia beans can be found still hanging on the trees at all seasons. These BEANS, when pulverized and cooked as porridge, are highly sustaining food.

Some acacias produce a kind of gum on the bark of the tree, such as gum arabic which comes of ACACIA ARABICA. This GUM is highly nutritious and may be eaten like candy.

The roots of the acacia will also yield water. Locate the root 4 or 5 feet from the tree trunk, pry it out of the ground, cut it into 2- or 3-foot lengths, and peel off the bark. Drain each section into a container or suck out the water. Plants growing in hollows between ridges have the most water, and roots 1 to 2 inches thick are ideal in size. Water can be carried in these roots for some distance by plugging one end with soil.

WHERE FOUND:

Tropics—Scrub and thorn forest.
Temperate—Coniferous forest.
Temperate—Steppe.
Any climatic zone—Desert scrub and waste.

About 500 kinds of acacia occur, especially in desert areas of the New and Old Worlds. These plants are especially prevalent in Africa, southern Asia and Australia, but many kinds occur in the warmer and drier parts of America. The sweet acacia illustrated here is found over a wide area in the drier parts of the Old World and may be considered a typical example of this kind of plant.

Figure A1-33. Acacia

171

Green male flowers

To 40' Tall

RF

SS

EDIBLE FRUIT
(Dark red to black)

WHERE FOUND:

Tropics—Rain forest.
Tropics—Semievergreen seasonal forest.

The bignay occurs wild from the Himalayas to Ceylon and eastward through Indonesia to northern Australia. This shrub or tree is frequently cultivated elsewhere in tropical climates and about 70 known varieties exist. They are found in open places and in secondary forests.

APPEARANCE. These are shrubs to small trees, 12-40 feet tall, with leaves 6 inches long, shiny and pointed at the tip. The flowers are small and green.

WHAT TO EAT. The fleshly, currantlike fruit is about ½ inch in diameter. The FRUIT, which is dark red to black in color, acid, and with a single seed, can be eaten raw.

Figure A1-34. Bignay

Wild Blueberry (Vaccinium), Huckleberry, Mountain Cranberry, Whortleberry

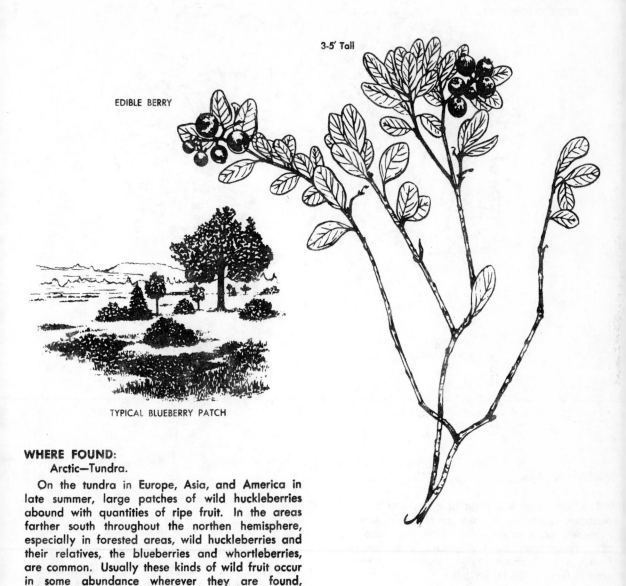

3-5' Tall

EDIBLE BERRY

TYPICAL BLUEBERRY PATCH

WHERE FOUND:
Arctic—Tundra.

On the tundra in Europe, Asia, and America in late summer, large patches of wild huckleberries abound with quantities of ripe fruit. In the areas farther south throughout the northen hemisphere, especially in forested areas, wild huckleberries and their relatives, the blueberries and whortleberries, are common. Usually these kinds of wild fruit occur in some abundance wherever they are found, whether it be on the tundra or in forested areas.

APPEARANCE. On the tundra, these wild berries grow on low bushes which are sometimes only a few inches tall. The varieties which grow farther south are produced on taller shrubs which may reach 6 feet in height. The ripe berries are blue, black, or red. These berries are sufficiently common to afford an abundance of fruit during late summer.

WHAT TO EAT. The RIPE BERRIES are eaten fresh from the bush or they may be cooked, which makes some kinds more palatable. Certain kinds may be dried and eaten like raisins during periods when little else is available.

Figure A1-35. Blueberry, Cranberry, Huckleberry, Whortleberry

T

6-12" Tall

EDIBLE YELLOW FRUIT

WHERE FOUND:
   Arctic—Tundra.
   The cloudberry is a plant of the tundra areas of Scandinavia, northern Asia, and North America. Anywhere north of 60° N. latitude, the cloudberry often covers many acres of ground. It is sometimes found in mountainous regions considerably farther south—often to 45° N. latitude.

APPEARANCE. The ripe cloudberry grows on an erect plant which seldom grows over a foot in height in the southern limit of its distribution and only a few inches tall on the arctic tundra. The plants have a few undivided, rounded, scalloped leaves. The fruit is borne at the top of the plant, first pink, then amber, at last yellow and very juicy and soft.

WHAT TO EAT. The SOFT RIPE FRUIT has a flavor strongly suggestive of poorly flavored baked apples. A taste must be developed for the cloudberry, but once acquired, large quantities can be consumed in season, usually late summer.
   The cloudberry is only one of several kinds of wild berries related to the blackberry, raspberry, and dewberries, which the survivor can expect to find in northern regions.

Figure A1-36. Cloudberry (Arctic Raspberry)

Manioc (Manihot utillissima)

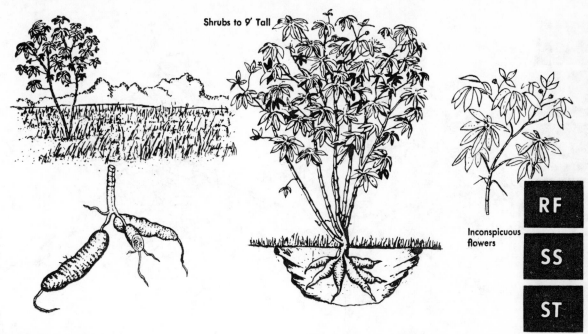

Shrubs to 9' Tall

Inconspicuous flowers

RF

SS

ST

WHERE FOUND:

Tropics—Rain forest.
Tropics—Semievergreen seasonal forest.
Tropics—Scrub and thorn forest.

Manioc is widespread in all tropical climates, especially in the moister districts. Although cultivated extensively in most parts, it will be found in abandoned gardens and growing wild over wide areas.

APPEARANCE. Manioc is a perennial shrubby plant, 3-9 feet tall, with jointed stems, and deep green fingerlike leaves. This plant has large fleshy rootstalks.

WHAT TO EAT. The ROOTSTALKS are full of starch and high in food value and are the part eaten. Manioc is known by many names, including manioca, mandioc, manihot, cassava, casabi, yuca, and rumu. Commercial tapioca and a sauce which forms the basis of Worcestershire sauce are derived from this plant.

Two kinds of manioc are known, bitter and sweet. Both kinds are edible, but THE BITTER VARIETY IS POISONOUS IF EATEN UNCOOKED.

The BITTER MANIOC is the common variety in many areas. Its poisonous properties are due to minute quantities of hydrocyanic acid. To test for

bitterness, just nibble on a piece of the rootstalk, and if it tastes bitter, prepare it in the following manner: First, grind the fresh manioc root into a pulp, then cook it for at least 1 hour. The poisonous properties will have been driven off completely, leaving the manioc quite safe and edible. The wet pulp can then be flattened into cakes and baked as a kind of bread.

Another method is to cook the roots in large pieces, for at least 1 hour, after which they can be grated and peeled. Press this pulp and knead it with a little water to remove the milky white juice. Steam it and then pound it into a plastic mass. Roll the paste into small balls and flatten into thin cakes by means of a bamboo or wooden roller. Dry the cakes in the sun. These can be eaten baked or roasted with salt or sugar added, if available.

One of the great advantages of manioc is its keeping qualities. Both manioc flour and manioc cakes keep almost indefinitely if they can be protected from insects and dampness. Manioc flour seems immune to weevils or moulds if packed in baskets lined with banana leaves.

The roots of the SWEET MANIOC are not bitter and may be eaten raw, roasted as a vegetable, made into flour, or boiled in dumplings. Roasted manioc has an agreeable flavor faintly resembling chestnuts.

Figure A1-37. Manioc

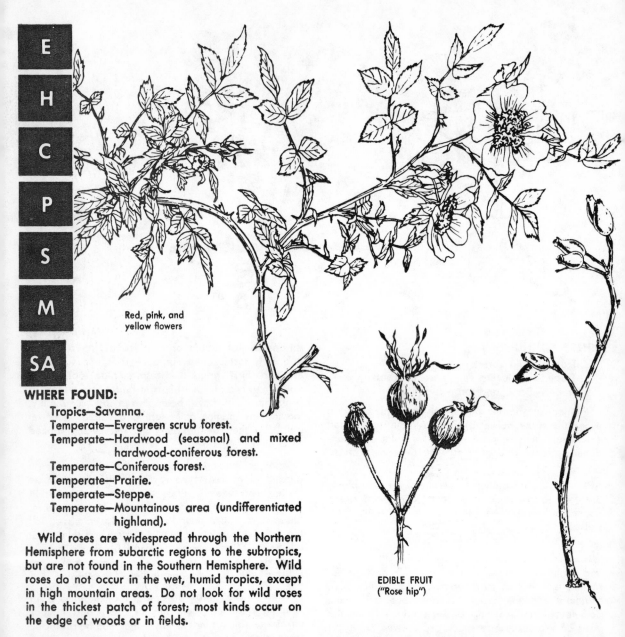

E
H
C
P
S
M
SA

Red, pink, and
yellow flowers

EDIBLE FRUIT
("Rose hip")

WHERE FOUND:

Tropics—Savanna.
Temperate—Evergreen scrub forest.
Temperate—Hardwood (seasonal) and mixed
     hardwood-coniferous forest.
Temperate—Coniferous forest.
Temperate—Prairie.
Temperate—Steppe.
Temperate—Mountainous area (undifferentiated
     highland).

Wild roses are widespread through the Northern Hemisphere from subarctic regions to the subtropics, but are not found in the Southern Hemisphere. Wild roses do not occur in the wet, humid tropics, except in high mountain areas. Do not look for wild roses in the thickest patch of forest; most kinds occur on the edge of woods or in fields.

APPEARANCE. Wild roses form low and arching shrubs up to 10 feet tall, or else they grow as extremely large and vigorous climbers. All wild roses have divided leaves similar to the cultivated rose. Their stems or canes are almost always thorny. The edible rose fruits are produced at the tips of branches in arching clusters. The fruit is usually red or orange, and rarely yellow, and is more or less bottle-shaped.

WHAT TO EAT. The RIPE FRUIT is called the "rose hip." These ripen from late summer to autumn and should not be eaten until quite soft; they remain on the bush nearly all winter. Some sorts taste flat, but others are quite sweet. The pulp only should be eaten. Rose hips are a very good source of vitamin A, and many kinds are good antiscorbutics (preventing scurvy).

Figure A1-38. Wild Rose

176

──── Saxaul (Haloxylon ammodendron) ────

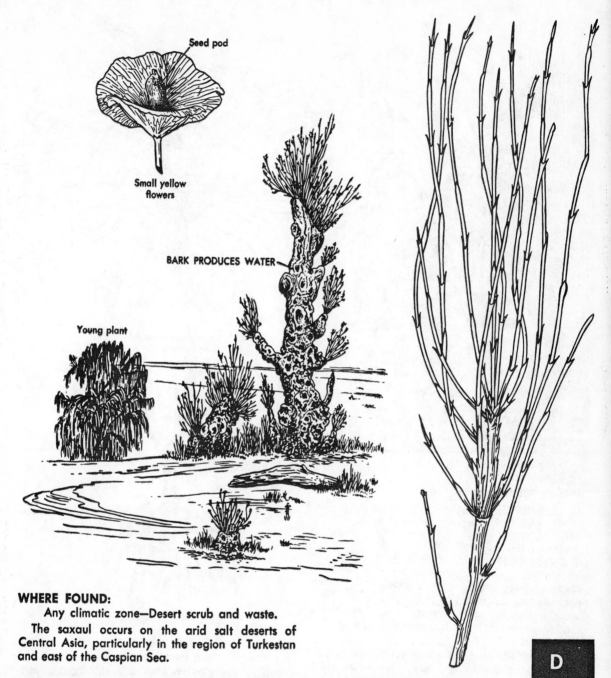

Seed pod

Small yellow flowers

BARK PRODUCES WATER

Young plant

D

WHERE FOUND:

Any climatic zone—Desert scrub and waste.

The saxaul occurs on the arid salt deserts of Central Asia, particularly in the region of Turkestan and east of the Caspian Sea.

APPEARANCE. The saxaul is found either as a small tree or as a large shrub with heavy, coarse wood and spongy, water-soaked bark. The branches of the young trees are vivid green and pendulous. The flowers are small and yellow.

WHAT TO EAT. The thick BARK acts as a water storage organ. By pressing quantities of the bark, drinking water may be obtained. This plant is an important source of water in the arid regions in which it grows.

Figure A1-39. Saxaul

177

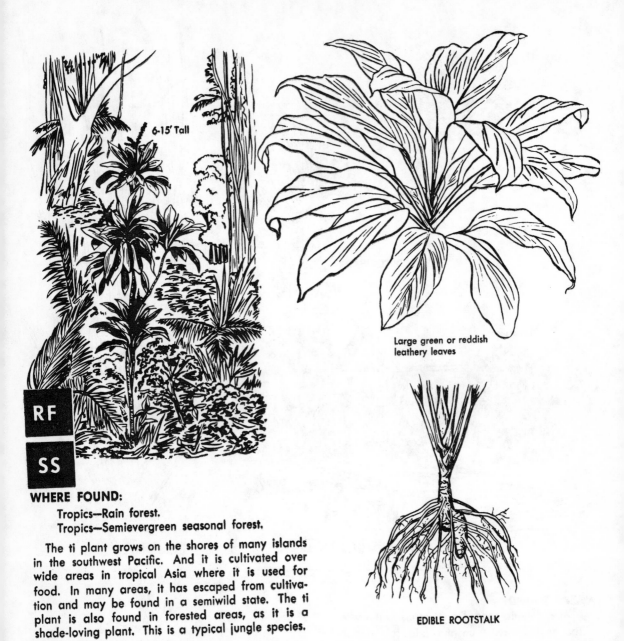

6-15' Tall

Large green or reddish
leathery leaves

EDIBLE ROOTSTALK

WHERE FOUND:

Tropics—Rain forest.
Tropics—Semievergreen seasonal forest.

The ti plant grows on the shores of many islands in the southwest Pacific. And it is cultivated over wide areas in tropical Asia where it is used for food. In many areas, it has escaped from cultivation and may be found in a semiwild state. The ti plant is also found in forested areas, as it is a shade-loving plant. This is a typical jungle species.

APPEARANCE. The ti plant may become a fairly tall shrub from 6-15 feet tall. The large, rather coarse, shiny, leathery leaves are arranged in a crowded fashion at the tips of the thick, rather succulent stems. The leaves are usually green or sometimes reddish. The flowers are borne at the apex of the plant in large plumelike clusters which are usually drooping. The ripe berries are red.

WHAT TO EAT. The large fleshy ROOTSTALK is the principal edible part. The root is full of starch, and for best results, should be oven-baked in the manner described for taro. In the East Indies, the natives eat the young unopened LEAVES cooked with rice.

Figure A1-40. Ti Plant

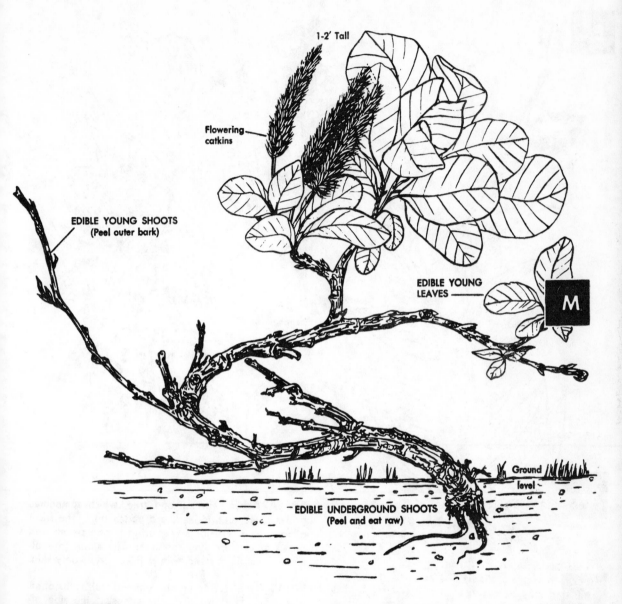

1-2' Tall

Flowering catkins

EDIBLE YOUNG SHOOTS
(Peel outer bark)

EDIBLE YOUNG LEAVES

M

Ground level

EDIBLE UNDERGROUND SHOOTS
(Peel and eat raw)

WHERE FOUND:

Arctic—Tundra.

Temperate—Mountainous area (undifferentiated highlands).

The Arctic willow is common on all tundra areas in North America, Europe, and Asia.

APPEARANCE. The Arctic willow is a shrub which never exceeds more than 1 or 2 feet in height and grows in clumps, which form dense mats on the tundra.

WHAT TO EAT. The succulent, TENDER YOUNG SHOOTS of the Arctic willow can be collected in early spring. Strip off the outer bark of the new shoots and eat the inner portion raw.

The young underground shoots of any of the various kinds of Arctic willow can be peeled and eaten raw. Young willow LEAVES are one of the richest sources of vitamin C, containing 7-10 times more than an orange.

T

Figure A1-41. Arctic Willow

Almond (Prunus amygdalus)

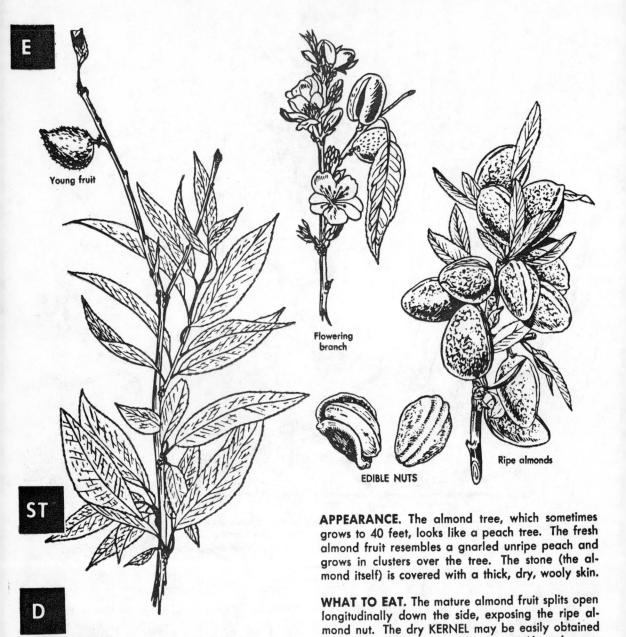

Young fruit

Flowering branch

EDIBLE NUTS

Ripe almonds

WHERE FOUND:

    Tropics—Scrub and thorn forest.
    Temperate—Evergreen scrub forest.
    Any climatic zone—Desert scrub and waste.

    The wild almond occurs in the semidesert areas of the Old World in southern Europe, the eastern Mediterranean, Iran, Arabia, China, Madeira, the Azores, and the Canary Islands.

APPEARANCE. The almond tree, which sometimes grows to 40 feet, looks like a peach tree. The fresh almond fruit resembles a gnarled unripe peach and grows in clusters over the tree. The stone (the almond itself) is covered with a thick, dry, wooly skin.

WHAT TO EAT. The mature almond fruit splits open longitudinally down the side, exposing the ripe almond nut. The dry KERNEL may be easily obtained by simply cracking open the stone. Almond meats are rich in food value, like all nuts, and should be gathered in large quantities and shelled for further use as survival food. Subsistence for rather long periods could be maintained solely from almonds. They may be boiled, in which case the outer covering of the kernel comes off and only the white meat remains.

Figure A1-42. Almond

─────Indian or Tropical Almond (Terminala catappa)─────

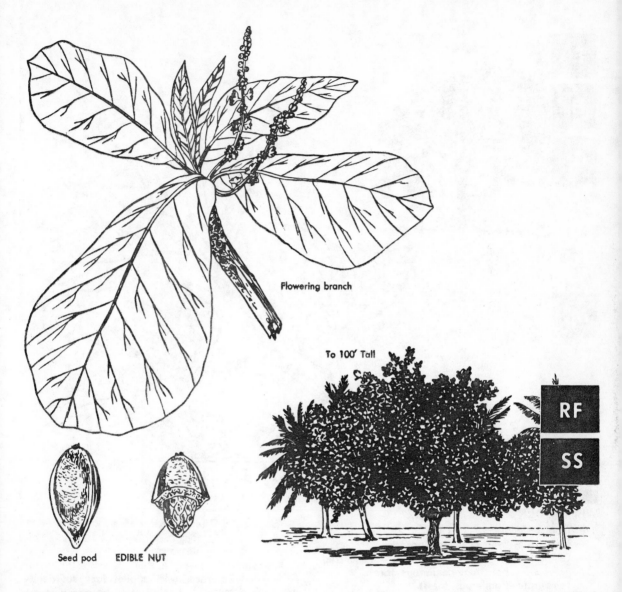

Flowering branch

To 100' Tall

RF

SS

Seed pod   EDIBLE NUT

WHERE FOUND:
   Tropics—Rain forest.
   Tropics—Semievergreen seasonal forest.

   The Indian almond is native to tropical southeastern Asia, northern Australia, and Polynesia. In its native habitat, the Indian almond is found only upon sandy seacoasts. However, it is now widely dispersed in all tropical countries around the globe and has become semiwild in many tropical areas where it can be found in abandoned fields, gardens, and along roadsides.

APPEARANCE. The Indian almond is a tall tree, growing to 100 feet in height. The edible seeds or kernels are surrounded by a spongy, husklike covering from 1 to 3 inches long. These fruits are produced at the tips of the branches. The leaves of the Indian almond are clustered at the ends of the young branches.

WHAT TO EAT. The KERNELS of the fruit are of a fine almondlike consistency and flavor.

Figure A1-43.   Indian or Tropical Almond

181

Wild Crabapple, Wild Apple (Malus)

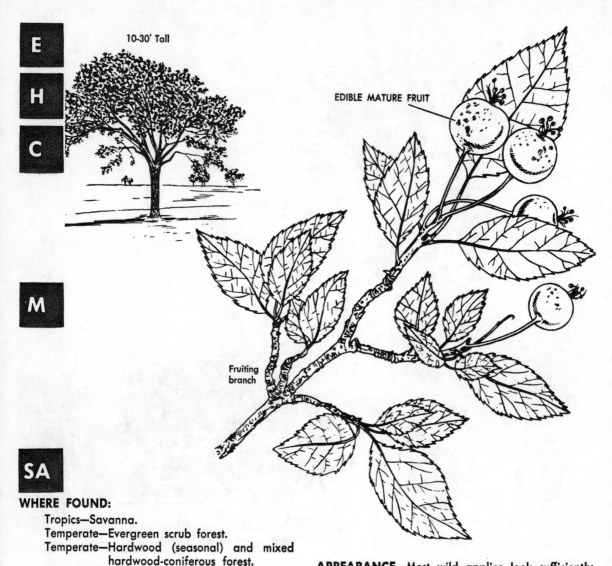

E

H

C

10-30' Tall

EDIBLE MATURE FRUIT

M

Fruiting
branch

SA

WHERE FOUND:

    Tropics—Savanna.

    Temperate—Evergreen scrub forest.

    Temperate—Hardwood (seasonal) and mixed
          hardwood-coniferous forest.

    Temperate—Coniferous forest.

    Temperate—Mountainous area (undifferentiated
          highland).

The common apple known in cultivation came from
Europe. Many kinds of wild apples, all relatives of
the common apple, occur in the United States, especially the eastern part, and a few kinds occur in
western United States. Wild apples are common
throughout the temperate parts of Asia and also in
Europe. Wild apples are found in open woodlands,
and rarely can be found in densely forested regions.
Most frequently, they occur on the edge of woods or
in fields.

APPEARANCE. Most wild applies look sufficiently
like their domesticated relatives to be easily recognized by the survivor, whether it be in Turkey or in
China. The size of wild apple varieties is considerably smaller than cultivated kinds; the largest kinds
usually do not exceed 2 to 3 inches in diameter, and
most often less.

WHAT TO EAT. Wild apples may be prepared in
the same manner for eating as cultivated kinds; that
is, they may be eaten either fresh when ripe or
cooked. If it becomes necessary to store up food
for some time, the apples can be cut into thin slices
and dried.

Figure A1-44. Wild Apple, Wild Crabapple

Bael Fruit (Aegle marmelos)

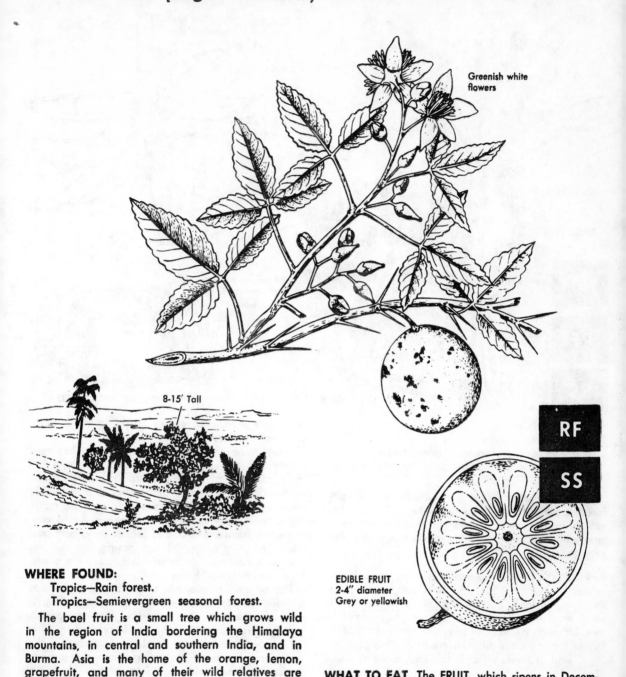

Greenish white flowers

8-15' Tall

RF

SS

EDIBLE FRUIT
2-4" diameter
Grey or yellowish

WHERE FOUND:

Tropics—Rain forest.

Tropics—Semievergreen seasonal forest.

The bael fruit is a small tree which grows wild in the region of India bordering the Himalaya mountains, in central and southern India, and in Burma. Asia is the home of the orange, lemon, grapefruit, and many of their wild relatives are found in this region. The bael fruit is an example of citrus fruit which is generally unknown in America.

APPEARANCE. The tree is 8-15 feet tall with a dense and spiny growth. The fruit is 2-4 inches in diameter, gray or yellowish, and full of seeds.

WHAT TO EAT. The FRUIT, which ripens in December, is at its best when just turning ripe. The juice of the ripe fruit, diluted with water and mixed with a small quantity of tamarind and sweetening, makes a delicious and cooling drink. The fruit, if eaten fresh, is sour but refreshing and, like other citrus fruits, is rich in vitamin C.

Figure A1-45. Bael Fruit

183

Bananas and Plantains (Musa)

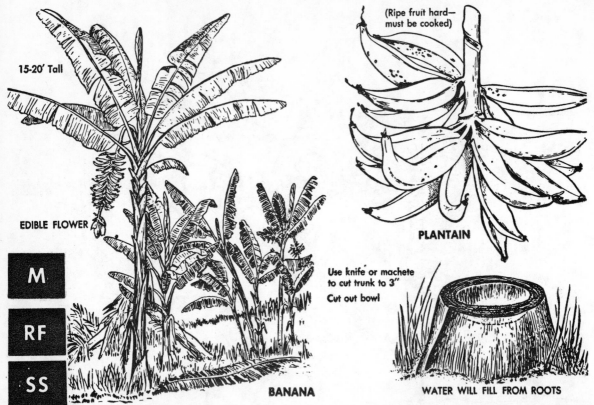

15-20' Tall

EDIBLE FLOWER

M

RF

SS

BANANA

(Ripe fruit hard—must be cooked)

PLANTAIN

Use knife or machete to cut trunk to 3"

Cut out bowl

WATER WILL FILL FROM ROOTS

WHERE FOUND:
  Tropics—Rain forest.
  Tropics—Semievergreen seasonal forest.
  Temperate—Mountainous area (undifferentiated highland).

Bananas and plantains grow mostly in the rain forest areas from sea level to 3,000-4,000 feet elevation. In the jungles of Asia wild bananas are common, although many wild forms are tough and not very palatable.

APPEARANCE. The banana and plantain look essentially alike. The banana is a soft, sweet fruit that is eaten fresh, but the plantain has a hard fruit which must be cooked. The banana plant is not a tree, although it looks like one. The large, undivided leaves overlap each other at the base, thus producing a kind of trunk, which is soft and easily broken.

WHAT TO EAT. In areas where bananas grow, they should be used for food as much as possible. They are extremely nourishing, and a diet of them alone would sustain life.

Fully ripe bananas may be cut in slices, sun-dried, and then thoroughly smoked over a fire. When prepared in this manner, they look like dried figs and keep very well. The smoke seems to be a slight deterrent to insects.

Plantains never soften, even when ripe. They must be roasted or boiled. When roasted, plantains become very dry and mealy. Large coarse plantains can be dried when green and boiled as a vegetable when needed. The dried fruit may also be made into a meal. This meal is about the color and consistency of graham flour and makes very tasty porridge, but it is not good for making bread. This meal can, however, be formed into round flat cakes, fried, and eaten with sugar.

The banana or plantain trunk can be made into an ideal source of water with a few cuts from a knife or machete. Cut the trunk, leaving approximately three inches of the trunk protruding from the ground. Cut out a bowl-like reservoir in the three inches of trunk protruding above the ground. Water will immediately flow into the bowl from the roots. This water will taste bitter; however, if the bowl is allowed to fill and be scooped out three times, the fourth filling will be palatable and a continuing source. The same trunk can be used continuously for periods of up to 4 days. When the bowl is not in use, it should be covered with a banana leaf to keep insects out of the water.

Figure A1-46. Banana and Plantain

Baobab (Adansonia digitata)

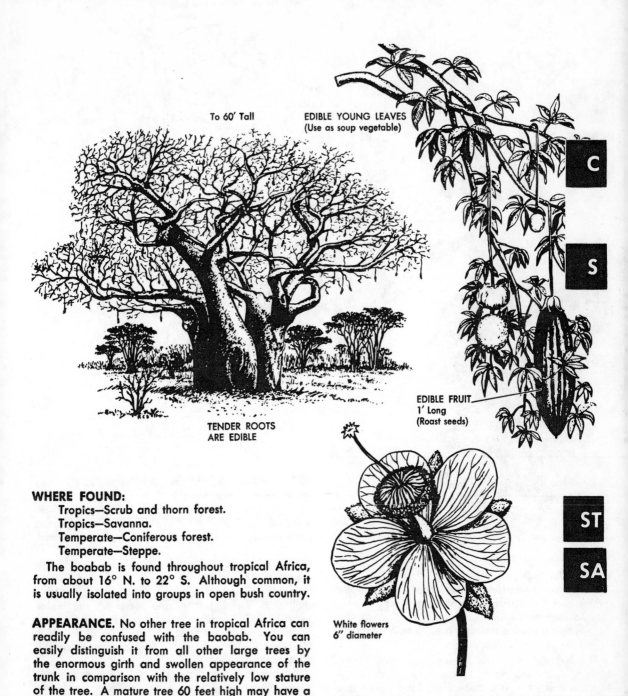

To 60' Tall

EDIBLE YOUNG LEAVES
(Use as soup vegetable)

C

S

TENDER ROOTS
ARE EDIBLE

EDIBLE FRUIT
1' Long
(Roast seeds)

ST

SA

White flowers
6" diameter

WHERE FOUND:
    Tropics—Scrub and thorn forest.
    Tropics—Savanna.
    Temperate—Coniferous forest.
    Temperate—Steppe.

    The boabab is found throughout tropical Africa, from about 16° N. to 22° S. Although common, it is usually isolated into groups in open bush country.

APPEARANCE. No other tree in tropical Africa can readily be confused with the baobab. You can easily distinguish it from all other large trees by the enormous girth and swollen appearance of the trunk in comparison with the relatively low stature of the tree. A mature tree 60 feet high may have a trunk 30 feet in diameter. The flowers are large and white, about 3 inches across, and hang loosely from the tree. The mature fruit is filled with a mealy pulp and numerous seeds.

WHAT TO EAT. The PULP and SEEDS of the fruit are edible. The young LEAVES can be used as a soup vegetable. The tender ROOT of the young baobab tree is also edible.

Figure A1-47. Baobab

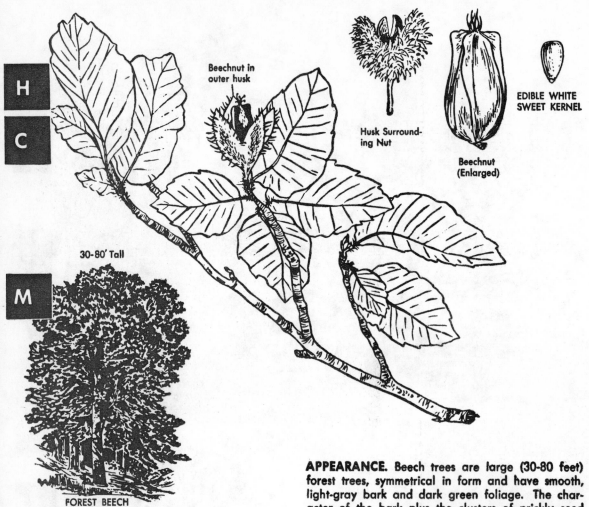

H

C

M

Beechnut in
outer husk

Husk Surround-
ing Nut

Beechnut
(Enlarged)

EDIBLE WHITE
SWEET KERNEL

30-80' Tall

FOREST BEECH
(Smooth, light bark)

WHERE FOUND:
Temperate—Hardwood (seasonal) and mixed
hardwood-coniferous forest.
Temperate—Coniferous forest.
Temperate—Mountainous area (undifferentiated
highland).

The beech tree is wild in eastern United States,
Europe, Asia, and north Africa. The beech occurs
in moist areas and is a tree of the forest. This tree
is common throughout southeastern Europe and
across temperate Asia. It does not occur in tropical
or subarctic areas. Beech relatives occur in Chile,
New Guinea, and New Zealand.

APPEARANCE. Beech trees are large (30-80 feet)
forest trees, symmetrical in form and have smooth,
light-gray bark and dark green foliage. The character of the bark plus the clusters of prickly seed
pods clearly distinguish the beech tree in the field.

WHAT TO EAT. The mature beechnuts readily fall
out of the husklike seed pods. These dark brown
triangular nuts may be eaten by breaking the thin
shell with the fingernail and removing the white,
sweet KERNEL inside. Beechnuts are one of the most
delicious of all wild nuts, and because of the high
oil content of the kernels, they are considered a
most useful survival food.

A secondary use of beechnuts is as a coffee substitute. They may be roasted so that the kernel
becomes golden brown and quite hard. The kernel
is then pulverized and, after boiling or steeping in
hot water, a passable substitute for coffee is the
result.

Figure A1:48. Beech

Breadfruit (Artocarpus incisa)

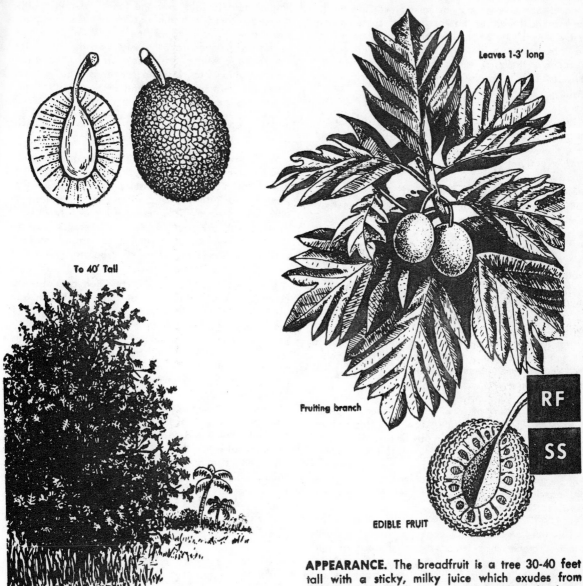

Leaves 1-3' long

To 40' Tall

Fruiting branch

RF

SS

EDIBLE FRUIT

APPEARANCE. The breadfruit is a tree 30-40 feet tall with a sticky, milky juice which exudes from fresh wounds. The leaves are 1-3 feet long, leathery, and the upper part has 3-9 lobes. The trees are frequently found near human habitation.

WHAT TO EAT. *Ripe breadfruits can be eaten raw. Scrape lightly with a shell to remove the skin, pick off the lumps of flesh with your fingers, separating the seeds, and discarding the hard outer covering.

WHERE FOUND:

Tropics—Rain forest.
Tropics—Semievergreen seasonal forest.

The breadfruit grows in most tropical countries, but is is especially common throughout the southwest Pacific, Indonesia, New Guinea, and tropical Asia and America. It is less common in Africa.

Figure A1-49. Breadfruit

When a sufficient quantity has been prepared in this manner, squeeze the FLESH into a container to form a mash. Some water may be mixed with this mash. The mashed breadfruit has a greenish color caused by the inner layer of skin, which is not removed by the light scraping. The fruit is now ready for eating in coconut shells. This preparation is surprisingly delicious and is considered quite as delectable as any good fruit salad.

Whole breadfruit can be cooked also. After light scraping and removal of the stalk, breadfruit may be grilled on embers of an open fire, or on heated coral spread out without any subsequent cover.

There are four other methods of cooking breadfruit in the mature, or firm stage. The first method consists of packing pieces of breadfruit, grated to a creamy consistency, into a GREEN coconut shell and cooking it. Remove the stalk end of the green nut by cracking around the shell. Remove the flesh around the upper edge of the main shell, as it is likely to come off in lumps and spoil the consistency. Pour out all but a small amount of fluid. Then place the grated breadfruit and coconut meat into the shell. Some of the fluid may be poured back until it rises to within a short distance of the rim. Replace the top part of the shell as a cover. The coconut shell container then acts as a natural casserole when placed in the oven.

A second method of cooking is with coconut cream in a MATURE nut casserole. For this preparation, cook the sliced breadfruit in an uncovered mature coconut shell with coconut cream added. Coconut cream can be prepared by grating ripe coconut with a jagged shell or piece of coral, placing the gratings in a porous cloth, and then squeezing out the juice (cream).

The third method is to cook the breadfruit with coconut cream in a wrapping of breadfruit and banana leaves as a receptacle on a green coconut-leaf platter. To construct this platter, arrange whole breadfruit leaves first with their stalks down, then sections of breadfruit leaves, and finally sections of banana leaf for the inner layer. Place pieces of breadfruit or taro in the leaf receptacle, leaving enough leaf to fold over the food. Pour in freshly prepared coconut cream until it is seen rising toward the upper level of the food. Fold the tips of the leaves over from the sides and the ends. Tie the package with a green coconut leaf. The usual way of tying is to twist the two ends together and shove the twist under the band formed by the leaf. When the tie is unfastened and the coconut-leaf receptacle removed, the opened-out leaves serve as a dish from which to eat.

A fourth way of preparation is cooking the breadfruit in a leaf wrapping, pounding it and then mixing it with grated meat of mature coconuts. Cut the breadfruit or taro into small pieces, wrap it in leaves, and cook in an oven. Then pound it in a bowl and grind it with a wooden mallet until soft. All lumps should be eliminated. Then add grated mature coconut flesh and mix thoroughly before eating.

Breadfruit in a SOFT RIPE condition can also be cooked. The breadfruit can be thinly peeled or left as it is. Pat the fruit with the hands to loosen the core. Grip the stalk with your teeth and gently pull the fruit away to withdraw the core, which can be discarded. Wrap the fruit in three breadfruit leaves with the tips downward. Fold the tips upward on opposite ends, reaching to just beyond the middle of the breadfruit. Tie the middle of the bundle transversely with a strip of pandanus leaf or hibiscus fiber. Fold the stalk ends of the leaves which project above the fruit downward to clear the opening made by the removal of the core. Pour coconut cream through the opening to fill the cavity. Pinch a lump of ripe breadfruit off the side and plug it into the opening as a stopper. Straighten out the stalk ends and tie with another strip of pandanus or hibiscus to seal the package, which is now ready for the oven. (See Chapter 2 for construction of oven.)

After about 2 hours, the food is ready to be removed from the oven. THIS METHOD FOR BREADFRUIT IS ADAPTABLE FOR OTHER KINDS OF TROPICAL FRUITS.